Sally Sondheim and Suzannah Sloan

THE
ACCIDENTAL GOURMET
Weekends and Holidays

FESTIVE MEALS FOR FAMILY AND FRIENDS

SIMON & SCHUSTER
NEW YORK • LONDON • TORONTO • SYDNEY • SINGAPORE

SIMON AND SCHUSTER
Rockefeller Center
1230 Avenue of the Americas
New York, NY 10020

For information regarding special discounts for bulk purchases,
please contact Simon & Schuster Special Sales at
1-800-456-6798 or business@simonandschuster.com

Designed by Joy O'Meara Battista

Manufactured in the United States of America

1   3   5   7   9   10   8   6   4   2

Library of Congress Cataloging-in-Publication Data
Sondheim, Sally.
The accidental gourmet : weekends and holidays /
Sally Sondheim and Suzannah Sloan.
p.   cm.
Includes index.
1. Dinners and dining.   2. Quick and easy cookery.
3. Holiday cookery. I. Sloan, Suzannah.   II. Title.
TX737.S65297   2003
641.5'4—dc21   2003045678

ISBN 0-7432-2781-6

To our mothers

In loving memory

It was because of them that we learned to cook . . .

ACKNOWLEDGMENTS

We would like to express our profound appreciation to our brave testers and tasters and our staunch supporters and contributors, without whom this tome would have fallen flat and the task would have been far too overwhelming to undertake:

Kim Aiello

Cindy, Claudio, and Adriana Bucceri

Tom and Janice Geisness

Roger Haydon

Molly Hobson

Jo Howe

Sue Klein

Blossom Landau

Cathy, Wilson, Ceanna, and Trevor,
and Jarrett Leake

Tom and Louise McCloskey

Sandy Phelan

Susan Roth

Sara Scribner

Robert Sondheim

Hal Sparks

Linda Wise

We would also like to thank the staff at the Town & Country Thriftway, Bainbridge Island, Washington. In particular:

Mike Anderson

Bryan Biggs

Katy Cunningham

Todd Kowalski

Rick Nakata

Felix Narte

Linda Papineau

Gary Reese

Su Reith

Steve Vadset

And our sincere gratitude to the helpful folks at Safeway Food & Drug, Bainbridge Island, Washington.

THE
ACCIDENTAL GOURMET

Weekends and Holidays

INTRODUCTION

First came *The Accidental Gourmet* for weeknights, which gave you complete and delicious dinner menus for every Monday through Friday for an entire year. Now we bring you the companion volume—*The Accidental Gourmet* for weekends and holidays which offers festive meals for family and friends. The year is now complete.

If you are already using *The Accidental Gourmet,* then you are familiar with the stress-free, fuss-free pleasure of preparing the evening meal. If not, read on and see for yourself how effortlessly this cookbook will redefine your relationship with your kitchen.

Like *Weeknights, Weekends and Holidays* is designed to complement the way we do things in today's hectic society. Because we believe that an overcommitted lifestyle does not have to shortchange the family, we show you how, even with limited time and resources, you can produce a terrific dinner every single Saturday, Sunday, and holiday of the year. The secret is simple. We have redesigned old-fashioned home cooking to fit perfectly into today's more fragmented existence. In other words, the taste that used to take our grandmothers days to prepare can now be produced by you in a matter of hours.

Statistics show that 70 percent of the families in this country prefer to home-cook on a regular basis. But if you're one of those who have depended on fast-food restaurants or packaged entrees for a quick fix, you're not home-cooking. Instead, you're paying a high premium for something filled with sodium, preservatives, and empty calories. For a little more time and a lot less money, you can have a complete, health-conscious meal instead. By using our foolproof method for putting meals on the table, you can make an evening memorable and have even the cook looking forward to dinner.

Every meal is composed of main, side, and dessert dishes that have been carefully chosen to complement one another and allow you to minimize your time but maximize your enjoyment. Each dinner comes with a step-by-step countdown to ensure that the entire meal is on the table at the right time and at the right temperature. And we provide a complete and organized shopping list for every menu. You can use this cookbook every single weekend. You can use it once or twice a month. You can use it as a reference. However you choose to use it, *The Accidental Gourmet* will work for you. Its easy-to-follow format will allow cooks of all levels to achieve spectacular results every time.

The Accidental Gourmet presents 52 Saturday night meals that are geared toward elegant entertaining—in case the boss and his wife are invited to dinner—52 Sunday night meals that are designed with family comfort in mind, and 23 holiday meals that can be expanded to feed a crowd.

In looking over the menus, you will notice that not only does each dish fit perfectly into its meal but when combined with *The Accidental Gourmet* for weeknights, each meal is carefully positioned within its week, each week is properly balanced within its season, and four distinct seasons of fresh fruits, vegetables, fish, and meat make up an entire year of cooking variety and pleasure.

In our efforts to simplify the entire dinner process, we have made the ritual of purchasing the ingredients every bit as important as the ritual of preparing the meal itself. Hence, the convenient and comprehensive shopping list, which provides you with all the ingredients you will need to create each meal, organized into general categories that correspond with the placement of products in the majority of markets across the country.

In addition to the products to be purchased for each meal, we have identified a number of nonperishable ingredients used throughout the book as staple items. We recommend that you keep these items on hand at all times, and that before you shop you take stock of the staples that will be used for each meal and add them to your shopping list if necessary. Nothing is more frustrating than starting to prepare a meal only to discover that you either lack or lack enough of a necessary ingredient.

While we have made every effort to be consistent, product availability does vary across the country, and you may find it necessary to make occasional substitutions. For example, products in cans and jars that may vary an ounce or two depending on the manufacturer can be substituted in recipes with no harm whatsoever. Different kinds of fish can be exchanged for whatever similar variety is available in your area.

You will notice that we use a great deal of fish in our cookbooks. It is always best to use fresh fish, but if you plan to shop ahead for those meals, look for fresh fish that has not been previously frozen, which you can freeze and then thaw the day before you are going to use it. Or you can purchase already frozen fish and thaw it the day before you use it. Or your fishmonger may agree to provide you with frozen fish that would ordinarily be thawed before being sold. Having said this, however, please keep in mind that shellfish such as clams and mussels must be purchased fresh and used within a day. If this is not possible, due to your location or your time availability, use canned clams instead.

Among the best things about creating a cookbook for an entire year is that we get to make full use of the fresh seasonal products that are showing up in more and more markets across the country. Even so, there may be some items that your market simply does not carry. Feel free to substitute. A small melon will stand in for a papaya; lettuce may be used instead of spinach. You are also free to choose a frozen vegetable if fresh is not available. Similarly with berries. We love fresh berries, as you will see by the frequency with which we use them. If you find any of them not available or cost-effective, you may always use frozen berries and simply adjust the instructions.

Breads are another item that can easily be interchanged. French and Italian loaves will always substitute for each other, as will country loaves and sourdough loaves. And peasant bread, rye bread, and pumpernickel are sufficiently similar to swap out.

It is always a joy to cook with fresh herbs because they so enhance the flavor and aroma of foods. We use them frequently—it's one of our rare extravagances. However, they can be costly, so you may omit them, if you prefer, by using the dried variety on a ratio of three parts fresh to one part dried. We use one herb, parsley, with abandon, because it does wonderful things for food, is relatively inexpensive, is available all year long, and can be found in every market in the country. There is a dried version, but it's no substitute.

Garlic is another herb we use liberally. It not only makes everything taste wonderful, it's good for you. You are of course free to omit it, but be prewarned that the dish will not be nearly as flavorful.

Because herbs and spices are such a delicious and healthy way to flavor foods, we almost never call for just plain salt and pepper. However, we invite you to season to taste in whatever way you choose. Play with the dishes. Adapt them to your particular taste. Experiment. Have fun. You can rarely go wrong.

While we have created *The Accidental Gourmet* to be a delicious, nutritious way to feed your family, we make no pretensions about it being a diet cookbook. It is instead a cookbook for the way most Americans prefer to eat. You are always free to use low-fat alternatives to such ingredients as milk, cream, cheeses, and oils, and you may certainly substitute margarine for butter. Desserts are always optional. However, there are now many low-fat pound cakes and cookies on the market, as well as low-fat and fat-free ice creams and frozen yogurts, that will allow you to enjoy many of our desserts without feeling guilty.

Because no two kitchens are exactly alike, and cooks vary so greatly in style, it would be nearly impossible for us to suggest a single list of equipment that would suit every home. Instead, we will briefly discuss the equipment that we used in creating the recipes for this cookbook, and then leave the details up to you.

For openers, there are a few small appliances without which we couldn't function. Tops on the list is an electric mixer, indispensable for mixing, beating, and blending chores that make preparing cakes and puddings seem easy. We love the wok for fast and healthy food preparation. There are stovetop versions as well as electric versions. Both work equally well. A blender is also indispensable. From fabulous soups to super sauces to perfect desserts, it's a miracle worker. We love stews almost as much as we love soups. This means a prominent place in our kitchen is reserved for the Dutch oven. And we prefer using a double boiler for rice. You bring water to a boil in the bottom, put your ingredients in the top, cover it up, and leave it alone. You end up with perfect results every time. An electric rice cooker also delivers fuss-free results, if you happen to have one. If you have an electric steaming appliance for vegetables, by all means use it. If not, you might want to consider the inexpensive stainless-steel fan-style insert for a saucepan, or the bamboo type that is used in a wok or skillet.

Every kitchen has its supply of basic pots and pans. We use them all, and probably more. We call for skillets in small, medium, and large sizes. On occasion, we even call for more than one of the same size at the same time. It's a good idea to have tight-fitting lids for all your skillets, but if you don't, aluminum foil can sometimes come to the rescue.

As with skillets, we use small, medium, and large saucepans. All the time. And a good-sized stockpot for cooking pasta. And a colander to drain it. As with the skillets, all of the saucepans should have tight-fitting lids.

You'll notice that we bake quite a bit in this cookbook, everything from biscuits to puddings, fish to fowl, and casseroles to cakes. So we use baking pans, baking dishes, baking sheets, muffin tins, and casseroles to delightful excess.

We also mix a lot, beat a lot, blend a lot. You can never have too many mixing bowls. We use everything from half-quart bowls to five-quart bowls, as often as possible.

Kitchen knives are definitely our weapons of choice. Get good quality, keep them clean and sharp, and they'll be worth their weight in steel for years to come. You can resort to expensive food processors, but we prefer doing it the old-fashioned way. It may take a little more time, but you control the results, and the cleanup is a lot easier.

Then there are all the miscellaneous utensils that make preparing a meal possible. We couldn't survive without a whisk in our kitchen. From sauces to salad dressings, it's a must. A vegetable brush, a vegetable peeler, and vegetable, citrus, and cheese graters all come under the necessary category. Something as simple as a pastry brush makes all sorts of jobs easy. Tongs to turn things, a mallet for crushing things, a melon-baller, an ice-cream scoop—just a few of the items that keep the food coming but rarely get much praise. From spoons to spreaders to spatulas, everything has its purpose. And a kitchen can't be called a real kitchen without a complete set of both liquid and dry measures. Unless you're uncommonly good at guessing, you'll use them every single evening.

We have made a deliberate choice not to include microwave oven recipes in *The Accidental Gourmet*. We're never sure how many cooks truly feel comfortable using the appliance for anything other than defrosting and reheating. If you're one that does, however, you can save time and produce spectacular results by baking fish and steaming vegetables in your microwave oven. You'll find that adapting our recipes is easy.

It's not enough for a cookbook author to tell you that you can put a whole dinner on the table at the right time and temperature. The truth is, unless you're a super-well-organized cook, the vegetables are likely to get cold while you're waiting for the meat. Or you're trying to bake the casserole at the same time as the dessert—at different temperatures. Trying to prepare a meal that consists of several different dishes, each with its own set of cooking instructions, isn't always easy. So we don't just tell you that you can get that whole meal on the table—we show you exactly how.

We call it the Countdown, and it's a chronology of cooking steps, covering every dish in the dinner, that will guide you through the preparation with the confidence of knowing that it will all be ready when you are. Just as we've taken the stress out of planning the meal, and the hassle out of buying the ingredients, we've now taken all the confusion out of the cooking, because that should be the last thing for you to have to worry about. With the entire meal in full view, following the Countdown is easy. We're with you every step of the way, from the moment you walk into your kitchen to the moment you sit down at the table. In fact, we've done everything for you but the dishes.

Now let's get started.

Weekend One Saturday

MEAT & POULTRY

2 Rock Cornish game hens

FRESH PRODUCE

VEGETABLES
1-1/2 pounds new red potatoes
1 pound Brussels sprouts
1 medium onion
4 cloves garlic

HERBS
2 tablespoons parsley (when chopped)

FRUIT
1 large lemon

CANS, JARS & BOTTLES

SOUP
1 can (14 ounces) chicken broth

PACKAGED GOODS

DRIED FRUITS & NUTS
1/2 cup sliced almonds

DESSERT & BAKING NEEDS
1-1/4 cups graham cracker crumbs

REFRIGERATED PRODUCTS

DAIRY
3 eggs

CHEESE
3 packages (8 ounces each)
cream cheese

FROZEN GOODS

FRUIT
1 package (16 ounces) whole
raspberries

STAPLES

☐ Butter
☐ Cornstarch
☐ Granulated sugar
☐ Vegetable oil
☐ Tarragon vinegar
☐ Dijon mustard
☐ Dried basil
☐ Dried tarragon
☐ Ground cinnamon
☐ Pepper
☐ Salt
☐ Vanilla extract

Weekend One Saturday

My Little Chickadees

4 cloves garlic
1 medium onion
1/3 cup tarragon vinegar
1 tablespoon Dijon mustard
1 teaspoon dried tarragon
1 teaspoon granulated sugar
3 tablespoons vegetable oil
1/4 cup chicken broth
2 Rock Cornish game hens
Seasoning to taste

Mae Wests

1-1/2 pounds new red potatoes
2 tablespoons fresh parsley (when chopped)
1-1/2 cups chicken broth
1/2 teaspoon dried basil
Seasoning to taste

Hustle Your Brussels

1/2 cup sliced almonds
1 pound Brussels sprouts
2 tablespoons butter
Seasoning to taste

Cheesecake

5 tablespoons butter
1-1/4 cups graham cracker crumbs
1 cup granulated sugar
1 large lemon
3 packages (8 ounces each) cream cheese
1 teaspoon vanilla extract
1/4 teaspoon ground cinnamon
3 eggs
1 package (16 ounces) frozen whole raspberries
2 tablespoons cornstarch
2 tablespoons water

EQUIPMENT

Electric mixer	Small mixing bowl
Blender	Baster
Large covered saucepan	Vegetable brush
Medium saucepan	Vegetable grater
Large skillet	Citrus grater
9 × 13-inch glass baking dish	Citrus juicer
Springform pan	Kitchen knives
Baking sheet	Measuring cups and spoons
Large mixing bowl	Cooking utensils

My Little Chickadees

1. Peel the garlic. Peel and quarter the onion.

2. In a blender, combine the garlic, the onion, the vinegar, the mustard, the tarragon, and the sugar. Gradually add the oil and the broth, and process until smooth.

3. Cut the game hens in half, rinse, and pat dry, and season to taste. Lay the hens in the 9 × 13-inch baking dish, skin side down. Spoon the tarragon mixture over the hens, and let stand for 10 minutes. Turn the hens over, and let stand for 10 minutes longer.

4. Increase the oven temperature to 400°F.

5. Bake until the hens are tender, basting occasionally, 40 to 45 minutes.

Mae Wests

1. Scrub the potatoes, prick each one several times with a fork, and cut them in half. Rinse and chop the parsley.

2. In a large saucepan, combine the potatoes with the broth, the basil, and enough water to cover. Bring to a boil, cover the pan, and cook until the potatoes are tender, about 20 minutes.

3. Drain the potatoes. Season them to taste and sprinkle them with the parsley.

Hustle Your Brussels

1. Preheat the oven to 350°F.

2. Spread the almonds on a baking sheet and toast lightly, about 5 minutes. Remove and reserve.

3. Wash, trim, and coarsely grate the Brussels sprouts.

4. Melt the butter in a large skillet. Sauté the sprouts until tender, about 5 minutes. Season to taste, and top with the toasted almonds.

Cheesecake

1. Melt 4 tablespoons of the butter.

2. Combine the graham cracker crumbs and 1/4 cup of the granulated sugar in a small bowl. Add the melted butter and mix well. Press this mixture into the bottom and sides of a springform pan, and place it in the refrigerator to chill for 15 minutes.

3. Preheat the oven to 325°F.

4. Grate the lemon peel and squeeze 2 tablespoons of lemon juice.

5. In a large bowl, combine the cream cheese and 1/2 cup of the sugar, and beat with an electric mixer to blend. Add the vanilla, the cinnamon, the lemon peel,

and the lemon juice. Add the eggs, one at a time, and beat until the mixture is smooth. Remove the pan from the refrigerator, and pour the cheese mixture into it.

6. Bake the cheesecake until the edges are firm when tapped with a spoon, and the center is still soft, about 40 minutes.

7. Remove the cheesecake from the oven and let stand for 10 minutes. Then refrigerate it until you are ready to serve.

8. Set the raspberries out to thaw.

9. Combine the remaining 1/4 cup sugar, the cornstarch, the water, and the remaining 1 tablespoon butter in a medium saucepan until well blended. Add the raspberries and their juice and bring the mixture to a boil, stirring constantly, until the liquid is clear and thick, 1 to 2 minutes. Set aside to cool.

10. Remove the sides of the pan, set the cheesecake on a plate, and spoon the berry mixture over the cake, letting it run down the sides.

COUNTDOWN

1. Assemble the ingredients and the equipment.
2. Do Steps 1–7 of *Cheesecake*.
3. Do Steps 1–2 of *Hustle Your Brussels*.
4. Do Steps 1–5 of *My Little Chickadees*.
5. Do Steps 1–2 of *Mae Wests*.
6. Do Steps 8–9 of *Cheesecake*.
7. Do Steps 3–4 of *Hustle Your Brussels*.
8. Do Step 3 of *Mae Wests*.
9. Do Step 10 of *Cheesecake*.

Weekend One Sunday

SHOPPING LIST

MEAT & POULTRY

1 pound lean ground beef

FRESH PRODUCE

VEGETABLES

1 medium head lettuce
1 medium cucumber
1 medium red bell pepper
1 medium white radish
1 medium onion

FRUIT

4 medium ripe pears
1 small orange

CANS, JARS & BOTTLES

SOUP

1 can (14 ounces) beef broth

VEGETABLES

1 can (14-1/2 ounces) diced tomatoes
1 can (15 ounces) kidney beans
1 can (15 ounces) pinto beans
1 can (11 ounces) whole kernel corn

SPREADS

3 tablespoons red currant jelly

PACKAGED GOODS

PASTA, RICE & GRAINS

1 cup long-grain white rice

REFRIGERATED PRODUCTS

DAIRY

3/4 cup milk
1/4 cup sour cream

STAPLES

❏ Butter
❏ Flour
❏ Baking powder
❏ Olive oil
❏ Vegetable oil
❏ Balsamic vinegar
❏ Dried cilantro
❏ Chili powder
❏ Ground cinnamon
❏ Ground cumin
❏ Pepper
❏ Salt

Weekend One Sunday

Chilly Chili

1 medium onion
1 medium red bell pepper
1 can (15 ounces) kidney beans
1 can (15 ounces) pinto beans
1 can (11 ounces) whole kernel corn
2 tablespoons olive oil
1 pound lean ground beef
1 can (14-1/2 ounces) diced tomatoes
1 can (14 ounces) beef broth
1 cup water
1 cup long-grain white rice
1 tablespoon chili powder
1 teaspoon ground cumin
1 tablespoon dried cilantro
Seasoning to taste
1/4 cup sour cream

Real Cool Salad

1 medium head lettuce
1 medium cucumber
1 medium white radish
3 tablespoons vegetable oil
1 tablespoon balsamic vinegar
1 tablespoon orange juice (see Breezy
   Biscuits)
Seasoning to taste

Breezy Biscuits

1 small orange
2 cups flour
1 tablespoon baking powder
3 tablespoons butter
3/4 cup milk

Pears On the Go

4 medium ripe pears
2 tablespoons butter
3 tablespoons red currant jelly
1 teaspoon ground cinnamon

EQUIPMENT

Dutch oven
9 × 9-inch glass baking dish
Baking sheet
Breadboard
2 large mixing bowls
Small mixing bowl
Whisk
Vegetable peeler
Citrus grater
Citrus juicer
Pastry blender
Biscuit cutter
Pastry brush
Aluminum foil
Kitchen knives
Measuring cups and spoons
Cooking utensils

Chilly Chili

1. Peel and chop the onion. Rinse, stem, seed, and chunk the bell pepper. Drain and rinse the beans. Drain the corn.

2. Heat the oil in a Dutch oven and sauté the ground beef for 3 minutes.

3. Add the onion and the bell pepper, and sauté until the onion is soft and the beef is cooked through, about 5 minutes.

4. Add the tomatoes, the beans, the corn, the broth, the water, the rice, the chili powder, the cumin, and the cilantro. Stir to blend and season to taste.

5. Cover and simmer, stirring occasionally, for 30 minutes.

6. Top with dollops of sour cream.

Real Cool Salad

1. Wash and dry the lettuce and tear it into bite-sized pieces. Peel and slice the cucumber. Peel, halve, and slice the radish. Place the vegetables in a large bowl.

2. In a small bowl, whisk together the oil, the vinegar, and the orange juice. Season to taste.

3. Toss the salad with the dressing.

Breezy Biscuits

1. Preheat the oven to 425°F. Flour the breadboard. Lightly flour a biscuit cutter.

2. Grate 2 tablespoons of orange peel, and squeeze 1 tablespoon of orange juice for the salad.

3. Combine the flour, the baking powder, and the butter in a large bowl, cutting the butter into the flour with a pastry blender until the mixture is crumbly.

4. Add the orange peel and the milk, and blend well. Form the mixture into a ball.

5. Place the ball on the breadboard and knead until smooth, 7–8 times. Roll or pat the dough to a 3/4-inch thickness.

6. Cut into rounds with the biscuit cutter.

7. Arrange the biscuits on an ungreased baking sheet, 1 inch apart.

8. Bake until the biscuits are light and golden, 10 to 12 minutes.

Pears On the Go

1. Preheat the broiler.

2. Peel, core, and halve the pears and place them, cut side down, in a 9 × 9-inch glass baking dish.

3. Melt the butter, and brush half of it over the pears. Place the dish under the broiler and broil for 5 minutes.

4. Turn the pears, brush them with the remaining butter, and broil for 3 minutes longer.

5. Cover the baking dish with aluminum foil to keep the pears warm.

6. Fill each pear half with the jelly, and lightly dust with the cinnamon.

COUNTDOWN

1. Assemble the ingredients and the equipment.
2. Do Steps 1–5 of *Pears On the Go.*
3. Do Steps 1–5 of *Chilly Chili.*
4. Do Steps 1–8 of *Breezy Biscuits.*
5. Do Steps 1–3 of *Real Cool Salad.*
6. Do Step 6 of *Chilly Chili.*
7. Do Step 6 of *Pears On the Go.*

Weekend Two Saturday

MEAT & POULTRY

4 lean boneless pork chops
  (about 1-1/2 pounds)

FRESH PRODUCE

VEGETABLES

4 medium carrots
1 small head lettuce
1 small red bell pepper
1 small onion
2 cloves garlic
1/4 cup chives (when chopped)

HERBS

2 tablespoons cilantro (when chopped)

FRUIT

1 large tart green apple
1 large lemon

CANS, JARS & BOTTLES

SOUP

2 cans (14 ounces each) chicken broth
1 can (14 ounces) vegetable broth

VEGETABLES

1 can (15 ounces) julienne beets

PACKAGED GOODS

PASTA, RICE & GRAINS

1 cup couscous

DRIED FRUITS & NUTS

1/4 cup pecan bits

DESSERT & BAKING NEEDS

1 square (1 ounce) semisweet chocolate

WINES & SPIRITS

1/2 cup dry white wine
1/4 cup dry sherry
1 tablespoon rum

REFRIGERATED PRODUCTS

DAIRY

1/2 cup half-and-half
1 cup whipping cream

- ❏ Butter
- ❏ Flour
- ❏ Granulated sugar
- ❏ Powdered sugar
- ❏ Chocolate syrup
- ❏ Vegetable oil
- ❏ Apple cider vinegar
- ❏ Worcestershire sauce
- ❏ Ground cloves
- ❏ Lemon-pepper seasoning
- ❏ Ground nutmeg
- ❏ Pepper
- ❏ Salt

Weekend Two Saturday

MENU

Soup Ahoy

4 medium carrots
1 small onion
2 tablespoons fresh cilantro (when chopped)
2 tablespoons butter
2 tablespoons flour
2 cans (14 ounces each) chicken broth
1/2 cup half-and-half
1/4 cup dry sherry
1 teaspoon granulated sugar
Seasoning to taste

Pork Authority

2 cloves garlic
1 large lemon
2 tablespoons butter
4 lean boneless pork chops (about 1-1/2 pounds)
1 tablespoon lemon-pepper seasoning
1/2 cup dry white wine
1/4 cup pecan bits
Seasoning to taste

Couscous Cargo

1/4 cup fresh chives (when chopped)
1 small red bell pepper
1 tablespoon vegetable oil
1/2 cup water
1 can (14 ounces) vegetable broth
1 cup couscous
1/4 teaspoon Worcestershire sauce
Seasoning to taste

Bedecked Salad

1 can (15 ounces) julienne beets
4 tablespoons apple cider vinegar
1/4 teaspoon ground cloves
1/4 teaspoon ground nutmeg
1 small head lettuce
1 large tart green apple

Rum Runners

1 cup whipping cream
2/3 cup chocolate syrup
1 tablespoon rum
2 tablespoons powdered sugar
1 square (1 ounce) semisweet chocolate

EQUIPMENT

Electric mixer	Vegetable brush
Blender	Citrus grater
Medium covered saucepan	Citrus juicer
Medium saucepan	Grater
Small saucepan	Plastic wrap
Large covered skillet	Kitchen knives
2 medium mixing bowls	Measuring cups and spoons
Whisk	Cooking utensils

Weekend Two Saturday

RECIPES

Soup Ahoy

1. Scrub and chop the carrots. Peel and chop the onion. Rinse and chop the cilantro.

2. Melt the butter in a medium saucepan. Sauté the carrots and the onion on low heat until the onion is translucent, but not brown, 5 to 10 minutes.

3. Stir in the flour and gradually add the broth. Bring to a boil, reduce the heat, and simmer for 10 minutes.

4. Place half the mixture in a blender, and process until smooth. Pour into a medium bowl. Repeat.

5. Return the soup to the saucepan, add the half-and-half, and whisk to blend. Blend in the sherry and the sugar, season to taste, and heat through, but do not boil.

6. Sprinkle with the cilantro.

Pork Authority

1. Peel and mince the garlic. Cut the lemon in half. Grate the peel from one half, and juice it. Slice the other half and reserve.

2. Melt the butter in a large skillet. Add the garlic and sauté for 2 minutes. Season both sides of the pork chops with the lemon-pepper seasoning and sauté them until they are golden brown, about 7 minutes per side.

3. Add the wine to the skillet, cover, reduce the heat, and simmer until the chops are cooked throughout, about 20 minutes.

4. Remove the chops to a platter, sprinkle with nuts, and cover to keep warm.

5. Add the lemon juice and the lemon peel to the pan juices and cook for 1 minute, scraping up any browned bits from the bottom. Season to taste and pour the sauce over the chops. Top each chop with a lemon slice.

Couscous Cargo

1. Rinse and chop the chives. Rinse, stem, seed, and chop the bell pepper.

2. Heat the oil in a medium saucepan. Sauté the bell pepper until it is soft, about 3 minutes. Remove the bell pepper and reserve.

3. Bring the water and the broth to a boil in the saucepan.

4. Add the couscous and the Worcestershire sauce. Return the mixture to a boil, cover, remove from the heat, and let stand until all the liquid has been absorbed, about 5 minutes.

5. Add the bell pepper and the chives, season to taste, and fluff with a fork.

Bedecked Salad

1. Drain the beets, reserving the juice.

2. In a small saucepan, combine the beet juice with the vinegar, the cloves, and the nutmeg. Bring the mixture to a boil, add the

beets, return to a boil, immediately remove from the heat, and chill.

3. Wash and dry the lettuce, separate it into leaves, and arrange the leaves on individual salad plates. Rinse and core the apple, cut it in quarters, and thinly slice.

4. Place the beet mixture in the center of the lettuce leaves. Arrange the apple slices around the beets.

Rum Runners

1. Chill a medium bowl and the beaters of an electric mixer in the refrigerator for at least 10 minutes.

2. In the chilled bowl, whip the cream with the chocolate syrup until stiff peaks form.

3. Fold in the rum and the powdered sugar, cover the bowl with plastic wrap, and refrigerate until you are ready to use.

4. Grate the chocolate.

5. Spoon the mixture into individual dessert glasses and top with the chocolate shavings.

COUNTDOWN

1. Assemble the ingredients and the equipment.
2. Do Steps 1–4 of *Rum Runners*.
3. Do Steps 1–2 of *Bedecked Salad*.
4. Do Step 1 of *Soup Ahoy*.
5. Do Step 1 of *Pork Authority*.
6. Do Step 1 of *Couscous Cargo*.
7. Do Steps 2–3 of *Pork Authority*.
8. Do Steps 2–3 of *Soup Ahoy*.
9. Do Steps 2–4 of *Couscous Cargo*.
10. Do Steps 4–5 of *Soup Ahoy*.
11. Do Steps 3–4 of *Bedecked Salad*.
12. Do Steps 4–5 of *Pork Authority*.
13. Do Step 5 of *Couscous Cargo*.
14. Do Step 6 of *Soup Ahoy*.
15. Do Step 5 of *Rum Runners*.

Weekend Two Sunday

SHOPPING LIST

MEAT & POULTRY

1 ham hock

FRESH PRODUCE

VEGETABLES
2 large carrots
2 stalks celery
1 medium head red leaf lettuce
2 small ripe avocados
1 medium cucumber
1 medium yellow bell pepper
1 medium onion
1 small red onion

CANS, JARS & BOTTLES

SOUP
3 cans (14 ounces each) beef broth

VEGETABLES
1 can (14-1/2 ounces) diced tomatoes
2 cans (15 ounces each) navy beans

PACKAGED GOODS

PASTA, RICE & GRAINS
2 cups Rice Krispies cereal

DESSERT & BAKING NEEDS
8 ounces chocolate chips

REFRIGERATED PRODUCTS

DAIRY
1 cup milk
2 eggs

FROZEN GOODS

DESSERTS
1 quart chocolate ice cream

STAPLES

- [ ] Butter
- [ ] Flour
- [ ] Baking powder
- [ ] Cornmeal
- [ ] Granulated sugar
- [ ] Chocolate syrup
- [ ] Olive oil
- [ ] Vegetable oil
- [ ] Balsamic vinegar
- [ ] Tabasco sauce
- [ ] Dijon mustard
- [ ] Bay leaf
- [ ] Dried tarragon
- [ ] Dried thyme
- [ ] Ground cumin
- [ ] Pepper
- [ ] Salt
- [ ] Peppermint extract

Weekend Two Sunday

Don't Ask, Don't Tell

1 medium onion
2 stalks celery
2 large carrots
2 cans (15 ounces each) navy beans
2 tablespoons vegetable oil
1 can (14-1/2 ounces) diced tomatoes
3 cans (14 ounces each) beef broth
1 ham hock
1/2 teaspoon dried thyme
1 bay leaf
1/2 teaspoon ground cumin
1/2 teaspoon Tabasco sauce
Seasoning to taste

Hush-Hush Salad

1 medium head red leaf lettuce
1 medium yellow bell pepper
1 medium cucumber
2 small ripe avocados
1 small red onion
3 tablespoons olive oil
2 tablespoons balsamic vinegar
1/4 teaspoon granulated sugar
1/2 teaspoon Dijon mustard
1/2 teaspoon dried tarragon
Seasoning to taste

Ambiguous Bread

1 cup flour
1 cup cornmeal
2 tablespoons granulated sugar
4 teaspoons baking powder
2 eggs
1 cup milk
1/4 cup vegetable oil

Cryptic Crisp

1 quart chocolate ice cream
2 tablespoons butter
8 ounces chocolate chips
2 cups Rice Krispies cereal
1 teaspoon peppermint extract
1/2 cup chocolate syrup

EQUIPMENT

Dutch oven

Medium saucepan

9 × 9-inch baking pan

Pie plate

2 large mixing bowls

2 small mixing bowls

Whisk

Vegetable peeler

Plastic wrap

Kitchen knives

Measuring cups and spoons

Cooking utensils

Don't Ask, Don't Tell

1. Peel and chop the onion. Rinse, trim, and chop the celery. Peel and chop the carrots. Drain and rinse the navy beans.

2. Heat the oil in a Dutch oven and sauté the onion, the celery, and the carrots until the onion is soft, about 5 minutes.

3. Add the tomatoes, the beans, the broth, the ham hock, the thyme, the bay leaf, and the cumin. Bring to a boil.

4. Reduce the heat, add the Tabasco sauce and season to taste. Cover and simmer until the flavors have blended, 20 to 25 minutes.

5. Remove the bay leaf and the ham hock, cut the meat off the bone, chop the meat, and return it to the soup.

6. Cover and simmer until you are ready to serve.

Hush-Hush Salad

1. Wash and dry the lettuce. Arrange 4 leaves on individual salad plates.

2. Tear the remaining lettuce into bite-sized pieces. Rinse, stem, seed, and slice the bell pepper. Peel and slice the cucumber. Peel, pit, and slice the avocados. Peel and chop the onion. Combine the vegetables in a large bowl.

3. In a small bowl, whisk together the oil, the vinegar, the sugar, the mustard, and the tarragon. Season to taste, and toss with the vegetables.

4. Spoon the mixture over the lettuce leaves.

Ambiguous Bread

1. Preheat the oven to 425°F. Grease a 9 × 9-inch baking pan.

2. In a large bowl, combine the flour, the cornmeal, the sugar, and the baking powder.

3. In a small bowl, whisk together the eggs, the milk, and the oil.

4. Make a well in the center of the dry ingredients and pour the egg mixture into it all at once. Blend well, and pour the mixture into the baking pan.

5. Bake until the bread is golden brown, 20 to 25 minutes.

Cryptic Crisp

1. Set the ice cream out to soften.

2. Melt the butter in a medium saucepan. Add the chocolate chips and heat, stirring constantly, until melted. Add the cereal and toss to coat. Remove the saucepan from the heat, and let it cool for 5 minutes.

3. Press the chocolate mixture into a pie plate, covering the bottom and sides evenly. Set it in the freezer to harden, at least 30 minutes.

4. Stir the peppermint extract into the softened ice cream, and mix well to blend. Spoon the ice cream into the chocolate crust until it mounds slightly.

5. Cover the pie with plastic wrap and return it to the freezer until you are ready to serve.

6. Cut the pie into wedges and drizzle with the chocolate syrup.

COUNTDOWN

1. Assemble the ingredients and the equipment.
2. Do Steps 1–3 of *Cryptic Crisp*.
3. Do Steps 1–4 of *Don't Ask, Don't Tell*.
4. Do Steps 4–5 of *Cryptic Crisp*.
5. Do Steps 1–5 of *Ambiguous Bread*.
6. Do Steps 1–3 of *Hush-Hush Salad*.
7. Do Steps 5–6 of *Don't Ask, Don't Tell*.
8. Do Step 4 of *Hush-Hush Salad*.
9. Do Step 6 of *Cryptic Crisp*.

Weekend Three Saturday

MEAT & POULTRY

1 pound mild Italian sausage
4 chicken drumsticks

FISH

1 pound medium shrimp, shelled
  and deveined
1/2 pound scallops
12 small steamer clams
12 mussels

FRESH PRODUCE

VEGETABLES

1 medium head green leaf lettuce
1 small bunch watercress
1 medium tomato
1 medium onion
2 cloves garlic

HERBS

4 tablespoons parsley (when chopped)

CANS, JARS & BOTTLES

SOUP

1 can (14 ounces) vegetable broth

CONDIMENTS

1 jar (6-1/2 ounces) marinated
  artichoke hearts
1 can (3-1/2 ounces) pitted black olives
2 tablespoons capers

PACKAGED GOODS

PASTA, RICE & GRAINS

1 cup long-grain white rice

DESSERT & BAKING NEEDS

1 small package instant vanilla pudding
  mix
6 ounces butterscotch chips

WINES & SPIRITS

1/2 cup dry white wine

REFRIGERATED PRODUCTS

DAIRY

2 cups milk
3/4 cup sour cream
6 eggs

DELI

4 slices bacon

FROZEN GOODS

VEGETABLES

1 package (10 ounces) green peas

STAPLES

❏ Butter
❏ Flour
❏ Baking powder
❏ Granulated sugar
❏ Olive oil
❏ Tarragon vinegar
❏ Worcestershire sauce
❏ Dijon mustard
❏ Cayenne pepper
❏ Paprika
❏ Pepper
❏ Saffron threads
❏ Salt
❏ Almond extract
❏ Vanilla extract

Weekend Three Saturday

MENU

Spanish Indecision

1 pound mild Italian sausage
1 package (10 ounces) frozen green peas
2 cloves garlic
1 medium onion
4 tablespoons fresh parsley (when chopped)
4 slices bacon
4 chicken drumsticks
1 pound medium shrimp, shelled and deveined
1/2 pound scallops
12 small steamer clams
12 mussels
2 tablespoons olive oil
1 cup long-grain white rice
1/4 teaspoon saffron threads
1 teaspoon paprika
1/8 teaspoon cayenne pepper
1/2 teaspoon Worcestershire sauce
1/2 cup dry white wine
1 can (14 ounces) vegetable broth
Seasoning to taste
2 tablespoons capers

Salador Dalí

1 medium head green leaf lettuce
1 small bunch watercress
1 medium fresh tomato
1 jar (6-1/2 ounces) marinated artichoke hearts
1 can (3-1/2 ounces) pitted black olives
3 tablespoons olive oil
2 tablespoons tarragon vinegar
1 teaspoon Dijon mustard
Seasoning to taste

Malagraina

4 tablespoons butter
1/2 cup granulated sugar
2 eggs
1 teaspoon vanilla extract
2/3 cup milk
2 cups flour
4 teaspoons baking powder

Minarets

1 small package instant vanilla pudding mix
1-1/4 cups + 3 tablespoons milk
3/4 cup sour cream
1 teaspoon almond extract
10 tablespoons butter
1 cup water
1 cup flour
4 eggs
6 ounces butterscotch chips

EQUIPMENT

Electric mixer	2 small mixing bowls
Medium saucepan	
Small saucepan	Whisk
Large covered ovenproof skillet	Kitchen knives
Muffin tin	Measuring cups and spoons
Baking sheet	Cooking utensils
Large mixing bowl	
2 medium mixing bowls	

Spanish Indecision

1. Set the sausage in the freezer for 10 minutes.

2. Set the package of peas in a small bowl of hot water to thaw.

3. Peel and mince the garlic. Peel and chop the onion. Rinse and chop the parsley.

4. Cut the sausage into 1/2-inch rounds. Dice the bacon. Rinse and pat dry the chicken. Rinse and pat dry the shrimp. Rinse and pat dry the scallops. Scrub the clams, and scrub and debeard the mussels, discarding any shellfish that does not close when tapped lightly.

5. Heat the oil in a large ovenproof skillet. Sauté the sausage with the bacon until the sausage is lightly browned and the bacon is crisp, about 5 minutes. Remove the sausage and the bacon with a slotted spoon, drain on paper towels, and reserve.

6. Add the chicken to the skillet and sauté for 5 minutes on each side or until lightly browned. Remove and reserve.

7. Add the garlic and the onion to the skillet and sauté for 5 minutes. Add the shrimp and the scallops, and sauté until the shrimp turn pink, 1 to 2 minutes. Remove and reserve.

8. Return the bacon to the skillet, add the rice, the saffron, the paprika, the cayenne pepper, and the Worcestershire sauce. Mix well to coat the rice and blend.

9. Add the wine and the broth, season to taste, and cook, covered, until most of the liquid is absorbed, 15 to 20 minutes.

10. Arrange the peas, the sausage, the chicken, the shrimp, the scallops, the clams, and the mussels over the rice in the skillet. Cover, add to the oven, and bake until the shellfish open, about 10 minutes.

11. Discard any clams and mussels that did not open. Sprinkle with the parsley and the capers.

Salador Dalí

1. Rinse the lettuce and the watercress in very cold water to crisp. Dry between paper towels. Tear the lettuce into bite-sized pieces. Separate and stem the watercress. Rinse and chop the tomato. Drain and chop the artichoke hearts. Drain the olives. Combine the vegetables in a large bowl.

2. In a small bowl, whisk together the oil, the vinegar, and the mustard. Season to taste.

3. Toss the salad with the dressing.

Malagraina

1. Preheat the oven to 375°F. Grease a muffin tin.

2. In a medium bowl, cream the butter and the sugar together until well blended. Beat in the eggs. Add the vanilla and the milk, and mix well.

3. Add the flour and the baking powder, and stir gently to blend.

4. Divide the batter evenly among the muffin cups. Bake until golden and firm to the touch, about 20 minutes.

Minarets

1. Combine the pudding mix, 1-1/4 cups of the milk, and the sour cream in a medium bowl and beat with an electric mixer until well blended, about 2 minutes. Fold in the almond extract and refrigerate for at least 20 minutes.

2. Preheat the oven to 375°F. Grease a baking sheet.

3. In a medium saucepan, melt 8 tablespoons of the butter with the water and bring the mixture to a boil. Remove the saucepan from the heat and add the flour all at once. Return the saucepan to the heat and beat vigorously until the mixture forms a ball and no longer sticks to the sides of the pan, about 3 minutes.

4. Remove the saucepan from the heat. Add the eggs, one at a time, beating well after each addition, until the mixture is very smooth.

5. Spoon the dough onto the baking sheet in 4 equal portions, making a little swirl at the top of each portion.

6. Bake until lightly browned, about 40 minutes.

7. Remove the puffs from the oven and turn the oven off.

8. With the tip of a sharp knife, make a small slit in the side of each puff to let the steam escape, return them to the oven, and let them dry for 5 minutes. Remove the puffs from the oven and let them cool.

9. In a small saucepan, melt the butterscotch chips and the remaining butter with the remaining milk, stirring until smooth.

10. Slice the tops off the cooled puffs and fill them with the pudding. Replace the tops and drizzle the butterscotch sauce over the top. Refrigerate until you are ready to serve.

COUNTDOWN

1. Assemble the ingredients and the equipment.
2. Do Steps 1–10 of *Minarets*.
3. Do Steps 1–9 of *Spanish Indecision*.
4. Do Steps 1–4 of *Malagraina*.
5. Do Step 10 of *Spanish Indecision*.
6. Do Steps 1–3 of *Salador Dalí*.
7. Do Step 11 of *Spanish Indecision*.

Weekend Three Sunday

MEAT & POULTRY

3 pounds chicken pieces

FRESH PRODUCE

VEGETABLES

3 medium carrots
3 stalks celery
1 package (10 ounces) mixed salad
  greens
1 small ripe avocado
1 medium cucumber
1 medium onion
2 scallions (green onions)
1 clove garlic

HERBS

2 tablespoons parsley (when chopped)

FRUIT

2 medium oranges

CANS, JARS & BOTTLES

SPREADS

1 cup raspberry jam

PACKAGED GOODS

DRIED FRUITS & NUTS

1/2 cup walnut bits

DESSERT & BAKING NEEDS

1 cup graham cracker crumbs

REFRIGERATED PRODUCTS

DAIRY

2/3 cup milk
1/2 cup half-and-half
1/4 cup whipped cream
3 eggs

STAPLES

- ❏ Flour
- ❏ Bisquick
- ❏ Granulated sugar
- ❏ Dark brown sugar
- ❏ Olive oil
- ❏ Red wine vinegar
- ❏ White wine vinegar
- ❏ Chicken bouillon cubes
- ❏ Bay leaf
- ❏ Whole allspice
- ❏ Ground nutmeg
- ❏ Pepper
- ❏ Salt
- ❏ Vanilla extract

Weekend Three Sunday

Fowling Around

3 pounds chicken pieces
2 chicken bouillon cubes
1 medium onion
3 medium carrots
3 stalks celery
1 clove garlic
1 bay leaf
3 whole allspice
Seasoning to taste
2 tablespoons fresh parsley (when chopped)
1/4 cup flour
1/2 cup half-and-half
2 cups Bisquick
2/3 cup milk

It Was Just One of Those Greens

1 package (10 ounces) mixed salad greens
2 scallions (green onions)
2 medium oranges
1 small ripe avocado
1 medium cucumber
3 tablespoons olive oil
1 teaspoon granulated sugar
1/4 teaspoon ground nutmeg
2 tablespoons white wine vinegar
1 teaspoon red wine vinegar
Seasoning to taste

Jelly's Last Jam

3 eggs
1/2 cup granulated sugar
1/2 cup dark brown sugar
1 teaspoon vanilla extract
1 cup graham cracker crumbs
1/2 cup walnuts bits
1 cup raspberry jam
1/4 cup whipped cream

EQUIPMENT

Electric mixer

Dutch oven

9 × 9-inch glass baking dish

2 medium mixing bowls

2 small mixing bowls

Whisk

Vegetable peeler

Kitchen knives

Measuring cups and spoons

Cooking utensils

Weekend Three Sunday

Fowling Around

1. Rinse and pat dry the chicken pieces.

2. Barely cover the chicken and the bouillon cubes with water in a Dutch oven. Bring to a boil.

3. Reduce the heat and simmer, covered, for 15 minutes.

4. Peel and quarter the onion, peel and chunk the carrots, and rinse, trim, and chunk the celery. Peel and mince the garlic.

5. Add the vegetables to the chicken. Add the bay leaf and the allspice. Season to taste and continue to simmer, covered, for 15 minutes more.

6. Rinse and chop the parsley.

7. In a small bowl, combine the flour with the half-and-half, whisk until smooth, and slowly blend into the Dutch oven.

8. In a medium bowl, mix together the Bisquick and the milk until a soft dough forms. Fold in the parsley.

9. Spoon the mixture over the chicken and vegetables. Cook, uncovered, for 10 minutes.

10. Cover the Dutch oven and cook 10 minutes longer.

11. Remove the bay leaf and the allspice before serving.

It Was Just One of Those Greens

1. Wash and dry the salad greens. Trim and slice the scallions. Peel and slice the oranges. Peel and slice the avocado. Peel and slice the cucumber.

2. Arrange the salad greens on individual salad plates.

3. Arrange the orange, the avocado, and the cucumber slices over the greens. Sprinkle the scallions over the top.

4. In a small bowl, whisk together the oil, the sugar, the nutmeg, and both vinegars. Season to taste.

5. Drizzle the dressing over the salad.

Jelly's Last Jam

1. Preheat the oven to 350°F. Grease and flour a 9 × 9-inch glass baking dish.

2. In a medium bowl, beat the eggs with an electric mixer until light and lemon-colored, about 3 minutes. Beat in the granulated sugar, the brown sugar, and the vanilla.

3. Fold in the graham cracker crumbs and the walnuts.

4. Pour the mixture into the baking dish and bake until a toothpick inserted in the center comes out clean, 20 to 25 minutes.

5. Spread the jam over the top of the torte. Cut into squares and garnish with dollops of whipped cream before serving.

COUNTDOWN

1. Assemble the ingredients and the equipment.
2. Do Steps 1–4 of *Jelly's Last Jam*.
3. Do Steps 1–9 of *Fowling Around*.
4. Do Steps 1–3 of *It Was Just One of Those Greens*.
5. Do Step 10 of *Fowling Around*.
6. Do Steps 4–5 of *It Was Just One of Those Greens*.
7. Do Step 11 of *Fowling Around*.
8. Do Step 5 of *Jelly's Last Jam*.

Weekend Four Saturday

SHOPPING LIST

MEAT & POULTRY

1 lean sirloin steak (about 2 pounds)

FRESH PRODUCE

VEGETABLES
1-1/2 pounds baby new red potatoes
1 medium shallot

HERBS
5 tablespoons chives (when chopped)
2 tablespoons dill (when chopped)

FRUIT
2 large oranges

CANS, JARS & BOTTLES

VEGETABLES
1 can (15 ounces) sliced beets

FRUIT
1 can (29 ounces) sliced peaches
1 maraschino cherry

WINES & SPIRITS

1/2 cup dry red wine

REFRIGERATED PRODUCTS

DAIRY
1/2 cup milk
1/4 cup whipped cream
1 egg

STAPLES

- ❏ Butter
- ❏ Flour
- ❏ Baking powder
- ❏ Cornstarch
- ❏ Granulated sugar
- ❏ Dark brown sugar
- ❏ Vegetable oil
- ❏ Red wine vinegar
- ❏ Celery seed
- ❏ Ground cinnamon
- ❏ Ground ginger
- ❏ Pepper
- ❏ Salt
- ❏ Vanilla extract

Weekend Four Saturday

Mistaken Identity

1 medium shallot
5 tablespoons fresh chives (when chopped)
1 lean sirloin steak (about 2 pounds)
2 tablespoons vegetable oil
1 tablespoon red wine vinegar
1/2 cup dry red wine
2 tablespoons butter
Seasoning to taste

Baby Faces

1-1/2 pounds baby new red potatoes
2 tablespoons fresh dill (when chopped)
Seasoning to taste
1 tablespoon butter
1/2 teaspoon celery seed

Beeting the Rap

1 can (15 ounces) sliced beets
2 large oranges
1 teaspoon vegetable oil
1/4 teaspoon ground ginger
1 tablespoon cornstarch
Seasoning to taste

Impeached

2 tablespoons butter
2 tablespoons dark brown sugar
1 can (29 ounces) sliced peaches
1 teaspoon ground cinnamon
1 maraschino cherry
1-1/4 cups flour

3/4 cup granulated sugar
2 teaspoons baking powder
1/4 cup vegetable oil
1/2 cup milk
1 egg
2 teaspoons vanilla extract
1/4 cup whipped cream

EQUIPMENT

Electric mixer

Medium saucepan

Large covered skillet

Large skillet

8-inch cake pan

Large mixing bowl

Vegetable brush

Citrus grater

Citrus juicer

Kitchen knives

Measuring cups and spoons

Cooking utensils

Weekend Four Saturday

Mistaken Identity

1. Peel and mince the shallot. Rinse and chop the chives. Trim any fat off the meat.

2. Heat the oil in a large skillet. Add the steak and brown, 4 to 5 minutes per side for rare, or 6 to 7 minutes per side for medium.

3. Remove the steak from the skillet and cover to keep it warm.

4. Add the shallot to the skillet and sauté for 1 minute. Add half of the chives and sauté for 30 seconds. Add the vinegar and the wine, and simmer for 1 minute. Add the butter, season to taste, blend well, and simmer for 1 minute more.

5. Slice the steak crosswise into 1/2-inch-thick slices.

6. Top the slices with the sauce and sprinkle with the remaining chives.

Baby Faces

1. Scrub the potatoes. Rinse and chop the dill.

2. Bring water to a boil in a large skillet.

3. Add the potatoes and season to taste. Cover and cook until the potatoes can be pierced easily with a sharp knife, 10 to 15 minutes.

4. Drain the potatoes and return them to the skillet. Toss with the butter, the dill, and the celery seed. Cover to keep warm.

Beeting the Rap

1. Drain the beets. Grate 1 tablespoon of orange peel and juice the oranges.

2. Heat the oil in a medium saucepan. Add the orange peel, the orange juice, the ginger, and the cornstarch. Season to taste and heat through.

3. Add the beets and simmer, stirring, until the sauce thickens, about 5 minutes.

Impeached

1. Preheat the oven to 350°F. Grease and flour an 8-inch cake pan.

2. In the oven, melt the butter with the brown sugar in the cake pan. Remove the pan and blend well.

3. Drain the peaches and arrange the slices in the pan to form the petals of a flower. Sprinkle with the cinnamon. Place the cherry in the center.

4. In a large bowl, combine the flour, the granulated sugar, the baking powder, the oil, and the milk. Blend with an electric mixer until smooth. Add the egg and the vanilla and beat until well blended, about 1-1/2 minutes.

5. Pour the mixture over the peaches and bake until the cake is golden and springs back when lightly touched, 40 to 45 minutes.

6. Let the cake stand for 10 minutes, then invert it onto a cake plate.

7. Serve with dollops of whipped cream.

COUNTDOWN

1. Assemble the ingredients and the equipment.
2. Do Steps 1–6 of *Impeached*.
3. Do Step 1 of *Beeting the Rap*.
4. Do Steps 1–3 of *Baby Faces*.
5. Do Steps 1–3 of *Mistaken Identity*.
6. Do Steps 2–3 of *Beeting the Rap*.
7. Do Step 4 of *Baby Faces*.
8. Do Steps 4–6 of *Mistaken Identity*.
9. Do Step 7 of *Impeached*.

Weekend Four Sunday

FRESH PRODUCE

VEGETABLES
1 medium carrot
1 small head red cabbage
1 medium cucumber

HERBS
1/4 cup chives (when chopped)

FRUIT
1 large lemon

CANS, JARS & BOTTLES

SOUP
1 can (10-3/4 ounces)
   Cheddar cheese soup
1 can (10-3/4 ounces) cream of
   broccoli soup
1 can (10-3/4 ounces) cream of
   celery soup

VEGETABLES
1 can (11 ounces) whole kernel corn

FISH
1 can (6 ounces) solid white tuna
1 tin (4 ounces) boneless, skinless
   sardines

CONDIMENTS
1 jar (2 ounces) diced pimiento

PACKAGED GOODS

PASTA, RICE & GRAINS
12 ounces elbow macaroni

BAKED GOODS
1 large French baguette

DESSERT & BAKING NEEDS
1 package (1 pound 2 ounces)
   yellow cake mix
1 small package lemon gelatin

REFRIGERATED PRODUCTS

DAIRY
1-3/4 cups milk
4 eggs

CHEESE
1 package (8 ounces) Laughing Cow
   Swiss cheese spread

DELI
3 slices bacon

FROZEN GOODS

VEGETABLES
1 package (10 ounces) green peas and
   pearl onions

STAPLES LIST

❏ Butter
❏ Granulated sugar
❏ Powdered sugar
❏ Vegetable oil
❏ Apple cider vinegar
❏ Plain breadcrumbs
❏ Paprika
❏ Pepper
❏ Salt

Weekend Four Sunday

Loony Tuna

1 package (10 ounces) frozen green
peas and pearl onions
1 can (10-3/4 ounces) Cheddar cheese
soup
1 can (10-3/4 ounces) cream of broccoli
soup
1 can (10-3/4 ounces) cream of celery
soup
1 cup milk
1 jar (2 ounces) diced pimiento
12 ounces elbow macaroni
1 can (11 ounces) whole kernel corn
1 can (6 ounces) solid white tuna
1 tin (4 ounces) boneless, skinless sardines
Seasoning to taste
1 cup plain breadcrumbs
1 tablespoon butter
1 teaspoon paprika

Silly Slaw

3 slices bacon
1 small head red cabbage
1 medium carrot
1 medium cucumber
3 tablespoons vegetable oil
2 tablespoons apple cider vinegar
1/2 teaspoon granulated sugar
Seasoning to taste

Batty Bread

1 package (8 ounces) Laughing Cow
Swiss cheese spread
1/4 cup fresh chives (when chopped)
1 large French baguette

Crazy Cake

1 package (1 pound 2 ounces) yellow
cake mix
1 small package lemon gelatin
4 eggs
3/4 cup vegetable oil
3/4 cup milk
1 large lemon
2 cups powdered sugar

EQUIPMENT

Electric mixer	3 small mixing bowls
Stockpot	Whisk
Large saucepan	Vegetable peeler
Small skillet	Vegetable grater
2-quart casserole	Citrus grater
9 × 13-inch baking pan	Citrus juicer
Baking sheet	Kitchen knives
Colander	Measuring cups and spoons
2 large mixing bowls	Cooking utensils

Loony Tuna

1. Set the package of peas and onions in a small bowl of hot water to thaw.

2. Bring water for the pasta to a boil in a stockpot.

3. In a large saucepan, combine the soups and the milk, whisking to blend until smooth. Mix in the undrained pimiento and the thawed peas and onions.

4. Cook the pasta until it is almost tender, about 8 minutes.

5. Drain the corn. Drain and flake the tuna. Drain and flake the sardines. Blend the corn into the soup mixture. Blend the fish into the soup mixture. Season to taste.

6. Drain the pasta. Place half of it in a 2-quart casserole. Layer half the fish sauce over the macaroni. Repeat. Top with the breadcrumbs. Cut the butter into pats and dot the top of the casserole with them. Sprinkle with the paprika.

7. Bake at 350°F until hot and bubbly, about 30 minutes.

Silly Slaw

1. Dice the bacon and sauté it in a small skillet until crisp, about 7 minutes. Drain the bacon on paper towels.

2. Trim and grate the cabbage. Peel and grate the carrot. Peel and chop the cucumber.

Combine the vegetables in a large bowl. Mix in the bacon.

3. In a small bowl, whisk together the oil, the vinegar, and the sugar. Season to taste and toss with the salad.

Batty Bread

1. Set the cheese out to soften.

2. Rinse, pat dry, and chop the chives.

3. Slice the baguette in half lengthwise, and cut each half into four sections.

4. Spread the cheese over the cut sides of the bread. Sprinkle with the chives. Lay the bread, cut sides up, on a baking sheet.

5. Preheat the broiler.

6. Broil the bread until the cheese is just bubbly, 1–2 minutes.

Crazy Cake

1. Preheat the oven to 350°F. Grease and flour a 9 × 13-inch baking pan.

2. In a large bowl, combine the cake mix, the gelatin, the eggs, the oil, and the milk. Beat with an electric mixer until well blended, about 5 minutes.

3. Pour the mixture into the baking pan and bake until golden, about 35 minutes.

4. Grate the lemon peel and juice the lemon. In a small bowl, combine the peel and the juice with the powdered sugar. Set aside.

5. While the cake is still hot, pierce it all over the top with the tines of a fork. Pour the lemon frosting over the cake.

6. Let cool before serving.

COUNTDOWN

1. Assemble the ingredients and the equipment.
2. Do Step 1 of *Batty Bread*.
3. Do Steps 1–4 of *Crazy Cake*.
4. Do Steps 1–7 of *Loony Tuna*.
5. Do Steps 5–6 of *Crazy Cake*.
6. Do Steps 2–4 of *Batty Bread*.
7. Do Steps 1–3 of *Silly Slaw*.
8. Do Steps 5–6 of *Batty Bread*.

Weekend Five Saturday

MEAT & POULTRY

1 capon (about 5 pounds)

FRESH PRODUCE

VEGETABLES

1-1/2 pounds small new red potatoes
1-1/2 pounds asparagus
1 medium head red leaf lettuce
1 bunch radishes
1 large onion

HERBS

1/4 cup parsley (when chopped)

CANS, JARS & BOTTLES

SOUP

1 can (10-1/2 ounces) beef consommé

VEGETABLES

1 can (14-1/2 ounces) hearts of palm

FRUIT

1 can (16 ounces) pitted dark cherries
  in syrup

WINES & SPIRITS

3 tablespoons dry sherry

REFRIGERATED PRODUCTS

DAIRY

1 cup milk
1 tablespoon half-and-half
1 egg

FROZEN GOODS

BAKED GOODS

1 pound cake

- ❏ Butter
- ❏ Flour
- ❏ Cornstarch
- ❏ Granulated sugar
- ❏ Powdered sugar
- ❏ Cocoa powder
- ❏ Olive oil
- ❏ Vegetable oil
- ❏ White wine vinegar
- ❏ Prepared horseradish
- ❏ Dried oregano
- ❏ Dried rosemary
- ❏ Dried tarragon
- ❏ Dried thyme
- ❏ Pepper
- ❏ Salt
- ❏ Vanilla extract

Weekend Five Saturday

Charlie Chapon

1 capon (about 5 pounds)
1 large onion
1-1/2 pounds small new red potatoes
1 can (16 ounces) pitted dark cherries in syrup
4 tablespoons butter
1 can (10-1/2 ounces) beef consommé
2 tablespoons cornstarch
3 tablespoons dry sherry
1/2 teaspoon dried oregano
Seasoning to taste

Slapsticks

1-1/2 pounds fresh asparagus
1 tablespoon vegetable oil
1/2 teaspoon dried thyme
1/2 teaspoon dried rosemary

Palms Up

1 medium head red leaf lettuce
1 can (14-1/2 ounces) hearts of palm
1 bunch radishes
1/4 cup fresh parsley (when chopped)
3 tablespoons olive oil
2 tablespoons white wine vinegar
1/2 teaspoon prepared horseradish
1 teaspoon dried tarragon
Seasoning to taste

Pie In Your Face

1 frozen pound cake
1/4 cup flour

1/4 cup granulated sugar
1 egg
1 teaspoon vanilla extract
1 cup milk
1 tablespoon butter
1 cup powdered sugar
3 tablespoons cocoa powder
1 tablespoon half-and-half

EQUIPMENT

Medium covered saucepan

Medium saucepan

Small saucepan

Medium skillet

Large roasting pan

Roasting rack

Steamer insert

Large mixing bowl

2 small mixing bowls

Vegetable brush

Vegetable peeler

Whisk

Meat thermometer

Kitchen knives

Measuring cups and spoons

Cooking utensils

Charlie Chapon

1. Preheat the oven to 400°F.

2. Rinse and pat dry the capon. Peel and slice the onion. Scrub the potatoes and peel a thin strip around the middle of each one. Drain the cherries, reserving 3 tablespoons of the syrup.

3. Place the capon, breast side down, on a rack in a large roasting pan. Rub the skin with 2 tablespoons of the butter and season to taste.

4. Reduce the oven to 375°F and roast the capon until it is golden, about 1 hour.

5. Turn the capon over, insert a meat thermometer, place the potatoes around the bird, and roast until the potatoes are tender and the internal temperature of the capon reads 175°F, about 2 hours.

6. Melt 2 tablespoons of butter in a medium skillet and sauté the onion until it is soft, about 5 minutes. Add the consommé. Combine the cornstarch with the reserved cherry syrup and add it to the skillet. Cook until the mixture begins to thicken and becomes clear, about 5 minutes.

7. Blend in the sherry and the cherries. Add the oregano and season to taste, and remove the skillet from the heat.

8. Remove the bird and let it stand for 10 minutes.

9. Carve the capon and serve with the potatoes and the sauce.

Slapsticks

1. Rinse the asparagus and break off the tough ends.

2. Bring water to a boil in a medium saucepan.

3. Arrange the asparagus in a steamer insert. Place the insert in the saucepan, cover, and cook until crisp-tender, 3 to 8 minutes, depending on thickness.

4. Drain the asparagus and the saucepan. Return the asparagus to the saucepan and toss with the oil, the thyme, and the rosemary. Cover to keep warm.

Palms Up

1. Wash and dry the lettuce and tear it into bite-sized pieces. Drain and thinly slice the hearts of palm. Rinse, stem, and thinly slice the radishes. Rinse and chop the parsley. Combine the vegetables in a large bowl.

2. In a small bowl, whisk together the oil, the vinegar, the horseradish, and the tarragon. Season to taste.

3. Toss the salad with the dressing.

Pie In Your Face

1. Set the pound cake out to thaw.

2. Slice the cake lengthwise into thirds.

3. In a small bowl, combine the flour and the granulated sugar. Add the egg and the vanilla, and blend well.

4. Heat the milk in a medium saucepan just to boiling. Slowly add the flour mixture to the milk and cook, stirring, until it comes to a boil and thickens. Remove the saucepan from the heat and let the filling cool.

5. Melt the butter in a small saucepan. Add the powdered sugar, the cocoa, and the half-and-half, and blend well. The mixture should be the consistency of chocolate syrup. If necessary, add more half-and-half, a tablespoon at a time.

6. Spread half of the custard filling on the bottom third of the cake. Place the second cake layer over the filling. Spread the rest of the filling on top of the second cake layer. Lay the third layer of cake on top. Drizzle the chocolate glaze over the cake, letting it run down the sides. Chill in the refrigerator until you are ready to serve.

COUNTDOWN

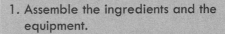

1. Assemble the ingredients and the equipment.
2. Do Steps 1–4 of *Charlie Chapon*.
3. Do Steps 1–6 of *Pie In Your Face*.
4. Do Steps 5–7 of *Charlie Chapon*.
5. Do Steps 1–2 of *Palms Up*.
6. Do Step 8 of *Charlie Chapon*.
7. Do Steps 1–4 of *Slapsticks*.
8. Do Step 9 of *Charlie Chapon*.
9. Do Step 3 of *Palms Up*.

Weekend Five Sunday

SHOPPING LIST

MEAT & POULTRY
1/2 pound mild Italian sausage

FRESH PRODUCE

VEGETABLES
2 stalks celery
1 medium head lettuce
2 small tomatoes
1 small green bell pepper
1 small red onion
3 scallions (green onions)
1 clove garlic

HERBS
2 tablespoons chives (when chopped)

FRUIT
1 medium lemon

CANS, JARS & BOTTLES

SOUP
1 can (14 ounces) chicken broth

PACKAGED GOODS

PASTA, RICE & GRAINS
12 ounces ziti

BAKED GOODS
2 small Boboli pizza crusts

DESSERT & BAKING NEEDS
1 small package lemon gelatin
1-1/2 cups graham cracker crumbs

WINES & SPIRITS
3/4 cup dry white wine

REFRIGERATED PRODUCTS

CHEESE
1 container (15 ounces) ricotta cheese

DAIRY
1 egg

FROZEN GOODS

DESSERTS
1 pint vanilla yogurt

STAPLES LIST

❑ Butter
❑ Flour
❑ Granulated sugar
❑ Olive oil
❑ Vegetable oil
❑ Red wine vinegar
❑ Grated Parmesan cheese
❑ Poppy seeds
❑ Dried tarragon
❑ Italian seasoning
❑ Paprika
❑ Pepper
❑ Salt

Weekend Five Sunday

MENU

Ziti Slickers

1 clove garlic
2 tablespoons fresh chives (when chopped)
1/2 pound mild Italian sausage
3 tablespoons butter
3 tablespoons flour
1 can (14 ounces) chicken broth
3/4 cup dry white wine
12 ounces ziti
1 egg
1 cup grated Parmesan cheese
1 container (15 ounces) ricotta cheese
Seasoning to taste
2 tablespoons olive oil

Hayseed Salad

1 medium head lettuce
2 stalks celery
3 scallions (green onions)
1 small green bell pepper
3 tablespoons vegetable oil
2 tablespoons red wine vinegar
1 teaspoon granulated sugar
1 teaspoon paprika
1/2 teaspoon dried tarragon
1/2 teaspoon poppy seeds
Seasoning to taste

Bippity Boboli Boo

2 small fresh tomatoes
1 small red onion
2 tablespoons olive oil
2 small Boboli pizza crusts
2 teaspoons Italian seasoning

Lemon Yo

1-1/2 cups graham cracker crumbs
1 medium lemon
1-1/4 cups water
1 small package lemon gelatin
Ice cubes
1 pint vanilla frozen yogurt

EQUIPMENT

Blender

Stockpot

2 medium skillets

9 × 13-inch glass
   baking dish

9 × 9-inch glass
   baking dish

Baking sheet

Colander

2 large mixing
   bowls

Medium mixing
   bowl

Small mixing bowl

Whisk

Citrus grater

Citrus juicer

Pastry brush

Aluminum foil

Kitchen knives

Measuring cups
   and spoons

Cooking utensils

Ziti Slickers

1. Preheat the oven to 350°F. Butter a 9 × 13-inch glass baking dish.

2. Bring water for the pasta to a boil in a stockpot.

3. Peel and mince the garlic. Rinse and chop the chives. Remove and discard the casings from the sausage and break the meat into small pieces.

4. Melt 2 tablespoons of the butter in a medium skillet. Slowly mix in the flour and whisk until well blended and thick.

5. Slowly blend in the broth. Add the wine and continue whisking to keep the mixture smooth. Simmer for 15 minutes.

6. Cook the pasta until it is almost tender, 8 to 10 minutes.

7. In a medium bowl, beat the egg. Add the cheeses, fold in 1 tablespoon of the chives, and season to taste.

8. Drain the pasta and toss with the remaining 1 tablespoon butter.

9. Heat the oil in another medium skillet.

10. Add the garlic and the sausage, and sauté until the sausage is brown, about 5 minutes.

11. Place a third of the pasta in the baking dish. Cover it with half of the sauce and half of the cheese mixture. Add another third of the pasta and the remaining sauce and cheese. Spread the rest of the pasta over the cheese, and top it with the sausage and remaining 1 tablespoon chives.

12. Cover the dish with aluminum foil and bake it for 35 minutes.

Hayseed Salad

1. Rinse and dry the lettuce and tear it into bite-sized pieces. Rinse, trim, and chop the celery. Trim and chop the scallions. Rinse, stem, and seed the bell pepper and slice it into rings. Combine the vegetables in a large bowl.

2. In a small bowl, whisk together the oil, the vinegar, the sugar, the paprika, the tarragon, and the poppy seeds. Season to taste.

3. Toss the salad with the dressing.

Bippity Boboli Boo

1. Rinse and chop the tomatoes. Peel and chop the onion.

2. Brush the oil over the Bobolis. Top them with the tomatoes and onions. Sprinkle with the Italian seasoning. Place them on a baking sheet.

3. Preheat the broiler.

4. Broil the Bobolis for 3 minutes.

Lemon Yo

1. Grease a 9 × 9-inch glass baking dish.

2. Place half of the graham cracker crumbs in the baking dish.

3. Grate 1 tablespoon of peel from the lemon and squeeze 3 tablespoons of lemon juice.

4. Bring 3/4 cup of the water to a boil. Pour it into a blender, add the gelatin, cover, and process until the gelatin is completely dissolved, about 30 seconds.

5. Combine the remaining 1/2 cup water with the ice cubes to make 1-1/4 cups. Add the ice to the gelatin and stir until it is partially melted. Then process for 30 seconds.

6. Pour the gelatin into a large bowl. Add the lemon juice. Fold in the frozen yogurt. Add the lemon peel. Pour the mixture evenly over the graham cracker crumbs in the baking dish, and top with the remaining crumbs. Place in the freezer until you are ready to serve, at least 1 hour.

COUNTDOWN

1. Assemble the ingredients and the equipment.
2. Do Steps 1–6 of *Lemon Yo.*
3. Do Steps 1–12 of *Ziti Slickers.*
4. Do Steps 1–2 of *Hayseed Salad.*
5. Do Steps 1–4 of *Bippity Boboli Boo.*
6. Do Step 3 of *Hayseed Salad.*

Weekend Six Saturday

SHOPPING LIST

MEAT & POULTRY

4 loin pork chops (about 1-1/2 pounds)

FRESH PRODUCE

VEGETABLES
1 large bunch broccoli
3 scallions (green onions)

HERBS
2 tablespoons chives (when chopped)

FRUIT
2 medium ripe pears
2 medium oranges

CANS, JARS & BOTTLES

SOUP
1 can (10-1/2 ounces) beef consommé

PACKAGED GOODS

PASTA, RICE & GRAINS
1 cup long-grain white rice

BAKED GOODS
1 package (3 ounces) ladyfingers

DRIED FRUITS & NUTS
1/4 cup raisins
1/2 cup walnut bits

DESSERT & BAKING NEEDS
1 envelope unflavored gelatin
3 squares (1 ounce each)
   unsweetened chocolate

WINES & SPIRITS

2 tablespoons dry sherry

REFRIGERATED PRODUCTS

DAIRY
1 cup whipping cream
4 eggs

FROZEN GOODS

VEGETABLES
1 package (10 ounces) wax beans

STAPLES

- ☐ Butter
- ☐ Granulated sugar
- ☐ Apple cider vinegar
- ☐ Soy sauce
- ☐ Dried marjoram
- ☐ Candied ginger
- ☐ Ground ginger
- ☐ Pepper
- ☐ Salt
- ☐ Vanilla extract

Weekend Six Saturday

Incompearable Pork

4 loin pork chops (about 1-1/2 pounds)
Seasoning to taste
2 medium ripe pears
2 medium oranges
1 teaspoon candied ginger (when chopped)
1/4 cup apple cider vinegar
1/4 teaspoon ground ginger
1/4 cup raisins

A Slice of Rice

3 scallions (green onions)
2 tablespoons butter
1 cup long-grain white rice
1 can (10-1/2 ounces) beef consommé
1/2 cup water
2 tablespoons dry sherry
1 tablespoon soy sauce
Seasoning to taste

Broccoli Bouquet

1 package (10 ounces) frozen wax beans
1 large bunch broccoli
2 tablespoons fresh chives (when chopped)
2 tablespoons butter
1/4 cup water
1 teaspoon dried marjoram
Seasoning to taste

Lady Be Good

1 envelope unflavored gelatin
1/2 cup + 2 tablespoons water
3 squares (1 ounce each) unsweetened chocolate
1 cup whipping cream
4 eggs
3/4 cup granulated sugar
1 teaspoon vanilla extract
1/2 cup walnut bits
1 package (3 ounces) ladyfingers

EQUIPMENT

Electric mixer	2 small mixing bowls
Large covered saucepan	Citrus grater
2 medium covered saucepans	Citrus juicer
Small saucepan	Plastic wrap
Medium covered skillet	Kitchen knives
Springform pan	Measuring cups and spoons
Large mixing bowl	Cooking utensils
2 medium mixing bowls	

Weekend Six Saturday

Incompearable Pork

1. Trim any excess fat from the pork chops and season them to taste.

2. Peel, core, and chop the pears. Grate 2 teaspoons of peel from the oranges and juice them. Chop the candied ginger.

3. Place the orange peel, the orange juice, the vinegar, and the ground ginger in a medium saucepan. Bring the mixture to a boil. Add the pears and the raisins, and cook until the mixture begins to thicken and get syrupy, 10 to 15 minutes.

4. Preheat the broiler.

5. Broil the pork chops for 10 minutes.

6. Remove the saucepan from the heat. Add the candied ginger. Cover the chutney to keep it warm.

7. Turn the chops and broil until the pork is tender and white throughout, about 6 minutes more.

8. Spoon the chutney over the chops.

A Slice of Rice

1. Trim and slice the scallions.

2. Melt the butter in a medium skillet. Sauté the rice in the butter until it is lightly browned, about 5 minutes.

3. Add the consommé, the water, the sherry, and the soy sauce. Cover the skillet, reduce the heat, and simmer until the liquid is absorbed and the rice is tender, 15 to 20 minutes.

4. Fold in the scallions, season to taste, and fluff with a fork.

Broccoli Bouquet

1. Set the package of wax beans in a small bowl of hot water to thaw.

2. Rinse and trim the broccoli and cut it into bite-sized florets. Rinse and chop the chives.

3. Melt the butter in a large saucepan. Add the broccoli and toss to coat. Add the water, cover the saucepan, and steam for 3 minutes. Stir in the wax beans and the marjoram. Season to taste and cook until the vegetables are crisp-tender, 2 to 3 minutes.

4. Drain the vegetables and sprinkle with the chives.

Lady Be Good

1. Chill a medium bowl and the beaters of an electric mixer in the refrigerator for at least 10 minutes.

2. In a small bowl, soften the gelatin in 2 tablespoons of the water.

3. In a small saucepan, melt the chocolate with the remaining water, stirring constantly. Remove the saucepan from the heat and stir in the gelatin. Blend to dissolve.

4. Beat the cream in the chilled bowl until stiff, about 3 minutes.

5. Separate the eggs, placing the yolks in a medium bowl and the whites in a large bowl.

6. Beat the yolks until light and frothy. Gradually beat in 1/2 cup of the sugar. Fold in the vanilla. Blend the melted chocolate into the yolk mixture.

7. Beat the egg whites until soft peaks form, about 3 minutes. Gradually beat in the remaining 1/4 cup sugar. Fold in the chocolate mixture. Fold in the whipped cream. Fold in the walnuts.

8. Line the bottom of a springform pan with single ladyfingers. Stand the remaining ladyfingers on end around the pan. Pour the chocolate mixture into the pan, smoothing the top.

9. Cover with plastic wrap and freeze until set, about 1 hour.

COUNTDOWN

1. Assemble the ingredients and the equipment.
2. Do Steps 1–9 of *Lady Be Good*.
3. Do Step 1 of *Broccoli Bouquet*.
4. Do Steps 1–4 of *Incompearable Pork*.
5. Do Steps 1–3 of *Slice of Rice*.
6. Do Steps 5–6 of *Incompearable Pork*.
7. Do Steps 2–3 of *Broccoli Bouquet*.
8. Do Step 7 of *Incompearable Pork*.
9. Do Step 4 of *Broccoli Bouquet*.
10. Do Step 4 of *Slice of Rice*.
11. Do Step 8 of *Incompearable Pork*.

Weekend Six Sunday

SHOPPING LIST

MEAT & POULTRY

3 pounds chicken pieces

FRESH PRODUCE

VEGETABLES

6 medium red potatoes
1 pound Brussels sprouts
1 medium parsnip
1 medium head iceberg lettuce
1 medium green bell pepper
1 medium yellow bell pepper
1 small shallot

FRUIT

4 medium cooking apples
1 small lemon

CANS, JARS & BOTTLES

SOUP

1 can (14 ounces) chicken broth

VEGETABLES

1 jar (4 ounces) sun-dried tomatoes

FRUIT

1 can (8 ounces) crushed pineapple

WINES & SPIRITS

1 cup dry white wine

REFRIGERATED PRODUCTS

DAIRY

1/3 cup milk
1 cup half-and-half
1 cup sour cream
2 eggs

FROZEN GOODS

PASTRY

1 sheet puff pastry

STAPLES

- [ ] Butter
- [ ] Flour
- [ ] Baking powder
- [ ] Baking soda
- [ ] Granulated sugar
- [ ] Dark brown sugar
- [ ] Vegetable oil
- [ ] Lemon juice
- [ ] Poppy seeds
- [ ] Dried basil
- [ ] Dried thyme
- [ ] Cayenne pepper
- [ ] Ground cinnamon
- [ ] Paprika
- [ ] Pepper
- [ ] Saffron threads
- [ ] Salt
- [ ] Rum extract

Weekend Six Sunday

Slim Chickens

6 medium red potatoes
1 medium parsnip
1 small shallot
1 small lemon
1 pound Brussels sprouts
1 medium green bell pepper
1 medium yellow bell pepper
1 jar (4 ounces) sun-dried tomatoes
3 pounds chicken pieces
1/2 cup flour
3 tablespoons vegetable oil
1 can (14 ounces) chicken broth
1 cup dry white wine
1/2 teaspoon dried basil
1/2 teaspoon dried thyme
1 tablepoon saffron threads
1 cup half-and-half
Seasoning to taste

Tom Mix

1 medium head iceberg lettuce
1/2 cup vegetable oil
1 egg
3 tablespoons lemon juice
1/2 teaspoon paprika
1 teaspoon granulated sugar
1/8 teaspoon cayenne pepper
1 tablespoon poppy seeds
Seasoning to taste

Flimflam Muffins

2 cups flour
1/4 cup granulated sugar
1 tablespoon baking powder
1/2 teaspoon baking soda
1/4 teaspoon salt
1 egg
1/3 cup milk
1/4 cup vegetable oil
1 cup sour cream

Apple Dumpling Gang

1 sheet puff pastry
4 medium cooking apples
1 tablespoon granulated sugar
1 teaspoon ground cinnamon
3 tablespoons butter
1 can (8 ounces) crushed pineapple
2 tablespoons dark brown sugar
1 teaspoon rum extract

EQUIPMENT

Blender	Small mixing bowl
Dutch oven	Citrus juicer
Small saucepan	Vegetable peeler
9 × 9-inch glass baking dish	Kitchen knives
Muffin tin	Measuring cups and spoons
Large mixing bowl	Cooking utensils
Large shallow bowl	

Weekend Six Sunday

Slim Chickens

1. Rinse and quarter the potatoes. Peel and chunk the parsnip. Peel and mince the shallot. Juice the lemon. Rinse and trim the Brussels sprouts. Rinse, stem, seed, and julienne the bell peppers. Drain the tomatoes and cut them into thin strips.

2. Rinse and pat dry the chicken.

3. Place the flour in a large shallow bowl and lightly dredge the chicken pieces in it.

4. Heat the oil in a Dutch oven and sauté the chicken pieces until lightly browned, about 15 minutes.

5. Add the potatoes, the parsnip, the shallot, the broth, the lemon juice, the wine, the basil, the thyme, and the saffron. Bring to a boil, reduce the heat, cover, and simmer until the chicken and potatoes are almost tender, about 40 minutes.

6. Add the Brussels sprouts, the bell peppers, the tomatoes, and the half-and-half. Season to taste and continue simmering for 15 minutes more.

Tom Mix

1. Wash and dry the lettuce, cut it into four wedges, and place them on individual salad plates.

2. In a blender, process the oil, the egg, and the lemon juice until thick, 1–2 minutes.

3. Blend in the paprika, the sugar, the cayenne pepper, the poppy seeds, and season to taste.

4. Drizzle the dressing over the lettuce wedges,

Flimflam Muffins

1. Grease a muffin tin.

2. In a large bowl, combine the flour, the sugar, the baking powder, the baking soda, and the salt. Make a well in the center.

3. In a small bowl, combine the egg, the milk, the oil, and the sour cream and blend well. Pour the egg mixture into the well in the flour mixture and stir to blend. Divide the batter evenly among the muffin cups.

4. Bake at 400°F until the muffins are lightly golden around the edges and the tops are firm, about 20 minutes.

Apple Dumpling Gang

1. Set the puff pastry out to thaw.

2. Preheat the oven to 400°F.

3. Rinse and core the apples. Combine the granulated sugar and the cinnamon, and spoon the mixture into the apple cavities. Dot each apple with 1/2 tablespoon of the butter.

4. Cut the puff pastry sheet into quarters. Set an apple on each square and wrap the pastry around the apple, pinching to seal. Set the wrapped apples in a 9 × 9-inch glass baking dish.

5. In a small saucepan, combine the undrained pineapple, the brown sugar, the remaining 1 tablespoon butter, and the rum extract. Bring the mixture to a boil, reduce the heat, and simmer until the sugar is completely dissolved, 3 to 4 minutes.

6. Pour the syrup over the apples and bake until the apples are cooked and the pastry is golden, about 20 minutes.

COUNTDOWN

1. Assemble the ingredients and the equipment.
2. Do Steps 1–5 of *Slim Chickens*.
3. Do Steps 1–6 of *Apple Dumpling Gang*.
4. Do Steps 1–4 of *Flimflam Muffins*.
5. Do Step 6 of *Slim Chickens*.
6. Do Steps 1–4 of *Tom Mix*.

Weekend Seven Saturday

SHOPPING LIST

FISH
4 salmon steaks (about 1-1/2 pounds)

FRESH PRODUCE

VEGETABLES
1 pound baby carrots
2 stalks celery
1 medium head lettuce
1 medium cucumber
1 bunch radishes
1 cup bean sprouts

HERBS
2 tablespoons parsley (when chopped)

PACKAGED GOODS

DESSERT & BAKING NEEDS
3 squares (1 ounce each)
  semisweet chocolate

WINES & SPIRITS
1/3 cup dry sherry

REFRIGERATED PRODUCTS

DAIRY
1 cup milk
1/2 cup half-and-half
2 eggs

JUICE
2 tablespoons orange juice

STAPLES

❏ Butter
❏ Vegetable shortening
❏ Flour
❏ Baking soda
❏ Granulated sugar
❏ Dark brown sugar
❏ Powdered sugar
❏ Cocoa powder
❏ Multicolored sprinkles
❏ Vegetable oil
❏ Rice vinegar
❏ Steak sauce
❏ Sesame seeds
❏ Ground cloves
❏ Whole black peppercorns
❏ Pepper
❏ Salt
❏ Peppermint extract

Weekend Seven Saturday

Savory Salmon

4 salmon steaks (about 1-1/2 pounds)
3 tablespoons steak sauce
1 teaspoon ground cloves
1 tablespoon dark brown sugar
2 tablespoons orange juice
1/4 cup whole black peppercorns (when crushed)
2 tablespoons vegetable oil

Complementary Carrots

1 pound baby carrots
2 tablespoons fresh parsley (when chopped)
2 tablespoons butter
1/3 cup water
1/3 cup dry sherry
Seasoning to taste

Select Salad

1 medium head lettuce
1 cup fresh bean sprouts
2 stalks celery
1 medium cucumber
1 bunch radishes
3 tablespoons vegetable oil
2 tablespoons rice vinegar
1/2 teaspoon sesame seeds
Seasoning to taste

Conspicuous Cake

3 squares (1 ounce each) semisweet chocolate
1-3/4 cups flour
1-1/3 cups granulated sugar
1 teaspoon baking soda
1/2 teaspoon salt
1 cup milk
1/2 cup vegetable shortening
2 eggs
2 teaspoons peppermint extract
4 tablespoons butter
2 cups powdered sugar
1/2 cup half-and-half
6 tablespoons cocoa powder
Multicolored sprinkles

EQUIPMENT

Electric mixer	Small mixing bowl
Medium covered saucepan	Whisk
Small saucepan	Vegetable peeler
Large skillet	Mallet
2 round cake pans	Plastic bag
2 large mixing bowls	Kitchen knives
Large shallow bowl	Measuring cups and spoons
Medium mixing bowl	Cooking utensils

Savory Salmon

1. Rinse and pat dry the salmon steaks.

2. In a large shallow bowl, combine the steak sauce, the cloves, the brown sugar, and the orange juice. Add the fish and marinate it for 30 minutes, turning several times.

3. Place the peppercorns in a plastic bag and pound them with a mallet until crushed.

4. Heat the oil in a large skillet. Dredge the salmon steaks in the crushed peppercorns and cook until the steaks are golden and flake easily with a fork, about 5 minutes per side.

5. Remove the fish and cover to keep warm.

6. Add the marinade to the skillet and bring the mixture to a boil. Spoon the sauce over the fish.

Complementary Carrots

1. Rinse the carrots. Rinse and chop the parsley.

2. In a medium saucepan, combine the carrots, the butter, the water, and the sherry. Season to taste. Bring the mixture to a boil, cover, reduce the heat, and simmer for 10 minutes.

3. Toss the carrots in the saucepan and continue cooking until the liquid is absorbed and the carrots are tender, about 5 minutes

4. Sprinkle with the parsley.

Select Salad

1. Wash and dry the lettuce and tear it into bite-sized pieces. Rinse and dry the bean sprouts. Rinse, trim, and chop the celery. Peel and slice the cucumber. Rinse, trim, and slice the radishes. Combine the vegetables in a large bowl.

2. In a small bowl, whisk together the oil, the vinegar, and the sesame seeds. Season to taste.

3. Toss the salad with the dressing.

Conspicuous Cake

1. Preheat the oven to 350°F. Grease and flour two round cake pans.

2. Slowly heat the chocolate in a small saucepan until it is melted.

3. In a large mixing bowl, combine the flour, the granulated sugar, the baking soda, and the salt. Add 3/4 cup of the milk and the shortening, and beat with an electric mixer for 2 minutes. Add the melted chocolate, the eggs, and the remaining 1/4 cup milk, blend well, and beat until smooth, about 2 minutes longer. Fold in 1 teaspoon of the peppermint extract and divide the mixture between the two cake pans.

4. Bake until the cakes spring back when lightly touched in the center, 30 to 35 minutes.

5. Remove the cakes from the oven and let them cool.

6. In a medium mixing bowl, cream the butter until soft and fluffy, about 2 minutes. Add the remaining teaspoon of peppermint extract and the powdered sugar, and blend well. Add the half-and-half and the cocoa powder, and beat until smooth, about 2 minutes.

7. Invert one cake layer onto a serving plate. Smooth on a layer of the frosting. Put the second layer on top and cover the top and sides with the remaining frosting. Top with the sprinkles.

COUNTDOWN

1. Assemble the ingredients and the equipment.
2. Do Steps 1–7 of *Conspicuous Cake*.
3. Do Steps 1–2 of *Select Salad*.
4. Do Steps 1–4 of *Savory Salmon*.
5. Do Steps 1–3 of *Complementary Carrots*.
6. Do Steps 5–6 of *Savory Salmon*.
7. Do Step 4 of *Complementary Carrots*.
8. Do Step 3 of *Select Salad*.

Weekend Seven Sunday

MEAT & POULTRY

2 lean cooked ham steaks
   (about 3/4 pound each)

FRESH PRODUCE

VEGETABLES
2 pounds baking potatoes
1 pound green beans
1 medium green bell pepper
3 scallions (green onions)
2 cloves garlic

HERBS
1/4 cup chives (when chopped)

FRUIT
1 pound rhubarb

PACKAGED GOODS

PASTA, RICE & GRAINS
1/3 cup rolled oats

WINES & SPIRITS

2 tablespoons rum

REFRIGERATED PRODUCTS

DAIRY
1 container (6 ounces) plain yogurt
1 cup small-curd cottage cheese

FROZEN GOODS

FRUIT
1 package (10 ounces) strawberries

☐ Butter
☐ Flour
☐ Cornstarch
☐ Granulated sugar
☐ Dark brown sugar
☐ Maple syrup
☐ Olive oil
☐ Tarragon vinegar
☐ Dijon mustard
☐ Dried rosemary
☐ Ground cinnamon
☐ Ground cumin
☐ Pepper
☐ Salt
☐ Vanilla extract

Weekend Seven Sunday

Ham to Mouth

2 lean cooked ham steaks (about 3/4 pound each)
3 tablespoons maple syrup
2 tablespoons rum
1 teaspoon dried rosemary

Penniless Potatoes

2 pounds baking potatoes
1/4 cup fresh chives (when chopped)
1 clove garlic
1 tablespoon butter
1 cup small-curd cottage cheese
1 container (6 ounces) plain yogurt
Seasoning to taste

Green With Envy

1 pound fresh green beans
1 clove garlic
1 medium green bell pepper
3 scallions (green onions)
2 tablespoons olive oil
1 teaspoon Dijon mustard
2 tablespoons tarragon vinegar
1 teaspoon ground cumin
Seasoning to taste

Cocky Crisp

1 package (10 ounces) frozen straw-berries
1 pound fresh rhubarb
1/4 cup granulated sugar

2 teaspoons cornstarch
4 tablespoons butter
1/4 cup dark brown sugar
1/3 cup rolled oats
1/3 cup flour
1/2 teaspoon ground cinnamon
1 teaspoon vanilla extract

EQUIPMENT

Large saucepan

Medium covered saucepan

1-quart casserole

8 × 8-inch glass baking dish

Baking sheet

2 large mixing bowls

2 small mixing bowls

Vegetable peeler

Pastry brush

Kitchen knives

Measuring cups and spoons

Cooking utensils

Weekend Seven Sunday

Ham to Mouth

1. Pat the ham steaks dry with paper towels, cut them in half, and place them on a baking sheet.

2. In a small bowl, combine the maple syrup, the rum, and the rosemary.

3. Preheat the broiler.

4. Brush the ham steaks with half of the mixture and broil, 3 to 4 inches from the heat, until the syrup begins to bubble, 2 to 3 minutes.

5. Turn the steaks over, brush them with the remaining maple mixture, and broil until the syrup bubbles, 2 to 3 minutes more.

Penniless Potatoes

1. Bring water to a boil in a large saucepan.

2. Peel and cube the potatoes. Rinse and chop the chives. Peel and mince the garlic.

3. Cook the potatoes until they are just tender, about 10 minutes.

4. Grease a 1-quart casserole.

5. Drain the potatoes well and turn them into the casserole. Add the butter, the garlic, the chives, the cheese, and the yogurt. Season to taste and mix to blend.

6. Bake at 350°F for 30 minutes.

7. Remove the casserole from the oven and cover to keep warm.

Green With Envy

1. Trim and string the beans. Peel and mince the garlic. Rinse, stem, and seed the bell pepper and cut it into thin strips. Trim and chop the scallions.

2. Bring 1 inch of water to a boil in a medium saucepan.

3. Cook the beans in the saucepan until they are crisp-tender, 4 to 5 minutes.

4. Drain the beans and set them aside.

5. Heat the oil in the saucepan and sauté the garlic, the bell pepper, and the scallions for 2 minutes.

6. Stir in the mustard, the vinegar, and the cumin.

7. Return the beans to the saucepan, season to taste, and toss to combine and heat through.

8. Remove the pan from the heat and cover to keep warm.

Cocky Crisp

1. Set the package of strawberries in a small bowl of warm water to thaw.

2. Preheat the oven to 350°F. Grease an 8 × 8-inch glass baking dish.

3. Rinse and chop the rhubarb.

4. In a large bowl, combine the strawberries and their syrup, the granulated sugar, and the cornstarch. Blend well. Add the rhubarb and toss to coat. Pour the mixture into the baking dish.

5. Melt the butter.

6. In a large bowl, combine the brown sugar, the oats, the flour, the cinnamon, and the vanilla. Mix well. Add the melted butter and mix until crumbly. Spread the mixture over the fruit.

7. Bake until the crust is lightly brown and the fruit is bubbly, 30 to 35 minutes.

COUNTDOWN

1. Assemble the ingredients and the equipment.
2. Do Steps 1–7 of *Cocky Crisp*.
3. Do Steps 1–6 of *Penniless Potatoes*.
4. Do Steps 1–3 of *Green With Envy*.
5. Do Steps 1–2 of *Ham to Mouth*.
6. Do Steps 4–8 of *Green With Envy*.
7. Do Step 7 of *Penniless Potatoes*.
8. Do Steps 3–5 of *Ham to Mouth*.

Weekend Eight Saturday

MEAT & POULTRY
1 whole turkey (about 8 pounds)

FRESH PRODUCE

VEGETABLES
4 medium yams
1 pound green beans
1 large carrot
2 stalks celery
4 medium onions
2 cloves garlic

HERBS
1 tablespoon basil (when chopped)
1/4 cup chives (when chopped)

FRUIT
4 medium green apples

PACKAGED GOODS

DRIED FRUITS & NUTS
1/2 cup walnut bits

DESSERT & BAKING NEEDS
2 squares (1 ounce each)
   unsweetened chocolate

WINES & SPIRITS
1 cup dry white wine

REFRIGERATED PRODUCTS

DAIRY
3/4 cup milk
1/2 cup sour cream
1 egg

❑ Butter
❑ Flour
❑ Baking powder
❑ Granulated sugar
❑ Dark brown sugar
❑ Olive oil
❑ Soy sauce
❑ Bay leaf
❑ Whole allspice
❑ Candied ginger
❑ Pepper
❑ Salt
❑ Vanilla extract

Talkin' Turkey

1 whole turkey (about 8 pounds)
Seasoning to taste
4 medium green apples
4 medium onions
1 large carrot
2 stalks celery
4 tablespoons butter
1 cup water
2 tablespoons soy sauce
1 cup dry white wine
1 bay leaf
3 whole allspice

All Yammed Up

4 medium yams
1/4 cup fresh chives (when chopped)
2 tablespoons candied ginger (when chopped)
1/2 cup sour cream
2 tablespoons butter

Notable Beans

1 pound fresh green beans
2 cloves garlic
1 tablespoon fresh basil (when chopped)
1 tablespoon butter
1 tablespoon olive oil
Seasoning to taste

Downbeat Cake

5 tablespoons butter
3 tablespoons dark brown sugar

1/2 cup walnut bits
2 squares (1 ounce each) unsweetened chocolate
2 tablespoons water
1 egg
1 cup granulated sugar
1 cup flour
1 tablespoon baking powder
1 teaspoon vanilla extract
3/4 cup milk

EQUIPMENT

Electric mixer

Large roasting pan

Small saucepan

Medium covered skillet

8-inch round cake pan

Roasting rack

Large mixing bowl

2 small mixing bowls

Baster

Meat thermometer

Vegetable brush

Aluminum foil

Kitchen knives

Measuring cups and spoons

Cooking utensils

Weekend Eight Saturday

Talkin' Turkey

1. Preheat the oven to 375°F.

2. Rinse and pat dry the turkey and season it to taste.

3. Rinse and quarter the apples. Peel and quarter the onions. Scrub the carrot. Rinse the celery.

4. Stuff the apples and the onions into the turkey cavity. Place the bird, breast side down, on a rack in a roasting pan. Add the carrot and the celery to the pan.

5. Melt the butter and brush it over the turkey.

6. In a small bowl, combine the water, the soy sauce, and the wine. Pour the mixture over the turkey. Add the bay leaf and the allspice to the pan.

7. Roast the bird, basting frequently, for 1 hour.

8. Turn the turkey breast side up. Reduce the temperature to 350°F and continue roasting until the turkey is golden and a meat thermometer carefully inserted between the breast and the thigh, so as not to touch the bone, registers 175°F, about 1-1/2 hours more.

All Yammed Up

1. Scrub and trim the potatoes and prick them several times with a fork. Wrap them individually in sheets of foil, add them to the oven, and bake until they are slightly soft to the touch, about 1 hour.

2. Rinse and chop the chives. Finely chop the ginger.

3. In a small bowl, combine the chives, the ginger, and the sour cream.

4. Remove the foil from the potatoes, cut them open, and add the butter.

5. Serve with the sour cream topping.

Notable Beans

1. Rinse and trim the beans. Peel and mince the garlic. Rinse and chop the basil.

2. Melt the butter with the oil in a medium skillet. Add the garlic and the beans, and sauté until the beans are crisp-tender, 4 to 5 minutes.

3. Stir in the basil and toss to combine. Season to taste and cover to keep warm.

Downbeat Cake

1. Preheat the oven to 350°F.

2. In an 8-inch round cake pan, combine 3 tablespoons of the butter with the brown sugar and the nuts. Place the pan in the oven while it is heating. When the butter is melted, remove the pan and spread the mixture evenly around the bottom. Set aside.

3. In a small saucepan, slowly melt the chocolate with the water. Set aside to cool.

4. In a large bowl, cream the remaining 2 tablespoons butter. Add the egg and blend well. Add the melted chocolate, the granulated sugar, the flour, the baking powder, and the vanilla. Slowly add the milk and beat with an electric mixer until smooth. Pour over the brown sugar mixture and bake until a toothpick inserted in the center comes out clean, 30 to 40 minutes.

5. Remove the cake from the oven and let it cool.

6. To serve, invert the cake onto a cake plate.

COUNTDOWN

1. Assemble the ingredients and the equipment.
2. Do Steps 1–5 of *Downbeat Cake*.
3. Do Steps 1–8 of *Talkin' Turkey*.
4. Do Step 1 of *All Yammed Up*.
5. Do Steps 1–3 of *Notable Beans*.
6. Do Steps 2–5 of *All Yammed Up*.
7. Do Step 6 of *Downbeat Cake*.

Weekend Eight Sunday

FRESH PRODUCE

VEGETABLES
1 medium head green leaf lettuce
1 medium ripe avocado
1 medium white radish
1 medium onion
3 scallions (green onions)
3 cloves garlic

HERBS
1/4 cup chives (when chopped)
1/2 cup cilantro (when chopped)

FRUIT
1 ripe mango
1 small pink grapefruit

CANS, JARS & BOTTLES

SOUP
2 cans (14 ounces each) chicken broth

VEGETABLES
1 can (14-1/2 ounces) diced tomatoes
1 can (15 ounces) red kidney beans
1 can (15 ounces) great Northern beans
1 can (11 ounces) whole kernel corn
   with bell peppers

INTERNATIONAL FOODS
1 can (4 ounces) chopped green chilies

PACKAGED GOODS

BAKED GOODS
4 graham cracker tart shells

DESSERT & BAKING NEEDS
1/4 cup flaked coconut

WINES & SPIRITS
2 tablespoons dry sherry

REFRIGERATED PRODUCTS

DAIRY
1/2 cup milk
1 egg

JUICE
1/2 cup orange juice

CHEESE
1 cup shredded Cheddar cheese

FROZEN GOODS

DESSERTS
1 pint mango sorbet

- ❏ Flour
- ❏ Cornmeal
- ❏ Baking soda
- ❏ Granulated sugar
- ❏ Olive oil
- ❏ Vegetable oil
- ❏ Red wine vinegar
- ❏ Tabasco sauce
- ❏ Ground cumin
- ❏ Pepper
- ❏ Salt

Weekend Eight Sunday

Samba Soup

2 cloves garlic
1/2 cup fresh cilantro (when chopped)
1/4 cup fresh chives (when chopped)
2 cans (14 ounces each) chicken broth
1/2 cup orange juice
2 tablespoons dry sherry
Seasoning to taste

Mexican Hat Dance

1 medium onion
1 clove garlic
1 can (15 ounces) red kidney beans
1 can (15 ounces) great Northern beans
1 can (4 ounces) chopped green chilies
1 can (11 ounces) whole kernel corn with
    bell peppers
6 tablespoons vegetable oil
1 tablespoon flour
1 can (14-1/2 ounces) diced tomatoes
1/4 teaspoon Tabasco sauce
Seasoning to taste
1 egg
1/2 cup milk
2/3 cup cornmeal
1/4 teaspoon baking soda
2 tablespoons granulated sugar
1 teaspoon ground cumin
1 cup shredded Cheddar cheese

Rumba Salad

1 medium head green leaf lettuce
3 scallions (green onions)

1 medium white radish
1 small pink grapefruit
1 medium ripe avocado
2 tablespoons olive oil
2 tablespoons red wine vinegar
1 teaspoon granulated sugar
Seasoning to taste

Mango Mambo

1 pint mango sorbet
1 ripe mango
4 graham cracker tart shells
1/4 cup flaked coconut

EQUIPMENT

Blender

Large saucepan

Medium covered saucepan

2-quart casserole

Strainer

3 medium mixing bowls

2 small mixing bowls

Whisk

Kitchen knives

Measuring cups and spoons

Cooking utensils

Samba Soup

1. Peel and coarsely chop the garlic. Rinse, pat dry, trim, and chop the cilantro. Rinse, pat dry, and chop the chives.

2. In a medium saucepan, combine the garlic, the cilantro, the broth, the orange juice, and the sherry. Season to taste and bring to a boil.

3. Reduce the heat, cover, and simmer for 15 minutes.

4. Strain the soup, and serve with the chives.

Mexican Hat Dance

1. Preheat the oven to 350°F. Grease a 2-quart casserole.

2. Peel and chop the onion. Peel and mince the garlic. Drain the beans. Drain the chilies. Drain the corn.

3. Heat 2 tablespoons of the oil in a large saucepan. Sauté the onion and the garlic until the onion is soft, about 5 minutes.

4. Stir in the flour. Add the beans, the chilies, the tomatoes, and the Tabasco sauce, and stir to combine. Season to taste, remove the saucepan from the heat, and set it aside.

5. In a small bowl, beat the egg with the milk.

6. In a medium bowl, combine the cornmeal, the baking soda, the sugar, and the remaining 4 tablespoons oil. Add the egg and milk mixture. Add the corn and mix well. Blend in the cumin.

7. Pour two-thirds of the cornmeal mixture into the casserole. Sprinkle with the cheese. Add the bean mixture. Spoon the remaining cornmeal mixture around the edges of the casserole.

8. Bake, uncovered, until hot and bubbly, 30 to 35 minutes.

Rumba Salad

1. Wash and dry the lettuce and arrange the leaves on individual salad plates.

2. Trim and chop the scallions. Trim and slice the radish. Peel and section the grapefruit and cut it into bite-sized pieces. Peel, pit, and chunk the avocado. Combine the fruit in a medium bowl.

3. In a small bowl, whisk together the oil, the vinegar, and the sugar. Season to taste and toss with the fruit. Top the lettuce with the fruit mixture.

Mango Mambo

1. Set the sorbet out to soften.

2. Peel and pit the mango and puree it in a blender.

3. In a medium bowl, fold the mango puree into the softened sorbet and freeze until you are ready to serve.

4. Spoon the mixture into the tart shells and sprinkle with the coconut.

COUNTDOWN

1. Assemble the ingredients and the equipment.
2. Do Steps 1–3 of *Mango Mambo*.
3. Do Steps 1–8 of *Mexican Hat Dance*.
4. Do Steps 1–3 of *Samba Soup*.
5. Do Steps 1–3 of *Rumba Salad*.
6. Do Step 4 of *Samba Soup*.
7. Do Step 4 of *Mango Mambo*.

Weekend Nine Saturday

SHOPPING LIST

MEAT & POULTRY

1 boneless center cut pork loin
   (about 3-1/2 pounds)

FRESH PRODUCE

VEGETABLES

1 pound sugar-snap peas

FRUIT

4 large cooking apples

CANS, JARS & BOTTLES

SOUP

1 can (10-1/2 ounces) beef broth
1 can (10-1/2 ounces) chicken broth

JUICE

1 can (6 ounces) apple juice

PACKAGED GOODS

PASTA, RICE & GRAINS

12 ounces curly egg noodles

BAKED GOODS

1 graham cracker pie shell

DESSERT & BAKING NEEDS

1 envelope unflavored gelatin

WINES & SPIRITS

1/4 cup dry sherry
2 tablespoons crème de cacao
3 tablespoons brandy

REFRIGERATED PRODUCTS

DAIRY

1 cup whipping cream
3 eggs

STAPLES

- ☐ Butter
- ☐ Flour
- ☐ Granulated sugar
- ☐ Dark brown sugar
- ☐ Powdered sugar
- ☐ Ground cinnamon
- ☐ Ground nutmeg
- ☐ Pepper
- ☐ Salt
- ☐ Vanilla extract

Weekend Nine Saturday

Any Pork In a Storm

1 boneless center cut pork loin (about
    3-1/2 pounds)
Seasoning to taste
1 cup flour
1/4 cup dry sherry
1 can (10-1/2 ounces) beef broth
1 can (10-1/2 ounces) chicken broth
12 ounces curly egg noodles

High Peas

1 pound sugar-snap peas
2 tablespoons butter
1/2 teaspoon ground nutmeg

Tempest Sauced

4 large cooking apples
1 can (6 ounces) apple juice
1/4 cup dark brown sugar
1/2 teaspoon ground cinnamon
1 teaspoon vanilla extract

Pie Winds

1 envelope unflavored gelatin
1/2 cup water
3 eggs
2/3 cup granulated sugar
2 tablespoons crème de cacao

3 tablespoons brandy
1 cup whipping cream
1 graham cracker pie shell
2 tablespoons powdered sugar

EQUIPMENT

Electric mixer

Stockpot

Medium saucepan

Small saucepan

Large skillet

Medium roasting pan

Roasting rack

Meat thermometer

Large mixing bowl

2 medium mixing bowls

Colander

Waxed paper

Whisk

Kitchen knives

Measuring cups and spoons

Cooking utensils

Any Pork In a Storm

1. Preheat the oven to 400°F.

2. Place the pork on a sheet of waxed paper. Season to taste, rubbing around all sides and both ends. Sprinkle with the flour, rubbing around all sides and both ends. Reserving the seasoned flour on the waxed paper, place the pork on a rack in a roasting pan, and roast until a meat thermometer inserted in the middle reads 170°F, about 1-1/2 hours.

3. Bring water for the noodles to a boil in a stockpot.

4. Remove the pork from the pan and slice it. Place the pan over the heat and add the sherry. Bring it to a boil, scraping up any browned bits from the bottom. Reserve 1 cup of the beef broth and add the rest to the pan. Reserve 1 cup of the chicken broth and add the rest to the pan. Bring the mixture to a boil.

5. Whisk the reserved beef broth with half of the reserved seasoned flour until smooth. Slowly add it to the pan, whisking constantly until the mixture begins to thicken, about 1 minute. Whisk the reserved chicken broth with the remaining seasoned flour until smooth, and slowly add it to the pan, whisking constantly until the mixture is thick and smooth, about 3 minutes.

6. Return the pork to the pan, coating the slices with the gravy.

7. Cook the noodles in the stockpot until they are almost tender, 5 to 7 minutes.

8. Drain the noodles and arrange them around the edge of a serving platter. Arrange the pork slices in the middle of the platter. Serve the pork and noodles with the gravy.

High Peas

1. Rinse and string the snap peas.

2. Melt the butter in a large skillet. Stir in the nutmeg until well blended. Add the snap peas and sauté until they are crisp-tender, about 3 minutes.

Tempest Sauced

1. Peel, core, and chunk the apples.

2. Combine the apples and the apple juice in a medium saucepan and cook over medium heat until the apples are very soft, about 15 minutes.

3. Mash the apples with a spoon to break them up. Add the brown sugar, the cinnamon, and the vanilla, and blend well.

Pie Winds

1. Chill a medium bowl in the refrigerator until you are ready to use.

2. Combine the gelatin and the water in a small saucepan and let it stand for 2 minutes.

3. Heat the mixture to dissolve the gelatin and remove the saucepan from the heat.

4. Separate the eggs, placing the yolks in a medium bowl and the whites in a large bowl.

5. With an electric mixer, beat the yolks with the granulated sugar until lemon-colored, about 3 minutes. Add the mixture to the gelatin and stir over medium heat until the mixture comes to a boil, about 3 minutes more.

6. Remove the saucepan from the heat and add the crème de cacao and the brandy. Pour the mixture back into the bowl and chill until the mixture thickens, about 25 minutes.

7. Beat the egg whites until they are very stiff, about 3 minutes. Fold the chilled filling into the egg whites.

8. Beat the whipping cream in the chilled bowl until it is stiff, about 3 minutes. Fold half of the whipped cream into the filling and turn the mixture into the graham cracker pie shell.

9. Add the powdered sugar to the remaining whipped cream, and mix to combine. Smooth the mixture over the pie. Refrigerate for at least 30 minutes.

C O U N T D O W N

1. Assemble the ingredients and the equipment.
2. Do Steps 1–2 of *Any Pork In a Storm.*
3. Do Steps 1–9 of *Pie Winds.*
4. Do Steps 1–2 of *Tempest Sauced.*
5. Do Step 1 of *High Peas.*
6. Do Steps 3–7 of *Any Pork In a Storm.*
7. Do Step 3 of *Tempest Sauced.*
8. Do Step 2 of *High Peas.*
9. Do Step 8 of *Any Pork In a Storm.*

Weekend Nine Sunday

FISH

4 sole fillets (about 1-1/2 pounds)

FRESH PRODUCE

VEGETABLES

1 pound asparagus
1 medium head lettuce
1 small shallot
2 scallions (green onions)

FRUIT

2 medium ripe pears
2 medium pink grapefruits
3 small mandarin oranges
1/2 pound seedless green grapes

CANS, JARS & BOTTLES

VEGETABLES

2 cans (11 ounces each) whole kernel
  corn

JUICE

1 can (6 ounces) tomato juice

CONDIMENTS

1 jar (2 ounces) diced pimiento

PACKAGED GOODS

DRIED FRUITS & NUTS

1/2 cup pecan bits

DESSERT & BAKING NEEDS

2 squares (1 ounce each) semisweet
  chocolate

WINES & SPIRITS

1/4 cup dry white wine

REFRIGERATED PRODUCTS

DAIRY

2 tablespoons milk
2 eggs

CHEESE

1/2 cup shredded Colby/Monterey Jack
cheese

STAPLES LIST

- ❏ Butter
- ❏ Flour
- ❏ Cornstarch
- ❏ Granulated sugar
- ❏ Dark brown sugar
- ❏ Powdered sugar
- ❏ Cocoa powder
- ❏ Vegetable oil
- ❏ Raspberry vinegar
- ❏ Honey
- ❏ Dijon mustard
- ❏ Prepared horseradish
- ❏ Celery seed
- ❏ Cayenne pepper
- ❏ Pepper
- ❏ Salt
- ❏ Vanilla extract

Weekend Nine Sunday

Shoes of the Fisherman

1 pound fresh asparagus
1 small shallot
4 sole fillets (about 1-1/2 pounds)
Seasoning to taste
2 tablespoons butter
1/4 cup dry white wine
1 can (6 ounces) tomato juice
2 teaspoons prepared horseradish
1 teaspoon granulated sugar
2 teaspoons cornstarch
1 tablespoon water
1/2 cup shredded Colby/Monterey
   Jack cheese

Corn of Plenty

2 scallions (green onions)
2 cans (11 ounces each) whole kernel
   corn
1 jar (2 ounces) diced pimiento
2 tablespoons butter
1/2 teaspoon cayenne pepper
Seasoning to taste

Fruitility

1 medium head lettuce
2 medium pink grapefruits
3 small mandarin oranges
1/2 pound seedless green grapes
2 medium ripe pears
3 tablespoons vegetable oil
2 tablespoons raspberry vinegar
1 tablespoon honey
1 teaspoon Dijon mustard

1 teaspoon celery seed
Seasoning to taste

Earth Tones

2 squares (1 ounce each) semisweet
   chocolate
7 tablespoons butter
1-1/2 cups dark brown sugar
1 cup flour
2 eggs
1 teaspoon vanilla extract
1/2 cup pecan bits
1 cup powdered sugar
1/3 cup cocoa powder
2 tablespoons milk

EQUIPMENT

Large saucepan

Large skillet

Medium skillet

9 × 13-inch glass baking dish

Muffin tin

4 small mixing bowls

Whisk

Kitchen knives

Measuring cups and spoons

Cooking utensils

Weekend Nine Sunday

RECIPES

Shoes of the Fisherman

1. Rinse and trim the asparagus to 6-inch lengths. Peel and mince the shallot. Rinse and pat dry the fish and season it to taste.

2. Melt the butter in a medium skillet and sauté the shallot for 1 minute.

3. Add the asparagus, toss to coat, and sauté for 3 to 5 minutes, depending on thickness.

4. Remove the asparagus and set it aside.

5. Add the wine, the tomato juice, and the horseradish to the skillet, and whisk to blend.

6. In a small bowl, combine the sugar and the cornstarch. Blend in the water and stir the mixture into the skillet. Cook until the mixture begins to thicken and is clear, 2 to 3 minutes.

7. Grease a 9 × 13-inch glass baking dish.

8. Arrange the fish in a single layer in the dish. Top with the asparagus. Pour the sauce over the top and sprinkle with the cheese.

9. Reduce the oven temperature to 325°F.

10. Bake until the fish flakes easily with a fork and the cheese is bubbly, 15 to 20 minutes.

Corn of Plenty

1. Trim and chop the scallions. Drain the corn. Drain the pimiento.

2. Melt the butter in a large skillet and sauté the scallions for 2 minutes. Add the corn, the pimiento, and the cayenne. Season to taste and cook until heated through.

Fruitility

1. Wash and dry the lettuce and arrange the leaves on individual salad plates.

2. Peel and section the grapefruits. Peel and section the oranges. Rinse and stem the grapes. Peel, core, and slice the pears.

3. Arrange the fruit over the lettuce leaves.

4. In a small bowl, whisk together the oil, the vinegar, the honey, the mustard, and the celery seed, and season to taste.

5. Spoon the dressing over the fruit.

Earth Tones

1. Preheat the oven to 350°F. Grease a muffin tin.

2. Slowly melt the chocolate with 4 table-spoons of the butter in a large saucepan, stirring to blend. Remove the saucepan from the heat and blend in the brown sugar and the flour.

3. Beat the eggs in a small bowl and add them to the saucepan. Add the vanilla and blend well. Fold in the nuts.

4. Spoon the mixture into the muffin tin, filling the cups half full.

5. Bake until a toothpick inserted into the center comes out clean, 20 to 25 minutes.

6. In a small bowl, combine the remaining 3 tablespoons butter, the powdered sugar, the cocoa, and the milk, and blend well. Spread the mixture over the cupcakes.

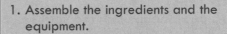

COUNTDOWN

1. Assemble the ingredients and the equipment.
2. Do Steps 1–5 of *Earth Tones*.
3. Do Steps 1–10 of *Shoes of the Fisherman*.
4. Do Steps 1–4 of *Fruitility*.
5. Do Steps 1–2 of *Corn of Plenty*.
6. Do Step 5 of *Fruitility*.
7. Do Step 6 of *Earth Tones*.

Weekend Ten Saturday

MEAT & POULTRY

4 lean beef tenderloins (about 2 pounds)

FRESH PRODUCE

VEGETABLES

1-1/2 pounds baby new red potatoes
1 medium head cauliflower
1 medium red onion
2 cloves garlic

HERBS

3 tablespoons basil (when chopped)
1 tablespoon rosemary (when chopped)
1 tablespoon thyme (when chopped)

CANS, JARS & BOTTLES

SOUP

1 can (10-1/2 ounces) beef consommé

FRUIT

1 can (15 ounces) sliced peaches in
    syrup

CONDIMENTS

1 jar (2 ounces) diced pimiento

PACKAGED GOODS

BAKED GOODS

4 individual meringue shells

DRIED FRUITS & NUTS

1/4 cup pecan bits

WINES & SPIRITS

3 tablespoons dry red wine
1/4 cup brandy
1/4 cup Kahlúa

REFRIGERATED PRODUCTS

DAIRY

1/4 cup whipping cream

FROZEN GOODS

DESSERTS

1 pint coffee ice cream

STAPLES

- ❑ Butter
- ❑ Cornstarch
- ❑ Granulated sugar
- ❑ Olive oil
- ❑ Vegetable oil
- ❑ Balsamic vinegar
- ❑ Lemon juice
- ❑ Whole black peppercorns
- ❑ Pepper
- ❑ Salt

Sir Loin

4 lean beef tenderloins (about 2 pounds)
3 tablespoons whole black peppercorns
3 tablespoons butter
1/4 cup brandy
3 tablespoons dry red wine
1/2 cup beef consommé
1/4 cup whipping cream
Seasoning to taste

Potentato

1-1/2 pounds baby new red potatoes
2/3 cup beef consommé
2 cloves garlic
3 tablespoons fresh basil (when chopped)
3 tablespoons olive oil
2 tablespoons lemon juice
Seasoning to taste

Caliphlower

1 medium red onion
1 medium head cauliflower
1 tablespoon fresh rosemary (when chopped)
1 tablespoon fresh thyme (when chopped)
1 jar (2 ounces) diced pimiento
2 tablespoons vegetable oil
1 tablespoon balsamic vinegar
1/2 teaspoon granulated sugar

Pontifical Peaches

1 can (15 ounces) sliced peaches in syrup
1/4 cup Kahlúa

2 teaspoons cornstarch
1 pint coffee ice cream
4 individual meringue shells
1/4 cup pecan bits

EQUIPMENT

Small covered saucepan

2 large covered skillets

Medium skillet

Whisk

Vegetable brush

Mallet

Ice cream scoop

Plastic bag

Kitchen knives

Measuring cups and spoons

Cooking utensils

Weekend Ten Saturday

Sir Loin

1. Rinse and pat dry the tenderloins.

2. Place the peppercorns in a plastic bag and coarsely crush them with a mallet. Press the peppercorns into both sides of each tenderloin.

3. Melt the butter in a medium skillet and sauté the tenderloins until done to taste, 2 minutes per side for rare.

4. Remove the tenderloins from the skillet and cover to keep them warm. They will continue to cook.

5. Add the brandy to the skillet, carefully flame it with a match, and cook for 1 minute.

6. Add the wine and the consommé, bring to a boil, and cook for 2 minutes, scraping up any browned bits.

7. Add the cream, blend well, season to taste, and cook for 1 minute more.

8. Spoon the sauce over the tenderloins.

Potentato

1. Scrub the potatoes and cut them in half. Place them in a large skillet with the consommé and enough water to cover. Bring to a boil and cook for 5 minutes.

2. Peel and mince the garlic. Rinse and chop the basil.

3. Drain the potatoes.

4. Heat the oil in the skillet and sauté the garlic for 1 minute.

5. Add the potatoes and sauté until they begin to brown, about 10 minutes.

6. Blend in the lemon juice and the basil and season to taste.

7. Remove the skillet from the heat and cover to keep warm.

Caliphlower

1. Peel and chop the onion. Rinse and trim the cauliflower and cut it into bite-sized florets. Rinse and chop the rosemary. Rinse and chop the thyme. Drain the pimiento.

2. Heat the oil in a large skillet and sauté the onion for 3 minutes.

3. Add the cauliflower, the rosemary, and the thyme, and sauté for 2 minutes.

4. Add the pimiento, the vinegar, and the sugar, and sauté until the cauliflower is crisp-tender, about 2 minutes more.

5. Remove the pan from the heat and cover it to keep warm.

Pontifical Peaches

1. Drain the peaches and set aside, reserving 1/4 cup of the syrup.

2. In a small saucepan, combine the reserved syrup, the Kahlúa, and the cornstarch. Bring the mixture to a boil and cook, whisking, until the cornstarch is dissolved and the sauce begins to thicken, about 2 minutes.

3. Remove the pan from the heat, cover, and set aside.

4. Place scoops of ice cream into the meringue shells. Top with the peaches and drizzle with the sauce. Garnish with the nuts.

COUNTDOWN

1. Assemble the ingredients and the equipment.
2. Do Steps 1–3 of *Pontifical Peaches*.
3. Do Steps 1–7 of *Potentato*.
4. Do Steps 1–5 of *Caliphlower*.
5. Do Steps 1–8 of *Sir Loin*.
6. Do Step 4 of *Pontifical Peaches*.

Weekend Ten Sunday

SHOPPING LIST

FRESH PRODUCE

VEGETABLES
1 medium eggplant
1 medium head lettuce
1 medium cucumber
1 large red bell pepper
1 large green bell pepper
1 medium onion
4 scallions (green onions)
4 cloves garlic

HERBS
1/4 cup basil (when chopped)
2 tablespoons parsley (when chopped)

CANS, JARS & BOTTLES

VEGETABLES
1 can (28 ounces) diced tomatoes

CONDIMENTS
1 jar (6-1/2 ounces) marinated
    artichoke hearts

PACKAGED GOODS

PASTA, RICE & GRAINS
1 package (9 ounces) lasagna noodles

BAKED GOODS
1 small loaf Italian bread

DRIED FRUITS & NUTS
1/4 cup walnut bits

DESSERTS & BAKING NEEDS
1 cup mini marshmallows

REFRIGERATED PRODUCTS

DAIRY
1/2 cup half-and-half
1 egg

CHEESE
1 container (15 ounces) ricotta cheese
2 cups shredded mozzarella cheese

FROZEN GOODS

DESSERTS
1 pint vanilla yogurt

STAPLES

- ❏ Butter
- ❏ Dark brown sugar
- ❏ Maple syrup
- ❏ Olive oil
- ❏ Tarragon vinegar
- ❏ Lemon juice
- ❏ Grated Parmesan cheese
- ❏ Celery seed
- ❏ Ground nutmeg
- ❏ Paprika
- ❏ Pepper
- ❏ Salt

Weekend Ten Sunday

MENU

Upon the Lasagna

1 medium eggplant
1 tablespoon salt
1 medium onion
2 cloves garlic
1 large red bell pepper
1 large green bell pepper
1/4 cup fresh basil (when chopped)
3 tablespoons olive oil
Seasoning to taste
1 package (9 ounces) lasagna noodles
1 container (15 ounces) ricotta cheese
1 egg
1 teaspoon ground nutmeg
1/2 cup grated Parmesan cheese
1 can (28 ounces) diced tomatoes
2 cups shredded mozzarella cheese

Beside the Salad

1 medium head lettuce
1 medium cucumber
4 scallions (green onions)
2 tablespoons fresh parsley (when chopped)
1 jar (6-1/2 ounces) marinated artichoke hearts
2 tablespoons tarragon vinegar
1/2 teaspoon celery seed
Seasoning to taste

Over the Bread

2 tablespoons butter
2 cloves garlic
1/2 teaspoon paprika
1 tablespoon lemon juice
1 small loaf Italian bread

Between the Dessert

2/3 cup dark brown sugar
1/2 cup half-and-half
1 cup mini marshmallows
2 tablespoons butter
1 tablespoon maple syrup
1/4 cup walnut bits
1 pint vanilla frozen yogurt

EQUIPMENT

Stockpot

Small saucepan

Large skillet

9 × 9-inch glass baking dish

Baking sheet

Colander

Large mixing bowl

2 medium mixing bowls

2 small mixing bowls

Whisk

Vegetable peeler

Ice cream scoop

Kitchen knives

Measuring cups and spoons

Cooking utensils

Weekend Ten Sunday

Upon the Lasagna

1. Trim, peel, and cut the eggplant into 1/4-inch-thick slices. Lay the slices on paper towels and sprinkle them with the salt. Let stand for 30 minutes.

2. Peel and chop the onion. Peel and mince the garlic. Rinse, stem, seed, and chop the bell peppers. Rinse and chop the basil.

3. Heat 1 tablespoon of the oil in a large skillet and sauté the onion and the garlic for 2 minutes. Add the bell peppers and sauté for 3 minutes. Scrape the mixture into a medium bowl, season to taste, and set aside.

4. Bring water for the pasta to a boil in a stockpot.

5. Squeeze the eggplant slices lightly to extract as much moisture as possible.

6. Heat the remaining 2 tablespoons oil in the skillet and sauté the eggplant until lightly browned, about 5 minutes per side. Drain the eggplant on paper towels.

7. Cook the pasta in the stockpot until it is almost tender, about 9 minutes.

8. Preheat the oven to 350°F. Lightly grease a 9 × 9-inch baking dish.

9. In a medium bowl, combine the ricotta cheese, the egg, the basil, the nutmeg, and 1 tablespoon of the Parmesan cheese.

10. Drain and rinse the pasta in cold water.

11. Spread a third of the tomatoes in the bottom of the baking dish. Add a third of the noodles, in a single layer, cutting them to fit. Add a third of the ricotta cheese mixture. Add a third of the eggplant. Add a third of the onion-pepper mixture. Sprinkle with a third of the mozzarella cheese and 2 tablespoons of the Parmesan cheese. Repeat twice.

12. Bake until the edges are golden and the cheese is hot and bubbly, about 45 minutes.

13. Let the lasagna stand for 10 minutes before cutting.

Beside the Salad

1. Wash and dry the lettuce and tear it into bite-sized pieces. Peel and slice the cucumber. Trim and chop the scallions. Rinse and chop the parsley. Drain the artichokes, reserving the marinade. Combine the vegetables in a large bowl.

2. In a small bowl, whisk the reserved artichoke marinade with the vinegar and the celery seed. Season to taste.

3. Toss the salad with the dressing.

Over the Bread

1. Set the butter out to soften.

2. Peel and mash the garlic.

3. In a small bowl, blend together the softened butter, the garlic, the paprika, and the lemon juice.

4. Slice the bread. Spread the slices with the garlic mixture.

5. Preheat the broiler. Lay the bread slices on a baking sheet and toast, about 2 minutes.

Between the Dessert

1. In a small saucepan, combine the brown sugar, the half-and-half, and the marshmallows, and cook until the sugar has dissolved and the mixture comes to a boil. Reduce the heat, blend in the butter, the maple syrup, and the nuts, and simmer until thick, about 5 minutes.

2. Remove the pan from the heat and set it aside.

3. Place scoops of yogurt in individual dessert bowls and top with the sauce.

COUNTDOWN

1. Assemble the ingredients and the equipment.
2. Do Steps 1–12 of *Upon the Lasagna*.
3. Do Steps 1–3 of *Over the Bread*.
4. Do Steps 1–2 of *Between the Dessert*.
5. Do Steps 1–2 of *Beside the Salad*.
6. Do Steps 4–5 of *Over the Bread*.
7. Do Step 13 of *Upon the Lasagna*.
8. Do Step 3 of *Beside the Salad*.
9. Do Step 3 of *Between the Dessert*.

SHOPPING LIST

MEAT & POULTRY

2 Rock Cornish game hens

FRESH PRODUCE

VEGETABLES

1 large bunch broccoli
1 medium carrot
2 stalks celery
1 medium onion
1 small red onion

FRUIT

2 medium limes

CANS, JARS & BOTTLES

SOUP

1 can (14 ounces) chicken broth

FRUIT

2 cans (11 ounces each)
    mandarin oranges

PACKAGED GOODS

PASTA, RICE & GRAINS

1 cup long-grain white rice

BAKED GOODS

1 graham cracker pie shell

DRIED FRUITS & NUTS

1/2 cup slivered almonds

WINES & SPIRITS

3 tablespoons dry white wine

REFRIGERATED PRODUCTS

DAIRY

1 cup sour cream
1-1/2 cups whipping cream

STAPLES

- ❏ Butter
- ❏ Cornstarch
- ❏ Granulated sugar
- ❏ Powdered sugar
- ❏ Lemon juice
- ❏ Soy sauce
- ❏ Chicken bouillon cube
- ❏ Bay leaf
- ❏ Whole allspice
- ❏ Ground ginger
- ❏ Pepper
- ❏ Salt
- ❏ Almond extract

Weekend Eleven Saturday

MENU

I'm Game If You Are

2 Rock Cornish game hens
Seasoning to taste
1 medium onion
2 stalks celery
1 chicken bouillon cube
3 whole allspice
1 bay leaf
1 cup water
2 cans (11 ounces each) mandarin
   oranges
2 tablespoons soy sauce
3 tablespoons dry white wine
3 tablespoons butter

Rice 'n' Shine

1 small red onion
1/4 cup slivered almonds
2 tablespoons butter
1 cup long-grain white rice
1 can (14 ounces) chicken broth
1 tablespoon lemon juice
Seasoning to taste

A Brazen Bunch

1 large bunch broccoli
1 medium carrot
2 tablespoons butter
1/4 teaspoon ground ginger
1/4 teaspoon granulated sugar
1 tablespoon lemon juice
Seasoning to taste

Tart of My Tart

2 medium limes
1 cup granulated sugar
3 tablespoons cornstarch
1-1/2 cups whipping cream
4 tablespoons butter
2 tablespoons powdered sugar
1 teaspoon almond extract
1 cup sour cream
1 graham cracker pie shell

EQUIPMENT

Electric mixer
Medium covered
   saucepan
Medium saucepan
Medium covered
   skillet
Medium roasting
   pan
Baking sheet
2 small mixing
   bowls
Whisk

Vegetable peeler
Vegetable grater
Citrus grater
Citrus juicer
Baster
Pastry brush
Kitchen knives
Measuring cups
   and spoons
Cooking utensils

I'm Game If You Are

1. Rinse and pat dry the game hens, and season them to taste.

2. Peel and quarter the onion. Rinse, trim, and chunk the celery. Arrange the vegetables in a medium roasting pan. Add the bouillon cube, the allspice, the bay leaf, and the water.

3. Drain the mandarin oranges, reserving 3/4 cup of the liquid. In a small bowl, combine the reserved liquid with the soy sauce and the wine, and set it aside.

4. Melt the butter.

5. Increase the oven temperature to 375°F.

6. Stuff the game hens with the oranges and place the birds in the roasting pan, breast side down. Brush them with the melted butter and bake for 25 minutes.

7. Turn the game hens breast side up, baste them with the butter, and brush them with the orange mixture.

8. Reduce the oven temperature to 350°F and bake, basting occasionally, until the hens are golden brown and the legs move easily, 30 to 35 minutes.

Rice 'n' Shine

1. Preheat the oven to 350°F.

2. Peel and mince the onion.

3. Lay the almonds on a baking sheet and bake until lightly toasted, 2 to 3 minutes. Set aside.

4. Melt the butter in a medium saucepan and sauté the onion until it is soft, about 5 minutes. Add the rice and toss to coat and brown lightly. Add the broth and the lemon juice. Season to taste, bring the mixture to a boil, cover, reduce the heat, and simmer until the liquid is absorbed and the rice is tender, 20 to 25 minutes.

5. Fold in the nuts and fluff the rice.

A Brazen Bunch

1. Rinse and trim the broccoli and cut it into bite-sized florets. Peel and grate the carrot.

2. Bring a small amount of water to a boil in a medium skillet.

3. Place the broccoli in the skillet, cover, and steam for 5 minutes.

4. Drain the broccoli.

5. Melt the butter with the ginger and the sugar in the skillet. Sauté the carrot for 1 minute. Return the broccoli to the skillet. Blend in the lemon juice and season to taste. Cover and simmer for 1 minute.

Tart of My Tart

1. Chill a small bowl and the beaters of an electric mixer in the refrigerator for at least 10 minutes.

2. Grate 1 tablespoon of lime peel and squeeze 1/3 cup lime juice.

3. In a medium saucepan, combine the sugar, the cornstarch, 1 cup of the whipping cream, the lime peel, the lime juice, and the butter. Bring the mixture to a boil, stirring to blend. Remove the saucepan from the heat and place it in the freezer for 5 minutes.

4. Beat the remaining 1/2 cup cream in the chilled bowl until stiff peaks form, about 3 minutes. Fold in the powdered sugar and the almond extract.

5. Fold the sour cream into the lime mixture and pour it into the pie shell. Spread the whipped cream over the lime mixture.

6. Chill the tart for at least 2 hours before serving.

COUNTDOWN

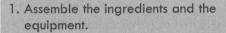

1. Assemble the ingredients and the equipment.
2. Do Steps 1–6 of *Tart of My Tart*.
3. Do Steps 1–3 of *Rice 'n' Shine*.
4. Do Steps 1–6 of *I'm Game If You Are*.
5. Do Step 1 of *A Brazen Bunch*.
6. Do Step 4 of *Rice 'n' Shine*.
7. Do Steps 7–8 of *I'm Game If You Are*.
8. Do Steps 2–5 of *A Brazen Bunch*.
9. Do Step 5 of *Rice 'n' Shine*.

Weekend Eleven Sunday

FRESH PRODUCE

VEGETABLES
1 large red onion
1 medium green bell pepper

HERBS
1/4 cup chives (when chopped)

FRUIT
3 medium bananas
1 large ripe pineapple
2 medium pink grapefruits
1 pound seedless green grapes

CANS, JARS & BOTTLES

SOUP
1 can (10-1/2 ounces) beef consommé

VEGETABLES
2 cups tomato juice

FRUIT
1 jar (6 ounces) maraschino cherries

JUICE
1 can (6 ounces) pineapple juice

PACKAGED GOODS

BAKED GOODS
1 large loaf French bread

DESSERT & BAKING NEEDS
1/2 cup flaked coconut

WINES & SPIRITS

3 tablespoons dry sherry

REFRIGERATED PRODUCTS

DAIRY
1-1/2 cups half-and-half
6 eggs

DELI
1/2 pound bacon
1/2 pound Canadian bacon
1/2 pound breakfast link sausage

STAPLES

- ❏ Granulated sugar
- ❏ Powdered sugar
- ❏ Maple syrup
- ❏ Worcestershire sauce
- ❏ Lemon juice
- ❏ Dried sage
- ❏ Ground cinnamon
- ❏ Pepper
- ❏ Salt
- ❏ Vanilla extract

Weekend Eleven Sunday

Strike Up the Soup

1/4 cup fresh chives (when chopped)
2 cups tomato juice
1 can (10-1/2 ounces) beef consommé
1 teaspoon granulated sugar
2 tablespoons lemon juice
1-1/2 teaspoons Worcestershire sauce
3 tablespoons dry sherry
Seasoning to taste

Toast of the Town

6 eggs
1-1/2 cups half-and-half
1 teaspoon ground cinnamon
1 teaspoon granulated sugar
1 teaspoon vanilla extract
1 large loaf French bread
1-1/2 cups maple syrup
1/2 cup powdered sugar

Banner Bacon

1/2 pound bacon
1/2 pound Canadian bacon
1/2 pound breakfast link sausage
1 large red onion
1 medium green bell pepper
1 teaspoon dried sage
Seasoning to taste

Salute to Fruit

1 large ripe pineapple
2 medium pink grapefruits
1 pound seedless green grapes
3 medium bananas
1 jar (6 ounces) maraschino cherries
1 can (6 ounces) pineapple juice
1/2 cup flaked coconut

EQUIPMENT

Medium covered saucepan

Small saucepan

Large skillet

10 × 15-inch baking pan

2 large mixing bowls

Small mixing bowl

Whisk

Plastic wrap

Kitchen knives

Measuring cups and spoons

Cooking utensils

Weekend Eleven Sunday

Strike Up the Soup

1. Rinse, pat dry, and chop the chives.

2. In a medium saucepan, combine the tomato juice, the consommé, the sugar, the lemon juice, the Worcestershire sauce, and the sherry.

3. Bring the mixture to a boil, reduce the heat, cover, and simmer for 15 minutes.

4. Sprinkle with the chives.

Toast of the Town

1. Preheat the oven to 400°F. Butter a 10 × 15-inch baking pan.

2. In a large bowl, whisk the eggs with the half-and-half.

3. Fold in the cinnamon, the sugar, and the vanilla.

4. Remove the ends from the bread, and cut the loaf into thick slices.

5. Dip the bread slices into the egg mixture, coating them well.

6. Arrange the bread slices in the baking pan.

7. Pour any remaining egg mixture over the bread.

8. Bake until the bread slices are golden, about 8 minutes.

9. Turn the bread slices and continue baking until the tops are golden, 3 to 4 minutes more.

10. Heat the maple syrup in a small saucepan.

11. Sprinkle the French toast with the powdered sugar and serve with the warm maple syrup.

Banner Bacon

1. Cut the bacon slices in half. Slice the Canadian bacon and cut the slices into strips. Separate the sausage links.

2. Peel and thinly slice the onion. Rinse, trim, seed, and chop the bell pepper.

3. Sauté the bacon slices and the Canadian bacon strips in a large skillet until crisp, about 7 minutes.

4. Drain the bacon on paper towels.

5. Sauté the sausage in the skillet until well browned, about 10 minutes.

6. Drain the sausage on paper towels.

7. Add the onion and the bell pepper to the skillet and sauté until the onion is soft, about 5 minutes.

8. Return the bacon and the sausage to the skillet, blend in the sage, season to taste, and toss until the mixture is combined and heated through, about 2 minutes.

Salute to Fruit

1. Peel, core, and chunk the pineapple. Peel and section the grapefruits. Rinse and stem the grapes. Peel and chunk the bananas. Combine the fruit in a large bowl.

2. Drain the cherries, reserving the juice in a small bowl. Scatter the cherries over the fruit.

3. Add the pineapple juice to the reserved cherry juice and drizzle the mixture over the fruit. Cover the bowl with plastic wrap and refrigerate it until you are ready to serve.

4. Top the fruit with the coconut.

COUNTDOWN

1. Assemble the ingredients and the equipment.
2. Do Steps 1–3 of *Salute to Fruit.*
3. Do Steps 1–7 of *Toast of the Town.*
4. Do Steps 1–3 of *Strike Up the Soup.*
5. Do Steps 1–6 of *Banner Bacon.*
6. Do Step 8 of *Toast of the Town.*
7. Do Step 7 of *Banner Bacon.*
8. Do Steps 9–10 of *Toast of the Town.*
9. Do Step 8 of *Banner Bacon.*
10. Do Step 4 of *Strike Up the Soup.*
11. Do Step 11 of *Toast of the Town.*
12. Do Step 4 of *Salute to Fruit.*

Weekend Twelve Saturday

FISH

4 sole fillets (about 1-1/2 pounds)
1/4 pound cooked baby shrimp

FRESH PRODUCE

VEGETABLES

6 medium carrots
1 stalk celery
4 medium mushrooms
1 small onion
2 scallions (green onions)

HERBS

1/4 cup chives (when chopped)

CANS, JARS & BOTTLES

SOUP

1 can (14 ounces) chicken broth

FRUIT

1 can (15 ounces) pineapple chunks

PACKAGED GOODS

PASTA, RICE & GRAINS

1 cup couscous

DRIED FRUITS & NUTS

1/2 cup pecan bits

DESSERT & BAKING NEEDS

1-1/2 cups vanilla wafer crumbs
12 ounces cinnamon chips

WINES & SPIRITS

2 tablespoons dry sherry

REFRIGERATED PRODUCTS

DAIRY

1/4 cup milk
1 cup sour cream
1/4 cup whipped cream
4 eggs

CHEESE

3 packages (8 ounces each)
   cream cheese

STAPLES

- ☐ Butter
- ☐ Flour
- ☐ Cornstarch
- ☐ Dark brown sugar
- ☐ Lemon juice
- ☐ Grated Parmesan cheese
- ☐ Plain breadcrumbs
- ☐ Dried tarragon
- ☐ Ground nutmeg
- ☐ Pepper
- ☐ Salt
- ☐ Vanilla extract

Weekend Twelve Saturday

MENU

Dear Sweet Sole

4 sole fillets (about 1-1/2 pounds)
1/4 pound cooked baby shrimp
1 small onion
4 medium mushrooms
1 stalk celery
3 tablespoons butter
2 tablespoons flour
1/4 cup milk
2 tablespoons dry sherry
1/2 cup grated Parmesan cheese
1 teaspoon dried tarragon
1/2 cup plain breadcrumbs
1 tablespoon lemon juice
Seasoning to taste

Precious Couscous

2 scallions (green onions)
1/4 cup fresh chives (when chopped)
1 can (14 ounces) chicken broth
1 cup couscous
Seasoning to taste

Catchy Carrots

6 medium carrots
1 can (15 ounces) pineapple chunks
1/2 cup + 1 tablespoon water
1/2 teaspoon ground nutmeg
2 teaspoons cornstarch
Seasoning to taste

Clever Cookie

3 packages (8 ounces each) cream
   cheese
4 tablespoons butter
1-1/2 cups vanilla wafer crumbs
   (when crushed)
1/2 cup pecan bits
1 cup dark brown sugar
4 eggs
2 teaspoons vanilla extract
2 tablespoons flour
1 cup sour cream
12 ounces cinnamon chips
1/4 cup whipped cream

EQUIPMENT

Electric mixer

2 medium covered saucepans

Medium skillet

9 × 13-inch glass baking dish

Springform pan

Large mixing bowl

Medium mixing bowl

Vegetable peeler

Aluminum foil

Kitchen knives

Measuring cups and spoons

Cooking utensils

Dear Sweet Sole

1. Rinse and pat dry the sole fillets. Rinse and pat dry the shrimp.

2. Peel and mince the onion. Rinse, pat dry, and mince the mushrooms. Rinse, string, and mince the celery.

3. Melt the butter in a medium skillet. Sauté the onion, the mushrooms, and the celery until the onion is soft, about 5 minutes. Add the shrimp and cook until heated, about 1 minute.

4. Stir in the flour and the milk, and blend well. Stir in the sherry, the cheese, and the tarragon. Cook until the cheese is melted and the sauce is very thick, 3 to 4 minutes.

5. Remove the skillet from the heat, add the breadcrumbs, blend well, and set aside to cool.

6. Reheat the oven to 400°F. Butter a 9 × 13-inch glass baking dish.

7. Place a quarter of the stuffing in the center of each fillet. Roll the fillet up and arrange it, seam side down, in the baking dish. Sprinkle the fillets with the lemon juice and season them to taste.

8. Cover the dish with aluminum foil and bake until the fish flakes easily with a fork, 15 to 20 minutes.

9. Remove the foil and bake, uncovered, for 5 minutes more.

Precious Couscous

1. Trim and chop the scallions. Rinse and chop the chives.

2. Bring the broth to a boil in a medium saucepan. Stir in the couscous and remove the saucepan from the heat. Add the scallions and the chives, cover, and let stand for 10 minutes.

3. Season to taste and fluff with a fork.

Catchy Carrots

1. Peel and julienne the carrots. Drain the pineapple, reserving the juice.

2. Bring 1/2 cup of the water and the pineapple juice to a boil in a medium saucepan. Add the carrots and the nutmeg, cover, and cook until they are crisp-tender, 5 to 6 minutes.

3. Blend the remaining water with the cornstarch and add the mixture to the carrots. Season to taste and blend well. Fold in the pineapple chunks.

Clever Cookie

1. Set the cream cheese and the butter out to soften.

2. Preheat the oven to 400°F. Grease a springform pan.

3. In a medium bowl, combine the wafer crumbs, the nuts, and the butter. Mix well and pat into the bottom of the springform pan and halfway up the sides.

4. In a large bowl, beat the cream cheese and the brown sugar with an electric mixer until well blended, 1 to 2 minutes. Beat in the eggs, one at a time. Add the vanilla and blend well. Add the flour and the sour cream, and beat until smooth. Stir in the cinnamon chips.

5. Pour the mixture evenly into the pan.

6. Bake for 15 minutes.

7. Reduce the oven temperature to 325°F and continue to bake until the cake is set around the edges but still soft in the middle, 25 to 30 minutes.

8. Remove the cake from the oven and cool for 10 minutes.

9. Refrigerate the cake for at least 1 hour.

10. Run a warmed knife around the edge of the cheesecake to loosen before removing it from the pan. Top with dollops of whipped cream.

COUNTDOWN

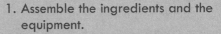

1. Assemble the ingredients and the equipment.
2. Do Steps 1–9 of *Clever Cookie*.
3. Do Steps 1–8 of *Dear Sweet Sole*.
4. Do Steps 1–2 of *Precious Couscous*.
5. Do Steps 1–3 of *Catchy Carrots*.
6. Do Step 3 of *Precious Couscous*.
7. Do Step 9 of *Dear Sweet Sole*.
8. Do Step 10 of *Clever Cookie*.

Weekend Twelve Sunday

MEAT & POULTRY

2 pounds lean beef stew meat

FRESH PRODUCE

VEGETABLES

1-1/2 pounds small new potatoes
4 medium carrots
4 stalks celery
2 medium turnips
1 medium head lettuce
1 medium tomato
1 medium cucumber
2 medium onions
1 clove garlic

HERBS

2 tablespoons parsley (when chopped)

CANS, JARS & BOTTLES

SOUP

1 can (14 ounces) beef broth

PACKAGED GOODS

BAKED GOODS

1 unbaked pie shell

REFRIGERATED PRODUCTS

DAIRY

2/3 cup milk

DELI

1 package (10 ounces) breadstick
  dough with garlic

- [ ] Butter
- [ ] Flour
- [ ] Bisquick
- [ ] Granulated sugar
- [ ] Molasses
- [ ] Vegetable oil
- [ ] White wine vinegar
- [ ] Dijon mustard
- [ ] Bay leaf
- [ ] Dried dill
- [ ] Dried rosemary
- [ ] Dried thyme
- [ ] Whole cloves
- [ ] Pepper
- [ ] Salt

Weekend Twelve Sunday

In a Stew

2 medium onions
5 whole cloves
4 stalks celery
4 medium carrots
2 medium turnips
1-1/2 pounds small new potatoes
2 tablespoons fresh parsley (when chopped)
1/3 cup flour
Seasoning to taste
2 pounds lean beef stew meat
4 tablespoons butter
1 can (14 ounces) beef broth
1-1/2 cups water
1 bay leaf
1-1/2 teaspoons dried thyme
2 cups Bisquick
2/3 cup milk

Salad Spin

1 medium head lettuce
1 medium cucumber
1 medium fresh tomato
1 clove garlic
3 tablespoons vegetable oil
2 tablespoons white wine vinegar
1/2 teaspoon Dijon mustard
Seasoning to taste

Stick to It

1 package (10 ounces) breadstick dough with garlic
2 tablespoons vegetable oil

1 teaspoon dried rosemary
1 teaspoon dried dill

Flick of the Wrist Pie

3/4 cup molasses
6 tablespoons cold water
1 heaping tablespoon flour
1 heaping tablespoon granulated sugar
1 unbaked pie shell

E Q U I P M E N T

Dutch oven
2 baking sheets
Large mixing bowl
2 medium mixing bowls
2 small mixing bowls
Whisk
Vegetable brush
Vegetable peeler
Pastry brush
Waxed paper
Kitchen knives
Measuring cups and spoons
Cooking utensils

Weekend Twelve Sunday

In a Stew

1. Peel and quarter the onions, sticking the whole cloves into one of the quarters. Rinse, trim, and slice the celery into 1-inch pieces. Peel the carrots and cut them into 1-inch chunks. Peel and quarter the turnips. Scrub the new potatoes, but do not peel. Rinse and chop the parsley.

2. Place the flour on a sheet of waxed paper. Season to taste and blend. Roll the beef cubes in the seasoned flour to coat well.

3. Melt the butter in a Dutch oven. Stir in the meat and brown it on all sides, about 20 minutes.

4. Add the onions, the broth, the water, the bay leaf, and the dried thyme.

5. Cover and simmer for 1 hour, stirring occasionally so that the meat does not stick.

6. Add the carrots, the turnips, the potatoes, and the celery, and cook for 1 more hour.

7. In a medium bowl, combine the Bisquick and the milk. Fold in the parsley and stir until a soft dough forms. Drop the dough by heaping tablespoons into the stew.

8. Cook, uncovered, for 10 minutes.

9. Cover the Dutch oven and cook for 10 minutes more. The dumplings should be light and puffy.

10. Remove the cloves and the bay leaf before serving.

Salad Spin

1. Wash and dry the lettuce and tear it into bite-sized pieces. Peel and chop the cucumber. Rinse and chop the tomato. Combine the vegetables in a large bowl.

2. Peel and mince the garlic. In a small bowl, whisk together the garlic, the oil, the vinegar, and the mustard, and season to taste.

3. Lightly toss the salad with the dressing.

Stick to It

1. Preheat the oven to 375°F.

2. Separate the breadsticks and place them on a baking sheet.

3. Brush the breadsticks with the oil.

4. Crush the rosemary into a small bowl. Blend in the dill.

5. Sprinkle the herb mixture over the breadsticks.

6. Bake until golden, about 10 minutes.

Flick of the Wrist Pie

1. Preheat the oven to 350°F.

2. In a medium bowl, combine the molasses, the water, the flour, and the sugar, and pour the mixture into the unbaked pie shell.

3. Place the pie on a baking sheet, and bake until the filling is firm, about 45 minutes.

COUNTDOWN

1. Assemble the ingredients and the equipment.
2. Do Steps 1–5 of *In a Stew.*
3. Do Steps 1–3 of *Flick of the Wrist Pie.*
4. Do Steps 6–8 of *In a Stew.*
5. Do Steps 1–2 of *Salad Spin.*
6. Do Step 9 of *In a Stew.*
7. Do Steps 1–6 of *Stick to It.*
8. Do Step 3 of *Salad Spin.*
9. Do Step 10 of *In a Stew.*

Weekend Thirteen Saturday

SHOPPING LIST

MEAT & POULTRY

1 whole duck (about 5 pounds)

FRESH PRODUCE

VEGETABLES

4 large red bell peppers
1 medium shallot
2 cloves garlic

HERBS

1/4 cup parsley (when chopped)

FRUIT

4 medium ripe pears
1 medium lemon

CANS, JARS & BOTTLES

SOUP

1 can (14 ounces) chicken broth

INTERNATIONAL FOODS

1 can (8 ounces) sliced water chestnuts

PACKAGED GOODS

PASTA, RICE & GRAINS

1 cup brown rice

DRIED FRUITS & NUTS

1/4 cup pecan bits

WINES & SPIRITS

3 tablespoons dry sherry
2 tablespoons brandy

REFRIGERATED PRODUCTS

DAIRY

1 cup half-and-half
3 eggs

STAPLES LIST

- ❏ Butter
- ❏ Flour
- ❏ Granulated sugar
- ❏ Dark brown sugar
- ❏ Vegetable oil
- ❏ Honey
- ❏ Soy sauce
- ❏ Sesame seeds
- ❏ Ground cinnamon
- ❏ Ground ginger
- ❏ Pepper
- ❏ Salt
- ❏ Almond extract

Sitting Duck

1 duck (about 5 pounds)
Seasoning to taste
2 cloves garlic
1 medium shallot
3 tablespoons soy sauce
3 tablespoons dry sherry
2 tablespoons honey
1 cup water

Rice to the Rescue

1/4 cup fresh parsley (when chopped)
1 tablespoon butter
1 can (14 ounces) chicken broth
1/2 cup water
1 cup brown rice
1/4 cup pecan bits

Precarious Peppers

4 large red bell peppers
1 medium lemon
1 can (8 ounces) sliced water chestnuts
2 tablespoons vegetable oil
1/4 teaspoon ground ginger
Seasoning to taste
2 teaspoons sesame seeds

Perilous Pie

4 medium ripe pears
6 tablespoons butter
1/2 cup dark brown sugar
2 tablespoons brandy
3 eggs

2/3 cup flour
1 cup half-and-half
1 teaspoon almond extract
1/2 cup granulated sugar
1/2 teaspoon ground cinnamon

EQUIPMENT

Blender

Medium covered saucepan

2 large skillets

Medium roasting pan

Pie plate

Roasting rack

Small mixing bowl

Citrus grater

Citrus juicer

Baster

Pastry brush

Kitchen knives

Measuring cups and spoons

Cooking utensils

Weekend Thirteen Saturday

RECIPES

Sitting Duck

1. Preheat the oven to 400°F.

2. Rinse and pat dry the duck, and season it to taste, inside and out.

3. Peel and mince the garlic. Peel and mince the shallot.

4. In a small bowl, combine the garlic and the shallot with the soy sauce and the sherry.

5. Divide the mixture in half and blend 1 tablespoon of the honey into each half. Brush half of the honey sauce on the duck.

6. Let the bird stand for 5 minutes and repeat with the remaining sauce.

7. Bring the water to a boil.

8. Place the bird on a rack in a medium roasting pan.

9. Blend the remaining soy mixture with the boiling water and pour it over the bird.

10. Roast the duck, basting occasionally, until it is browned and the legs move easily, 1-1/2 to 2 hours.

11. Let the duck stand for 10 minutes before carving.

Rice to the Rescue

1. Rinse and chop the parsley.

2. Melt the butter in a medium saucepan. Add the broth and the water, and bring the mixture to a boil.

3. Add the rice, cover the saucepan, reduce the heat, and simmer until the liquid is absorbed and the rice is tender, 20 to 25 minutes.

4. Fluff the rice and sprinkle with the parsley and the nuts.

Precarious Peppers

1. Rinse, stem, and seed the bell peppers and cut them into thin strips. Grate 2 teaspoons of lemon peel and juice the lemon. Drain the water chestnuts.

2. Heat the oil in a large skillet and sauté the peppers and the water chestnuts with the lemon peel until crisp-tender, about 3 minutes.

3. Add the lemon juice and the ginger, season to taste, toss to combine, and heat through, about 1 minute.

4. Sprinkle with the sesame seeds.

Perilous Pie

1. Butter a pie plate and place it in the oven to heat.

2. Peel, core, and thinly slice the pears.

3. Melt 2 tablespoons of the butter in a large skillet. Add the pears, the brown sugar, and the brandy, and cook until the pears are cooked and glazed on both sides, about 5 minutes.

4. Melt the remaining 4 tablespoons butter. Combine the butter, the eggs, the flour, the half-and-half, and the almond extract in a blender, and process until smooth.

5. Pour half of the batter into the pie plate. Arrange the pear slices over the batter, reserving the cooking juices. Pour the remaining batter over the pears and sprinkle with the sugar and the cinnamon.

6. Add the pie to the oven and bake until the pie is set, 25 to 30 minutes.

7. Just before serving, drizzle the pie with the reserved cooking juices.

COUNTDOWN

1. Assemble the ingredients and the equipment.
2. Do Steps 1–10 of *Sitting Duck*.
3. Do Steps 1–6 of *Perilous Pie*.
4. Do Steps 1–3 of *Rice to the Rescue*.
5. Do Step 11 of *Sitting Duck*.
6. Do Steps 1–4 of *Precarious Peppers*.
7. Do Step 4 of *Rice to the Rescue*.
8. Do Step 7 of *Perilous Pie*.

Weekend Thirteen Sunday

FRESH PRODUCE

VEGETABLES
2 medium zucchini
1 package (10 ounces) spinach
1 medium cucumber
1 medium onion
1 small red onion
1 clove garlic

HERBS
1/2 cup cilantro (when chopped)

FRUIT
2 medium bananas

CANS, JARS & BOTTLES

SOUP
1 can (10-1/2 ounces) onion soup

VEGETABLES
1 can (28 ounces) stewed tomatoes
1 can (15 ounces) garbanzo beans

PACKAGED GOODS

DRIED FRUIT & NUTS
1/2 cup sliced almonds

DESSERT & BAKING NEEDS
2 tablespoons chocolate chips
1/4 cup marshmallow crème

REFRIGERATED PRODUCTS

DAIRY
1-1/4 cups milk
1/2 cup half-and-half
1 egg

JUICE
2 tablespoons orange juice

CHEESE
1/2 cup shredded Colby/Monterey Jack cheese

DELI
1/2 pound bacon

FROZEN GOODS

DESSERTS
1 pint honey almond gelato

STAPLES

- ☐ Butter
- ☐ Flour
- ☐ Baking powder
- ☐ Granulated sugar
- ☐ Dark brown sugar
- ☐ Olive oil
- ☐ Lemon juice
- ☐ Grated Romano cheese
- ☐ Poppy seeds
- ☐ Dried basil
- ☐ Bay leaves
- ☐ Whole allspice
- ☐ Pepper
- ☐ Salt
- ☐ Vanilla extract

Weekend Thirteen Sunday

MENU

Jam-Packed Chowder

2 tablespoons butter
1 medium onion
2 medium zucchini
1 clove garlic
1 can (15 ounces) garbanzo beans
1 can (28 ounces) stewed tomatoes
1 can (10-1/2 ounces) onion soup
1 teaspoon dried basil
2 bay leaves
3 whole allspice
1 teaspoon granulated sugar
Seasoning to taste
1/2 cup shredded Colby/Monterey
   Jack cheese
1/2 cup grated Romano cheese
1/2 cup half-and-half

Solid Salad

1/2 pound bacon
1 package (10 ounces) fresh spinach
1/2 cup fresh cilantro (when chopped)
1 medium cucumber
1 small red onion
3 tablespoons olive oil
2 tablespoons lemon juice
Seasoning to taste

Stuffed Muffins

4 tablespoons butter
1-1/4 cups milk
1/4 cup poppy seeds
1/4 cup granulated sugar
1 egg

1 teaspoon vanilla extract
2 cups flour
4 teaspoons baking powder

Busy Bananas

2 tablespoons butter
2 tablespoons dark brown sugar
1/2 cup sliced almonds
1 pint honey almond gelato
2 medium bananas
2 tablespoons orange juice
2 tablespoons chocolate chips
1/4 cup marshmallow crème

EQUIPMENT

Blender
Dutch oven
Small skillet
Medium skillet
Muffin tin
Large mixing bowl
2 medium mixing bowls
3 small mixing bowls
Whisk
Vegetable brush
Vegetable peeler
Kitchen knives
Measuring cups and spoons
Cooking utensils

Weekend Thirteen Sunday

Jam-Packed Chowder

1. Preheat the oven to 375°F.

2. Melt the butter in an ovenproof Dutch oven.

3. Peel and chop the onion. Scrub and slice the zucchini. Peel and mince the garlic. Drain and rinse the beans. Combine the ingredients in the Dutch oven.

4. Mix in the tomatoes, the onion soup, the basil, the bay leaves, the allspice, and the sugar. Season to taste.

5. Cover and bake for 1 hour, stirring occasionally.

6. Blend in the cheeses and the half-and-half.

7. Cover and bake until the cheese is melted and the chowder is hot, about 5 minutes more.

8. Remove the bay leaves and the allspice before serving.

Solid Salad

1. Dice the bacon.

2. Sauté the bacon in a medium skillet until crisp, about 5 minutes.

3. Drain the bacon on paper towels.

4. Rinse and pat dry the spinach. Rinse and chop the cilantro. Peel and slice the cucumber. Peel and slice the onion. Combine the vegetables in a large bowl.

5. In a small bowl, whisk together the oil and the lemon juice. Season to taste.

6. Toss the salad with the dressing and sprinkle with the bacon.

Stuffed Muffins

1. Set the butter out to soften.

2. Grease a muffin tin.

3. Combine the milk and the poppy seeds in a small bowl for 10 minutes.

4. In a medium bowl, cream the butter with the sugar.

5. Add the egg, the vanilla, and the milk mixture.

6. In another medium bowl, combine the flour and the baking powder, and blend well.

7. Make a well in the center of the dry ingredients and pour the milk mixture into it. Stir to blend, but do not beat.

8. Fill the muffin cups three-quarters full.

9. Add the muffins to the oven and bake until they are golden, about 20 minutes.

Busy Bananas

1. Melt the butter with the brown sugar in a small skillet and sauté the nuts until well coated, about 3 minutes. Scrape into a small bowl and refrigerate for 10 minutes.

2. Set the gelato out to soften.

3. Combine the bananas and the orange juice in a blender.

4. Add the gelato and blend until smooth.

5. Fold in the nuts and the chocolate chips.

6. Pour the mixture into individual dessert glasses and freeze until you are ready to serve.

7. Top with dollops of marshmallow crème.

COUNTDOWN

1. Assemble the ingredients and the equipment.
2. Do Steps 1–6 of *Busy Bananas*.
3. Do Steps 1–5 of *Jam-Packed Chowder*.
4. Do Steps 1–9 of *Stuffed Muffins*.
5. Do Steps 1–4 of *Solid Salad*.
6. Do Steps 6–7 of *Jam-Packed Chowder*.
7. Do Steps 5–6 of *Solid Salad*.
8. Do Step 8 of *Jam-Packed Chowder*.
9. Do Step 7 of *Busy Bananas*.

Spring

Weekend One Saturday

MEAT & POULTRY
2 pounds lean beef

FRESH PRODUCE

VEGETABLES
6 medium new potatoes
1 pound baby carrots
1 small turnip
1 bunch arugula
1 head Belgian endive
1 head radicchio
4 scallions (green onions)
4 cloves garlic

HERBS
3 tablespoons parsley (when chopped)

FRUIT
1 large lemon

CANS, JARS & BOTTLES

SOUP
1 can (14 ounces) beef broth

VEGETABLES
1 can (4 ounces) button mushrooms

FRUIT
1 can (8 ounces) crushed pineapple

DESSERT & BAKING NEEDS
1 can (21 ounces) cherry pie filling

PACKAGED GOODS

BAKED GOODS
1 large French baguette
1 chocolate pie shell

DESSERT & BAKING NEEDS
1 small package raspberry gelatin

WINES & SPIRITS
1 cup dry red wine

REFRIGERATED PRODUCTS

DAIRY
1/2 cup sour cream
1/4 cup whipped cream

CHEESE
8 ounces Gruyère cheese

DELI
6 slices bacon

FROZEN GOODS

VEGETABLES
1 package (16 ounces) whole baby
  onions

STAPLES

☐ Flour
☐ Cornstarch
☐ Granulated sugar
☐ Olive oil
☐ Red wine vinegar
☐ Dried tarragon
☐ Dried thyme
☐ Pepper
☐ Salt
☐ Almond extract

Viva la Beef

1 package (16 ounces) frozen whole baby onions
6 slices bacon
1 clove garlic
3 tablespoons fresh parsley (when chopped)
6 medium new potatoes
1 pound baby carrots
2 pounds lean beef
1/2 cup flour
1 can (14 ounces) beef broth
1 cup dry red wine
1/2 teaspoon dried thyme
1 can (4 ounces) button mushrooms
Seasoning to taste

Tricolor Salad

1 small turnip
1 bunch arugula
1 head Belgian endive
1 head radicchio
1 clove garlic
4 tablespoons olive oil
3 tablespoons red wine vinegar
1/2 teaspoon dried tarragon
Seasoning to taste

Pain de Paris

8 ounces Gruyère cheese
4 scallions (green onions)
2 cloves garlic
1 large lemon
1/2 cup sour cream
1 large French baguette

Mon Cherie

1 can (8 ounces) crushed pineapple
1 tablespoon cornstarch
1 small package raspberry gelatin
1 can (21 ounces) cherry pie filling
1/2 teaspoon almond extract
1/4 cup granulated sugar
1 chocolate pie shell
1/4 cup whipped cream

EQUIPMENT

Blender
Dutch oven
Large saucepan
Baking sheet
Large mixing bowl
2 small mixing bowls
Whisk
Citrus grater
Citrus juicer
Vegetable brush
Vegetable peeler
Waxed paper
Kitchen knives
Measuring cups and spoons
Cooking utensils

Weekend One Saturday

Viva la Beef

1. Set the package of onions in a small bowl of hot water to thaw.

2. Preheat the oven to 350°F.

3. In a Dutch oven, sauté the bacon until it is crisp and brown, about 8 minutes. Drain the bacon on paper towels.

4. Peel and mince the garlic. Rinse and chop the parsley. Scrub and halve the potatoes. Rinse the carrots.

5. Cut the beef into 1-inch cubes. Place the flour on a piece of waxed paper. Coat the beef well with the flour and sauté in the bacon drippings until well browned, 15 to 20 minutes.

6. Place the broth, the wine, the garlic, the thyme, and 1-1/2 tablespoons of the parsley in a blender and process until smooth. Pour the mixture over the beef, cover, and bake for 30 minutes.

7. Add the potatoes, the carrots, the onions, and the undrained mushrooms to the beef, and season to taste. Cover and bake for 30 minutes more.

8. Uncover and bake until the liquid has been absorbed, about 15 minutes longer.

9. Crumble the bacon over the top of the beef and sprinkle with the remaining 1-1/2 tablespoons parsley.

Tricolor Salad

1. Peel and slice the turnip. Rinse and trim the arugula. Rinse and slice the endive. Rinse and chop the radicchio. Combine the ingredients in a large bowl.

2. In a small bowl, whisk together the oil, the vinegar, and the tarragon. Season to taste.

3. Toss the salad with the dressing.

Pain de Paris

1. Set the cheese out to soften.

2. Trim and chop the scallions. Peel and mince the garlic. Grate 1 tablespoon of lemon peel and squeeze 3 tablespoons of lemon juice.

3. In a small bowl, combine the softened cheese, the scallions, the garlic, the lemon peel, the lemon juice, and the sour cream, and blend well.

4. Slice the baguette into inch-thick rounds, and lay them on a baking sheet.

5. Spread the cheese mixture over the baguette slices.

6. Preheat the broiler.

7. Broil the bread slices until bubbly, 1–2 minutes.

Mon Cherie

1. In a large saucepan, combine the undrained pineapple, the cornstarch, and the gelatin. Bring the mixture to a boil, stirring until it is thick and glossy, about 5 minutes, then remove it from the heat.

2. Stir the pie filling and the almond extract into the saucepan. Blend in the sugar and pour the mixture into the pie shell. Chill the pie until you are ready to serve, at least 1 hour.

3. Top each serving with a dollop of whipped cream.

COUNTDOWN

1. Assemble the ingredients and the equipment.
2. Do Steps 1–6 of *Viva la Beef.*
3. Do Steps 1–2 of *Mon Cherie.*
4. Do Step 7 of *Viva la Beef.*
5. Do Step 1 of *Pain de Paris.*
6. Do Steps 1–2 of *Tricolor Salad.*
7. Do Step 8 of *Viva la Beef.*
8. Do Steps 2–7 of *Pain de Paris.*
9. Do Step 3 of *Tricolor Salad.*
10. Do Step 9 of *Viva la Beef.*
11. Do Step 3 of *Mon Cherie.*

Weekend One Sunday

SHOPPING LIST

MEAT & POULTRY

1-1/2 pounds boneless, skinless chicken breast

FRESH PRODUCE

VEGETABLES

1 medium bunch broccoli
2 medium carrots
2 stalks celery
1 package (10 ounces) spinach
1 large ripe avocado
1 medium onion
1 medium red onion

HERBS

2 tablespoons parsley (when chopped)

CANS, JARS & BOTTLES

SOUP

2 cans (14 ounces each) chicken broth

SPREADS

1 jar (10 ounces) apple-mint jelly

DESSERT & BAKING NEEDS

1/4 cup marshmallow crème

PACKAGED GOODS

DESSERT & BAKING NEEDS

1 package active dry yeast

WINES & SPIRITS

2 tablespoons dry sherry

REFRIGERATED PRODUCTS

DAIRY

1 cup half-and-half
1 cup buttermilk

CHEESE

1/2 pound Jarlsberg cheese

FROZEN GOODS

DESSERTS

1 pint vanilla yogurt
1 pint lime sherbet

STAPLES

- ❐ Butter
- ❐ Flour
- ❐ Baking powder
- ❐ Baking soda
- ❐ Granulated sugar
- ❐ Olive oil
- ❐ Balsamic vinegar
- ❐ Lemon juice
- ❐ Dijon mustard
- ❐ Dried basil
- ❐ Italian seasoning
- ❐ Pepper
- ❐ Salt

Down On the Farm Soup

1 medium onion
2 medium carrots
2 stalks celery
1 medium bunch broccoli
2 tablespoons fresh parsley (when chopped)
1/2 pound Jarlsberg cheese
1-1/2 pounds boneless, skinless chicken breast
2 tablespoons butter
2 tablespoons dry sherry
1 teaspoon dried basil
1-1/2 teaspoons Italian seasoning
2 cans (14 ounces each) chicken broth
3 tablespoons flour
1 cup half-and-half
Seasoning to taste

Garden Patch Salad

1 package (10 ounces) fresh spinach
1 medium red onion
1 large ripe avocado
3 tablespoons olive oil
2 tablespoons lemon juice
1 teaspoon Dijon mustard
1 teaspoon balsamic vinegar
1/2 teaspoon granulated sugar
Seasoning to taste

Country Biscuits

4 tablespoons butter
1 package active dry yeast
1/4 cup warm water
2-1/2 cups flour
1 tablespoon granulated sugar
1 tablespoon baking powder
1/2 teaspoon baking soda
1 cup buttermilk

Sunday Sundaes

1 jar (10 ounces) apple-mint jelly
1/4 cup water
1 pint vanilla frozen yogurt
1 pint lime sherbet
1/4 cup marshmallow crème

EQUIPMENT

Stockpot	Cheese grater
Small saucepan	Rolling pin
Baking sheet	Pastry blender
Breadboard	Biscuit cutter
2 large mixing bowls	Ice cream scoop
3 small mixing bowls	Kitchen knives
Whisk	Measuring cups and spoons
Vegetable peeler	Cooking utensils

Weekend One Sunday

Down On the Farm Soup

1. Peel and chop the onion. Peel and chop the carrots. Rinse, trim, and chop the celery. Rinse the broccoli and cut it into bite-sized florets. Rinse and chop the parsley. Grate the cheese. Rinse, pat dry, and cube the chicken.

2. Melt the butter in a stockpot. Add the onion and sauté until it is soft, about 5 minutes.

3. Stir in the chicken and sauté until the cubes are opaque, about 3 minutes.

4. Add the carrots, the celery, the sherry, the basil, and the Italian seasoning, and sauté about 3 minutes.

5. Stir in the broth and bring to a boil.

6. Cover, reduce the heat, and simmer until the vegetables are crisp-tender, about 10 minutes.

7. Add the broccoli and simmer for 5 minutes more.

8. In a small bowl, whisk the flour into the half-and-half.

9. Slowly add the mixture to the soup, stirring to blend, and heat through.

10. Simmer until the soup begins to thicken, about 10 minutes.

11. Stir in the cheese and season to taste. Garnish with the parsley.

Garden Patch Salad

1. Rinse and tear the spinach into bite-sized pieces. Peel and slice the onion. Peel, pit, and slice the avocado. Combine the vegetables in a large bowl.

2. In a small bowl, whisk together the oil, the lemon juice, the mustard, the vinegar, and the sugar, and season to taste.

3. Toss the salad with the dressing.

Country Biscuits

1. Set the butter out to soften.

2. Preheat the oven to 400°F. Flour a breadboard. Flour a biscuit cutter.

3. In a small bowl, combine the yeast with the warm water and let it stand to dissolve, about 5 minutes.

4. In a large bowl, combine the flour, the sugar, the baking powder, and the baking soda.

5. Cut the softened butter into the mixture with a pastry blender until the dough resembles small peas.

6. Fold in the yeast mixture and the buttermilk, and blend well.

7. Turn the mixture out onto the breadboard and knead it until smooth, 8 to 10 times. Roll the dough out to a 3/4-inch thickness and cut it with the biscuit cutter.

8. Place the biscuits on a baking sheet and bake until they are golden, about 15 minutes.

Sunday Sundaes

1. Heat the apple-mint jelly with the water in a small saucepan, stirring until the jelly melts, about 4 minutes. Set the pan aside to cool.

2. Place 2 tablespoons of the jelly in the bottom of each individual dessert glass. Add a scoop of frozen yogurt and a scoop of sherbet. Add another tablespoon of the jelly, and top with marshmallow crème.

COUNTDOWN

1. Assemble the ingredients and the equipment.
2. Do Steps 1–6 of *Down On the Farm Soup.*
3. Do Steps 1–8 of *Country Biscuits.*
4. Do Step 7 of *Down On the Farm Soup.*
5. Do Step 1 of *Sunday Sundaes.*
6. Do Steps 8–10 of *Down On the Farm Soup.*
7. Do Steps 1–2 of *Garden Patch Salad.*
8. Do Step 11 of *Down On the Farm Soup.*
9. Do Step 3 of *Garden Patch Salad.*
10. Do Step 2 of *Sunday Sundaes.*

Weekend Two Saturday

FISH

4 shark steaks or other firm white fish
steaks (about 1-1/2 pounds)

FRESH PRODUCE

VEGETABLES
1-1/2 pounds asparagus
1 small onion

HERBS
2 tablespoons rosemary (when chopped)
2 tablespoons thyme (when chopped)

FRUIT
1 medium ripe honeydew melon
2 medium ripe peaches
1 pound seedless red grapes

CANS, JARS & BOTTLES

VEGETABLES
1 can (14-1/2 ounces) diced tomatoes

PACKAGED GOODS

PASTA, RICE & GRAINS
1 cup long-grain white rice

DESSERT & BAKING NEEDS
2 envelopes unflavored gelatin

WINES & SPIRITS

1 split dry champagne
3 tablespoons brandy

FROZEN GOODS

JUICE
6 ounces pink lemonade

- ☐ Butter
- ☐ Granulated sugar
- ☐ Powdered sugar
- ☐ Olive oil
- ☐ Balsamic vinegar
- ☐ Lemon juice
- ☐ Cayenne pepper
- ☐ Ground nutmeg
- ☐ Pepper
- ☐ Salt

Weekend Two Saturday

MENU

Shark Symphony

4 shark steaks or other firm white fish steaks (about 1-1/2 pounds)
2 tablespoons fresh thyme (when chopped)
2 tablespoons fresh rosemary (when chopped)
2 tablespoons olive oil
Seasoning to taste
2 tablespoons balsamic vinegar

Prelude to Rice

1-1/4 cups water
1 small onion
1 cup long-grain white rice
1 can (14-1/2 ounces) diced tomatoes
1 teaspoon granulated sugar
1 teaspoon ground nutmeg

Asparagus Concerto

1-1/2 pounds fresh asparagus
4 tablespoons butter
1/4 cup water
1 tablespoon lemon juice
1/8 teaspoon cayenne pepper
Seasoning to taste

Champagne Sonata

6 ounces frozen pink lemonade
2 envelopes unflavored gelatin
1/2 cup water
1 medium ripe honeydew melon
2 medium ripe peaches

1 pound seedless red grapes
3 tablespoons brandy
1 split dry champagne
2 tablespoons powdered sugar

EQUIPMENT

Electric mixer
Medium saucepan
Large covered skillet
9 × 13-inch glass baking dish
1-quart casserole
3-cup ring mold
Large mixing bowl
Medium mixing bowl
Small mixing bowl
Pastry brush
Melon baller
Kitchen knives
Measuring cups and spoons
Cooking utensils

Weekend Two Saturday

Shark Symphony

1. Place a 9 × 13-inch glass baking dish under the broiler and preheat.

2. Rinse and pat dry the shark steaks.

3. Rinse, pat dry, and chop the thyme. Rinse, pat dry, and chop the rosemary.

4. Combine the thyme, the rosemary, and the oil in a small bowl.

5. Brush the shark on both sides with the herb mixture.

6. Place the steaks in the hot dish and broil until they are firm to the touch, 4 to 5 minutes. Do not turn them over.

7. Season to taste and drizzle with the vinegar.

Prelude to Rice

1. Preheat the oven to 350°F. Grease a 1-quart casserole.

2. Bring the water to a boil.

3. Peel and mince the onion.

4. In the casserole, combine the onion, the water, the rice, the tomatoes, the sugar, and the nutmeg.

5. Cover the casserole and bake until the liquid is absorbed and the rice is tender, about 30 minutes.

Asparagus Concerto

1. Rinse the asparagus and remove the tough ends.

2. In a large skillet, melt the butter with the water, the lemon juice, and the cayenne pepper.

3. Add the asparagus to the skillet, season to taste, cover, and steam until the spears are crisp-tender, 3 to 8 minutes, depending on their thickness.

Champagne Sonata

1. Set the lemonade out to thaw.

2. Combine the gelatin with the water in a medium saucepan and let stand for 5 minutes.

3. Place the saucepan over low heat and stir until the gelatin is dissolved, about 2 minutes.

4. Remove the saucepan from the heat and let it cool.

5. Blend in the lemonade. Turn the mixture into a medium bowl and chill for 30 minutes.

6. Cut the melon in half and remove the seeds. Using a melon baller, scoop out the melon flesh. Peel and slice the peaches. Rinse and stem the grapes. Combine the fruit in a large bowl and toss it with the brandy.

7. Remove the gelatin mixture from the refrigerator and beat in the champagne.

8. Grease a 3-cup ring mold.

9. Place half the gelatin mixture in the mold. Add half of the fruit. Top with the remaining gelatin mixture, and chill until you are ready to serve, at least 2 hours. Chill the remaining fruit until you are ready to serve.

10. Unmold the fruit ring onto a plate and fill the center with the remaining fruit. Dust with the powdered sugar.

C O U N T D O W N

1. Assemble the ingredients and the equipment.
2. Do Steps 1–9 of *Champagne Sonata.*
3. Do Steps 1–5 of *Prelude to Rice.*
4. Do Steps 1–3 of *Asparagus Concerto.*
5. Do Steps 1–7 of *Shark Symphony.*
6. Do Step 10 of *Champagne Sonata.*

Weekend Two Sunday

SHOPPING LIST

MEAT & POULTRY

1 lean beef pot roast
(about 3-1/2 pounds)

FRESH PRODUCE

VEGETABLES

2 large sweet potatoes
1 medium bunch broccoli
1 stalk celery
1/3 pound mushrooms
1 medium onion
3 scallions (green onions)
3 cloves garlic

CANS, JARS & BOTTLES

SOUP

1 can (14 ounces) beef broth

FRUIT

1 can (15 ounces) pineapple chunks

PACKAGED GOODS

DRIED FRUITS & NUTS

2 tablespoons sliced almonds

DESSERT & BAKING NEEDS

1 small package instant coconut cream
pudding mix

REFRIGERATED PRODUCTS

DAIRY

1-1/4 cups milk
3/4 cup sour cream

STAPLES

- [ ] Butter
- [ ] Cornstarch
- [ ] Dark brown sugar
- [ ] Vegetable oil
- [ ] White wine vinegar
- [ ] Soy sauce
- [ ] Sesame seeds
- [ ] Ground ginger
- [ ] Ground nutmeg
- [ ] Pepper
- [ ] Salt
- [ ] Almond extract

Weekend Two Sunday

Playful Pot Roast

1 lean beef pot roast (about 3-1/2 pounds)
1/3 pound fresh mushrooms
1 medium onion
2 tablespoons vegetable oil
1 can (15 ounces) pineapple chunks
1/4 cup soy sauce
1-1/2 teaspoons ground ginger
1 tablespoon cornstarch
1 can (14 ounces) beef broth
Seasoning to taste

Puckish Potatoes

2 large sweet potatoes
3 scallions (green onions)
1 stalk celery
3 tablespoons vegetable oil
2 tablespoons white wine vinegar
Seasoning to taste

Blatant Broccoli

3 cloves garlic
1 medium bunch broccoli
3 tablespoons butter
1 teaspoon sesame seeds
Seasoning to taste

Prankish Pudding

1 small package instant coconut cream pudding mix
1-1/4 cups milk
3/4 cup sour cream
1 teaspoon almond extract
1/2 teaspoon ground nutmeg
2 tablespoons sliced almonds
1 tablespoon dark brown sugar

EQUIPMENT

Electric mixer
Dutch oven
Large skillet
Medium covered skillet
Medium mixing bowl
Small mixing bowl
Vegetable peeler
Whisk
Kitchen knives
Measuring cups and spoons
Cooking utensils

Weekend Two Sunday

RECIPES

Playful Pot Roast

1. Trim any excess fat from the roast. Rinse, pat dry, and slice the mushrooms. Peel and slice the onion.

2. Heat the oil in a Dutch oven.

3. Sear the roast on all sides until lightly browned, about 10 minutes.

4. Drain the pineapple, reserving the juice in a small bowl. Add the soy sauce, the ginger, and the cornstarch to the reserved pineapple juice and whisk to blend well.

5. Add the onion and the broth to the roast. Season to taste. Cover and simmer until the roast is tender, 3 to 4 hours.

6. Remove the roast from the Dutch oven and cover to keep warm.

7. Add the pineapple juice mixture to the Dutch oven. Stir until the mixture thickens, about 5 minutes.

8. Add the pineapple chunks and the mushrooms and heat through.

9. Slice the roast and return the slices to the Dutch oven.

10. Serve the meat with the sauce.

Puckish Potatoes

1. Peel the potatoes, cut them in half lengthwise, and slice them thinly. Trim and chop the scallions. Rinse, trim, and dice the celery.

2. Heat the oil in a large skillet and sauté the potatoes for 3 minutes.

3. Add the celery and sauté for 2 minutes more.

4. Add the scallions and sauté for 1 minute more.

5. Stir in the vinegar, season to taste, and continue to sauté until the potatoes are crisp-tender, 1 to 2 minutes longer.

Blatant Broccoli

1. Peel and mince the garlic. Rinse and trim the broccoli and cut it into bite-sized florets.

2. Melt the butter in a medium skillet, and sauté the garlic and the sesame seeds for 3 minutes.

3. Add the broccoli and sauté until crisp-tender, about 5 minutes.

4. Season to taste and cover to keep warm.

Prankish Pudding

1. In a medium bowl, beat the pudding mix with the milk and the sour cream until well blended.

2. Fold in the almond extract and the nutmeg.

3. Pour the mixture into individual dessert bowls and chill until you are ready to serve.

4. Top each pudding with a sprinkling of nuts and brown sugar.

COUNTDOWN

1. Assemble the ingredients and the equipment.
2. Do Steps 1–5 of *Playful Pot Roast.*
3. Do Steps 1–3 of *Prankish Pudding.*
4. Do Step 1 of *Puckish Potatoes.*
5. Do Step 1 of *Blatant Broccoli.*
6. Do Steps 6–10 of *Playful Pot Roast.*
7. Do Steps 2–4 of *Blatant Broccoli.*
8. Do Steps 2–5 of *Puckish Potatoes.*
9. Do Step 4 of *Prankish Pudding.*

Weekend Three Saturday

MEAT & POULTRY

4 chicken breast halves
(about 2-1/2 pounds)

FRESH PRODUCE

VEGETABLES

1/2 pound mushrooms
1 medium head romaine lettuce
1 medium green bell pepper
1 medium onion
3 cloves garlic

FRUIT

7 large cooking apples

CANS, JARS & BOTTLES

VEGETABLES

1 can (14-1/2 ounces) diced tomatoes

SAUCES

1 can (6 ounces) tomato paste

FISH

1 tin (2 ounces) anchovy fillets (optional)

PACKAGED GOODS

PASTA, RICE & GRAINS

1 pound linguini

BAKED GOODS

1 cup seasoned croutons

WINES & SPIRITS

1/2 cup dry white wine

REFRIGERATED PRODUCTS

DAIRY

1/4 cup whipped cream
1 egg

FROZEN GOODS

PASTRY

1 sheet puff pastry

STAPLES

☐ Butter
☐ Flour
☐ Granulated sugar
☐ Dark brown sugar
☐ Cocoa powder
☐ Olive oil
☐ Red wine vinegar
☐ Lemon juice
☐ White Worcestershire sauce
☐ Tabasco sauce
☐ Dijon mustard
☐ Grated Parmesan cheese
☐ Dried basil
☐ Dried oregano
☐ Ground cinnamon
☐ Pepper
☐ Salt

Weekend Three Saturday

MENU

Show Off Chicken

4 chicken breast halves (about
   2-1/2 pounds)
1 medium onion
1 medium green bell pepper
1/2 pound fresh mushrooms
2 cloves garlic
1/4 cup flour
2 tablespoons olive oil
1 can (14-1/2 ounces) diced tomatoes
1 can (6 ounces) tomato paste
1/2 teaspoon dried basil
1/4 teaspoon dried oregano
1/2 cup dry white wine
Seasoning to taste
1 pound linguini

Sid Caesar Salad

1 clove garlic
1 tin (2 ounces) anchovy fillets (optional)
1 egg
2 tablespoons lemon juice
2 tablespoons red wine vinegar
1/2 tablespoon Dijon mustard
1/4 teaspoon white Worcestershire
   sauce
1/8 teaspoon Tabasco sauce
Seasoning to taste
6 tablespoons olive oil
1 medium head romaine lettuce
1/4 cup grated Parmesan cheese
1 cup seasoned croutons

Imogene Coca Crisp

1 sheet frozen puff pastry
6 tablespoons butter
6 tablespoons dark brown sugar
7 large cooking apples
1 tablespoon granulated sugar
1 teaspoon ground cinnamon
1/4 cup whipped cream
2 tablespoons cocoa powder

EQUIPMENT

Dutch oven

Stockpot

Small saucepan

9-inch round cake pan

Colander

Large mixing bowl

Small mixing bowl

Breadboard

Whisk

Rolling pin

Waxed paper

Kitchen knives

Measuring cups and spoons

Cooking utensils

Weekend Three Saturday

Show Off Chicken

1. Preheat the oven to 350°F.

2. Rinse and pat dry the chicken breasts.

3. Peel and chop the onion. Rinse, stem, seed, and chop the bell pepper. Rinse, pat dry, and slice the mushrooms. Peel and mince the garlic.

4. Place the flour on a sheet of waxed paper and dredge the chicken in the flour.

5. Heat the oil in a Dutch oven and lightly brown the chicken breasts on both sides, about 10 minutes.

6. Remove the Dutch oven from the heat.

7. Add the onion, the bell pepper, the mushrooms, the garlic, the undrained tomatoes, the tomato paste, the basil, and the oregano. Blend in the wine and season to taste.

8. Cover and bake in the oven for 1 hour.

9. Bring water for the pasta to a boil in a stockpot.

10. Cook the pasta until it is almost tender, 2 to 3 minutes if you are using fresh pasta, 6 to 7 minutes if you are using dry pasta.

11. Drain the pasta and serve under the chicken.

Sid Caesar Salad

1. Bring water to a boil in a small saucepan.

2. Peel and mince the garlic. Drain and chop the anchovy fillets.

3. Boil the egg for 1 minute.

4. Crack the egg into a small bowl. Add the garlic, the anchovies, the lemon juice, the vinegar, the mustard, the Worcestershire sauce, and the Tabasco sauce. Season to taste and combine. Add the oil and whisk to blend.

5. Wash and dry the romaine, tear it into bite-sized pieces, and place it in a large bowl.

6. Toss the romaine with the dressing and top with the cheese and the croutons.

Imogene Coca Crisp

1. Set the puff pastry out to thaw.

2. Preheat the oven to 425°F. Flour a breadboard.

3. Cut the butter into pieces and lay the pieces around a 9-inch round cake pan. Sprinkle the brown sugar over the butter.

4. Peel, core, and quarter 6 of the apples, and arrange them on end around the pan in a double row. Peel and core the remaining apple, and place it in the center of the pan.

5. Cook over low heat until the butter melts. Increase the heat to medium, and cook, shaking the pan occasionally, until the sugar caramelizes, about 5 minutes.

6. Roll the puff pastry out on the breadboard to a 9-inch round. Place it over the apples and press down lightly. Dust the dough with the granulated sugar and the cinnamon.

7. Place the pan in the oven and bake until the pastry has risen and is golden, 25 to 30 minutes.

8. Remove the pan from the oven and let stand for 5 minutes.

9. Carefully run a knife around the edge of the cake pan and invert the crisp onto a plate.

10. Top with dollops of whipped cream and dust with the cocoa powder.

COUNTDOWN

1. Assemble the ingredients and the equipment.
2. Do Steps 1–9 of *Imogene Coca Crisp.*
3. Do Steps 1–8 of *Show Off Chicken.*
4. Do Steps 1–5 of *Sid Caesar Salad.*
5. Do Steps 9–10 of *Show Off Chicken.*
6. Do Step 6 of *Sid Caesar Salad.*
7. Do Step 11 of *Show Off Chicken.*
8. Do Step 10 of *Imogene Coca Crisp.*

Weekend Three Sunday

FISH

1 pound cod fillets
1/2 pound cooked crabmeat

FRESH PRODUCE

VEGETABLES

4 medium baking potatoes
2 stalks celery
1 medium head lettuce
1 small daikon radish
1 medium onion
1 medium red onion

HERBS

2 tablespoons fresh parsley
  (when chopped)

FRUIT

2 small pink grapefruit
2 large oranges

CANS, JARS & BOTTLES

VEGETABLES

1 can (11 ounces) whole kernel corn
1 can (15 ounces) sliced beets

JUICE

8 ounces clam juice

PACKAGED GOODS

DESSERT & BAKING NEEDS

8 squares (1 ounce each)
  semisweet chocolate

REFRIGERATED PRODUCTS

DAIRY

2 cups + 1 tablespoon milk
2 cups half-and-half
4 eggs

JUICE

1 teaspoon orange juice

DELI

4 slices bacon

STAPLES

- ☐ Butter
- ☐ Flour
- ☐ Bisquick
- ☐ Granulated sugar
- ☐ Light corn syrup
- ☐ Olive oil
- ☐ Vegetable oil
- ☐ Balsamic vinegar
- ☐ Poppy seeds
- ☐ Lemon-pepper seasoning
- ☐ Pepper
- ☐ Salt
- ☐ Orange extract
- ☐ Vanilla extract

Weekend Three Sunday

Flying Fish Chowder

4 slices bacon
1 medium onion
2 stalks celery
4 medium baking potatoes
2 tablespoons fresh parsley (when chopped)
1 can (11 ounces) whole kernel corn
1 pound cod fillets
1/2 pound cooked crabmeat
8 ounces clam juice
1 cup water
2 cups half-and-half
1 teaspoon granulated sugar
1/2 teaspoon lemon-pepper seasoning
3 tablespoons flour
2 cups milk
Seasoning to taste

Silly Little Salad

1 small daikon radish
2 small pink grapefruit
1 medium red onion
1 medium head lettuce
1 can (15 ounces) sliced beets
1 teaspoon orange juice
3 tablespoons olive oil
2 tablespoons balsamic vinegar
Seasoning to taste

Mild-Mannered Muffins

2 large oranges
2 tablespoons vegetable oil

1 egg
1 teaspoon orange extract
2 cups Bisquick
2 tablespoons granulated sugar
1 tablespoon poppy seeds

Big Brownie Pie

1/2 cup + 2 tablespoons light corn syrup
9 tablespoons butter
8 squares (1 ounce each) semisweet chocolate
1/4 cup granulated sugar
3 eggs
2 teaspoons vanilla extract
1 cup flour
1 tablespoon milk

Flying Fish Chowder

1. Chop the bacon. Peel and chop the onion. Rinse, trim, and chop the celery. Peel and dice the potatoes. Rinse and chop the parsley. Drain the corn.

2. Rinse and pat dry the cod and cut it into chunks. Rinse and pick over the crabmeat to remove any shell or cartilage.

3. Sauté the bacon, the onion, and the celery in a Dutch oven until the bacon is cooked and the onion is soft, about 5 minutes. Add the potatoes, the clam juice, and the water. Bring to a boil, cover, and simmer until the potatoes are tender, 10 to 15 minutes.

4. Add the fish and cook for 5 minutes more.

5. Add the crab, the corn, the half-and-half, the sugar, and the lemon-pepper seasoning. Heat through, about 5 minutes.

6. In a small bowl, whisk together the flour with 1/4 cup of the milk, and add it to the Dutch oven. Season to taste. Simmer the chowder, slowly adding the rest of the milk and stirring until the chowder has thickened slightly, about 6 minutes.

7. Cover and heat through, but do not let it boil.

8. Sprinkle with the parsley.

Silly Little Salad

1. Peel and slice the daikon. Peel and section the grapefruit. Peel and thinly slice the onion. Wash and dry the lettuce, tear it into bite-sized pieces, and distribute it among individual salad plates. Drain, rinse, and drain the beets again.

2. Arrange the daikon, the grapefruit sections, and the onion slices over the lettuce. Arrange the beets over each salad.

3. In a small bowl, whisk together the orange juice, the oil, and the vinegar. Season to taste.

4. Drizzle the dressing over each salad.

Mild-Mannered Muffins

1. Preheat the oven to 400°F. Grease a muffin tin.

2. Grate the orange peel and juice the oranges.

3. In a large bowl, combine the orange juice, the orange peel, the oil, and the egg, and blend well. Fold in the orange extract.

4. Fold in the Bisquick, the sugar, and the poppy seeds.

5. Divide the batter evenly among the muffin cups.

6. Bake until golden, 15–20 minutes.

Big Brownie Pie

1. Preheat the oven to 350°F. Grease and flour a 9-inch round cake pan.

2. In a large saucepan, combine 1/2 cup of the corn syrup and 8 tablespoons of the butter. Stir to blend and bring the mixture to a boil. Remove the saucepan from the heat and blend in 5 squares of the chocolate, stirring until it is melted.

3. Blend in the sugar. Whisk in the eggs, one at a time. Blend in the vanilla. Fold in the flour. Mix well. Pour the batter into the cake pan, and bake until a toothpick inserted in the center comes out clean, about 30 minutes.

4. Remove the cake pan from the oven and let cool for 5 minutes.

5. In a small saucepan, melt the remaining 3 squares chocolate with the remaining 1 tablespoon butter. Fold in the remaining 2 tablespoons corn syrup and the milk. Remove the saucepan from the heat and pour the glaze over the cooled brownie.

COUNTDOWN

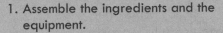

1. Assemble the ingredients and the equipment.
2. Do Steps 1–5 of *Big Brownie Pie*.
3. Do Steps 1–3 of *Flying Fish Chowder*.
4. Do Steps 1–6 of *Mild-Mannered Muffins*.
5. Do Steps 1–3 of *Silly Little Salad*.
6. Do Steps 4–7 of *Flying Fish Chowder*.
7. Do Step 4 of *Silly Little Salad*.
8. Do Step 8 of *Flying Fish Chowder*.

Weekend Four Saturday

SHOPPING LIST

MEAT & POULTRY
4 loin pork chops (about 1-1/2 pounds)

FRESH PRODUCE

VEGETABLES
1-1/2 pounds asparagus
1 large green bell pepper
1 small onion
1 clove garlic

CANS, JARS & BOTTLES

SOUP
1 can (14 ounces) chicken broth

CONDIMENTS
1 jar (2 ounces) diced pimiento

PACKAGED GOODS

PASTA, RICE & GRAINS
1 cup brown rice

WINES & SPIRITS
1/4 cup dry white wine
1/4 cup dry sherry

REFRIGERATED PRODUCTS

DAIRY
1 cup whipping cream

CHEESE
1 cup small-curd cottage cheese

FROZEN GOODS

FRUIT
1 package (16 ounces) whole
  raspberries

STAPLES

☐ Butter
☐ Cornstarch
☐ Dark brown sugar
☐ Vegetable oil
☐ Lemon juice
☐ Honey
☐ Dried tarragon
☐ Ground allspice
☐ Ground cinnamon
☐ Lemon-pepper seasoning
☐ Pepper
☐ Salt
☐ Vanilla extract

Weekend Four Saturday

Praise the Pork

1 clove garlic
1 tablespoon cornstarch
2 tablespoons lemon juice
2 tablespoons butter
4 loin pork chops (about 1-1/2 pounds)
1/4 cup dry white wine
3 tablespoons honey
1/2 cup chicken broth
1 teaspoon lemon-pepper seasoning
Seasoning to taste

Revere the Rice

1 small onion
1 tablespoon vegetable oil
1 teaspoon dried tarragon
1 cup brown rice
1-1/4 cups chicken broth
1 cup water
1/4 cup dry sherry
1 jar (2 ounces) diced pimientos
Seasoning to taste

Applaud the Pepper

1-1/2 pounds fresh asparagus
1 large green bell pepper
2 tablespoons butter
1/2 teaspoon ground allspice
Seasoning to taste

Commend the Cream

1 package (16 ounces) frozen whole
  raspberries
1 cup small-curd cottage cheese
1/3 cup dark brown sugar
1/2 teaspoon ground cinnamon
1 cup whipping cream
1 teaspoon vanilla extract

EQUIPMENT

Electric mixer

Blender

Medium covered saucepan

2 large covered skillets

Medium covered skillet

Medium mixing bowl

Small mixing bowl

Kitchen knives

Measuring cups and spoons

Cooking utensils

Praise the Pork

1. Peel and mince the garlic. In a small bowl, combine the cornstarch and the lemon juice.

2. Melt the butter in a large skillet. Add the garlic and sauté for 1 minute.

3. Add the pork chops and brown them, 5 to 6 minutes per side.

4. Add the wine, cover the skillet, and cook until the chops are tender and cooked through, 15 to 20 minutes.

5. Remove the chops and keep them warm.

6. Combine the honey, the broth, and the lemon-pepper seasoning with the cornstarch mixture and add it to the skillet. Bring to a boil and cook, stirring, until the sauce thickens to a glaze, about 5 minutes.

7. Season to taste and spoon the glaze over the pork chops.

Revere the Rice

1. Peel and mince the onion.

2. Heat the oil in a medium saucepan.

3. Sauté the onion with the tarragon until the onion is soft, about 5 minutes.

4. Add the rice and sauté for 1 minute.

5. Add the broth, the water, the sherry, and the pimiento, and season to taste.

6. Cover the saucepan, reduce the heat, and simmer until the liquid is absorbed and the rice is tender, 20 to 25 minutes.

7. Fluff the rice before serving.

Applaud the Pepper

1. Bring a small amount of water to a boil in a medium skillet.

2. Remove and discard the tough ends of the asparagus and cut the spears into 1-inch pieces. Rinse, stem, seed, and chunk the bell pepper.

3. Add the asparagus to the skillet and cook, covered, until crisp-tender, about 5 minutes.

4. Melt the butter with the allspice in a large skillet. Sauté the bell pepper until crisp-tender, about 3 minutes.

5. Drain the asparagus and toss with the bell pepper. Season to taste and cover to keep warm.

Commend the Cream

1. Set the raspberries out to thaw.

2. Chill a medium bowl and the beaters of an electric mixer in the refrigerator for at least 10 minutes.

3. Place the cottage cheese in a blender and process until smooth and creamy, about 1 minute. Add the brown sugar and the cinnamon and blend well, about 30 seconds.

4. In the chilled bowl, whip the cream until stiff peaks form, about 5 minutes. Fold in the vanilla.

5. Fold the cheese mixture into the whipped cream.

6. Reserve a handful of whole berries. Place half of the remaining berries in the bottoms of individual dessert glasses. Spoon half of the cream mixture over the berries. Repeat. Top with the reserved berries. Refrigerate until you are ready to serve.

COUNTDOWN

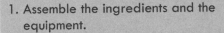

1. Assemble the ingredients and the equipment.
2. Do Steps 1–6 of *Commend the Cream.*
3. Do Steps 1–4 of *Praise the Pork.*
4. Do Steps 1–6 of *Revere the Rice.*
5. Do Steps 1–5 of *Applaud the Pepper.*
6. Do Steps 5–7 of *Praise the Pork.*
7. Do Step 7 of *Revere the Rice.*

Weekend Four Sunday

MEAT & POULTRY

3 pounds chicken pieces

FRESH PRODUCE

VEGETABLES

1 medium carrot
1 stalk celery
1 medium head red cabbage
1 small onion

HERBS

1/4 cup parsley (when chopped)

FRUIT

4 large ripe pears

CANS, JARS & BOTTLES

VEGETABLES

1 can (14-1/2 ounces) stewed tomatoes

PACKAGED GOODS

DESSERT & BAKING NEEDS

2 teaspoons instant tapioca

REFRIGERATED PRODUCTS

DAIRY

1 cup milk
1-1/2 cups buttermilk
1/2 cup plain yogurt
1 egg

DELI

2 slices bacon

FROZEN GOODS

VEGETABLES

1 package (10 ounces) lima beans

STAPLES

- ❏ Butter
- ❏ Vegetable shortening
- ❏ Flour
- ❏ Baking powder
- ❏ Cornmeal
- ❏ Granulated sugar
- ❏ Dark brown sugar
- ❏ Molasses
- ❏ Vegetable oil
- ❏ Rice vinegar
- ❏ Honey
- ❏ Grated Parmesan cheese
- ❏ Plain breadcrumbs
- ❏ Celery seed
- ❏ Dried dill
- ❏ Dried oregano
- ❏ Cayenne pepper
- ❏ Ground cinnamon
- ❏ Ground nutmeg
- ❏ Pepper
- ❏ Salt
- ❏ Vanilla extract

Weekend Four Sunday

MENU

Chickendale

3 pounds chicken pieces
1/4 cup fresh parsley (when chopped)
1-1/2 cups buttermilk
2 tablespoons honey
1/2 teaspoon dried oregano
1/4 teaspoon cayenne pepper
3 tablespoons vegetable oil
1 cup plain breadcrumbs
3 tablespoons grated Parmesan cheese
Seasoning to taste

Dilly-Dally

1 package (10 ounces) frozen lima beans
2 slices bacon
1 small onion
1 can (14-1/2 ounces) stewed tomatoes
1/2 teaspoon dried dill
1 tablespoon molasses
Seasoning to taste

See-Slaw

1 medium head red cabbage
1 medium carrot
1 stalk celery
1/2 cup plain yogurt
2 teaspoons rice vinegar
1/2 teaspoon celery seed
1/4 teaspoon granulated sugar
Seasoning to taste

Cornfounded

4 tablespoons butter
3/4 cup cornmeal
1 cup flour
1/4 cup granulated sugar
1 tablespoon baking powder
1 egg
1 cup milk

Impearfection

1/2 cup flour
1/4 teaspoon salt
2 tablespoons vegetable shortening
1-1/2 tablespoons very cold water
4 large ripe pears
3 tablespoons dark brown sugar
2 teaspoons instant tapioca
1/4 teaspoon ground cinnamon
1/4 teaspoon ground nutmeg
1 teaspoon vanilla extract
1 tablespoon granulated sugar

EQUIPMENT

Large skillet
9 × 13-inch glass baking dish
8 × 8-inch glass baking dish
4 individual baking cups
Breadboard
Large shallow bowl
3 large mixing bowls
2 medium mixing bowls
3 small mixing bowls
Whisk
Vegetable peeler
Vegetable grater
Rolling pin
Plastic wrap
Kitchen knives
Measuring cups and spoons
Cooking utensils

Weekend Four Sunday

Chickendale

1. Rinse and pat dry the chicken. Rinse and chop the parsley.

2. In a large shallow bowl, combine the buttermilk, the honey, the oregano, and the cayenne pepper. Add the chicken pieces, cover with plastic wrap, and refrigerate for at least 1 hour, turning to coat several times.

3. Decrease the oven temperature to 350°F.

4. Drizzle the oil around a 9 × 13-inch glass baking dish.

5. In a medium bowl, combine the parsley, the breadcrumbs, and the Parmesan cheese. Season to taste. Dredge the chicken in the breadcrumb mixture and place the pieces in the baking dish. Drizzle with the oil and bake until the chicken is cooked throughout and the juice runs clear, 40 to 50 minutes.

Dilly-Dally

1. Set the package of lima beans in a small bowl of hot water to thaw.

2. Cook the bacon in a large skillet until crisp. Drain the bacon on paper towels, reserving the bacon drippings.

3. Peel and chop the onion.

4. Sauté the onion in the reserved bacon drippings until tender, about 5 minutes.

Add the beans, the tomatoes, the dill, and the molasses. Season to taste. Toss lightly and heat through, about 4 minutes.

5. Crumble the bacon and sprinkle over the top of the beans.

See-Slaw

1. Trim and grate the cabbage. Peel and grate the carrot. Rinse, trim, and mince the celery. Combine the vegetables in a large bowl.

2. In a small bowl, combine the yogurt, the vinegar, the celery seed, and the sugar. Season to taste and toss with the cabbage mixture.

Cornfounded

1. Grease an 8 × 8-inch glass baking dish. Flour a breadboard.

2. Melt the butter.

3. In a large bowl, combine the cornmeal, the flour, the sugar, and the baking powder.

4. In a small bowl, whisk together the egg and the milk. Blend in the butter. Add the egg mixture to the cornmeal mixture and blend well.

5. Turn the batter into the baking dish, add to the oven, and bake until golden, 30 to 35 minutes.

Impearfection

1. Preheat the oven to 400°F.

2. In a medium bowl, combine the flour and the salt. Add the shortening and blend with a fork. Sprinkle in the cold water and mix gently to form a ball of dough. Let the dough sit for 10 minutes.

3. Peel and core the pears and cut them into thin slices. Put the slices in a large bowl. Add the brown sugar, the tapioca, the cinnamon, the nutmeg, and the vanilla. Stir to combine. Divide the pear mixture among 4 individual baking cups.

4. Place the dough on the breadboard. Roll out the dough and cut it into rounds to fit the top of each baking cup. Place the pastry over the pear mixture, sealing the edges. Cut several slits in the pastry to let steam escape. Sprinkle the top of each with the granulated sugar.

5. Bake until bubbly and golden, 30 to 35 minutes.

COUNTDOWN

1. Assemble the ingredients and the equipment.
2. Do Steps 1–2 of *Chickendale*.
3. Do Steps 1–5 of *Impearfection*.
4. Do Steps 3–5 of *Chickendale*.
5. Do Steps 1–5 of *Cornfounded*.
6. Do Steps 1–2 of *See-Slaw*.
7. Do Steps 1–5 of *Dilly-Dally*.

Weekend Five Saturday

SHOPPING LIST

MEAT & POULTRY

4 lean beef tenderloins
(about 2 pounds)

FRESH PRODUCE

VEGETABLES

8 stalks celery
4 medium mushrooms
1 medium onion
2 medium shallots
1 bunch scallions (green onions)

HERBS

2 tablespoons thyme (when minced)

CANS, JARS & BOTTLES

SOUP

1 can (14 ounces) beef broth

FRUIT

1 can (11 ounces) mandarin oranges

PACKAGED GOODS

PASTA, RICE & GRAINS

1 cup long-grain white rice

DESSERT & BAKING NEEDS

1 envelope unflavored gelatin

WINES & SPIRITS

1/3 cup dry white wine

REFRIGERATED PRODUCTS

DAIRY

1/4 cup half-and-half
3 eggs

JUICE

1 cup orange juice

STAPLES LIST

- ❑ Butter
- ❑ Flour
- ❑ Cornstarch
- ❑ Cream of tartar
- ❑ Granulated sugar
- ❑ Dark brown sugar
- ❑ Multicolored sprinkles
- ❑ Vegetable oil
- ❑ Sesame seeds
- ❑ Paprika
- ❑ Pepper
- ❑ Salt
- ❑ Orange extract

The Thyme of Your Life

2 medium shallots
2 tablespoons fresh thyme (when minced)
1 tablespoon vegetable oil
4 lean beef tenderloins (about 2 pounds)
1/3 cup dry white wine
3 tablespoons butter
2 teaspoons flour
1/2 cup beef broth
1/4 cup half-and-half
Seasoning to taste

I'd Rather Be Rice

1 medium onion
4 medium mushrooms
2 tablespoons butter
1 cup long-grain white rice
1-1/4 cups beef broth
1 cup water
Seasoning to taste
1 teaspoon paprika

The Odd Couple

8 stalks celery
1 bunch scallions (green onions)
2 tablespoons butter
1 teaspoon sesame seeds
4 tablespoons water
2 teaspoons dark brown sugar
1 teaspoon cornstarch
Seasoning to taste

California Sweet

1 cup orange juice
1 envelope unflavored gelatin
3 eggs
1/2 teaspoon orange extract
1/2 cup granulated sugar
1 teaspoon cream of tartar
1 can (11 ounces) mandarin oranges
Multicolored sprinkles for garnish

EQUIPMENT

Electric mixer

Medium covered saucepan

Small saucepan

Large covered skillet

Medium skillet

Medium mixing bowl

Whisk

Aluminum foil

Kitchen knives

Measuring cups and spoons

Cooking utensils

The Thyme of Your Life

1. Peel and mince the shallots. Rinse and mince the thyme.

2. Heat the oil in a medium skillet and sauté the tenderloins according to taste, about 4 minutes per side for rare.

3. Reserving the cooking juices, remove the tenderloins and cover them with aluminum foil to keep them warm.

4. Add the wine to the skillet and deglaze it. Add the butter, the shallots, and the thyme, and sauté for 1 minute. Blend in the flour. Add the broth and combine. Add the half-and-half, season to taste, and stir until the mixture thickens and reduces slightly, 5 to 6 minutes. Do not let it boil.

5. Spoon the sauce over the tenderloins.

I'd Rather Be Rice

1. Peel and mince the onion. Rinse, pat dry, and chop the mushrooms.

2. Melt the butter in a medium saucepan. Add the onion and sauté until it is soft, about 5 minutes.

3. Add the rice and sauté until the rice is golden, about 3 minutes.

4. Stir in the broth and the water, bring the mixture to a boil, cover the pan, reduce the heat, and simmer for 10 minutes.

5. Add the mushrooms, season to taste, and continue cooking until the liquid is absorbed and the rice is tender, 10 to 12 minutes.

6. Fluff the rice with a fork and sprinkle with the paprika.

The Odd Couple

1. Rinse and trim the celery and cut it into 4-inch lengths. Cut each piece into strips that are the same thickness as the scallions. Rinse and trim the scallions, cutting the white tops into 4-inch lengths and reserving the green stems.

2. Bring a small amount of water to a boil and pour it over the green scallion stems. Immediately plunge the green stems into cold water and pat them dry on paper towels.

3. Combine the celery and the white scallion tops, and divide evenly into 4 bundles. Tie each bundle firmly together with the green scallion stems.

4. Melt the butter in a large skillet. Sauté the bundles for 2 minutes on each side. Remove the bundles. Add the sesame seeds, the water, and the brown sugar to the skillet. Stir in the cornstarch, season to taste, and blend well. Add the celery bundles and coat with the sauce. Cover to keep warm.

California Sweet

1. Combine the orange juice and the gelatin in a small saucepan and let stand for 5 minutes.

2. Warm the mixture until the gelatin dissolves, about 2 minutes.

3. Separate the eggs, adding the yolks to the gelatin and placing the whites in a medium bowl.

4. Whisk the yolks into the gelatin and cook for 2 minutes.

5. Remove the saucepan from the heat and fold in the orange extract.

6. Beat the egg whites with an electric mixer until stiff, about 5 minutes.

7. Gradually add the sugar and the cream of tartar, beating until the whites are very stiff and glossy, 2 to 3 minutes more.

8. Drain the mandarin oranges and fold them into the egg whites. Fold in the gelatin, and spoon the mixture into individual dessert glasses. Chill until set, about 1 hour.

9. Garnish with the sprinkles.

COUNTDOWN

1. Assemble the ingredients and the equipment.
2. Do Steps 1–8 of *California Sweet*.
3. Do Steps 1–4 of *I'd Rather Be Rice*.
4. Do Steps 1–3 of *The Odd Couple*.
5. Do Step 5 of *I'd Rather Be Rice*.
6. Do Step 4 of *The Odd Couple*.
7. Do Steps 1–4 of *The Thyme of Your Life*.
8. Do Step 6 of *I'd Rather Be Rice*.
9. Do Step 5 of *The Thyme of Your Life*.
10. Do Step 9 of *California Sweet*.

Weekend Five Sunday

FISH
4 halibut steaks (about 1-1/2 pounds)

FRESH PRODUCE

VEGETABLES
1 small red onion
1 small shallot
1 clove garlic

HERBS
2 tablespoons cilantro (when chopped)
2 tablespoons parsley (when chopped)

CANS, JARS & BOTTLES

VEGETABLES
1 can (14-1/2 ounces) diced tomatoes

PACKAGED GOODS

PASTA, RICE & GRAINS
8 ounces curly egg noodles

DESSERT & BAKING NEEDS
1 cup flaked coconut

REFRIGERATED PRODUCTS

DAIRY
1 cup buttermilk
3 tablespoons half-and-half
3 eggs

DELI
2 slices bacon

FROZEN GOODS

VEGETABLES
1 package (10 ounces) wax beans

- [ ] Butter
- [ ] Vegetable shortening
- [ ] Flour
- [ ] Baking powder
- [ ] Baking soda
- [ ] Granulated sugar
- [ ] Dark brown sugar
- [ ] Vegetable oil
- [ ] Worcestershire sauce
- [ ] White wine vinegar
- [ ] Dried tarragon
- [ ] Ground allspice
- [ ] Ground cinnamon
- [ ] Ground nutmeg
- [ ] Pepper
- [ ] Salt
- [ ] Vanilla extract

Weekend Five Sunday

MENU

Halibets Are Off

1 clove garlic
1 small shallot
4 halibut steaks (about 1-1/2 pounds)
Seasoning to taste
2 tablespoons butter
2 tablespoons vegetable oil
2 tablespoons flour
1 can (14-1/2 ounces) diced tomatoes
2 tablespoons white wine vinegar
2 teaspoons Worcestershire sauce
1/2 teaspoon granulated sugar
1/2 teaspoon dried tarragon

No Nonsense Noodle

2 tablespoons fresh cilantro (when chopped)
8 ounces curly egg noodles
2 tablespoons butter

Keen Bean

1 package (10 ounces) frozen wax beans
2 slices bacon
1 small red onion
2 tablespoons fresh parsley (when chopped)
Seasoning to taste

Reciprocake

1/2 cup vegetable shortening
1-1/2 cups granulated sugar
3 eggs
2 cups flour
1 teaspoon ground cinnamon
1 teaspoon ground nutmeg
1 teaspoon ground allspice
2 teaspoons baking powder
1 teaspoon baking soda
1 teaspoon vanilla extract
1 cup buttermilk
4 tablespoons butter
1 cup flaked coconut
2/3 cup dark brown sugar
3 tablespoons half-and-half

EQUIPMENT

Electric mixer

Large covered saucepan

Small saucepan

Large skillet

Medium skillet

9 × 13-inch glass baking dish

9 × 13-inch baking pan

Colander

Large mixing bowl

Medium mixing bowl

2 small mixing bowls

Aluminum foil

Kitchen knives

Measuring cups and spoons

Cooking utensils

Weekend Five Sunday

RECIPES

Halibets Are Off

1. Grease a 9 × 13-inch glass baking dish.

2. Peel and mince the garlic. Peel and mince the shallot.

3. Rinse and pat dry the halibut steaks, season them to taste, and arrange them in the baking dish.

4. Melt the butter with the oil in a large skillet, and sauté the garlic and the shallot for 5 minutes.

5. Add the flour and blend until smooth. Blend in the tomatoes, the vinegar, the Worcestershire sauce, the sugar, and the tarragon. Reduce the heat and simmer until the sauce begins to thicken, about 10 minutes.

6. Increase the oven temperature to 400°F.

7. Pour the sauce over the fish, cover with a sheet of aluminum foil, and bake until the fish flakes easily with a fork, about 30 minutes.

No Nonsense Noodle

1. Bring water for the noodles to a boil in a large saucepan.

2. Rinse and chop the cilantro.

3. Cook the noodles until they are almost tender, 4 to 5 minutes.

4. Drain the noodles and return them to the saucepan. Toss with the butter and the cilantro. Cover to keep warm.

Keen Bean

1. Set the package of wax beans in a small bowl of hot water to thaw.

2. Dice the bacon. Peel and chop the onion. Rinse and chop the parsley.

3. Sauté the bacon in a medium skillet for 2 minutes.

4. Add the onion and sauté until the onion is soft and the bacon is almost crisp, about 5 minutes.

5. Add the beans and sauté until heated through, about 2 minutes.

6. Season to taste and sprinkle with the parsley.

Reciprocake

1. Preheat the oven to 350°F. Grease and flour a 9 × 13-inch baking pan.

2. In a large bowl, combine the shortening and the sugar, and beat with an electric mixer until well blended and fluffy, about 3 minutes.

3. Add the eggs, one at a time, beating well after each addition.

4. In a medium bowl, combine the flour, the cinnamon, the nutmeg, the allspice, the baking powder, and the baking soda.

5. In a small bowl, combine the vanilla and the buttermilk.

6. With the mixer on low speed, blend a little of the flour mixture into the egg mixture. Then blend a little of the buttermilk mixture into the egg mixture. Repeat until all the ingredients are combined and the batter is smooth.

7. Pour the batter into the pan and bake until the cake is golden and springs back lightly when touched in the center, 35 to 40 minutes.

8. Melt the butter in a small saucepan. Stir in the coconut, the brown sugar, and the half-and-half. Simmer just until the mixture comes to a boil and the sugar is dissolved, about 5 minutes.

9. Spread the frosting over the cake.

COUNTDOWN

1. Assemble the ingredients and the equipment.
2. Do Steps 1–8 of *Reciprocake*.
3. Do Steps 1–7 of *Halibets Are Off*.
4. Do Steps 1–2 of *No Nonsense Noodle*.
5. Do Step 1 of *Keen Bean*.
6. Do Step 3 of *No Nonsense Noodle*.
7. Do Step 2 of *Keen Bean*.
8. Do Step 4 of *No Nonsense Noodle*.
9. Do Steps 3–6 of *Keen Bean*.
10. Do Step 9 of *Reciprocake*.

Weekend Six Saturday

SHOPPING LIST

FISH

1-1/2 pounds medium shrimp, shelled
and deveined

FRESH PRODUCE

VEGETABLES
1-1/2 pounds asparagus
1 small red onion

HERBS
1 tablespoon parsley (when chopped)

CANS, JARS & BOTTLES

FRUIT
1 can (30 ounces) whole purple plums

SPREADS
5 tablespoons orange marmalade

PACKAGED GOODS

PASTA, RICE & GRAINS
1 cup long-grain white rice

WINES & SPIRITS

3 tablespoons dry sherry

REFRIGERATED PRODUCTS

DAIRY
1/2 cup + 2 tablespoons milk
1 cup half-and-half

PASTRY
1 package (2) unbaked pie shells

STAPLES

- ❏ Butter
- ❏ Flour
- ❏ Cornstarch
- ❏ Granulated sugar
- ❏ Red wine vinegar
- ❏ Lemon juice
- ❏ White Worcestershire sauce
- ❏ Ketchup
- ❏ Ground allspice
- ❏ Lemon-pepper seasoning
- ❏ Pepper
- ❏ Saffron threads
- ❏ Salt
- ❏ Vanilla extract

Weekend Six Saturday

Shrimp Esther Newberg

1-1/2 pounds medium shrimp, shelled and deveined
3 tablespoons butter
3 tablespoons flour
1/2 cup milk
1 cup half-and-half
2 tablespoons ketchup
1 teaspoon lemon juice
1 teaspoon white Worcestershire sauce
3 tablespoons dry sherry
Seasoning to taste

Ten Percent Rice

1 tablespoon fresh parsley (when chopped)
1 cup long-grain white rice
2 cups water
2 teaspoons saffron threads

Best-Selling Asparagus

1 cup water
1-1/2 pounds fresh asparagus
1 small red onion
1 teaspoon lemon-pepper seasoning
2 tablespoons red wine vinegar
1/2 teaspoon granulated sugar
Seasoning to taste

Little Jack Horner Pie

1 can (30 ounces) whole purple plums
1/4 cup + 1 tablespoon granulated sugar
1-1/2 tablespoons cornstarch
1 teaspoon vanilla extract
1/4 teaspoon ground allspice
1 package (2) unbaked pie shells
5 tablespoons orange marmalade
2 tablespoons milk

EQUIPMENT

Double boiler

Medium saucepan

Small saucepan

2 large covered skillets

Pie plate

Whisk

Kitchen knives

Measuring cups and spoons

Cooking utensils

Shrimp Esther Newberg

1. Rinse and pat dry the shrimp.

2. Melt the butter in a large skillet.

3. Stir in the flour.

4. Reduce the heat and gradually stir in the milk and the half-and-half, stirring continuously until the mixture thickens, about 4 minutes.

5. Blend in the ketchup, the lemon juice, and the Worcestershire sauce.

6. Add the shrimp and the sherry, and toss to coat. Season to taste and sauté until the shrimp turn pink, about 2 minutes.

7. Remove from the heat and cover to keep warm.

Ten Percent Rice

1. Bring water to a boil in the bottom of a double boiler.

2. Rinse and chop the parsley.

3. Combine the rice, the 2 cups water, and the saffron in the top of the double boiler. Cover, reduce the heat, and simmer until the liquid is absorbed and the rice is tender, 30 to 40 minutes.

4. Fluff the rice with a fork and fold in the parsley.

Best-Selling Asparagus

1. Bring the water to a boil in a large skillet.

2. Remove and discard the tough ends from the asparagus and trim the spears to an equal length. Peel and thinly slice the onion.

3. Lay the asparagus in the skillet, cover, reduce the heat, and steam until the spears are bright green and crisp-tender, 5 to 8 minutes, depending on their thickness.

4. In a small saucepan, whisk together the lemon-pepper seasoning, the vinegar, and the sugar. Season to taste and bring the mixture just to a boil.

5. Drain the asparagus. Lay the onion slices over the spears. Drizzle with the sauce.

Little Jack Horner Pie

1. Preheat the oven to 400°F.

2. Drain the plums, cut them in half, and pit them, reserving 1-1/4 cups of the juice.

3. In a medium saucepan, combine the reserved plum juice with 1/4 cup of the sugar and the cornstarch. Cook, stirring constantly, until the mixture is thick and clear, about 5 minutes.

4. Remove the saucepan from the heat and blend in the vanilla and the allspice.

5. Press one pie shell into a pie plate, pricking the bottom all over with a fork. Spread the marmalade over the shell. Arrange the plums over the marmalade. Pour the syrup over the plums. Invert the second pie shell over the filling, crimping the edges to seal. Cut several slits in the top to let steam escape. Brush the top with the milk and sprinkle with the remaining 1 tablespoon sugar.

6. Bake until the crust is golden, about 20 minutes.

COUNTDOWN

1. Assemble the ingredients and the equipment.
2. Do Steps 1–6 of *Little Jack Horner Pie*.
3. Do Steps 1–3 of *Ten Percent Rice*.
4. Do Step 1 of *Shrimp Esther Newberg*.
5. Do Steps 1–3 of *Best-Selling Asparagus*.
6. Do Steps 2–7 of *Shrimp Esther Newberg*.
7. Do Steps 4–5 of *Best-Selling Asparagus*.
8. Do Step 4 of *Ten Percent Rice*.

Weekend Six Sunday

FRESH PRODUCE

VEGETABLES
2 large carrots
1 medium head cabbage
1 small head lettuce
1 medium onion
2 scallions (green onions)
3 cloves garlic

HERBS
2 tablespoons parsley (when chopped)

FRUIT
1 small ripe honeydew melon
2 ripe kiwifruits
1/4 pound seedless red grapes
1 large banana

CANS, JARS & BOTTLES

SOUP
3 cans (14 ounces each) beef broth
1 can (10-1/2 ounces) beef consommé

PACKAGED GOODS

PASTA, RICE & GRAINS
1 pound spinach ravioli

BAKED GOODS
1 loaf Italian bread

DESSERT & BAKING NEEDS
2 squares (1 ounce each) unsweetened
   chocolate
1 cup chocolate chips

WINES & SPIRITS
3 tablespoons dry sherry

REFRIGERATED PRODUCTS

DAIRY
2 eggs

DELI
6 slices bacon

FROZEN GOODS

DESSERTS
1 pint vanilla ice cream

STAPLES

- ❏ Butter
- ❏ Flour
- ❏ Granulated sugar
- ❏ Chocolate syrup
- ❏ Olive oil
- ❏ Vegetable oil
- ❏ Rice vinegar
- ❏ Lemon juice
- ❏ Dijon mustard
- ❏ Honey
- ❏ Grated Parmesan cheese
- ❏ Poppy seeds
- ❏ Dried basil
- ❏ Dried rosemary
- ❏ Pepper
- ❏ Salt
- ❏ Vanilla extract

Weekend Six Sunday

MENU

Rambunctious Ravioli Soup

6 slices bacon
1 medium onion
2 cloves garlic
2 tablespoons fresh parsley (when chopped)
1 medium head cabbage
2 large carrots
3 cans (14 ounces each) beef broth
1 can (10-1/2 ounces) beef consommé
1/2 cup lemon juice
3 tablespoons dry sherry
1 teaspoon granulated sugar
1 teaspoon dried basil
1 pound spinach ravioli
Seasoning to taste
1/2 cup grated Parmesan cheese

Rapscallion Salad

1 small head lettuce
2 ripe kiwifruits
1/4 pound seedless red grapes
1 large banana
1 small ripe honeydew melon
2 scallions (green onions)
3 tablespoons vegetable oil
2 tablespoons rice vinegar
1/2 teaspoon Dijon mustard
1 tablespoon poppy seeds
1 teaspoon honey

Boisterous Bread

1 loaf Italian bread
1 clove garlic
2 tablespoons olive oil
1/2 teaspoon dried rosemary

Disorderly Dessert

4 tablespoons butter
2 squares (1 ounce each) unsweetened chocolate
1 cup granulated sugar
2 eggs
1/2 cup flour
1 teaspoon vanilla extract
1 cup chocolate chips
1 pint vanilla ice cream
1/2 cup chocolate syrup

EQUIPMENT

Dutch oven	Melon baller
Large saucepan	Pastry brush
8 × 8-inch baking pan	Ice cream scoop
Large mixing bowl	Aluminum foil
Small mixing bowl	Kitchen knives
Whisk	Measuring cups and spoons
Vegetable peeler	Cooking utensils
Vegetable grater	

Rambunctious Ravioli Soup

1. Chop the bacon into 1/2-inch pieces. Peel and chop the onion. Peel and mince the garlic. Rinse and chop the parsley. Core and grate the cabbage. Peel and slice the carrots.

2. Cook the bacon in a Dutch oven until soft, about 3 minutes.

3. Add the onion, the garlic, and the parsley, and sauté until the onion is lightly browned, about 7 minutes.

4. Add the broth, the consommé, the cabbage, and the carrot. Bring the mixture to a boil and add the lemon juice, the sherry, the sugar, and the basil.

5. Cover, reduce the heat, and simmer for 10 minutes.

6. Stir in the ravioli, and cook until it is tender, 10 minutes if you are using fresh ravioli, 12 minutes if you are using frozen. Season to taste.

7. Top with the cheese.

Rapscallion Salad

1. Wash and dry the lettuce and arrange the leaves on individual salad plates.

2. Peel and slice the kiwifruits. Rinse and stem the grapes. Peel and slice the banana. Cut the melon in half, discard the seeds, and, with a melon baller, scoop out the fruit. Combine the fruit in a large bowl.

3. Trim and chop the scallions.

4. In a small bowl, whisk together the oil, the vinegar, the mustard, the poppy seeds, and the honey.

5. Place the fruit mixture on the lettuce leaves, and spoon the dressing over the top.

6. Sprinkle with the scallions.

Boisterous Bread

1. Slice the bread in half lengthwise. Peel and finely mince the garlic.

2. Brush the cut side of the bread with the oil, and sprinkle it with the garlic and the rosemary.

3. Put the two halves of the bread together and wrap the loaf tightly in aluminum foil.

4. Bake at 350°F until hot, 10 to 12 minutes.

Disorderly Dessert

1. Preheat the oven to 350°F. Grease an 8 × 8-inch baking pan.

2. Combine the butter and the chocolate squares in a large saucepan, and melt slowly, stirring to blend. Remove the saucepan from the heat and gradually add the sugar. Add the eggs, one at a time, beating well after each egg is added. Fold in the flour. Blend well. Add the vanilla and the chocolate chips.

3. Pour the mixture into the baking pan and bake until set, 25 to 30 minutes. Do not overcook. The top should be soft when touched.

4. Cut into squares, top each brownie with a scoop of ice cream, and drizzle with the chocolate syrup.

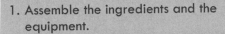

COUNTDOWN

1. Assemble the ingredients and the equipment.
2. Do Steps 1–3 of *Disorderly Dessert*.
3. Do Steps 1–5 of *Rambunctious Ravioli Soup*.
4. Do Steps 1–3 of *Boisterous Bread*.
5. Do Step 6 of *Rambunctious Ravioli Soup*.
6. Do Step 4 of *Boisterous Bread*.
7. Do Steps 1–6 of *Rapscallion Salad*.
8. Do Step 7 of *Rambunctious Ravioli Soup*.
9. Do Step 4 of *Disorderly Dessert*.

Weekend Seven Saturday

SHOPPING LIST

MEAT & POULTRY

1 boneless ham (about 3-1/2 pounds)

FRESH PRODUCE

VEGETABLES

3/4 pound sugar-snap peas
2 medium sweet onions
2 medium red onions
8 small shallots
10 scallions (green onions)
8 cloves garlic

FRUIT

3 pints strawberries

CANS, JARS & BOTTLES

VEGETABLES

1 can (11 ounces) whole kernel corn

FRUIT

1 can (8 ounces) sliced pineapple

CONDIMENTS

1 jar (2 ounces) diced pimiento

PACKAGED GOODS

BAKED GOODS

1 shortbread pie shell

WINES & SPIRITS

1 split champagne

REFRIGERATED PRODUCTS

DAIRY

1/4 cup whipped cream

STAPLES

☐ Butter
☐ Cornstarch
☐ Granulated sugar
☐ Dark brown sugar
☐ Olive oil
☐ Vegetable oil
☐ Balsamic vinegar
☐ Dijon mustard
☐ Honey
☐ Ground ginger
☐ Pepper
☐ Salt

Weekend Seven Saturday

Handsome Ham

1 boneless ham (about 3-1/2 pounds)
1 cup dark brown sugar
1 split champagne
1-1/2 tablespoons honey
2 teaspoons ground ginger
2 teaspoons Dijon mustard
1 can (8 ounces) sliced pineapple

Aristocratic Corn

3/4 pound sugar-snap peas
1 can (11 ounces) whole kernel corn
1 jar (2 ounces) diced pimiento
2 tablespoons vegetable oil
1/2 teaspoon granulated sugar
Seasoning to taste

Elegant Onions

8 cloves garlic
8 small shallots
2 medium sweet onions
2 medium red onions
10 scallions (green onions)
3 tablespoons butter
2 tablespoons olive oil
1 tablespoon balsamic vinegar

Sophisticated Strawberries

3 pints fresh strawberries
1 cup granulated sugar
3-1/2 tablespoons cornstarch
1/2 cup water
1 shortbread pie shell
1/4 cup whipped cream

EQUIPMENT

Large saucepan

Small saucepan

Large covered skillet

Medium skillet

Medium roasting pan

Roasting rack

Medium mixing bowl

Baster

Kitchen knives

Measuring cups and spoons

Cooking utensils

Weekend Seven Saturday

RECIPES

Handsome Ham

1. Preheat the oven to 325°F.

2. Score the top fat on the ham with the tip of a sharp knife.

3. Place the ham on a rack in a medium roasting pan. Spread the top of the ham with half of the brown sugar. Drizzle half of the champagne over the sugar.

4. Bake until heated through, about 2 hours.

5. In a small saucepan, combine the remaining 1/2 cup brown sugar, the remaining champagne, the honey, the ginger, and the mustard. Bring the mixture to a boil and baste the ham with the mixture every 15 minutes.

6. Drain the pineapple.

7. For the final 10 minutes of baking, arrange the pineapple slices over the ham, securing with toothpicks, if necessary.

Aristocratic Corn

1. Rinse and string the snap peas. Drain the corn. Drain the pimiento.

2. Heat the oil with the sugar in a medium skillet and sauté the snap peas for 3 minutes.

3. Add the corn and the pimiento, season to taste, and sauté until the snap peas are crisp-tender and the corn is heated through, about 3 minutes more.

Elegant Onions

1. Peel and halve the garlic cloves. Peel the shallots. Peel and quarter the sweet onions. Peel and quarter the red onions. Trim the scallions and cut them in half.

2. Melt the butter with the oil in a large skillet and sauté the garlic, the shallots, the sweet onions, and the red onions for 5 minutes.

3. Cover the skillet, reduce the heat, and simmer, stirring occasionally, until just tender, about 40 minutes.

4. Add the scallions and sauté until they are just tender, about 5 minutes more.

5. Remove the garlic. Drizzle with the vinegar.

Sophisticated Strawberries

1. Wash and hull the berries.

2. In a medium bowl, mash enough berries to make 2 cups.

3. In a large saucepan, blend together the sugar, the cornstarch, and the water. Add the mashed berries and cook, stirring constantly, until the mixture comes to a boil. Boil until the mixture is thick and clear, about 2 minutes.

4. Set the saucepan aside and let the mixture cool for 10 minutes.

5. Fold in the whole berries, and turn the mixture into the pie shell. Chill for at least 1 hour.

6. To serve, garnish with dollops of whipped cream.

COUNTDOWN

1. Assemble the ingredients and the equipment.
2. Do Steps 1–5 of *Handsome Ham*.
3. Do Steps 1–5 of *Sophisticated Strawberries*.
4. Do Steps 1–3 of *Elegant Onions*.
5. Do Steps 6–7 of *Handsome Ham*.
6. Do Step 1 of *Aristocratic Corn*.
7. Do Step 4 of *Elegant Onions*.
8. Do Steps 2–3 of *Aristocratic Corn*.
9. Do Step 5 of *Elegant Onions*.
10. Do Step 6 of *Sophisticated Strawberries*.

Weekend Seven Sunday

FRESH PRODUCE

VEGETABLES
3 medium zucchini
2 medium carrots
1 package (10 ounces) spinach
4 medium mushrooms
1 medium head red leaf lettuce
1 small yellow bell pepper
1 small bunch radishes
1 small onion
2 scallions (green onions)
1 clove garlic

FRUIT
1 medium ripe cantaloupe
1 medium orange
4 medium bananas

CANS, JARS & BOTTLES

VEGETABLES
1 can (28 ounces) crushed tomatoes

PACKAGED GOODS

PASTA, RICE & GRAINS
12 ounces curly egg noodles

DESSERT & BAKING NEEDS
1-1/2 cups flaked coconut
1 jar (12 ounces) hot fudge sauce

REFRIGERATED PRODUCTS

DAIRY
1/2 cup sour cream

CHEESE
1 container (15 ounces) ricotta cheese
2 cups shredded mozzarella cheese

- ☐ Granulated sugar
- ☐ Olive oil
- ☐ Vegetable oil
- ☐ Tarragon vinegar
- ☐ Dried basil
- ☐ Dried oregano
- ☐ Ground nutmeg
- ☐ Pepper
- ☐ Salt
- ☐ Orange extract

Weekend Seven Sunday

Noodling Up

1 clove garlic
2 medium carrots
1 small onion
3 medium zucchini
1 package (10 ounces) fresh spinach
12 ounces curly egg noodles
3 tablespoons olive oil
1 can (28 ounces) crushed tomatoes
1 teaspoon granulated sugar
1/2 teaspoon dried basil
Seasoning to taste
1 container (15 ounces) ricotta cheese
2 cups shredded mozzarella cheese

Fork Over the Salad

1 medium head red leaf lettuce
2 scallions (green onions)
1 small bunch radishes
1 small yellow bell pepper
4 medium fresh mushrooms
3 tablespoons vegetable oil
2 tablespoons tarragon vinegar
1/4 teaspoon ground nutmeg
1/2 teaspoon dried oregano
Seasoning to taste

Coconuts

1 medium orange
1 medium ripe cantaloupe
4 medium bananas
1 teaspoon orange extract
1/2 cup sour cream
1-1/2 cups flaked coconut
1 jar (12 ounces) hot fudge sauce

EQUIPMENT

Stockpot	Vegetable brush
Small saucepan	Vegetable peeler
Large skillet	Citrus grater
9 × 9-inch glass baking dish	Citrus juicer
Colander	Waxed paper
Large shallow bowl	Plastic wrap
Large mixing bowl	Kitchen knives
Small mixing bowl	Measuring cups and spoons
Whisk	Cooking utensils

Weekend Seven Sunday

Noodling Up

1. Bring water for the pasta to a boil in a stockpot.

2. Peel and mince the garlic. Peel and slice the carrots. Peel and mince the onion. Scrub, trim, and slice the zucchini. Wash, dry, and stem the spinach.

3. Cook the noodles in the stockpot until almost tender, about 7 minutes.

4. Heat the oil in a large skillet and sauté the garlic for 1 minute.

5. Add the carrots and the onion, and sauté for 5 minutes.

6. Add the zucchini and sauté for 2 minutes.

7. Add the tomatoes, the sugar, and the basil. Season to taste, blend well, reduce the heat, and simmer for 2 minutes.

8. Drain the noodles and run them under cold water to cool.

9. Preheat the oven to 350°F. Grease a 9 × 9-inch glass baking dish.

10. Spoon a small amount of the tomato mixture into the bottom of the dish. Add a layer of noodles, a layer of ricotta cheese, and a layer of spinach. Top with half of the remaining tomato mixture. Repeat. Sprinkle with the mozzarella cheese.

11. Bake until hot and bubbly, 45 to 50 minutes.

12. Let sit for 10 minutes before serving.

Fork Over the Salad

1. Wash and dry the lettuce and tear it into bite-sized pieces. Trim and chop the scallions. Rinse, trim, and slice the radishes. Rinse, stem, seed, and slice the bell pepper. Rinse, pat dry, and slice the mushrooms. Combine the vegetables in a large bowl.

2. In a small bowl, whisk together the oil, the vinegar, the nutmeg, and the oregano. Season to taste.

3. Toss the salad with the dressing.

Coconuts

1. Grate 1 tablespoon of orange peel. Juice the orange. Halve the melon, removing the seeds and the rind, and cut the melon into chunks. Peel and chunk the bananas.

2. In a large shallow bowl, combine the orange peel, the orange juice, and the orange extract with the sour cream. Lay the coconut out on a sheet of waxed paper.

3. Roll the bananas in the sour cream mixture and then in the coconut. Place the chunks on a plate, cover the plate with plastic wrap, and refrigerate it until you are ready to serve.

4. Roll the cantaloupe chunks in the sour cream mixture and then in the coconut. Place the chunks on a plate, cover it with plastic wrap, and refrigerate it until you are ready to serve.

5. Heat the hot fudge sauce in a small saucepan.

6. Arrange the fruit on individual dessert plates and drizzle with the hot fudge sauce.

COUNTDOWN

1. Assemble the ingredients and the equipment.
2. Do Steps 1–11 of *Noodling Up*.
3. Do Steps 1–4 of *Coconuts*.
4. Do Step 12 of *Noodling Up*.
5. Do Steps 1–3 of *Fork Over the Salad*.
6. Do Steps 5–6 of *Coconuts*.

Weekend Eight Saturday

SHOPPING LIST

MEAT & POULTRY

1 whole duck (about 5 pounds)

FRESH PRODUCE

VEGETABLES

4 medium baking potatoes
1 large bunch broccoli
1 medium head romaine lettuce
1 small green bell pepper
1 small red onion
2 cloves garlic

FRUIT

1 small ripe peach
2 ripe kiwifruits
1/2 pint raspberries
1/2 pint blueberries
1 large lemon

CANS, JARS & BOTTLES

SOUP

1 can (10-1/2 ounces) beef broth

FISH

1 tin (2 ounces) anchovy fillets (optional)

SPREADS

1/3 cup red currant jelly

PACKAGED GOODS

BAKED GOODS

4 individual chocolate tart shells

DESSERT & BAKING NEEDS

1 small package instant French vanilla
   pudding mix

REFRIGERATED PRODUCTS

DAIRY

1-1/4 cups milk
3/4 cup sour cream
1/4 cup whipped cream

STAPLES

❏ Granulated sugar
❏ Dark brown sugar
❏ Vegetable oil
❏ White wine vinegar
❏ Lemon juice
❏ Kitchen Bouquet
❏ Dried sage
❏ Ground cinnamon
❏ Dry mustard
❏ Paprika
❏ Pepper
❏ Salt
❏ Vanilla extract

Weekend Eight Saturday

MENU

Duck Be a Lady Tonight

1 whole duck (about 5 pounds)
2 cloves garlic
4 medium baking potatoes
1 can (10-1/2 ounces) beef broth
2 tablespoons dark brown sugar
2 teaspoons dried sage
2 tablespoons Kitchen Bouquet

Sit Down, You're Broccoling the Boat

1 large bunch broccoli
1 large lemon
1/4 teaspoon ground cinnamon
Seasoning to taste

A Poisson Could Develop a Cold

1 medium head romaine lettuce
1 small green bell pepper
1 small red onion
1 tin (2 ounces) anchovy fillets (optional)
3 tablespoons vegetable oil
2 tablespoons white wine vinegar
1/4 teaspoon dry mustard
1/4 teaspoon granulated sugar
1/4 teaspoon paprika
Seasoning to taste

Pies and Dolls

1 small package instant French vanilla
   pudding mix
1-1/4 cups milk
3/4 cup sour cream
1 teaspoon vanilla extract
4 individual chocolate tart shells
1/3 cup red currant jelly
1 tablespoon lemon juice
1 small ripe peach
2 ripe kiwifruits
1/2 pint fresh raspberries
1/2 pint fresh blueberries
1/4 cup whipped cream

EQUIPMENT

Electric mixer	Whisk
Medium covered saucepan	Citrus grater
Small saucepan	Citrus juicer
Medium roasting pan	Vegetable peeler
Steamer insert	Kitchen knives
Medium mixing bowl	Measuring cups and spoons
Small mixing bowl	Cooking utensils

Duck Be a Lady Tonight

1. Preheat the oven to 450°F.

2. Rinse and pat dry the duck and split it into quarters.

3. Peel and slice the garlic. Slip the slices under the skin of the duck pieces.

4. Peel the potatoes and cut them into 1-1/2-inch cubes.

5. Put the broth in the bottom of a medium roasting pan. Add the potatoes.

6. Place the hind quarters of the duck over the potatoes. Sprinkle with half of the sugar and half of the sage, and brush on half of the Kitchen Bouquet. Roast for 10 minutes.

7. Add the breast quarters to the pan. Sprinkle with the remaining 1 tablespoon sugar, the remaining 1 teaspoon sage, and the remaining 1 tablespoon Kitchen Bouquet.

8. Reduce the oven heat to 400°F and roast until the duck is golden and the potatoes are golden and crunchy, about 30 minutes more.

Sit Down, You're Broccoling the Boat

1. Bring a small amount of water to a boil in a medium saucepan.

2. Rinse and trim the broccoli and cut it into spears.

3. Grate 2 tablespoons of lemon peel, and cut the lemon in half.

4. Arrange the broccoli spears in a steamer insert and place the insert in the saucepan. Squeeze the juice of half the lemon over the broccoli and sprinkle with the cinnamon. Cover the saucepan and steam for 8 minutes.

5. Sprinkle the lemon peel over the broccoli, season to taste, and continue steaming for 2 minutes more.

6. Slice the remaining half lemon and serve with the broccoli.

A Poisson Could Develop a Cold

1. Wash, dry, and trim the romaine and arrange the leaves on individual salad plates. Rinse, stem, seed, and slice the bell pepper. Peel and slice the onion. Arrange the bell pepper and onion slices over the lettuce.

2. Drain and blot the anchovies and place one on each salad.

3. In a small bowl, whisk together the oil, the vinegar, the mustard, the sugar, and the paprika. Season to taste.

4. Drizzle the dressing over the salads.

Pies and Dolls

1. In a medium bowl, beat the pudding mix, the milk, and the sour cream with an electric mixer until well blended, about 2 minutes. Fold in the vanilla. Spoon the mixture into individual tart shells and refrigerate for 10 minutes.

2. In a small saucepan, melt the currant jelly with the lemon juice, then set aside.

3. Peel, pit, and slice the peach. Peel, halve, and slice the kiwifruits. Rinse and pat dry the berries.

4. Lay the peach slices over the pudding. Lay the kiwi slices over the peach slices. Lay the berries over the kiwi slices. Drizzle the currant glaze over the fruit and refrigerate until you are ready to serve.

5. Garnish with dollops of whipped cream.

COUNTDOWN

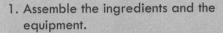

1. Assemble the ingredients and the equipment.
2. Do Steps 1–4 of *Pies and Dolls.*
3. Do Steps 1–8 of *Duck Be a Lady Tonight.*
4. Do Steps 1–3 of *A Poisson Could Develop a Cold.*
5. Do Steps 1–6 of *Sit Down, You're Broccoling the Boat.*
6. Do Step 4 of *A Poisson Could Develop a Cold.*
7. Do Step 5 of *Pies and Dolls.*

Weekend Eight Sunday

SHOPPING LIST

FISH

1/2 pound salmon fillets
1/2 pound sole fillets
1/2 pound medium shrimp,
    shelled and deveined
1/2 pound scallops

FRESH PRODUCE

VEGETABLES
4 medium red potatoes
4 medium carrots
4 stalks celery
1 medium head green leaf lettuce
1 medium cucumber
1 large onion

HERBS
1 tablespoon parsley (when chopped)

FRUIT
3 medium bananas

CANS, JARS & BOTTLES

SOUP
1 can (14 ounces) chicken broth

VEGETABLES
1 can (28 ounces) crushed tomatoes

JUICE
2 cups clam juice

PACKAGED GOODS

BAKED GOODS
1 shortbread pie shell

WINES & SPIRITS

1/2 cup dry red wine

REFRIGERATED PRODUCTS

DAIRY
2/3 cup buttermilk

DELI
2 slices bacon

FROZEN GOODS

DESSERTS
1 pint Rocky Road ice cream
1 carton (8 ounces) whipped topping

STAPLES

❑ Vegetable shortening
❑ Flour
❑ Baking powder
❑ Baking soda
❑ Granulated sugar
❑ Chocolate sprinkles
❑ Olive oil
❑ Red wine vinegar
❑ Worcestershire sauce
❑ Dijon mustard
❑ Ketchup
❑ Dried rosemary
❑ Dried thyme
❑ Pepper
❑ Salt

Weekend Eight Sunday

Wild Soup

1/2 pound salmon fillets
1/2 pound sole fillets
1/2 pound medium shrimp, shelled and deveined
1/2 pound scallops
2 slices bacon
1 large onion
4 medium carrots
4 stalks celery
4 medium red potatoes
1 tablespoon fresh parsley (when chopped)
1 can (28 ounces) crushed tomatoes
2 cups clam juice
1 can (14 ounces) chicken broth
1/2 cup dry red wine
2 tablespoons ketchup
1 tablespoon Worcestershire sauce
1/4 teaspoon dried thyme
Seasoning to taste

Tame Toss

1 medium head green leaf lettuce
1 medium cucumber
3 tablespoons olive oil
2 tablespoons red wine vinegar
1/4 teaspoon Dijon mustard
Seasoning to taste

Brash Biscuits

1 teaspoon dried rosemary
2 cups flour
1 tablespoon granulated sugar
1 tablespoon baking powder
1/4 teaspoon baking soda
1/2 teaspoon salt
1/2 cup vegetable shortening
2/3 cup buttermilk

Crazy Pie

1 pint Rocky Road ice cream
1 carton (8 ounces) frozen whipped topping
3 medium bananas
1 shortbread pie shell
Chocolate sprinkles for garnish

EQUIPMENT

Dutch oven
Baking sheet
Breadboard
Large mixing bowl
Pastry blender
Small mixing bowl
Vegetable peeler
Whisk
Biscuit cutter
Plastic wrap
Kitchen knives
Measuring cups and spoons
Cooking utensils

Wild Soup

1. Rinse and pat dry the salmon and the sole, and cut them into chunks. Rinse and pat dry the shrimp and the scallops.

2. Dice the bacon.

3. Peel and chop the onion. Peel and chunk the carrots. Rinse, trim, and slice the celery. Peel and chunk the potatoes. Rinse and chop the parsley.

4. Cook the bacon in a Dutch oven until it is crisp. Drain the bacon on paper towels and reserve the drippings in the pan.

5. In the bacon drippings, sauté the onion until it is soft, about 5 minutes.

6. Add the carrots, the potatoes, the celery, the tomatoes, the clam juice, the broth, the wine, the ketchup, the Worcestershire sauce, and the thyme.

7. Bring the mixture to a boil. Cover the Dutch oven, reduce the heat, and simmer for 45 minutes.

8. Add the salmon and the sole chunks and season to taste. Return the soup to a boil, cover, and cook for 10 minutes.

9. Add the shrimp and the scallops, and cook for 5 minutes more. Season to taste.

10. Sprinkle with the bacon and the parsley.

Tame Toss

1. Rinse and dry the lettuce and tear it into bite-sized pieces. Peel and slice the cucumber. Arrange the vegetables on individual salad plates.

2. In a small bowl, whisk together the oil, the vinegar, and the mustard. Season to taste.

3. Drizzle the dressing over the salad.

Brash Biscuits

1. Preheat the oven to 450°F. Flour a breadboard. Flour a biscuit cutter.

2. Crumble the rosemary.

3. In a large bowl, combine the flour, the sugar, the baking powder, the baking soda, the salt, and the rosemary.

4. Add the shortening to the bowl and cut it in with a pastry blender until the mixture resembles fine crumbs.

5. Add the buttermilk and stir to combine until the dough forms a ball.

6. Turn the dough out onto the floured breadboard and roll to coat. Knead the dough until it is smooth, 8 to 10 times.

7. Pat the dough out into a half-inch thickness, cut with the biscuit cutter, and arrange the biscuits on a baking sheet.

8. Bake until golden, 10–12 minutes.

Crazy Pie

1. Set the ice cream and the whipped topping out to soften slightly.

2. Peel and slice the bananas and arrange them in the bottom of the pie shell.

3. Spread the softened ice cream over the bananas. Spoon the whipped topping over the ice cream. Cover the pie with plastic wrap and freeze it for at least 30 minutes.

4. Remove the pie from the freezer 5 minutes before serving. Garnish with the chocolate sprinkles.

COUNTDOWN

1. Assemble the ingredients and the equipment.
2. Do Steps 1–3 of *Crazy Pie*.
3. Do Steps 1–7 of *Wild Soup*.
4. Do Steps 1–7 of *Brash Biscuits*.
5. Do Step 8 of *Wild Soup*.
6. Do Step 8 of *Brash Biscuits*.
7. Do Steps 1–2 of *Tame Toss*.
8. Do Step 9 of *Wild Soup*.
9. Do Step 3 of *Tame Toss*.
10. Do Step 10 of *Wild Soup*.
11. Do Step 4 of *Crazy Pie*.

Weekend Nine Saturday

SHOPPING LIST

MEAT & POULTRY

1 pound bulk sausage
1 whole chicken (about 4 pounds)

FRESH PRODUCE

VEGETABLES
1-1/4 pounds Brussels sprouts
1 large onion

FRUIT
1 large lemon

CANS, JARS & BOTTLES

SOUP
1 can (14 ounces) chicken broth

SPREADS
1/4 cup red currant jelly

PACKAGED GOODS

PASTA, RICE & GRAINS
8 ounces wild rice

DESSERT & BAKING NEEDS
1 envelope unflavored gelatin

WINES & SPIRITS

1/2 cup brandy

REFRIGERATED PRODUCTS

DAIRY
1 cup whipping cream
4 eggs

JUICE
2 tablespoons orange juice

STAPLES

- ❑ Butter
- ❑ Cream of tartar
- ❑ Granulated sugar
- ❑ Vegetable oil
- ❑ Dijon mustard
- ❑ Honey
- ❑ Pepper
- ❑ Salt

Weekend Nine Saturday

MENU

There's No Fowl Like an Old Fowl

1 can (14 ounces) chicken broth
1-1/2 cups water
8 ounces wild rice
1 large onion
1 tablespoon vegetable oil
1 pound bulk sausage
1/2 cup brandy
1 whole chicken (about 4 pounds)
Seasoning to taste
3 tablespoons butter
1/4 cup red currant jelly

Something to Sprout About

1-1/4 pounds Brussels sprouts
2 tablespoons orange juice
2 teaspoons Dijon mustard
1 tablespoon honey

It's a Lemon

1 large lemon
1 envelope unflavored gelatin
3/4 cup granulated sugar
1/2 teaspoon salt
4 eggs
1/2 cup cold water
1 cup whipping cream
1 teaspoon cream of tartar

EQUIPMENT

Electric mixer
Double boiler
2 medium covered saucepans
Small saucepan
Large skillet
1-quart covered casserole
Medium roasting pan
Steamer insert
Meat thermometer
Skewers
Strainer
Large mixing bowl
Medium mixing bowl
Small mixing bowl
Citrus grater
Citrus juicer
Whisk
Pastry brush
Kitchen knives
Measuring cups and spoons
Cooking utensils

There's No Fowl Like an Old Fowl

1. Bring the broth and 1 cup of the water to a boil in a medium saucepan.

2. Rinse the rice.

3. Add the rice to the saucepan, cover, reduce the heat, and simmer until the liquid is absorbed and the rice is tender, 40 to 45 minutes.

4. Peel and mince the onion.

5. Heat the oil in a large skillet and sauté the onion and the sausage until the meat is browned, about 10 minutes. Add the brandy and cook until the liquid has almost evaporated, about 2 minutes.

6. Blend the sausage mixture into the rice and let it cool for 10 minutes.

7. Preheat the oven to 375°F.

8. Rinse and pat dry the chicken. Season it to taste, inside and out.

9. Stuff some of the rice mixture into the chicken and secure the opening with skewers.

10. Place the remaining rice mixture in a 1-quart casserole.

11. Pour the remaining 1/2 cup water into a medium roasting pan. Add the chicken, breast side down.

12. In a small saucepan, melt the butter with the jelly. Brush some of it over the chicken and roast it for 40 minutes.

13. Turn the chicken, brush with the remaining jelly mixture, insert a meat thermometer into the fleshy part of the thigh, and roast until the temperature reads 180°F and the chicken is nicely browned, about 1-1/4 hours.

14. Cover the rice casserole and place it in the oven with the chicken for the final 15 minutes of cooking.

Something to Sprout About

1. Bring a small amount of water to a boil in a medium saucepan.

2. Rinse and trim the sprouts and cut them in half. Put the sprouts in a steamer insert, place the insert in the saucepan, cover the pan, and steam until the sprouts are crisp-tender, about 10 minutes.

3. Drain the sprouts. Combine the orange juice, the mustard, and the honey in the saucepan. Add the sprouts and toss them in the mixture to coat. Heat through.

It's a Lemon

1. Chill a medium bowl and the beaters of an electric mixer in the refrigerator for at least 10 minutes.

2. Grate the lemon peel. Juice the lemon.

3. Bring water to a boil in the bottom of a double boiler.

4. In the top of the double boiler, combine the gelatin, 1/4 cup of the sugar, and the salt.

5. Separate the eggs, placing the yolks in a small bowl and the whites in a large bowl.

6. To the yolks, add the water and the lemon juice, and whisk to blend. Add the egg yolk mixture to the gelatin mixture. Reduce the heat and cook, stirring constantly, until the mixture thickens, about 10 minutes.

7. Remove the top of the double boiler from the heat and fold in half of the lemon peel. Let the mixture cool for 20 minutes.

8. Whip the cream in the chilled bowl until stiff, about 3 minutes.

9. Whip the egg whites until soft peaks form, about 2 minutes. Gradually add the remaining 1/2 cup sugar and the cream of tartar, and continue beating until the sugar is dissolved and the egg whites are stiff and glossy, about 2 minutes more.

10. Fold the whipped cream into the egg whites. Add the lemon mixture, and blend well.

11. Pour the mixture into individual dessert glasses, sprinkle with the remaining lemon peel, and refrigerate for at least 1 hour.

COUNTDOWN

1. Assemble the ingredients and the equipment.
2. Do Steps 1–11 of *It's a Lemon*.
3. Do Steps 1–14 of *There's No Fowl Like an Old Fowl*.
4. Do Steps 1–3 of *Something to Sprout About*.

Weekend Nine Sunday

MEAT & POULTRY

1-1/2 pounds lean cooked ham steak

FRESH PRODUCE

VEGETABLES

1 pound baking potatoes
1-1/2 pounds green peas, unshelled
1 medium head red leaf lettuce
2 medium tomatoes
1 medium onion
1 small red onion
1 clove garlic

HERBS

2 tablespoons parsley (when chopped)

FRUIT

1 small lemon

CANS, JARS & BOTTLES

SOUP

1 can (10-1/2 ounces) chicken broth

DESSERT & BAKING NEEDS

1 can (21 ounces) blueberry pie filling

REFRIGERATED PRODUCTS

DAIRY

2-3/4 cups milk
1 cup sour cream
1 cup whipping cream
1 egg

- ❏ Butter
- ❏ Flour
- ❏ Baking powder
- ❏ Powdered sugar
- ❏ Olive oil
- ❏ Vegetable oil
- ❏ Lemon juice
- ❏ Honey
- ❏ Seasoned breadcrumbs
- ❏ Ground cinnamon
- ❏ Ground nutmeg
- ❏ Paprika
- ❏ Pepper
- ❏ Salt
- ❏ Vanilla extract

Clap Your Hams

1 pound baking potatoes
1 medium onion
2 tablespoons fresh parsley (when chopped)
1-1/2 pounds lean cooked ham steak
1/3 cup flour
Seasoning to taste
2 cups milk
1/2 cup seasoned breadcrumbs
1 tablespoon butter

Peas of Mind

1-1/2 pounds fresh green peas, unshelled
1 can (10-1/2 ounces) chicken broth
1/2 teaspoon paprika

Leaf of Faith

1 medium head red leaf lettuce
2 medium fresh tomatoes
1 small red onion
1 clove garlic
3 tablespoons olive oil
2 tablespoons lemon juice
Seasoning to taste

Muffoons

1 small lemon
3/4 cup milk
1/3 cup vegetable oil
1/4 cup honey
1 egg
2 cups flour
1 tablespoon baking powder
1/2 teaspoon salt
1/2 teaspoon ground cinnamon
1/4 teaspoon ground nutmeg

Blueberry Fool

1 cup whipping cream
2 tablespoons powdered sugar
1 teaspoon vanilla extract
1 cup sour cream
1 can (21 ounces) blueberry pie filling

EQUIPMENT

Electric mixer
2-quart covered casserole
Medium covered saucepan
Muffin tin
Large mixing bowl
Medium mixing bowl
2 small mixing bowls
Vegetable peeler
Citrus grater
Citrus juicer
Whisk
Kitchen knives
Measuring cups and spoons
Cooking utensils

Weekend Nine Sunday

Clap Your Hams

1. Preheat the oven to 350°F.

2. Peel and thinly slice the potatoes. Peel and slice the onion. Rinse and chop the parsley. Trim and cube the ham.

3. Layer half the ham in a 2-quart casserole. Cover with half of the potatoes and half of the onion. Sprinkle with half of the flour. Repeat. Season to taste, add the milk, cover, and bake until the potatoes are nearly tender, about 1 hour.

4. Increase the oven temperature to 400°F. Top the casserole with the breadcrumbs, dot with the butter, and sprinkle with the parsley. Bake, uncovered, until the breadcrumbs are golden, about 20 minutes more.

Peas of Mind

1. Shell the peas.

2. Bring the peas and the broth to a boil in a medium saucepan, cover, and cook until the peas are tender, 5 to 8 minutes.

3. Drain the peas and sprinkle with the paprika.

Leaf of Faith

1. Wash and dry the lettuce and distribute the leaves on individual salad plates.

2. Rinse and slice the tomatoes. Peel and thinly slice the onion. Arrange the tomatoes and the onion over the lettuce.

3. Peel and mince the garlic. In a small bowl, whisk together the garlic, the oil, and the lemon juice. Season to taste.

4. Spoon the dressing over the salad.

Muffoons

1. Preheat the oven to 400°F. Grease a muffin tin.

2. Grate the lemon peel and juice the lemon.

3. In a large bowl, combine the milk, the oil, the honey, the lemon peel, the lemon juice, and the egg, and beat until well blended.

4. In a small bowl, combine the flour, the baking powder, the salt, the cinnamon, and the nutmeg.

5. Fold the dry ingredients into the wet ingredients.

6. Divide the batter evenly among the muffin cups.

7. Bake until golden, about 20 minutes.

Blueberry Fool

1. Chill a medium bowl and the beaters of an electric mixer in the refrigerator for at least 10 minutes.

2. Whip the cream in the chilled bowl, until stiff peaks form, about 5 minutes. Fold in the powdered sugar and the vanilla. Fold in the sour cream.

3. Place a layer of the pie filling in the bottom of individual dessert glasses. Cover with half of the whipped cream mixture. Repeat. Chill in the refrigerator until you are ready to serve.

COUNTDOWN

1. Assemble the ingredients and the equipment.
2. Do Steps 1–3 of *Blueberry Fool*.
3. Do Steps 1–3 of *Clap Your Hams*.
4. Do Steps 1–3 of *Leaf of Faith*.
5. Do Steps 1–6 of *Muffoons*.
6. Do Step 4 of *Clap Your Hams*.
7. Do Step 7 of *Muffoons*.
8. Do Steps 1–3 of *Peas of Mind*.
9. Do Step 4 of *Leaf of Faith*.

Weekend Ten Saturday

MEAT & POULTRY

4 lean beef tenderloins (about 2 pounds)

FRESH PRODUCE

VEGETABLES

4 medium artichokes
1 stalk celery
8 medium mushrooms
1 medium onion

CANS, JARS & BOTTLES

SOUP

1 can (14 ounces) beef broth
1 can (14 ounces) chicken broth

PACKAGED GOODS

PASTA, RICE & GRAINS

1/2 cup wild rice
1/2 cup brown rice
1/2 cup long-grain white rice

BAKED GOODS

1 pound cake

DRIED FRUITS & NUTS

1/2 cup walnut bits

DESSERT & BAKING NEEDS

6 ounces chocolate chips

WINES & SPIRITS

3 tablespoons brandy

REFRIGERATED PRODUCTS

DAIRY

4 eggs

☐ Butter
☐ Powdered sugar
☐ Vegetable oil
☐ Lemon juice
☐ Worcestershire sauce
☐ Bay leaf
☐ Pepper
☐ Salt
☐ Rum extract

Weekend Ten Saturday

Brandish the Beef

1 medium onion
8 medium fresh mushrooms
3 tablespoons vegetable oil
4 lean beef tenderloins (about 2 pounds)
1 tablespoon Worcestershire sauce
3 tablespoons brandy
Seasoning to taste

Three-Rice Pilaf

1 stalk celery
1/2 cup walnut bits
1/2 cup wild rice
1/2 cup brown rice
1 can (14 ounces) beef broth
1 can (14 ounces) chicken broth
1/2 cup long-grain white rice

Thistle Please You

4 medium fresh artichokes
1-1/2 cups water
1/4 cup lemon juice
1 bay leaf
4 tablespoons butter

No Retort

6 ounces chocolate chips
8 tablespoons butter
1/4 cup hot water
4 eggs
1/4 cup powdered sugar
1 teaspoon rum extract
1 pound cake

E Q U I P M E N T

Double boiler

Medium covered saucepan

Medium saucepan

Large skillet

Medium skillet

Steamer insert

Whisk

Kitchen shears

Kitchen knives

Measuring cups and spoons

Cooking utensils

Brandish the Beef

1. Peel and chop the onion. Rinse, pat dry, and thinly slice the mushrooms.

2. Heat 2 tablespoons of the oil in a large skillet and brown the beef tenderloins quickly on one side. Turn the tenderloins and cook until they are almost done to taste, 5 to 6 minutes for rare.

3. Heat the remaining 1 tablespoon oil in a medium skillet and sauté the onion for 2 minutes.

4. Add the mushrooms and sauté for 3 minutes.

5. Add the Worcestershire sauce and the brandy to the mushroom mixture, blend well, and pour over the tenderloins, turning to coat them.

6. Season to taste and cook for 1 minute more.

Three-Rice Pilaf

1. Bring water to a boil in the bottom of a double boiler.

2. Rinse, trim, and mince the celery.

3. In the top of the double boiler, combine the celery, the walnut bits, the wild rice, the brown rice, and the broth.

4. Cover, reduce the heat, and simmer for 10 minutes.

5. Add the white rice to the top of the double boiler. Cover and simmer until the liquid is absorbed and the rice is tender, 30 to 40 minutes more.

Thistle Please You

1. Discard the stems and rough outer leaves of the artichokes and with kitchen shears trim the prickly points off the inner leaves.

2. Bring the water, the lemon juice, and the bay leaf to a boil in a medium saucepan.

3. Arrange the artichokes in a steamer insert and place the insert in the saucepan. Cover and steam until a leaf pulls easily from the stem, 30 to 35 minutes.

4. Melt the butter and serve it with the artichokes for dipping.

No Retort

1. In a medium saucepan, combine the chocolate, the butter, and the water, and slowly heat, stirring, until the chocolate is melted and the mixture is smooth, about 5 minutes. Whisk the eggs into the chocolate mixture and cook for 1 minute more. Remove the saucepan from the heat and let stand for 5 minutes.

2. Blend in the sugar, fold in the rum extract, and stir until smooth. Chill the mixture until it thickens, at least 40 minutes.

3. Carefully cut the cake into four equal layers.

4. Spread a little of the frosting on the bottom layer, add the next layer, and repeat. Continue repeating until all the layers are back together. Frost the top and sides of the entire tort, and refrigerate it until you are ready to serve.

COUNTDOWN

1. Assemble the ingredients and the equipment.
2. Do Steps 1–4 of *No Retort*.
3. Do Steps 1–4 of *Three-Rice Pilaf*.
4. Do Steps 1–2 of *Thistle Please You*.
5. Do Step 5 of *Three-Rice Pilaf*.
6. Do Step 3 of *Thistle Please You*.
7. Do Steps 1–6 of *Brandish the Beef*.
8. Do Step 4 of *Thistle Please You*.

Weekend Ten Sunday

MEAT & POULTRY

3 pounds chicken pieces

FRESH PRODUCE

VEGETABLES
1-1/2 pounds baby new red potatoes
1 small shallot
1 clove garlic

HERBS
1/4 cup chives (when chopped)

CANS, JARS & BOTTLES

SOUP
2 cans (10-1/2 ounces each) chicken broth

VEGETABLES
1 can (4 ounces) button mushrooms

DESSERT & BAKING NEEDS
1 jar (10 ounces) peach jam

PACKAGED GOODS

DRIED FRUITS & NUTS
1/2 cup pecan bits

DESSERT & BAKING NEEDS
1 small package instant French vanilla pudding mix

WINES & SPIRITS

2/3 cup dry red wine

REFRIGERATED PRODUCTS

DAIRY
1-1/4 cups milk
3/4 cup sour cream

FROZEN GOODS

VEGETABLES
1 package (16 ounces) cut green beans

STAPLES

- ❑ Butter
- ❑ Flour
- ❑ Vegetable oil
- ❑ Red wine vinegar
- ❑ Lemon juice
- ❑ Ketchup
- ❑ Kitchen Bouquet
- ❑ Bay leaf
- ❑ Dried tarragon
- ❑ Curry powder
- ❑ Ground nutmeg
- ❑ Pepper
- ❑ Salt

Weekend Ten Sunday

Sonja Henie

3 pounds chicken pieces
1 small shallot
1 clove garlic
4 tablespoons vegetable oil
1/2 cup flour
Seasoning to taste
2 cups chicken broth
2/3 cup dry red wine
1/2 cup ketchup
1/3 cup red wine vinegar
1 tablespoon Kitchen Bouquet
1 teaspoon dried tarragon
1 bay leaf
1/2 cup water

John Curry

1-1/2 pounds baby new red potatoes
1/4 cup fresh chives (when chopped)
3 tablespoons butter
1 tablespoon lemon juice
1/2 teaspoon curry powder
Seasoning to taste

Dick Buttons

1 package (16 ounces) frozen cut green
   beans
1/4 cup chicken broth
1 can (4 ounces) button mushrooms
1/2 teaspoon ground nutmeg
Seasoning to taste

Olympic Pudding

1 small package instant French vanilla
   pudding mix
1-1/4 cups milk
3/4 cup sour cream
1 jar (10 ounces) peach jam
1/2 cup pecan bits

EQUIPMENT

Electric mixer

Dutch oven

Large saucepan

Medium saucepan

Large skillet

2 medium mixing bowls

Small mixing bowl

Whisk

Vegetable brush

Plastic bag

Aluminum foil

Kitchen knives

Measuring cups and spoons

Cooking utensils

Weekend Ten Sunday

Sonja Henie

1. Preheat the oven to 350°F.

2. Rinse and pat dry the chicken pieces.

3. Peel and mince the shallot. Peel and mince the garlic.

4. Heat the oil in a large skillet, and sauté the shallot and the garlic for 1 minute.

5. Place the flour in a plastic bag. Season to taste. Dredge the chicken in the seasoned flour, a few pieces at a time. Reserve the remaining flour.

6. Sauté the chicken in the skillet until browned on all sides, 10 to 15 minutes. Place the chicken in a Dutch oven.

7. To the skillet, add the broth, the wine, the ketchup, the vinegar, the Kitchen Bouquet, the tarragon, and the bay leaf. Bring the mixture to a boil and pour it over the chicken.

8. Bake until the chicken is tender, 30 to 35 minutes.

9. Remove the chicken and cover it with aluminum foil to keep it warm. Remove the bay leaf. Place the Dutch oven over a burner and bring the liquid to a boil.

10. In a small bowl, whisk together the reserved seasoned flour and the water. Slowly pour the mixture into the hot liquid, and whisk until the gravy is smooth and thickened, about 7 minutes.

John Curry

1. Scrub the potatoes. Rinse and chop the chives.

2. Place the potatoes in a large saucepan and cover them with water. Bring to a boil and cook until they are tender, 10 to 15 minutes.

3. Drain the potatoes and return them to the saucepan, reduce the heat, and shake the potatoes gently over the burner until they are dry, about 3 minutes.

4. Add the butter, the lemon juice, and the curry powder. Season to taste and toss to combine.

5. Sprinkle with the chives.

Dick Buttons

1. Set the package of green beans in a medium bowl of hot water to thaw.

2. Combine the thawed beans, the broth, the undrained mushrooms, and the nutmeg in a medium saucepan. Season to taste, bring to a boil, reduce the heat, and simmer for 2 minutes.

Olympic Pudding

1. Combine the pudding mix, the milk, and the sour cream in a medium bowl and beat with an electric mixer until well blended, about 2 minutes.

2. Place a third of the pudding in the bottom of individual dessert glasses. Add half of the jam. Layer another third of the pudding. Add the remaining jam. Top with the remaining pudding and the nuts. Refrigerate until you are ready to serve.

COUNTDOWN

1. Assemble the ingredients and the equipment.
2. Do Step 1 of *Dick Buttons*.
3. Do Steps 1–8 of *Sonja Henie*.
4. Do Steps 1–2 of *John Curry*.
5. Do Steps 1–2 of *Olympic Pudding*.
6. Do Steps 9–10 of *Sonja Henie*.
7. Do Steps 3–4 of *John Curry*.
8. Do Step 2 of *Dick Buttons*.
9. Do Step 5 of *John Curry*.

Weekend Eleven Saturday

MEAT & POULTRY

2 pounds lean boneless pork loin

FRESH PRODUCE

VEGETABLES

1-1/2 pounds red potatoes
1 package (10 ounces) spinach
1 medium onion
1 medium red onion
1 medium shallot
2 cloves garlic

FRUIT

1 small orange
1/2 pound seedless red grapes

CANS, JARS & BOTTLES

SOUP

1 can (10-1/2 ounces) chicken broth
1 can (10-3/4 ounces) onion soup

FRUIT

1 can (21 ounces) lemon pie filling

WINES & SPIRITS

1/4 cup dry white wine

- [ ] Butter
- [ ] Vegetable shortening
- [ ] Flour
- [ ] Cornstarch
- [ ] Granulated sugar
- [ ] Dark brown sugar
- [ ] Vegetable oil
- [ ] Worcestershire sauce
- [ ] Dijon mustard
- [ ] Dry mustard
- [ ] Pepper
- [ ] Salt

Pork Avenue

2 pounds lean boneless pork loin
1 medium onion
1/2 pound seedless red grapes
1/4 cup flour
Seasoning to taste
2 tablespoons butter
1/2 cup chicken broth
1/4 cup dry white wine
1 tablespoon Dijon mustard
2 teaspoons dry mustard
2 tablespoons dark brown sugar

Penthouse Potatoes

1-1/2 pounds red potatoes
1 medium red onion
3 tablespoons vegetable oil
1 can (10-3/4 ounces) onion soup
Seasoning to taste

Presumptuous Spinach

2 cloves garlic
1 medium shallot
1 package (10 ounces) fresh spinach
1 tablespoon vegetable oil
2 teaspoons cornstarch
1/2 teaspoon Worcestershire sauce
3/4 cup chicken broth
Seasoning to taste

Uptown Pie

1 small orange
1-1/4 cups flour
1/2 teaspoon salt
4 tablespoons granulated sugar
1/2 cup vegetable shortening
1-1/2 tablespoons cold water
1 can (21 ounces) lemon pie filling

EQUIPMENT

Medium saucepan	Citrus juicer
2 large covered skillets	Pastry blender
	Rolling pin
Pie plate	Plastic wrap
Breadboard	Aluminum foil
Large shallow bowl	Kitchen knives
Large mixing bowl	Measuring cups and spoons
Vegetable brush	
Vegetable grater	Cooking utensils
Citrus grater	

Pork Avenue

1. Trim any excess fat from the pork and cut it into 8 equal slices. Peel and slice the onion. Rinse, pat dry, stem, and halve the grapes.

2. Place the flour in a large shallow bowl. Season to taste. Coat the pork slices on both sides with the seasoned flour.

3. Melt the butter in a large skillet. Add the pork and sauté until lightly browned, 3 to 4 minutes per side. Remove the pork and set it aside.

4. Add the onion to the skillet and sauté until soft, about 5 minutes.

5. Add the grapes, the broth, the wine, both mustards, and the brown sugar. Bring the mixture to a boil, cover, reduce the heat, and simmer until the sauce begins to thicken and is slightly reduced, about 10 minutes.

6. Return the pork slices to the skillet, cover, and simmer until the pork is tender and cooked throughout, about 8 minutes.

Penthouse Potatoes

1. Scrub and coarsely grate the potatoes. Peel and coarsely grate the onion.

2. Heat the oil in a large skillet and sauté the potatoes and the onion until the potatoes are lightly browned, about 5 minutes.

3. Blend in the soup, season to taste, and bring to a boil. Cover the skillet, reduce the heat, and simmer for 5 minutes.

4. Uncover the skillet, and continue simmering until the liquid is absorbed and the potatoes are cooked through, about 5 minutes more.

Presumptuous Spinach

1. Peel and mince the garlic. Peel and chop the shallot. Rinse, dry, and stem the spinach.

2. Heat the oil in a medium saucepan and sauté the garlic and the shallot for 5 minutes.

3. Blend the cornstarch and the Worcestershire sauce into the broth, add the mixture to the skillet, season to taste, and bring to a boil. Add the spinach and cook until just wilted, about 2 minutes.

Uptown Pie

1. Grate 1 teaspoon of orange peel and squeeze 1 tablespoon of orange juice.

2. Combine the flour, the salt, and half of the sugar in a large bowl. Using a pastry blender, cut the shortening into the flour mixture until it resembles coarse meal. Add the orange peel, the orange juice, and the cold water. Mix until the dough forms a ball. Cover with plastic wrap and refrigerate for 20 minutes.

3. Preheat the oven to 350°F. Flour a breadboard.

4. Roll out the dough on the breadboard. Press the dough into a pie plate, flute the edges, and prick the dough all over with a fork.

5. Bake until golden, about 20 minutes.

6. Remove the pie shell from the oven and let it cool for 10 minutes.

7. Fill the pie shell with the lemon filling. Sprinkle with the remaining 2 tablespoons sugar.

8. Preheat the broiler.

9. Cover the edges of the pie shell with aluminum foil. Place the pie under the broiler until the sugar has caramelized, about 2 minutes.

COUNTDOWN

1. Assemble the ingredients and the equipment.
2. Do Steps 1–9 of *Uptown Pie*.
3. Do Step 1 of *Penthouse Potatoes*.
4. Do Step 1 of *Presumptuous Spinach*.
5. Do Steps 1–5 of *Pork Avenue*.
6. Do Steps 2–3 of *Penthouse Potatoes*.
7. Do Step 6 of *Pork Avenue*.
8. Do Step 4 of *Penthouse Potatoes*.
9. Do Steps 2–3 of *Presumptuous Spinach*.

Weekend Eleven Sunday

FRESH PRODUCE

VEGETABLES
2 medium tomatoes
2 cloves garlic

HERBS
1/4 cup basil (when chopped)
2 tablespoons chives (when chopped)
1/4 cup parsley (when chopped)

CANS, JARS & BOTTLES

VEGETABLES
1 can (28 ounces) diced tomatoes

CONDIMENTS
1 jar (6-1/2 ounces) marinated
   artichoke hearts
1 jar (3-1/2 ounces) pitted black olives
1 jar (3 ounces) pimiento-stuffed
   green olives

PACKAGED GOODS

PASTA, RICE & GRAINS
1 pound spaghetti

BAKED GOODS
1 loaf Italian bread
8 ounces garlic croutons
1 package (3 ounces) ladyfingers

WINES & SPIRITS
1/2 cup dry red wine

REFRIGERATED PRODUCTS

DAIRY
2 eggs
1/4 cup whipped cream

CHEESE
1/2 pound pepper Jack cheese

DELI
1/2 pound sliced dry Italian salami

FROZEN GOODS

FRUIT
1 package (16 ounces) sliced peaches

STAPLES

❑ Granulated sugar
❑ Powdered sugar
❑ Olive oil
❑ Vegetable oil
❑ White wine vinegar
❑ Dried oregano
❑ Candied ginger
❑ Italian seasoning
❑ Pepper
❑ Salt
❑ Almond extract

Weekend Eleven Sunday

Egg 'Em On

2 eggs
2 medium fresh tomatoes
1/2 pound pepper Jack cheese
1 jar (6-1/2 ounces) marinated artichoke hearts
1 jar (3-1/2 ounces) pitted black olives
1 jar (3 ounces) pimiento-stuffed green olives
2 tablespoons olive oil
1 tablespoon white wine vinegar
1/8 teaspoon dried oregano
Seasoning to taste
1/2 pound sliced dry Italian salami
8 ounces garlic croutons

String 'Em Up

2 cloves garlic
1/4 cup fresh basil (when chopped)
1/4 cup fresh parsley (when chopped)
1/4 cup vegetable oil
1 can (28 ounces) diced tomatoes
1/2 teaspoon Italian seasoning
1/2 teaspoon granulated sugar
Seasoning to taste
1 pound spaghetti
1/2 cup dry red wine

Bread 'Em Out

1 loaf Italian bread
2 tablespoons fresh chives (when chopped)
Reserved artichoke marinade from Egg 'Em On

Peach and Choose

1 package (16 ounces) frozen sliced peaches
4 tablespoons candied ginger (when chopped)
1 package (3 ounces) ladyfingers
2 tablespoons powdered sugar
2 teaspoons almond extract
1/4 cup whipped cream

EQUIPMENT

Stockpot
2 small saucepans
Large covered skillet
9 × 9-inch glass baking dish
Baking sheet
Colander
Medium mixing bowl
2 small mixing bowls
Whisk
Kitchen knives
Measuring cups and spoons
Cooking utensils

Weekend Eleven Sunday

Egg 'Em On

1. Cover the eggs with water in a small sauce-pan and cook until hard–boiled, 10 to 12 minutes.

2. Drain the eggs, run them under cold water, and refrigerate for at least 10 minutes.

3. Rinse and quarter the tomatoes. Cube the cheese. Drain the artichokes, reserving the marinade for Bread 'Em Out. Drain the olives.

4. In a small bowl, whisk together the oil, the vinegar, and the oregano. Season to taste.

5. Arrange the salami, the tomatoes, the cheese, the artichokes, and the olives on individual salad plates. Quarter the eggs and arrange them on the plates. Top with the croutons, and drizzle with the dressing.

String 'Em Up

1. Peel and mince the garlic. Rinse and chop the basil. Rinse and chop the parsley.

2. Heat the oil in a large skillet and sauté the garlic for 3 minutes.

3. Add the basil, the undrained tomatoes, the Italian seasoning, and the sugar. Season to taste, bring the mixture to a boil, cover, reduce the heat, and simmer for 30 minutes.

4. Bring water for the pasta to a boil in a stockpot.

5. Cook the spaghetti until it is almost tender, 3 to 4 minutes if you are using fresh pasta, 7 to 8 minutes if you are using dry pasta.

6. Add the parsley and the wine to the skillet and let the sauce simmer for 5 minutes more.

7. Drain the pasta and top it with the sauce.

Bread 'Em Out

1. Preheat the oven to 350°F.

2. Cut the bread in half lengthwise. Rinse and chop the chives.

3. Spread the reserved artichoke marinade on the cut sides of the bread, and sprinkle the cut sides with the chives.

4. Place the bread on a baking sheet, cut side up, and bake until crisp and golden, about 10 minutes.

Peach and Choose

1. Set the package of peaches in a medium bowl of hot water to thaw.

2. Chop the ginger. Drain the peaches, reserving the juice.

3. Separate the ladyfingers. Arrange half of the ladyfingers, cut side up, in a 9 × 9-inch glass baking dish. Top with half of the peaches. Sprinkle with half of the powdered sugar and half of the ginger. Repeat.

4. In a small bowl, combine the reserved peach juice with the almond extract. Drizzle the mixture over the top of the peaches and refrigerate for at least 1 hour.

5. Top with dollops of whipped cream.

COUNTDOWN

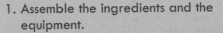

1. Assemble the ingredients and the equipment.
2. Do Steps 1–4 of *Peach and Choose*.
3. Do Step 1 of *Egg 'Em On*.
4. Do Steps 1–4 of *String 'Em Up*.
5. Do Steps 2–4 of *Egg 'Em On*.
6. Do Steps 1–4 of *Bread 'Em Out*.
7. Do Steps 5–6 of *String 'Em Up*.
8. Do Step 5 of *Egg 'Em On*.
9. Do Step 7 of *String 'Em Up*.
10. Do Step 5 of *Peach and Choose*.

Weekend Twelve Saturday

SHOPPING LIST

FISH

4 sole fillets (about 1-1/2 pounds)

FRESH PRODUCE

VEGETABLES

1-1/2 pounds asparagus
1 small head red leaf lettuce
1 small head Belgian endive
2 medium tomatoes
1 medium cucumber
1 medium shallot
1 clove garlic

HERBS

2 tablespoons parsley
  (when chopped)

FRUIT

2 medium oranges
2 ripe kiwifruits
1 pint strawberries

CANS, JARS & BOTTLES

JUICE

8 ounces clam juice

PACKAGED GOODS

BAKED GOODS

4 individual baguettes
1 loaf angel food cake

WINES & SPIRITS

1/2 cup dry white wine
2 tablespoons Grand Marnier

REFRIGERATED PRODUCTS

DAIRY

1/2 cup half-and-half
1/4 cup whipped cream

CHEESE

1 container (4 ounces) herbed
  cream cheese

STAPLES

- ❑ Butter
- ❑ Flour
- ❑ Granulated sugar
- ❑ Olive oil
- ❑ White wine vinegar
- ❑ Red wine vinegar
- ❑ Lemon juice
- ❑ Dijon mustard
- ❑ Honey
- ❑ Poppy seeds
- ❑ Bay leaf
- ❑ Dried tarragon
- ❑ Cayenne pepper
- ❑ Ground cinnamon
- ❑ Lemon-pepper seasoning
- ❑ Pepper
- ❑ Salt

Weekend Twelve Saturday

Sole Coward

4 sole fillets (about 1-1/2 pounds)
Seasoning to taste
1 medium shallot
2 medium fresh tomatoes
2 tablespoons fresh parsley (when chopped)
8 ounces clam juice
1 bay leaf
1/2 cup dry white wine
3 tablespoons flour
1/2 cup half-and-half
2 tablespoons butter
1 tablespoon lemon juice
1/4 teaspoon cayenne pepper

Blithe Spirits

1-1/2 pounds fresh asparagus
3 tablespoons butter
1 tablespoon Dijon mustard
1 teaspoon red wine vinegar
2 teaspoons lemon-pepper seasoning
1/2 teaspoon granulated sugar

Bittersweet

1 small head red leaf lettuce
1 small head Belgian endive
1 medium cucumber
1 clove garlic
3 tablespoons olive oil
2 tablespoons white wine vinegar
1/2 teaspoon honey
1/2 teaspoon dried tarragon
Seasoning to taste

Private Loaves

1 container (4 ounces) herbed cream cheese
4 individual baguettes
1 tablespoon poppy seeds

Fallen Angels

1 pint fresh strawberries
2 ripe kiwifruits
2 medium oranges
2 tablespoons Grand Marnier
1 loaf angel food cake
1/4 cup whipped cream
1 teaspoon ground cinnamon

EQUIPMENT

2 large covered skillets

Baking sheet

Large mixing bowl

2 small mixing bowls

Whisk

Vegetable peeler

Aluminum foil

Plastic wrap

Kitchen knives

Measuring cups and spoons

Cooking utensils

Sole Coward

1. Rinse and pat dry the fish fillets and season them to taste.

2. Peel and mince the shallot. Rinse and chop the tomatoes. Rinse and chop the parsley.

3. In a large skillet, combine the clam juice, the bay leaf, and the wine. Bring the mixture to a boil. Add the fillets, cover, and poach in the liquid until the fish flakes easily with a fork, about 8 minutes.

4. Remove the fish and cover it with aluminum foil to keep it warm.

5. In a small bowl, whisk together the flour and the half-and-half. Add the mixture to the skillet and simmer, stirring, until the sauce thickens slightly, about 7 minutes.

6. Blend in the butter, the lemon juice, and the cayenne pepper. Reduce the heat and simmer for 5 minutes.

7. Add the tomatoes and heat them through, about 2 minutes.

8. Remove the bay leaf. Spoon the sauce over the fish, arranging the tomatoes on top. Sprinkle with the parsley.

Blithe Spirits

1. Bring a small amount of water to a boil in a large skillet.

2. Rinse the asparagus and remove the tough ends. Place the spears in the skillet, cover, and steam until they are crisp-tender, 3 to 8 minutes, depending on their thickness.

3. Drain the asparagus.

4. Melt the butter in the skillet. Blend in the mustard, the vinegar, the lemon-pepper seasoning, and the sugar. Return the asparagus to the skillet and turn the spears to coat and heat through. Remove the skillet from the heat and cover it to keep warm.

Bittersweet

1. Wash and dry the lettuce and tear it into bite-sized pieces. Wash and dry the endive and tear it into bite-sized pieces. Peel and chop the cucumber. Distribute the vegetables among individual salad plates.

2. Peel and mince the garlic. In a small bowl, combine the garlic, the oil, the vinegar, the honey, and the tarragon. Season to taste.

3. Drizzle the dressing over the salad.

Private Loaves

1. Set the cream cheese out to soften.

2. Preheat the oven to 275°F.

3. Place the bread on a baking sheet in the oven to warm for 10 minutes.

4. Cut the loaves in half and spread the cut sides with the cheese. Sprinkle the cut sides with the poppy seeds.

Fallen Angels

1. Rinse, hull, and slice the strawberries. Peel and slice the kiwifruits. Peel and section the oranges and cut the sections in half. Combine the fruit in a large bowl and toss it with the Grand Marnier. Cover the bowl with plastic wrap and refrigerate it until you are ready to use.

2. Cut the cake into 8 slices. Arrange the slices on individual dessert plates. Spoon the fruit over the cake. Top with a dollop of whipped cream and dust with the cinnamon.

COUNTDOWN

1. Assemble the ingredients and the equipment.
2. Do Step 1 of *Fallen Angels*.
3. Do Step 1 of *Private Loaves*.
4. Do Steps 1–2 of *Bittersweet*.
5. Do Step 2 of *Private Loaves*.
6. Do Steps 1–3 of *Sole Coward*.
7. Do Step 3 of *Private Loaves*.
8. Do Steps 4–5 of *Sole Coward*.
9. Do Steps 1–3 of *Blithe Spirits*.
10. Do Step 6 of *Sole Coward*.
11. Do Step 4 of *Blithe Spirits*.
12. Do Step 4 of *Private Loaves*.
13. Do Steps 7–8 of *Sole Coward*.
14. Do Step 3 of *Bittersweet*.
15. Do Step 2 of *Fallen Angels*.

Weekend Twelve Sunday

SHOPPING LIST

MEAT & POULTRY
3 pounds chicken legs and thighs

FRESH PRODUCE

VEGETABLES
1 package (10 ounces) mixed salad
  greens
1 pint cherry tomatoes
1 medium ripe avocado
1 small red bell pepper
1 small green bell pepper
1 medium onion
2 cloves garlic

CANS, JARS & BOTTLES

VEGETABLES
1 can (14-1/2 ounces) diced tomatoes
1 can (11 ounces) whole kernel corn

DESSERT & BAKING NEEDS
1/4 cup marshmallow crème

PACKAGED GOODS

PASTA, RICE & GRAINS
1 cup Rice Krispies cereal
1 package (8 ounces) corn muffin mix

DRIED FRUITS & NUTS
1/3 cup pecan bits

WINES & SPIRITS
1/4 cup dry white wine

REFRIGERATED PRODUCTS

DAIRY
1/3 cup milk
1/4 cup sour cream
1 egg

FROZEN GOODS

DESSERTS
1 pint butter pecan ice cream

STAPLES

- [ ] Butter
- [ ] Granulated sugar
- [ ] Dark brown sugar
- [ ] Olive oil
- [ ] Vegetable oil
- [ ] Rice vinegar
- [ ] Chicken bouillon cubes
- [ ] Bay leaf
- [ ] Dried dill
- [ ] Ground cloves
- [ ] Ground coriander
- [ ] Ground ginger
- [ ] Ground nutmeg
- [ ] Paprika
- [ ] Pepper
- [ ] Salt
- [ ] Turmeric

Weekend Twelve Sunday

From Hen to Mouth

3 pounds chicken legs and thighs
2 cloves garlic
1 small red bell pepper
1 small green bell pepper
1 medium onion
2 tablespoons butter
2 tablespoons vegetable oil
1 teaspoon ground ginger
1 teaspoon turmeric
1 teaspoon ground cloves
1 teaspoon ground coriander
1 teaspoon ground nutmeg
1 can (14-1/2 ounces) diced tomatoes
1/4 cup dry white wine
2 chicken bouillon cubes
1 bay leaf
Seasoning to taste

Skinny Salad

1 package (10 ounces) mixed salad
    greens
1 pint cherry tomatoes
1 medium ripe avocado
3 tablespoons olive oil
2 tablespoons rice vinegar
1/2 teaspoon granulated sugar
1/2 teaspoon dried dill
Seasoning to taste

Meager Muffins

1 package (8 ounces) corn muffin mix
1 egg
1/3 cup milk

1 can (11 ounces) whole kernel corn
1/4 cup sour cream
1/4 teaspoon paprika

Crumby Dessert

1 cup Rice Krispies cereal
2 tablespoons butter
1/4 cup dark brown sugar
1/3 cup pecan bits
1 pint butter pecan ice cream
1/4 cup marshmallow crème

EQUIPMENT

Dutch oven

Small saucepan

Muffin tin

Large mixing bowl

Medium mixing bowl

2 small mixing bowls

Whisk

Ice cream scoop

Plastic bag

Kitchen knives

Measuring cups and spoons

Cooking utensils

Weekend Twelve Sunday

RECIPES

From Hen to Mouth

1. Rinse and pat dry the chicken.

2. Peel and mince the garlic. Rinse, stem, seed, and chop the bell peppers. Peel and chop the onion.

3. Melt the butter with the oil in a Dutch oven and sauté the garlic for 1 minute.

4. Add the ginger, the turmeric, the cloves, the coriander, and the nutmeg, and stir for 1 minute to blend.

5. Add the chicken pieces and sauté until golden, 10 to 12 minutes.

6. Add the onion and sauté until it is soft, about 5 minutes.

7. Stir in the bell peppers. Add the tomatoes, the wine, and the bouillon cubes, mashing to dissolve them. Add the bay leaf and season to taste.

8. Cover and simmer until the chicken is tender and cooked through, 30 to 35 minutes.

9. Remove the bay leaf before serving.

Skinny Salad

1. Wash and dry the salad greens. Rinse and halve the tomatoes. Peel, pit, and slice the avocado. Combine the vegetables in a large bowl.

2. In a small bowl, whisk together the oil, the vinegar, the sugar, and the dill.

3. Season to taste, and toss with the salad.

Meager Muffins

1. Preheat the oven to 400°F. Grease a muffin tin.

2. In a medium bowl, blend together the muffin mix, the egg, and the milk.

3. Divide the batter evenly among the muffin cups.

4. Drain the corn.

5. In a small bowl, combine the corn and the sour cream.

6. Spoon a teaspoon of the mixture into the center of each muffin. Sprinkle with the paprika.

7. Bake until the muffins are golden and slightly firm to the touch, 15 to 20 minutes.

Crumby Dessert

1. Place the Rice Krispies in a plastic bag and crush them.

2. Melt the butter in a small saucepan. Add the brown sugar and simmer, stirring, until blended. Fold in the cereal and stir to combine.

3. Remove the pan from the heat. Fold in the nuts.

4. Spoon a third of the mixture into individual dessert glasses. Add a scoop of ice cream. Add another layer of the cereal mixture and another scoop of ice cream. Top with the remaining cereal mixture. Freeze until you are ready to serve.

5. Top with a dollop of marshmallow crème.

COUNTDOWN

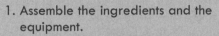

1. Assemble the ingredients and the equipment.
2. Do Steps 1–4 of *Crumby Dessert*.
3. Do Steps 1–8 of *From Hen to Mouth*.
4. Do Steps 1–7 of *Meager Muffins*.
5. Do Steps 1–3 of *Skimpy Salad*.
6. Do Step 9 of *From Hen to Mouth*.
7. Do Step 5 of *Crumby Dessert*.

Weekend Thirteen Saturday

MEAT & POULTRY

4 New York strip steaks (about 2 pounds)

FRESH PRODUCE

VEGETABLES

1 pound sugar-snap peas
3 medium yellow summer squash
1 medium leek

HERBS

1 tablespoon chives (when chopped)
2 tablespoons dill (when chopped)
1 tablespoon parsley (when chopped)

FRUIT

1 medium ripe Crenshaw melon
1 pint strawberries
1/2 pound seedless green grapes

PACKAGED GOODS

BAKED GOODS

1 chocolate pie shell

WINES & SPIRITS

1/4 cup dry red wine
1 teaspoon dry sherry
1 tablespoon crème de cacao

REFRIGERATED PRODUCTS

DAIRY

1/2 cup sour cream
1 cup whipping cream

JUICE

3 tablespoons orange juice

FROZEN GOODS

DESSERTS

1 quart peppermint ice cream

STAPLES

- [ ] Butter
- [ ] Powdered sugar
- [ ] Chocolate sprinkles
- [ ] Olive oil
- [ ] Balsamic vinegar
- [ ] Lemon juice
- [ ] Worcestershire sauce
- [ ] Honey
- [ ] Dried savory
- [ ] Ground cloves
- [ ] Dry mustard
- [ ] Pepper
- [ ] Salt

Weekend Thirteen Saturday

Let It Beef

4 New York strip steaks (about 2 pounds)
Seasoning to taste
1 tablespoon fresh chives (when chopped)
1 tablespoon fresh parsley (when chopped)
3 tablespoons butter
2 teaspoons dry mustard
2 tablespoons lemon juice
1/4 cup dry red wine
2 teaspoons Worcestershire sauce
1 tablespoon honey

Yellow Submarines

1 medium leek
3 medium yellow summer squash
2 tablespoons fresh dill (when chopped)
2 tablespoons olive oil
2 tablespoons balsamic vinegar
Seasoning to taste

Give Peas a Chance

1 pound sugar-snap peas
2 tablespoons butter
1/2 teaspoon ground cloves
1/2 teaspoon dried savory

Strawberry Fields

1 medium ripe Crenshaw melon
1 pint fresh strawberries
1/2 pound seedless green grapes
1/2 cup sour cream

3 tablespoons orange juice
1 teaspoon dry sherry

Sergeant Peppermint

1 quart peppermint ice cream
1 chocolate pie shell
1 cup whipping cream
2 tablespoons powdered sugar
1 tablespoon crème de cacao
Chocolate sprinkles for garnish

EQUIPMENT

Electric mixer
Small saucepan
Large covered skillet
Medium covered skillet
Medium mixing bowl
Small mixing bowl
Whisk
Plastic wrap
Kitchen knives
Measuring cups and spoons
Cooking utensils

Weekend Thirteen Saturday

Let It Beef

1. Prepare the grill or the broiler.

2. Trim any excess fat from the steaks and season them to taste. Rinse and chop the chives. Rinse and chop the parsley.

3. Grill or broil the steaks to taste, about 5 minutes per side for rare.

4. Melt the butter in a small saucepan. Blend in the mustard, the lemon juice, the wine, the Worcestershire sauce, and the honey. Heat through.

5. Drizzle the sauce over the steaks and top them with the chives and the parsley.

Yellow Submarines

1. Wash the leek thoroughly, removing all the dirt. Trim and remove the dark leaves and slice the leek into thin rounds. Rinse, stem, and julienne the squash. Rinse and chop the dill.

2. Heat the oil in a large skillet and sauté the leek until soft, about 5 minutes.

3. Add the squash and sauté until soft, about 3 minutes.

4. Stir in the vinegar and the dill, and season to taste.

5. Remove the skillet from the heat and cover to keep warm.

Give Peas a Chance

1. Rinse and string the snap peas.

2. Melt the butter with the cloves in a medium skillet. Sauté the snap peas until they are crisp-tender, about 3 minutes. Toss the peas with the savory. Remove the skillet from the heat and cover to keep warm.

Strawberry Fields

1. Cut the melon into quarters and remove the seeds. Thinly slice the quarters and remove the rind. Arrange the slices on individual salad plates.

2. Wash and stem the strawberries, cut them in half, and arrange them with the melon slices. Wash and stem the grapes, cut them in half, and arrange them on the salad plates.

3. In a small bowl, whisk together the sour cream, the orange juice, and the sherry.

4. Drizzle the dressing over the fruit.

Sergeant Peppermint

1. Set the ice cream out to soften slightly.

2. Pack the ice cream evenly into the pie shell. Cover it with plastic wrap and freeze until you are ready to use.

3. Chill a medium bowl and the beaters of an electric mixer in the refrigerator for at least 10 minutes.

4. Whip the cream in the chilled bowl until soft peaks form. Beat in the sugar. Fold in the crème de cacao. Continue beating until stiff, about 3 minutes. Cover the bowl with plastic wrap and refrigerate it until you are ready to use.

5. Top the pie with the whipped cream and garnish with the sprinkles.

COUNTDOWN

1. Assemble the ingredients and the equipment.
2. Do Steps 1–4 of *Sergeant Peppermint*.
3. Do Steps 1–2 of *Let It Beef*.
4. Do Step 1 of *Yellow Submarines*.
5. Do Step 1 of *Give Peas a Chance*.
6. Do Steps 1–3 of *Strawberry Fields*.
7. Do Step 3 of *Let It Beef*.
8. Do Steps 2–5 of *Yellow Submarines*.
9. Do Step 2 of *Give Peas a Chance*.
10. Do Steps 4–5 of *Let It Beef*.
11. Do Step 4 of *Strawberry Fields*.
12. Do Step 5 of *Sergeant Peppermint*.

Weekend Thirteen Sunday

SHOPPING LIST

FRESH PRODUCE

VEGETABLES
1 medium head red cabbage
2 scallions (green onions)
1 large sweet onion

HERBS
3 tablespoons chives (when chopped)

FRUIT
2 medium oranges

CANS, JARS & BOTTLES

FISH
1 can (6 ounces) solid white tuna

SAUCES
1 jar (16 ounces) roasted garlic Alfredo sauce

CONDIMENTS
1 jar (2 ounces) diced pimiento

PACKAGED GOODS

PASTA, RICE & GRAINS
8 ounces manicotti shells

BAKED GOODS
1 loaf Italian bread

DESSERT & BAKING NEEDS
6 ounces chocolate chips

REFRIGERATED PRODUCTS

DAIRY
1-1/4 cups half-and-half
1/4 cup whipped cream
3 eggs

CHEESE
1 container (15 ounces) ricotta cheese
1 cup shredded Cheddar cheese

FROZEN GOODS

VEGETABLES
1 package (12 ounces) spinach soufflé

STAPLES

- ❑ Butter
- ❑ Granulated sugar
- ❑ Dark brown sugar
- ❑ Vegetable oil
- ❑ Apple cider vinegar
- ❑ Lemon juice
- ❑ Prepared horseradish
- ❑ Sesame seeds
- ❑ Dry mustard
- ❑ Paprika
- ❑ Pepper
- ❑ Salt
- ❑ Rum extract

Weekend Thirteen Sunday

The Tuna the Better

1 package (12 ounces) frozen spinach soufflé
8 ounces manicotti shells
3 tablespoons fresh chives (when chopped)
1 jar (2 ounces) diced pimiento
1 can (6 ounces) solid white tuna
1 container (15 ounces) ricotta cheese
1 egg
1 tablespoon lemon juice
Seasoning to taste
1 jar (16 ounces) roasted garlic Alfredo sauce
1 cup shredded Cheddar cheese

Slaw Poke

1 medium head red cabbage
2 medium oranges
2 scallions (green onions)
3 tablespoons vegetable oil
2 tablespoons apple cider vinegar
1/2 teaspoon granulated sugar
1 teaspoon sesame seeds
Seasoning to taste

When All Is Bread and Done

1 large sweet onion
4 tablespoons butter
2 tablespoons vegetable oil
2 teaspoons dark brown sugar
2 tablespoons prepared horseradish

1/2 teaspoon dry mustard
1/4 teaspoon paprika
1 loaf Italian bread

Clogged Arteries

2 eggs
1/4 teaspoon salt
1 teaspoon rum extract
6 ounces chocolate chips
1-1/4 cups half-and-half
1/4 cup whipped cream

EQUIPMENT

Stockpot	2 small mixing bowls
Medium saucepan	Whisk
Large skillet	Vegetable grater
9 × 13-inch glass baking dish	Aluminum foil
Baking sheet	Plastic wrap
Colander	Kitchen knives
2 large mixing bowls	Measuring cups and spoons
Medium mixing bowl	Cooking utensils

Weekend Thirteen Sunday

The Tuna the Better

1. Set the package of spinach soufflé in a medium bowl of hot water to thaw.

2. Bring water for the pasta to a boil in a stockpot.

3. Cook the manicotti shells until almost tender, about 10 minutes.

4. Rinse and chop the chives. Drain the pimiento. Drain and flake the tuna. Combine the ingredients in a large bowl.

5. Blend in the ricotta cheese, the egg, and the lemon juice. Fold the spinach soufflé into the tuna mixture and season to taste.

6. Preheat the oven to 350°F.

7. Drain the manicotti shells and run them under cold water to cool.

8. Spoon half of the Alfredo sauce into the bottom of a 9 × 13–inch glass baking dish.

9. Fill the manicotti tubes with the tuna mixture, reserving the remainder, and lay the manicotti on top of the sauce. Spoon the rest of the Alfredo sauce over the manicotti, top with the remaining tuna mixture, and sprinkle with the cheese.

10. Cover the dish with aluminum foil and bake for 30 minutes.

11. Uncover and continue baking until hot and bubbly, about 5 minutes more.

Slaw Poke

1. Trim and grate the cabbage. Peel and chop the oranges. Trim and chop the scallions. Combine the ingredients in a large bowl.

2. In a small bowl, whisk together the oil, the vinegar, the sugar, and the sesame seeds. Season to taste and toss with the slaw.

When All Is Bread and Done

1. Peel and thinly slice the onion.

2. Melt 2 tablespoons of the butter with the oil and the sugar in a large skillet.

3. Sauté the onions until they are soft, about 5 minutes.

4. Blend in the horseradish, the mustard, and the paprika.

5. Cut the bread in half lengthwise and lay the halves, cut sides up, on a baking sheet. Spread the remaining butter over the cut sides.

6. Spread the onion mixture over the bread.

7. Bake at 350°F until hot and bubbly, about 5 minutes.

Clogged Arteries

1. In a small bowl, whisk together the eggs, the salt, and the rum extract until thick and light, about 3 minutes.

2. In a medium saucepan, combine the chocolate chips and the half-and-half, and heat to a simmer, stirring, until blended and smooth, about 5 minutes.

3. Gradually blend the egg mixture into the chocolate mixture and cook, stirring, until well blended and thick, about 5 minutes.

4. Pour the mixture into individual dessert bowls. Cover them with plastic wrap and chill for at least 1 hour.

5. Top with dollops of whipped cream.

COUNTDOWN

1. Assemble the ingredients and the equipment.
2. Do Steps 1–4 of *Clogged Arteries.*
3. Do Steps 1–10 of *The Tuna the Better.*
4. Do Steps 1–6 of *When All Is Bread and Done.*
5. Do Steps 1–2 of *Slaw Poke.*
6. Do Step 11 of *The Tuna the Better.*
7. Do Step 7 of *When All Is Bread and Done.*
8. Do Step 5 of *Clogged Arteries.*

Summer

Weekend One Saturday

MEAT & POULTRY

4 lean loin pork chops (about 2 pounds)

FRESH PRODUCE

VEGETABLES
1-1/2 pounds baking potatoes
1 medium head red cabbage
3 small shallots
3 cloves garlic

HERBS
2 tablespoons parsley (when chopped)

FRUIT
1 medium lemon
2 medium bananas

CANS, JARS & BOTTLES

FRUIT
1 can (8 ounces) crushed pineapple

CONDIMENTS
3 tablespoons capers

PACKAGED GOODS

DESSERT & BAKING NEEDS
2 cups chocolate chips

WINES & SPIRITS
1/4 cup dry white wine
2 tablespoons rum

REFRIGERATED PRODUCTS

DAIRY
1-1/2 cups milk
1/4 cup half-and-half
1/4 cup whipped cream
2 eggs

STAPLES

- ❏ Butter
- ❏ Flour
- ❏ Cornstarch
- ❏ Granulated sugar
- ❏ Dark brown sugar
- ❏ Chocolate sprinkles
- ❏ Vegetable oil
- ❏ Apple cider vinegar
- ❏ Beef bouillon cube
- ❏ Dried sage
- ❏ Paprika
- ❏ Pepper
- ❏ Salt
- ❏ Vanilla extract

Weekend One Saturday

Peerless Pork

1 clove garlic
3 small shallots
3 tablespoons capers
4 lean loin pork chops (about 2 pounds)
Seasoning to taste
2 tablespoons vegetable oil
1/4 cup dry white wine
1 beef bouillon cube
1/2 cup water
2 tablespoons flour
1/4 cup half-and-half

Paramount Potatoes

1-1/2 pounds baking potatoes
2 cloves garlic
2 tablespoons fresh parsley (when chopped)
1 medium lemon
3 tablespoons butter
1 teaspoon dried sage
1 teaspoon paprika
Seasoning to taste

Consummate Cabbage

1 medium head red cabbage
1 can (8 ounces) crushed pineapple
1 tablespoon cornstarch
2 tablespoons apple cider vinegar
2 tablespoons dark brown sugar
1/2 cup water
2 tablespoons butter

Ultimate Dessert

1-1/2 cups milk
2 cups chocolate chips
2 eggs
1/4 cup granulated sugar
1 teaspoon vanilla extract
2 tablespoons rum
2 medium bananas
1/4 cup whipped cream
Chocolate sprinkles

EQUIPMENT

Blender
Large covered saucepan
Large saucepan
Medium saucepan
Large covered skillet
Medium skillet
Small mixing bowl
Whisk
Citrus grater
Citrus juicer
Vegetable peeler
Kitchen knives
Measuring cups and spoons
Cooking utensils

Weekend One Saturday

Peerless Pork

1. Peel and mince the garlic. Peel and chop the shallots. Drain the capers.

2. Rinse and pat dry the pork chops and season them to taste.

3. Heat the oil in a large skillet and brown the pork chops, about 5 minutes per side.

4. Remove the chops from the skillet and set them aside.

5. Add the garlic and the shallots to the skillet and sauté for 4 minutes.

6. Add the capers, the wine, the bouillon cube, and the water.

7. Return the pork to the skillet, cover, reduce the heat, and simmer until the chops are tender and no longer pink inside, about 20 minutes.

8. Remove the pork and cover to keep warm.

9. Combine the flour and the half-and-half and add it to the skillet, whisking to blend. Heat the sauce through and spoon it over the chops.

Paramount Potatoes

1. Bring water to a boil in a large saucepan.

2. Peel and cube the potatoes. Peel and mince the garlic. Rinse and chop the parsley. Grate 1 tablespoon of lemon peel. Juice the lemon.

3. Boil the potatoes until they are tender, 10 to 15 minutes.

4. Drain the potatoes and set them aside.

5. Melt the butter in a medium skillet. Add the garlic and sauté for 1 minute.

6. Add the potatoes, the lemon juice, the lemon peel, the sage, and the paprika. Season to taste and sauté until the potatoes are lightly browned, about 5 minutes.

7. Sprinkle with the parsley.

Consummate Cabbage

1. Rinse, quarter, and slice the cabbage. Drain the pineapple, reserving the juice.

2. In a small bowl, combine the reserved pineapple juice, the cornstarch, the vinegar, and the brown sugar.

3. Bring the water to a boil in a large saucepan.

4. Add the cabbage, cover, and cook until it is tender, about 7 minutes.

5. Blend the butter into the cabbage. Blend in the brown sugar mixture. Add the pineapple and cook, stirring, until the cabbage is heated through and the sauce is bubbling, about 5 minutes.

Ultimate Dessert

1. Pour the milk into a medium saucepan and bring just to a boil. Remove the pan from the heat.

2. Place the chocolate chips, the eggs, the sugar, the vanilla, and the rum in a blender, and process for 30 seconds. Add the hot milk and process until smooth, about 1 minute. Pour the mixture into individual dessert glasses and refrigerate for at least 1 hour.

3. Peel and slice the bananas.

4. Top with the banana slices and garnish with dollops of whipped cream and a dash of sprinkles.

COUNTDOWN

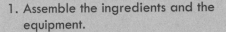

1. Assemble the ingredients and the equipment.
2. Do Steps 1–2 of *Ultimate Dessert*.
3. Do Steps 1–4 of *Peerless Pork*.
4. Do Steps 1–3 of *Paramount Potatoes*.
5. Do Steps 1–2 of *Consummate Cabbage*.
6. Do Steps 5–7 of *Peerless Pork*.
7. Do Steps 3–4 of *Consummate Cabbage*.
8. Do Steps 4–7 of *Paramount Potatoes*.
9. Do Step 5 of *Consummate Cabbage*.
10. Do Steps 8–9 of *Peerless Pork*.
11. Do Steps 3–4 of *Ultimate Dessert*.

Weekend One Sunday

SHOPPING LIST

FRESH PRODUCE

VEGETABLES
1 pound asparagus
1 medium green bell pepper

HERBS
2 tablespoons basil (when chopped)
4 tablespoons parsley (when chopped)
1 tablespoon thyme (when chopped)

FRUIT
1 pound apricots
2 medium oranges

CANS, JARS & BOTTLES

SOUP
1 can (10-1/2 ounces) beef broth
1 can (10-1/2 ounces) beef consommé

JUICE
2 cups tomato juice

PACKAGED GOODS

BAKED GOODS
4 English muffins

WINES & SPIRITS

2 tablespoons dry sherry

REFRIGERATED PRODUCTS

DAIRY
1/4 cup half-and-half
1/2 cup sour cream
9 eggs

FROZEN GOODS

DESSERTS
1 pint vanilla ice cream

STAPLES

☐ Butter
☐ Granulated sugar
☐ Lemon juice
☐ Worcestershire sauce
☐ Prepared horseradish
☐ Grated Parmesan cheese
☐ Poppy seeds
☐ Ground cardamom
☐ Ground cloves
☐ Pepper
☐ Salt

Weekend One Sunday

MENU

Sanctioned Soup

1 medium green bell pepper
1 can (10-1/2 ounces) beef broth
1 can (10-1/2 ounces) beef consommé
2 cups tomato juice
2 tablespoons lemon juice
1 teaspoon Worcestershire sauce
1 teaspoon granulated sugar
1/2 teaspoon ground cloves
Seasoning to taste

No Excuses

1 pound fresh asparagus
4 tablespoons fresh parsley (when chopped)
2 tablespoons fresh basil (when chopped)
1 tablespoon fresh thyme (when chopped)
9 eggs
1/4 cup half-and-half
Seasoning to taste
3 tablespoons butter
3 tablespoons grated Parmesan cheese

Justifiable Muffins

4 English muffins
1/2 cup sour cream
1/2 teaspoon prepared horseradish
1 teaspoon poppy seeds

Apricot Absolution

1 pound fresh apricots
2 medium oranges
1-1/2 cups water
1/2 cup granulated sugar
2 tablespoons dry sherry
2 teaspoons ground cardamom
1 pint vanilla ice cream

EQUIPMENT

Medium covered saucepan

Medium saucepan

Large skillet

Strainer

2 large mixing bowls

Medium bowl

Small mixing bowl

Citrus grater

Ice cream scoop

Kitchen knives

Measuring cups and spoons

Cooking utensils

Weekend One Sunday

Sanctioned Soup

1. Rinse, stem, seed, and mince the bell pepper.

2. In a medium saucepan, combine the bell pepper, the broth, the consommé, the tomato juice, the lemon juice, the Worcestershire sauce, the sugar, and the cloves. Season to taste, bring to a boil, cover, reduce the heat, and simmer until the bell pepper is tender, about 8 minutes.

3. Strain the soup into a large bowl and let it cool for 10 minutes.

4. Cover the bowl and refrigerate it for 1 hour.

No Excuses

1. Rinse the asparagus, remove and discard the tough ends, and cut the spears into 1-inch pieces. Rinse and chop the parsley, the basil, and the thyme.

2. Bring a small amount of water to a boil in a large skillet, and cook the asparagus until it is crisp-tender, 3 to 8 minutes, depending on thickness.

3. Drain the asparagus and set aside. Rinse out the skillet.

4. In a large bowl, beat the eggs with the half-and-half. Fold in the parsley, the basil, and the thyme. Season to taste.

5. Melt the butter in the skillet. Add the eggs and cook until they are almost set, about 5 minutes, turning the pan to cook the eggs evenly.

6. Arrange the asparagus on half of the egg and sprinkle with the cheese. Fold the other half of the egg over the cheese and asparagus, cover the skillet, remove from the heat, and let it stand until the cheese is melted, about 2 minutes.

Justifiable Muffins

1. Split the muffins in half and toast them lightly.

2. In a small bowl, combine the sour cream, the horseradish, and the poppy seeds.

3. Preheat the broiler.

4. Spread the sour cream mixture over the muffin halves and place them under the broiler until hot and bubbly, about 2 minutes.

Apricot Absolution

1. Peel, halve, and pit the apricots. Grate 2 tablespoons of orange peel. Peel and section the oranges.

2. In a medium saucepan, combine the water and the sugar. Bring the mixture to a boil, reduce the heat, and simmer until the liquid is reduced by half, about 10 minutes.

3. Add the orange sections, the sherry, and the cardamom to the saucepan and cook for 5 minutes.

4. Add the apricots to the saucepan, and cook until they are tender, about 3 minutes.

5. With a slotted spoon, remove the apricots and the oranges to a medium bowl.

6. Continue to simmer the liquid until it begins to thicken, about 5 minutes more.

7. Pour the liquid over the fruit, and sprinkle with the orange peel. Let stand.

8. Place scoops of the ice cream in individual dessert bowls, and spoon the fruit and sauce over the top.

COUNTDOWN

1. Assemble the ingredients and the equipment.
2. Do Steps 1–4 of *Sanctioned Soup*.
3. Do Steps 1–7 of *Apricot Absolution*.
4. Do Steps 1–2 of *No Excuses*.
5. Do Steps 1–3 of *Justifiable Muffins*.
6. Do Steps 3–5 of *No Excuses*.
7. Do Step 4 of *Justifiable Muffins*.
8. Do Step 6 of *No Excuses*.
9. Do Step 8 of *Apricot Absolution*.

Weekend Two Saturday

SHOPPING LIST

MEAT & POULTRY

1-1/2 pounds chicken livers

FRESH PRODUCE

VEGETABLES

1 small bunch beets
1 pound baby carrots
1 package (10 ounces) mixed salad
   greens
2 medium tomatoes
1 medium cucumber
1 medium onion

HERBS

3 tablespoons dill (when chopped)
2 tablespoons parsley (when chopped)

FRUIT

1 medium orange
1 pint raspberries

PACKAGED GOODS

PASTA, RICE & GRAINS

8 ounces wide egg noodles

BAKED GOODS

2 packages (3 ounces each) ladyfingers

WINES & SPIRITS

3 tablespoons dry sherry
2 tablespoons Kahlúa

REFRIGERATED PRODUCTS

DAIRY

1/2 cup sour cream
1 cup whipping cream

CHEESE

1 container (4 ounces) whipped
   cream cheese

STAPLES

- ❑ Butter
- ❑ Flour
- ❑ Dark brown sugar
- ❑ Powdered sugar
- ❑ Cocoa powder
- ❑ Vegetable oil
- ❑ Red wine vinegar
- ❑ Chicken bouillon cube
- ❑ Instant coffee
- ❑ Celery seed
- ❑ Dried tarragon
- ❑ Ground cardamom
- ❑ Paprika
- ❑ Pepper
- ❑ Salt
- ❑ Orange extract

Weekend Two Saturday

MENU

Special Delivery

1-1/2 pounds chicken livers
1 medium onion
2 medium fresh tomatoes
3 tablespoons fresh dill (when chopped)
2 tablespoons fresh parsley (when chopped)
1 chicken bouillon cube
4 tablespoons flour
1 tablespoon paprika
Seasoning to taste
4 tablespoons butter
8 ounces wide egg noodles
3 tablespoons dry sherry
1/2 cup sour cream

Convey the Carrots

1 pound baby carrots
1 tablespoon butter
1/4 teaspoon dark brown sugar
1/4 teaspoon ground cardamom

Dispatch the Salad

1 package (10 ounces) mixed salad greens
1 small bunch fresh beets
1 medium cucumber
1 medium orange
3 tablespoons vegetable oil
2 tablespoons red wine vinegar
1/2 teaspoon dried tarragon
1/2 teaspoon celery seed
Seasoning to taste

First-Class Raspberries

1 pint fresh raspberries
1 tablespoon instant coffee
1 tablespoon hot water
1 cup whipping cream
1 teaspoon orange extract
3 tablespoons powdered sugar
1 container (4 ounces) whipped cream cheese
2 tablespoons Kahlúa
3 tablespoons cocoa powder
2 packages (3 ounces each) ladyfingers

EQUIPMENT

Electric mixer	2 small mixing bowls
Large saucepan	Whisk
Medium covered saucepan	Citrus grater
Small saucepan	Vegetable peeler
Large covered skillet	Vegetable grater
Springform pan	Kitchen knives
Colander	Measuring cups and spoons
Large shallow bowl	Cooking utensils
Large mixing bowl	
2 medium mixing bowls	

Weekend Two Saturday

Special Delivery

1. Rinse and pat dry the chicken livers and cut them in half. Peel and mince the onion. Rinse and chop the tomatoes. Rinse and chop the dill. Rinse and chop the parsley.

2. Bring 1/2 cup water to a boil in a small saucepan. Dissolve the bouillon cube in the boiling water.

3. In a large shallow bowl, combine the flour and the paprika. Season to taste. Dredge the chicken livers in the flour mixture.

4. Bring water for the pasta to a boil in a large saucepan.

5. Melt 3 tablespoons of the butter in a large skillet and sauté the livers until they are golden brown and tender, about 5 minutes.

6. Remove and reserve the livers.

7. Cook the noodles in the boiling water until they are almost tender, about 7 minutes.

8. Add the onion to the skillet and sauté for 3 minutes. Stir in the tomatoes and the bouillon mixture. Cover the skillet, reduce the heat, and simmer for 5 minutes.

9. Drain the noodles, return them to the saucepan, and toss them with the remaining 1 tablespoon butter.

10. Blend the sherry, the sour cream, and the dill into the skillet. Return the livers to the skillet and heat through, about 2 minutes.

11. Serve the chicken livers over the noodles, and sprinkle with the parsley.

Convey the Carrots

1. Bring a small amount of water to a boil in a medium saucepan.

2. Rinse and trim the carrots, and cook them until they are crisp-tender, about 10 minutes, checking occasionally to make sure the water does not boil out.

3. Drain the carrots and return them to the saucepan. Toss them with the butter, the brown sugar, and the cardamom. Cover to keep warm.

Dispatch the Salad

1. Rinse and dry the salad greens and distribute them among individual salad plates.

2. Scrub, trim, and grate the beets and place them in a small bowl. Peel and slice the cucumber. Grate 1 tablespoon of the orange peel. Peel, section, and chop the orange. Combine the cucumber and the orange in a medium bowl.

3. In a small bowl, whisk together the orange peel, the oil, the vinegar, the tarragon, and the celery seed. Season to taste.

4. Top the salad greens with the cucumber and orange. Arrange the beets on top and drizzle the dressing over the salads.

First-Class Raspberries

1. Chill a medium bowl and the beaters of an electric mixer in the refrigerator for at least 10 minutes.

2. Rinse the raspberries and blot them on paper towels.

3. Dissolve the instant coffee in the hot water.

4. In the chilled bowl, whip the cream until stiff peaks form, about 5 minutes. Fold in the orange extract and the powdered sugar.

5. In a large bowl, combine the cream cheese, the Kahlúa, and the cocoa powder. Fold in half of the whipped cream.

6. Separate the ladyfingers. Cover the bottom of a springform pan with ladyfinger halves. Drizzle with the instant coffee. Spoon half of the cream cheese mixture over the ladyfingers.

7. Stand a row of ladyfinger halves around the sides of the pan. Layer half of the raspberries over the cream cheese mixture. Add another layer of ladyfinger halves over the raspberries. Spread the remaining cheese mixture over the ladyfingers. Top with the remaining whipped cream and the remaining raspberries. Refrigerate until you are ready to serve.

COUNTDOWN

1. Assemble the ingredients and the equipment.
2. Do Steps 1–7 of *First-Class Raspberries*.
3. Do Steps 1–3 of *Dispatch the Salad*.
4. Do Steps 1–4 of *Special Delivery*.
5. Do Steps 1–2 of *Convey the Carrots*.
6. Do Steps 5–8 of *Special Delivery*.
7. Do Step 3 of *Convey the Carrots*.
8. Do Steps 9–10 of *Special Delivery*.
9. Do Step 4 of *Dispatch the Salad*.
10. Do Step 11 of *Special Delivery*.

Weekend Two Sunday

FISH

1-1/2 pounds small shrimp,
  shelled and deveined

FRESH PRODUCE

VEGETABLES
1 medium head green leaf lettuce
2 large tomatoes
2 large ripe avocados
1 small bunch radishes
1 jalapeño pepper
1 medium onion
1 small red onion
2 cloves garlic

HERBS
1/4 cup chives (when chopped)

FRUIT
1 small ripe cantaloupe
1 small ripe casaba melon

CANS, JARS & BOTTLES

SOUP
1 can (14 ounces) chicken broth

VEGETABLES
1 can (15 ounces) black beans
1 can (11 ounces) whole kernel corn

FRUIT
1 jar (6 ounces) maraschino cherries

CONDIMENTS
1 can (3-1/2 ounces) sliced black olives

PACKAGED GOODS

INTERNATIONAL FOODS
8 taco shells

REFRIGERATED PRODUCTS

DAIRY
1 cup sour cream

CHEESE
2 cups shredded Cheddar cheese
1 package (3 ounces) cream cheese

FROZEN GOODS

DESSERTS
1 container (8 ounces) whipped topping

STAPLES

❏ Butter
❏ Powdered sugar
❏ Vegetable oil
❏ White wine vinegar
❏ White Worcestershire sauce
❏ Lime juice
❏ Ground cumin
❏ Pepper
❏ White pepper
❏ Salt
❏ Vanilla extract

Weekend Two Sunday

Avocado Cool

2 large ripe avocados
1 clove garlic
1/4 cup fresh chives (when chopped)
1 can (14 ounces) chicken broth
1 cup sour cream
1 tablespoon lime juice
1/4 teaspoon white Worcestershire
    sauce
1/4 teaspoon white pepper
Seasoning to taste

Taco Your Time

1 clove garlic
1-1/2 pounds small shrimp, shelled and
    deveined
2 large fresh tomatoes
1 small bunch radishes
1 small red onion
1 jalapeño pepper
1 can (3-1/2 ounces) sliced black olives
1 medium head green leaf lettuce
4 tablespoons vegetable oil
1 tablespoon lime juice
1 tablespoon white wine vinegar
Seasoning to taste
8 taco shells
2 cups shredded Cheddar cheese

It's Bean Done

1 medium onion
1 can (15 ounces) black beans
1 can (11 ounces) whole kernel corn

2 tablespoons butter
1 teaspoon ground cumin
Seasoning to taste

Minute Melon

1 package (3 ounces) cream cheese
1 container (8 ounces) frozen whipped
    topping
1 small ripe cantaloupe
1 small ripe casaba melon
1 jar (6 ounces) maraschino cherries
1 tablespoon powdered sugar
1 teaspoon vanilla extract

EQUIPMENT

Blender

Large skillet

Medium skillet

2 large mixing bowls

Medium mixing bowl

Small mixing bowl

Whisk

Plastic wrap

Kitchen knives

Measuring cups and spoons

Cooking utensils

Avocado Cool

1. Peel, pit, and quarter the avocados. Peel and mince the garlic. Rinse, trim, and chop the chives.

2. In a blender, combine the avocados, the garlic, and 1 cup of the broth. Process until smooth.

3. Pour the avocado mixture into a large bowl and blend in the remaining broth, the sour cream, the lime juice, the Worcestershire sauce, and the pepper. Season to taste, cover with plastic wrap, and refrigerate until you are ready to serve.

4. Sprinkle with the chopped chives.

Taco Your Time

1. Peel and mince the garlic. Rinse and pat dry the shrimp. Rinse and chop the tomatoes. Trim and slice the radishes. Peel and thinly slice the onion. Rinse, seed, and dice the jalapeño pepper.

2. Drain the olives.

3. Combine the tomatoes, the radishes, the onion, and the jalapeño in a large bowl.

4. Wash, dry, and shred the lettuce.

5. Heat 2 tablespoons of the oil in a large skillet and sauté the garlic for 1 minute.

6. Add the shrimp and sauté until they turn bright pink, 2 to 3 minutes.

7. Remove the skillet from the heat and set it aside.

8. In a small bowl, whisk together the lime juice, the vinegar, and the remaining 2 tablespoons of oil. Season to taste.

9. Combine the shrimp with the tomato mixture and toss with the dressing.

10. Spoon the filling into the taco shells, top with the lettuce, and sprinkle with the cheese.

It's Bean Done

1. Peel and mince the onion.

2. Drain the beans and the corn.

3. Melt the butter in a medium skillet, and sauté the onion for 5 minutes.

4. Add the beans and the corn to the skillet. Fold in the cumin, season to taste, and heat through.

Minute Melon

1. Set the cream cheese and the frozen whipped topping out to soften.

2. Peel, seed, and cut the melons into thin slices.

3. Alternate the cantaloupe and the casaba melon slices on individual dessert plates.

4. Cover the plates with plastic wrap and set them aside.

5. Drain and chop the cherries, reserving the juice.

6. In a medium bowl, combine the reserved cherry juice, the cream cheese, the powdered sugar, and the vanilla.

7. Fold in the whipped topping and the chopped cherries.

8. Cover the bowl with plastic wrap and refrigerate it until you are ready to use.

9. Spoon the topping over the melon slices.

COUNTDOWN

1. Assemble the ingredients and the equipment.
2. Do Steps 1–3 of *Avocado Cool.*
3. Do Steps 1–8 of *Minute Melon.*
4. Do Steps 1–7 of *Taco Your Time.*
5. Do Steps 1–4 of *It's Bean Done.*
6. Do Steps 8–10 of *Taco Your Time.*
7. Do Step 4 of *Avocado Cool.*
8. Do Step 9 of *Minute Melon.*

Weekend Three Saturday

FISH
1-1/2 pounds swordfish steaks

FRESH PRODUCE

VEGETABLES
1 medium bunch broccoli
1 stalk celery
1 medium head lettuce
1 medium cucumber
1 medium orange bell pepper
8 small boiling onions
1 medium shallot
3 scallions (green onions)

HERBS
2 tablespoons dill (when chopped)
3 tablespoons parsley (when chopped)

FRUIT
1 medium lime
1 pint strawberries

CANS, JARS & BOTTLES

SOUP
1 can (14 ounces) vegetable broth

VEGETABLES
1 can (4 ounces) button mushrooms

SPREADS
1/2 cup strawberry preserves

PACKAGED GOODS

PASTA, RICE & GRAINS
1/2 cup brown rice
1/2 cup wild rice

DRIED FRUITS & NUTS
1/4 cup walnut pieces

WINES & SPIRITS
1/4 cup dry sherry
1 tablespoon Grand Marnier

REFRIGERATED PRODUCTS

DAIRY
1-1/2 cups milk
1/4 cup whipped cream
3 eggs

JUICE
2 tablespoons orange juice

STAPLES

- ❏ Butter
- ❏ Flour
- ❏ Powdered sugar
- ❏ Cocoa powder
- ❏ Olive oil
- ❏ Vegetable oil
- ❏ Balsamic vinegar
- ❏ Dijon mustard
- ❏ Honey
- ❏ Dried rosemary
- ❏ Pepper
- ❏ Salt

Weekend Three Saturday

MENU

Excalibur

1-1/2 pounds swordfish steaks
1 medium lime
2 tablespoons fresh dill (when chopped)
1 medium orange bell pepper
1 medium bunch broccoli
8 small boiling onions
1 tablespoon olive oil
Seasoning to taste

Sir Ricelot

3 tablespoons fresh parsley (when
    chopped)
1 medium shallot
1 stalk celery
3 tablespoons butter
1/2 cup brown rice
1/2 cup wild rice
1 can (4 ounces) button mushrooms
1 can (14 ounces) vegetable broth
1/4 cup dry sherry
1/2 teaspoon dried rosemary
Seasoning to taste

Merlin's Mix

1 medium head lettuce
3 scallions (green onions)
1 medium cucumber
1/4 cup walnut pieces
1 tablespoon honey
1 teaspoon Dijon mustard
2 tablespoons vegetable oil
1 tablespoon balsamic vinegar
Seasoning to taste

Morgan le Crêpe

3 tablespoons butter
3 eggs
1/8 teaspoon salt
1 cup flour
1/4 cup cocoa powder
1-1/2 cups milk
1 pint fresh strawberries
1/4 cup powdered sugar
1/2 cup strawberry preserves
1 tablespoon Grand Marnier
2 tablespoons orange juice
1/4 cup whipped cream

EQUIPMENT

Blender	Whisk
Large covered saucepan	Citrus juicer
Small saucepan	Vegetable peeler
Medium skillet	4 large skewers
Small skillet	Waxed paper
Large shallow bowl	Kitchen knives
2 large mixing bowls	Measuring cups and spoons
Small mixing bowl	Cooking utensils

Weekend Three Saturday

RECIPES

Excalibur

1. Rinse and pat dry the swordfish, cut it into 1-1/2-inch cubes, and place the cubes in a large shallow bowl. Juice the lime. Rinse and chop the dill. Rinse, stem, and seed the bell pepper and cut it into chunks. Rinse and trim the broccoli and cut it into bite-sized florets. Peel and trim the onions.

2. Sprinkle the lime juice and the olive oil over the fish and refrigerate for 30 minutes.

3. Prepare the grill.

4. Bring water to a boil in a medium skillet. Add the broccoli and the onions and blanch until the broccoli turns bright green, about 1 minute. Remove the vegetables and rinse them in cold water.

5. Thread the fish cubes onto the skewers, alternating with the bell pepper, the broccoli, and the onions. Season to taste.

6. Grill the fish until it is opaque and flakes easily with a fork, 12 to 15 minutes, turning it occasionally.

Sir Ricelot

1. Rinse and chop the parsley. Peel and mince the shallot. Rinse, trim, and chop the celery.

2. Melt the butter in a large saucepan. Add the shallot, the celery, the brown rice, and the wild rice, and sauté for 3 minutes. Add the mushrooms and their liquid, the

broth, and the sherry. Bring to a boil, cover, reduce the heat, and simmer until the liquid is absorbed and the rice is tender, 35 to 40 minutes.

3. Fold in the parsley and the rosemary, season to taste, and fluff with a fork.

Merlin's Mix

1. Wash and dry the lettuce and tear it into bite-sized pieces. Trim and chop the scallions. Peel and chop the cucumber. Combine the vegetables in a large bowl. Fold in the walnut bits.

2. In a small bowl, whisk together the honey, the mustard, the oil, and the vinegar. Season to taste.

3. Toss the salad with the dressing.

Morgan le Crêpe

1. Melt 2 tablespoons of the butter.

2. Place the eggs, the salt, and the melted butter in a blender and process for 30 seconds. Gradually add the flour and the cocoa powder, and process until blended. Add the milk and process until smooth. Cover and set aside for 1 hour.

3. Melt 1 teaspoon of the remaining butter in a small skillet, swirling to coat the bottom and sides of the pan. Add 2 tablespoons of the batter to the skillet, tipping the skillet to let the mixture completely cover the

bottom. Cook until the crêpe is set and the edges are dry, about 1 minute.

4. Turn the crêpe over with a spatula and lightly brown it on the other side, about 20 seconds. Loosen the crepe and slide it onto a sheet of waxed paper. Repeat until you have made 8 crepes, adding more butter to the pan as needed. Cover the crêpes to keep them warm.

5. Rinse, hull, and slice the strawberries. Place them in a large bowl and sprinkle them with the powdered sugar.

6. In a small saucepan, combine the strawberry preserves, the Grand Marnier, and the orange juice, and heat until melted and well blended.

7. Spoon a portion of the berries onto each crêpe. Place a spoonful of whipped cream over the berries and roll up the crêpes. Lay the crêpes on individual dessert plates. Spoon the sauce over the crêpes and top with a dollop of whipped cream.

COUNTDOWN

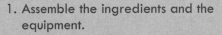

1. Assemble the ingredients and the equipment.
2. Do Steps 1–2 of *Morgan le Crêpe*.
3. Do Steps 1–3 of *Excalibur*.
4. Do Steps 3–5 of *Morgan le Crêpe*.
5. Do Steps 1–2 of *Sir Ricelot*.
6. Do Steps 1–2 of *Merlin's Mix*.
7. Do Steps 4–6 of *Excalibur*.
8. Do Step 3 of *Sir Ricelot*.
9. Do Step 3 of *Merlin's Mix*.
10. Do Steps 6–7 of *Morgan le Crêpe*.

Weekend Three Sunday

MEAT & POULTRY

3 pounds chicken pieces

FRESH PRODUCE

VEGETABLES

1 pound red potatoes
1 medium head lettuce
1 pint cherry tomatoes
1 medium cucumber
1 medium green bell pepper
1 small bunch radishes
1 large onion
2 cloves garlic

HERBS

2 tablespoons chives (when chopped)

FRUIT

2 medium ripe peaches
2 medium oranges

CANS, JARS & BOTTLES

SOUP

1 can (14 ounces) chicken broth

PACKAGED GOODS

BAKED GOODS

8 butterflake rolls
6 almond macaroons

DRIED FRUITS & NUTS

1/4 cup sliced almonds

REFRIGERATED PRODUCTS

DAIRY

1 cup whipping cream

FROZEN GOODS

DESSERTS

1 pint French vanilla ice cream

STAPLES

❑ Flour
❑ Granulated sugar
❑ Powdered sugar
❑ Olive oil
❑ Vegetable oil
❑ Red wine vinegar
❑ Mayonnaise
❑ Bay leaf
❑ Dried basil
❑ Ground allspice
❑ Paprika
❑ Pepper
❑ Salt
❑ Almond extract

Weekend Three Sunday

MENU

Sunday Chicken

1 large onion
2 cloves garlic
1 pound red potatoes
2 medium oranges
3 pounds chicken pieces
3 tablespoons vegetable oil
2 tablespoons flour
1 can (14 ounces) chicken broth
1 teaspoon ground allspice
1 bay leaf
Seasoning to taste

Lighthearted Salad

1 medium head lettuce
1 small bunch radishes
1 medium green bell pepper
1 medium cucumber
1 pint cherry tomatoes
1 teaspoon dried basil
1 teaspoon granulated sugar
3 tablespoons olive oil
2 tablespoons red wine vinegar
Seasoning to taste

Carefree Rolls

2 tablespoons fresh chives (when chopped)
1/3 cup mayonnaise
1/2 teaspoon paprika
8 butterflake rolls

Summer Soufflé

1 pint French vanilla ice cream
6 almond macaroons
1 cup whipping cream
1 tablespoon powdered sugar
1 teaspoon almond extract
2 medium ripe peaches
1/4 cup sliced almonds

EQUIPMENT

Electric mixer

Dutch oven

1-1/2-quart casserole

2 large mixing bowls

2 small mixing bowls

Whisk

Citrus grater

Citrus juicer

Vegetable brush

Vegetable peeler

Mallet

Plastic wrap

Plastic bag

Kitchen knives

Measuring cups and spoons

Cooking utensils

Weekend Three Sunday

RECIPES

Sunday Chicken

1. Peel and thinly slice the onion. Peel and mince the garlic. Scrub and chunk the potatoes. Grate 2 tablespoons of the orange peel. Juice the oranges. Rinse and pat dry the chicken pieces.

2. Heat the oil in a Dutch oven. Add the garlic, the onion, and the chicken, and sauté until the chicken is browned on all sides and almost cooked through, about 20 minutes.

3. Remove the chicken and set it aside.

4. Combine the flour and the orange juice and add the mixture to the Dutch oven. Add the broth and the potatoes. Bring to a boil, cover, reduce the heat, and simmer for 10 minutes.

5. Return the chicken to the Dutch oven and add the allspice and the bay leaf. Season to taste and cook until the potatoes and the chicken are tender, about 10 minutes.

6. Remove the chicken, the potatoes, and the onions, and cover to keep warm.

7. Bring the sauce to a boil and cook until it is reduced by half, about 5 minutes.

8. Discard the bay leaf. Pour the sauce over the chicken, the potatoes, and the onions, and sprinkle with the orange peel.

Lighthearted Salad

1. Wash and dry the lettuce and tear it into bite-sized pieces. Scrub, trim, and slice the radishes. Rinse, stem, and seed the bell pepper and cut it into thin rings. Peel and slice the cucumber. Rinse the tomatoes and cut them in half. Combine the vegetables in a large bowl.

2. In a small bowl, whisk together the basil, the sugar, the oil, and the vinegar. Season to taste.

3. Toss the salad with the dressing.

Carefree Rolls

1. Rinse and chop the chives.

2. In a small bowl, combine the chives, the mayonnaise, and the paprika.

3. Carefully open the sections of the rolls, and spread the mixture lightly between each section.

Summer Soufflé

1. Chill a large bowl and the beaters of an electric mixer in the refrigerator for at least 10 minutes.

2. Set the ice cream out to soften.

3. Place the macaroons in a plastic bag and crush them with a mallet.

4. In the chilled bowl, whip the cream until stiff, about 2 minutes. Fold in the powdered sugar and the almond extract. Fold in the ice cream. Fold in the macaroon crumbs. Spoon the mixture into a 1-1/2-quart casserole, cover with plastic wrap, and freeze until you are ready to serve.

5. Remove the soufflé from the freezer. Peel and slice the peaches, arrange them over the soufflé, and top with the almonds.

COUNTDOWN

1. Assemble the ingredients and the equipment.
2. Do Steps 1–4 of *Summer Soufflé*.
3. Do Steps 1–2 of *Carefree Rolls*.
4. Do Steps 1–5 of *Sunday Chicken*.
5. Do Steps 1–2 of *Lighthearted Salad*.
6. Do Step 3 of *Carefree Rolls*.
7. Do Steps 6–8 of *Sunday Chicken*.
8. Do Step 3 of *Lighthearted Salad*.
9. Do Step 5 of *Summer Soufflé*.

Weekend Four Saturday

MEAT & POULTRY

4 New York strip steaks (about 2 pounds)

FRESH PRODUCE

VEGETABLES

4 ears corn on the cob
2 small zucchini
1 small head Boston lettuce
4 large tomatoes
1 medium red onion
3 cloves garlic

HERBS

2 tablespoons basil (when chopped)
1/2 cup chives (when chopped)
1/4 cup parsley (when chopped)
1 tablespoon rosemary (when chopped)

FRUIT

2 large ripe nectarines
2 ripe kiwifruits
1 small lime
1 pint blueberries

PACKAGED GOODS

DESSERT & BAKING NEEDS

1 small package instant coconut cream
   pudding mix
1 envelope unflavored gelatin

WINES & SPIRITS

3 tablespoons dry sherry
3 tablespoons Grand Marnier

REFRIGERATED PRODUCTS

DAIRY

1 cup milk
1 cup + 2 tablespoons half-and-half

JUICE

1 cup orange juice

FROZEN GOODS

BAKED GOODS

1 pound cake

STAPLES LIST

- ❏ Butter
- ❏ Granulated sugar
- ❏ Vegetable oil
- ❏ Tarragon vinegar
- ❏ Lemon juice
- ❏ Dijon mustard
- ❏ Dried marjoram
- ❏ Dried thyme
- ❏ Whole black peppercorns
- ❏ Pepper
- ❏ Salt

Weekend Four Saturday

For Goodness Steaks

2 tablespoons whole black peppercorns
4 New York strip steaks (about 2 pounds)
2 cloves garlic
2 small zucchini
2 tablespoons fresh basil (when chopped)
1 tablespoon fresh rosemary (when chopped)
2 tablespoons butter
1 teaspoon Dijon mustard
3 tablespoons dry sherry
2 tablespoons half-and-half
Seasoning to taste

The Best Ears of Our Lives

1 small lime
4 ears fresh corn on the cob
3 tablespoons butter
1 teaspoon granulated sugar

The Red Salad

4 large tomatoes
I medium red onion
1 clove garlic
1/2 cup fresh chives (when chopped)
1/4 cup fresh parsley (when chopped)
2/3 cup vegetable oil
1/4 cup tarragon vinegar
1 teaspoon granulated sugar
1/2 teaspoon dried marjoram
1/2 teaspoon dried thyme
Seasoning to taste
1 small head Boston lettuce

The Fruit of All Evil

1 frozen pound cake
1 envelope unflavored gelatin
1/2 cup hot water
1 small package instant coconut cream pudding mix
1 cup milk
1 cup half-and-half
4 tablespoons granulated sugar
1 cup orange juice
2 large ripe nectarines
2 ripe kiwifruits
1 tablespoon lemon juice
1 pint fresh blueberries
3 tablespoons Grand Marnier

EQUIPMENT

Electric mixer	Citrus juicer
Medium saucepan	Vegetable brush
Small saucepan	Vegetable grater
Medium covered skillet	Pastry brush
Large trifle bowl	Plastic wrap
Large shallow bowl	Plastic bag
Medium mixing bowl	Aluminum foil
Small mixing bowl	Kitchen knives
Whisk	Measuring cups and spoons
Citrus grater	Cooking utensils

Weekend Four Saturday

For Goodness Steaks

1. Prepare the grill.

2. Place the peppercorns in a plastic bag and crush them lightly. Press the peppercorns into the steaks. Peel and mince the garlic. Scrub, trim, and grate the zucchini. Rinse and chop the basil. Rinse and chop the rosemary.

3. Melt the butter in a medium skillet. Add the garlic and the zucchini, and sauté until the zucchini is tender, about 1 minute. Stir in the mustard, the basil, the rosemary, the sherry, and the half-and-half. Blend well and season to taste. Cover the pan and set it aside.

4. Grill the steaks to desired doneness, 5 minutes per side for rare.

5. Spoon the zucchini sauce over the steaks.

The Best Ears of Our Lives

1. Grate 2 teaspoons of lime peel and juice the lime. Shuck the corn.

2. Melt the butter in a small saucepan. Blend in the lime peel, the lime juice, and the sugar.

3. Lay each ear of corn on a sheet of aluminum foil. Brush the ears with the lime mixture, seal the foil around each ear, place them on the edges of the grill, and cook until they are crisp-tender, about 5 minutes, turning as necessary.

The Red Salad

1. Rinse and slice the tomatoes. Peel and thinly slice the onion. Peel and mince the garlic. Rinse and chop the chives. Rinse and chop the parsley.

2. Place the tomatoes and the onion in a large shallow bowl. Sprinkle with the garlic.

3. In a small bowl, whisk together the oil, the vinegar, the sugar, the marjoram, and the thyme, and season to taste. Pour the mixture over the tomatoes, cover, and refrigerate for at least 1 hour.

4. Wash and dry the lettuce and arrange the leaves on individual salad plates.

5. Drain the tomato and onion mixture and arrange the slices over the lettuce leaves. Garnish with the chives and the parsley.

The Fruit of All Evil

1. Set the pound cake out to thaw.

2. Combine the gelatin and the hot water in a medium saucepan and let stand for 3 minutes.

3. Combine the pudding mix, the milk, and the half-and-half in a medium bowl and beat with an electric mixer until well blended, about 2 minutes. Cover the bowl

with plastic wrap and refrigerate it until you are ready to use.

4. Add the sugar to the gelatin, bring to a boil, and cook until the sugar has dissolved. Remove the pan from the heat, add the orange juice, blend well, and refrigerate until partially set, about 20 minutes.

5. Rinse, pit, and slice the nectarines. Peel, trim, and slice the kiwifruits. Sprinkle the fruit with the lemon juice to keep it from turning brown. Rinse and blot the blueberries on paper towels.

6. Slice the cake to cover the bottom of a large trifle bowl. Sprinkle the cake with the Grand Marnier. Spread half of the blueberries over the cake.

7. Spoon half of the gelatin over the cake. Add the pudding mixture. Top with the remaining gelatin. Arrange the nectarine slices around the edges of the bowl. Arrange the kiwifruit slices in the center. Sprinkle the remaining blueberries over the top. Cover the bowl with plastic wrap and refrigerate it until you are ready to serve.

COUNTDOWN

1. Assemble the ingredients and the equipment.
2. Do Steps 1–7 of *The Fruit of All Evil.*
3. Do Steps 1–3 of *The Red Salad.*
4. Do Steps 1–4 of *For Goodness Steaks.*
5. Do Steps 1–3 of *The Best Ears of Our Lives.*
6. Do Steps 4–5 of *The Red Salad.*
7. Do Step 5 of *For Goodness Steaks.*

Weekend Four Sunday

FRESH PRODUCE

VEGETABLES
1 medium carrot
1 package (10 ounces) spinach
1 small head lettuce
1 medium cucumber
2 medium green bell peppers
2 medium shallots
3 scallions (green onions)
4 cloves garlic

HERBS
2 tablespoons parsley (when chopped)

FRUIT
2 small ripe honeydew melons
1 pint strawberries

CANS, JARS & BOTTLES

CONDIMENTS
1 jar (6-1/2 ounces) marinated
   artichoke hearts
1 jar (10 ounces) roasted red peppers

PACKAGED GOODS

PASTA, RICE & GRAINS
1 pound linguini

DESSERT & BAKING NEEDS
1 envelope unflavored gelatin

BAKED GOODS
1 small loaf Italian bread

REFRIGERATED PRODUCTS

DAIRY
1/2 cup milk
1 cup sour cream
1 cup whipping cream

CHEESE
1 container (15 ounces) ricotta cheese

STAPLES

❏ Butter
❏ Granulated sugar
❏ White wine vinegar
❏ Worcestershire sauce
❏ Grated Parmesan cheese
❏ Dried oregano
❏ Pepper
❏ Salt
❏ Vanilla extract

Weekend Four Sunday

Pasta, Present, and Future

2 medium shallots
1 clove garlic
2 medium green bell peppers
2 tablespoons fresh parsley (when chopped)
1 jar (10 ounces) roasted red peppers
1 container (15 ounces) ricotta cheese
1/2 teaspoon dried oregano
1 pound linguini
Seasoning to taste

Nick of Time Salad

1 small head lettuce
1 package (10 ounces) fresh spinach
3 scallions (green onions)
1 medium cucumber
1 medium carrot
1 jar (6-1/2 ounces) marinated artichoke hearts
2 tablespoons white wine vinegar
1 teaspoon Worcestershire sauce
Seasoning to taste

Ready Bread

3 cloves garlic
4 tablespoons butter
1 small loaf Italian bread
1/2 cup grated Parmesan cheese

In the Sweet By-and-By

1 cup whipping cream
1 envelope unflavored gelatin
1/2 cup milk
1/2 cup granulated sugar
1 cup sour cream
2 teaspoons vanilla extract
2 small ripe honeydew melons
1 pint fresh strawberries

EQUIPMENT

Blender

Stockpot

Medium saucepan

Medium skillet

Small skillet

Colander

Large mixing bowl

Medium mixing bowl

Small mixing bowl

Whisk

Vegetable peeler

Vegetable grater

Pastry brush

Kitchen knives

Measuring cups and spoons

Cooking utensils

Pasta, Present, and Future

1. Peel and chop the shallots. Peel and mince the garlic. Rinse, stem, seed, and chop the bell peppers. Rinse and chop the parsley. Drain the roasted peppers, reserving the oil.

2. Bring water for the pasta to a boil in a stockpot.

3. Heat the reserved pepper oil in a medium skillet and sauté the shallots, the garlic, and the bell peppers for 4 minutes.

4. Combine the roasted peppers and the cheese in a blender and process until smooth.

5. Fold in the parsley and the oregano.

6. Cook the pasta until it is almost tender, 2 to 3 minutes if you are using fresh pasta, 6 to 7 minutes if you are using dry pasta.

7. Drain the pasta, return it to the stockpot, and toss it with the shallot mixture. Fold in the ricotta mixture. Season to taste and heat through.

Nick of Time Salad

1. Wash and dry the lettuce and arrange the leaves on individual salad plates.

2. Rinse the spinach and tear it into bite-sized pieces. Trim and chop the scallions. Peel and slice the cucumber. Peel and grate the carrot.

3. Drain the artichoke hearts, reserving the marinade in a small bowl, and cut them in half.

4. Combine the vegetables in a large bowl.

5. Whisk the vinegar and the Worcestershire sauce into the reserved artichoke marinade. Season to taste.

6. Toss the salad with the dressing and spoon it over the lettuce.

Ready Bread

1. Peel and mince the garlic.

2. Melt the butter in a small skillet and sauté the garlic for 2 minutes.

3. Slice the bread. Brush the slices with the butter mixture and sprinkle with the Parmesan cheese.

In the Sweet By-and-By

1. Heat the cream in a medium saucepan, but do not let it boil. Remove the pan from the heat.

2. Sprinkle the gelatin over the warm cream and let it stand for 5 minutes.

3. Return the cream mixture to the heat, add the milk and the sugar, and simmer, stirring, until the sugar is completely dissolved, about 3 minutes.

4. Pour the mixture into a medium bowl and refrigerate it for 30 minutes.

5. Fold the sour cream and the vanilla into the cream mixture, and refrigerate it until you are ready to serve.

6. Cut the melons in half and remove the seeds. Place each half on an individual dessert plate. Stem, hull, and slice the strawberries, reserving 4 whole berries. Spoon the sliced berries into the melon cavities and set them aside.

7. Top the fruit with the sauce and garnish with a whole berry.

COUNTDOWN

1. Assemble the ingredients and the equipment.
2. Do Steps 1–6 of *In the Sweet By-and-By.*
3. Do Steps 1–5 of *Nick of Time Salad.*
4. Do Steps 1–6 of *Pasta, Present, and Future.*
5. Do Steps 1–3 of *Ready Bread.*
6. Do Step 7 of *Pasta, Present, and Future.*
7. Do Step 6 of *Nick of Time Salad.*
8. Do Step 7 of *In the Sweet By-and-By.*

Weekend Five Saturday

SHOPPING LIST

MEAT & POULTRY
4 lean boneless loin pork chops
(about 1-1/2 pounds)

FRESH PRODUCE

VEGETABLES
1-1/2 pounds sweet potatoes
1 pound asparagus
2 stalks celery
1 large shallot
1 scallion (green onion)
1 clove garlic

HERBS
4 tablespoons chives (when chopped)
3 tablespoons parsley (when chopped)

FRUIT
2 pints strawberries

CANS, JARS & BOTTLES

SPREADS
1/4 cup raspberry preserves

CONDIMENTS
1 jar (2 ounces) diced pimiento
2 tablespoons sweet pickle relish

PACKAGED GOODS

DRIED FRUITS & NUTS
1/2 cup dried apricots

DESSERT & BAKING NEEDS
12 ounces cinnamon chips

WINES & SPIRITS
2 tablespoons dry sherry

REFRIGERATED PRODUCTS

DAIRY
1/4 cup half-and-half
1 cup sour cream
1/4 cup whipped cream

JUICE
1/4 cup orange juice

FROZEN GOODS

BAKED GOODS
1 cinnamon-swirl pound cake

STAPLES

- ❑ Butter
- ❑ Granulated sugar
- ❑ Dark brown sugar
- ❑ Vegetable oil
- ❑ Red wine vinegar
- ❑ Raspberry vinegar
- ❑ Lemon juice
- ❑ Soy sauce
- ❑ Dried tarragon
- ❑ Dry mustard
- ❑ Pepper
- ❑ Salt
- ❑ Vanilla extract

Weekend Five Saturday

Stuffed Shirts

1 large shallot
4 lean boneless loin pork chops (about
   1-1/2 pounds)
1/2 cup dried apricots
1/4 cup raspberry preserves
1 teaspoon dried tarragon
2 teaspoons dark brown sugar
1/4 cup orange juice
1/4 cup raspberry vinegar
1 tablespoon dry mustard
Seasoning to taste
2 tablespoons vegetable oil

Pompous Potatoes

1-1/2 pounds sweet potatoes
2 stalks celery
4 tablespoons fresh chives (when
   chopped)
1 jar (2 ounces) diced pimento
3 tablespoons fresh parsley (when
   chopped)
2 tablespoons sweet pickle relish
3 tablespoons vegetable oil
1 tablespoon red wine vinegar
2 tablespoons lemon juice
1 teaspoon granulated sugar
Seasoning to taste

Snobby Spears

1 pound fresh asparagus
1 clove garlic
1 scallion (green onion)

2 tablespoons dry sherry
1 teaspoon soy sauce
1 tablespoon butter

Boastful Berries

1 frozen cinnamon-swirl pound cake
12 ounces cinnamon chips
1/4 cup half-and-half
2 pints fresh strawberries
1 cup sour cream
1 teaspoon vanilla extract
1/4 cup whipped cream

EQUIPMENT

Large covered saucepan

Small saucepan

2 large covered skillets

Large mixing bowl

Medium mixing bowl

3 small mixing bowls

Whisk

Vegetable brush

Plastic wrap

Kitchen knives

Measuring cups and spoons

Cooking utensils

Stuffed Shirts

1. Peel and mince the shallot. Rinse, pat dry, and cut a deep pocket in the side of each pork chop.

2. Chop the apricots and combine them in a small bowl with the raspberry preserves. Spoon the mixture into the pork chop pockets. Close the pockets with toothpicks, if necessary.

3. In the same bowl, combine the tarragon, the brown sugar, the orange juice, the vinegar, and the mustard. Season to taste.

4. Heat the oil in a large skillet. Add the shallot and sauté for 1 minute. Add the pork chops and brown on one side, about 5 minutes.

5. Turn the chops and brown them for 5 minutes more.

6. Add the orange juice mixture. Cover the skillet, reduce the heat, and simmer until the chops are tender and cooked through, about 20 minutes.

Pompous Potatoes

1. Bring water to a boil in a large saucepan.

2. Scrub, trim, and quarter the potatoes.

3. Place the potatoes in the saucepan, cover, and cook until tender, about 15 minutes.

4. Rinse, trim, and chop the celery. Rinse and chop the chives. Drain the pimiento.

Combine the celery, the chives, and the pimiento in a large bowl. Rinse and chop the parsley.

5. Drain and rinse the potatoes under cold water. Set them aside to cool.

6. Peel and cube the potatoes and add them to the celery mixture.

7. In a small bowl, whisk together the pickle relish, the oil, the vinegar, the lemon juice, and the sugar. Season to taste and toss with the potato mixture. Top with the parsley, cover with plastic wrap, and refrigerate until you are ready to serve.

Snobby Spears

1. Bring a small amount of water to a boil in a large skillet.

2. Rinse the asparagus and remove and discard the tough ends. Peel and mince the garlic. Trim and chop the scallion.

3. Place the asparagus in the skillet, cover, and steam until the spears are crisp-tender, 3 to 8 minutes, depending on thickness.

4. In a small bowl, combine the sherry, the soy sauce, and the garlic.

5. Drain the asparagus, return it to the skillet, and toss it with the butter. Add the sherry mixture and toss until heated through, about 1 minute.

6. Garnish with the scallion.

Boastful Berries

1. Set the pound cake out to thaw.

2. Slowly melt the cinnamon chips with the half-and-half in a small saucepan. Remove the pan from the heat, and set it aside.

3. Reserve 4 whole strawberries for garnish, and rinse, stem, hull, and slice the remainder.

4. Place the sour cream in a medium bowl. Fold in the vanilla. Slowly blend in the melted cinnamon.

5. Cut the pound cake into 4 layers. Lightly spread the bottom layer with some of the melted cinnamon. Arrange a third of the strawberries over the cinnamon. Repeat twice. Spread the remaining cinnamon over the top and sides of the cake. Garnish with dollops of whipped cream and the reserved strawberries. Refrigerate the cake until you are ready to serve.

COUNTDOWN

1. Assemble the ingredients and the equipment.
2. Do Steps 1–5 of *Boastful Berries*.
3. Do Steps 1–7 of *Pompous Potatoes*.
4. Do Steps 1–6 of *Stuffed Shirts*.
5. Do Steps 1–6 of *Snobby Spears*.

Weekend Five Sunday

MEAT & POULTRY

3 pounds chicken pieces

FRESH PRODUCE

VEGETABLES

1 small bunch broccoli
2 medium carrots
1/2 pound mushrooms
1 medium head green leaf lettuce
1 medium cucumber
1 medium green bell pepper
1 small onion
3 scallions (green onions)
2 cloves garlic

HERBS

3 tablespoons chives (when chopped)
3 tablespoons dill (when chopped)
2 teaspoons parsley (when chopped)

FRUIT

2 medium bananas
1 large lime

CANS, JARS & BOTTLES

SOUP

1 can (14 ounces) chicken broth

PACKAGED GOODS

PASTA, RICE & GRAINS

1 cup couscous

DRIED FRUITS & NUTS

2 tablespoons pecan pieces

REFRIGERATED PRODUCTS

DAIRY

1/4 cup whipped cream

JUICE

2 tablespoons orange juice

FROZEN GOODS

DESSERTS

1 pint coffee ice cream

STAPLES

- ❏ Butter
- ❏ Granulated sugar
- ❏ Cocoa powder
- ❏ Olive oil
- ❏ Apple cider vinegar
- ❏ Prepared horseradish
- ❏ Celery seed
- ❏ Dried basil
- ❏ Paprika
- ❏ Pepper
- ❏ Salt

Weekend Five Sunday

Chickenitza

3 pounds chicken pieces
2 cloves garlic
1 small onion
1/2 pound fresh mushrooms
1 large lime
3 tablespoons fresh dill (when chopped)
4 tablespoons butter
1 teaspoon paprika
Seasoning to taste

Santa Cous

3 tablespoons fresh chives (when
   chopped)
2 teaspoons fresh parsley (when
   chopped)
2 tablespoons butter
1 cup couscous
1 can (14 ounces) chicken broth
Seasoning to taste

Greenada

1 small bunch broccoli
1 medium head green leaf lettuce
2 medium carrots
3 scallions (green onions)
1 medium cucumber
1 medium green bell pepper
4 tablespoons olive oil
3 tablespoons apple cider vinegar
1 tablespoon granulated sugar
1/2 teaspoon prepared horseradish
1 teaspoon dried basil

1/2 teaspoon celery seed
Seasoning to taste

Copabanana

2 medium bananas
2 tablespoons orange juice
1 pint coffee ice cream
1/4 cup whipped cream
1 tablespoon cocoa powder
2 tablespoons pecan pieces

EQUIPMENT

Dutch oven
Medium covered saucepan
Medium saucepan
Large mixing bowl
Small mixing bowl
Whisk
Citrus grater
Citrus juicer
Vegetable grater
Vegetable peeler
Ice cream scoop
Kitchen knives
Measuring cups and spoons
Cooking utensils

Weekend Five Sunday

Chickenitza

1. Rinse and pat dry the chicken pieces. Peel and chop the garlic. Peel and chop the onion. Rinse, pat dry, and slice the mushrooms. Grate 1 tablespoon of lime peel and juice the lime. Rinse and chop the dill.

2. Melt the butter in a Dutch oven, and sauté the garlic and the onion for 3 minutes.

3. Add the chicken and brown the pieces on all sides, about 20 minutes.

4. Add the lime juice and the paprika to the Dutch oven. Fold in the mushrooms. Season to taste.

5. Cover and simmer until the chicken is tender and no longer pink inside, about 30 minutes.

6. Fold in the dill and the lime peel and simmer for 5 minutes more.

Santa Cous

1. Rinse and chop the chives. Rinse and chop the parsley.

2. In a medium saucepan, combine the butter, the couscous, and the broth. Bring the mixture to a boil.

3. Cover the pan, remove it from the heat, and let it stand for 10 minutes.

4. Add the chives and the parsley and season to taste.

5. Fluff with a fork before serving.

Greenada

1. Bring a small amount of water to a boil in a medium saucepan.

2. Rinse and trim the broccoli and cut it into bite-sized florets. Place the broccoli in the saucepan, return to a boil, and cook for 1 minute.

3. Drain the broccoli and rinse it in cold water until cooled.

4. Wash and dry the lettuce and tear it into bite-sized pieces. Peel and grate the carrots. Trim and chop the scallions. Peel and slice the cucumber. Rinse, stem, seed, and chop the bell pepper. Combine the vegetables in a large bowl. Fold in the broccoli.

5. In a small bowl, whisk together the oil, the vinegar, the sugar, the horseradish, the basil, and the celery seed. Season to taste.

6. Toss the salad with the dressing.

Copabanana

1. Peel and slice the bananas and sprinkle them with the orange juice.

2. Distribute the bananas among individual dessert glasses, reserving 4 slices for garnish.

3. Spoon the ice cream over the banana slices. Top with dollops of whipped cream, and sprinkle with the cocoa powder and the nuts.

4. Garnish with the reserved banana slices.

COUNTDOWN

1. Assemble the ingredients and the equipment.
2. Do Steps 1–5 of *Chickenitza*.
3. Do Steps 1–3 of *Santa Cous*.
4. Do Steps 1–5 of *Greenada*.
5. Do Step 6 of *Chickenitza*.
6. Do Steps 4–5 of *Santa Cous*.
7. Do Step 6 of *Greenada*.
8. Do Steps 1–4 of *Copabanana*.

Weekend Six Saturday

FISH

4 Chilean sea bass fillets
(about 1-1/2 pounds)

FRESH PRODUCE

VEGETABLES
1 small head cauliflower
4 ears corn on the cob
1 stalk celery
1 medium head red leaf lettuce
2 medium tomatoes
1 small onion
2 medium ripe avocados
1 medium orange bell pepper
1 medium green bell pepper

HERBS
2 tablespoons chives (when chopped)
3 tablespoons cilantro (when chopped)
1/4 cup dill (when chopped)

FRUIT
1 large lemon
1 pint blueberries
1 pint raspberries

CANS, JARS & BOTTLES

SOUP
2 cans (10-1/2 ounces each) chicken
broth

VEGETABLES
1 can (14 ounces) whole artichoke hearts

CONDIMENTS
1 can (3-1/2 ounces) pitted black olives

PACKAGED GOODS

BAKED GOODS
4 individual meringue shells

REFRIGERATED PRODUCTS

DAIRY
1 container (8 ounces) blueberry yogurt

STAPLES

❑ Butter
❑ Flour
❑ Vegetable oil
❑ White wine vinegar
❑ Lemon juice
❑ White Worcestershire sauce
❑ Dijon mustard
❑ Honey
❑ Bay leaf
❑ Dried thyme
❑ Cayenne pepper
❑ Lemon-pepper seasoning
❑ Paprika
❑ Pepper
❑ Salt

Weekend Six Saturday

Spaced-Out Soup

1 small onion
1 stalk celery
1/4 cup fresh dill (when chopped)
1 large lemon
1 can (14 ounces) whole artichoke hearts
2 tablespoons butter
2 tablespoons flour
2 cans (10-1/2 ounces each) chicken broth
1 bay leaf
1/4 teaspoon dried thyme
1/4 teaspoon lemon-pepper seasoning
Seasoning to taste

Baffled Bass

4 Chilean sea bass fillets (about
   1-1/2 pounds)
2 medium fresh tomatoes
2 tablespoons fresh chives (when
   chopped)
3 tablespoons vegetable oil
2 tablespoons white wine vinegar
2 teaspoons Dijon mustard
Seasoning to taste

State of Cornfusion

4 ears fresh corn on the cob
1 medium orange bell pepper
1 medium green bell pepper
3 tablespoons fresh cilantro (when
   chopped)
4 tablespoons butter
1 teaspoon white Worcestershire sauce
1/4 teaspoon cayenne pepper
Seasoning to taste

Salad Snafu

1 medium head red leaf lettuce
1 small head cauliflower
2 medium ripe avocados
1 can (3-1/2 ounces) pitted black olives
3 tablespoons vegetable oil
2 tablespoons lemon juice
1/2 teaspoon paprika
Seasoning to taste

Bungled Berries

1 pint fresh blueberries
1 pint fresh raspberries
1 container (8 ounces) blueberry yogurt
2 tablespoons honey
4 individual meringue shells

EQUIPMENT

Blender	Citrus juicer
Medium saucepan	Whisk
Small saucepan	Aluminum foil
4 large skewers	Pastry brush
Large mixing bowl	Kitchen knives
3 small mixing bowls	Measuring cups and spoons
Citrus grater	Cooking utensils

Weekend Six Saturday

Spaced-Out Soup

1. Peel and chop the onion. Rinse, trim, and chop the celery. Rinse, pat dry, and chop the dill. Grate 2 teaspoons of lemon peel and squeeze 2 tablespoons of lemon juice. Drain and chop the artichokes.

2. Melt the butter in a medium saucepan and sauté the onion, the garlic, and the celery until the onion is soft, about 5 minutes.

3. Add the flour and cook, stirring, for two minutes.

4. Add the artichoke hearts, the broth, the bay leaf, the thyme, the lemon peel, and the lemon-pepper seasoning. Season to taste and bring to a boil. Reduce the heat and simmer for 20 minutes, stirring fequently.

5. Remove the bay leaf, place the soup in a blender, and puree.

6. Sprinkle with the dill.

Baffled Bass

1. Prepare the grill.

2. Rinse and pat dry the fish.

3. Rinse and chop the tomatoes. Rinse and chop the chives.

4. In a small bowl, combine the oil, the vinegar, and the mustard.

5. Lay the fish fillets on individual sheets of aluminum foil. Season to taste.

6. Brush the fillets with the mustard mixture.

7. Top the fillets with the tomatoes and the chives.

8. Seal the foil packets and grill them until the fish flakes easily with a fork, about 15 minutes.

State of Cornfusion

1. Shuck and trim the corn and cut it into 2-inch sections. Rinse, stem, seed, and cut the bell peppers into 2-inch squares. Rinse and chop the cilantro.

2. Melt the butter in a small saucepan.

3. Blend in the Worcestershire sauce and the cayenne pepper.

4. Remove the pan from the heat and fold in the cilantro.

5. Alternate the vegetables on 4 large skewers. Season to taste and brush them with some of the butter mixture.

6. Arrange the skewers on the side of the grill and cook, basting occasionally with the remaining butter mixture, until the vegetables are crisp-tender, about 15 minutes.

Salad Snafu

1. Wash and dry the lettuce. Arrange 4 large leaves on individual salad plates and tear the rest into bite-sized pieces.

2. Rinse and trim the cauliflower and cut it into bite-sized florets. Peel, pit, and slice the avocados. Drain the olives. Combine the vegetables in a large bowl. Add the remaining lettuce.

3. In a small bowl, whisk together the oil, the lemon juice, and the paprika. Season to taste.

4. Toss the salad with the dressing and spoon it onto the lettuce leaves.

Bungled Berries

1. Rinse the berries and blot them on paper towels.

2. In a small bowl, combine 1/2 cup of the blueberries with half of the yogurt and refrigerate until you are ready to use. Fold the honey into the remaining yogurt and refrigerate until you are ready to use.

3. Place the meringue shells on individual dessert plates. Spoon the blueberry-yogurt mixture into the shells. Top with the remaining blueberries and some of the raspberries.

4. Spoon the honey mixture over one corner of the shells and onto the plate. Sprinkle the remaining raspberries over the honey mixture.

COUNTDOWN

1. Assemble the ingredients and the equipment.
2. Do Step 1 of *Baffled Bass*.
3. Do Steps 1–2 of *Bungled Berries*.
4. Do Steps 1–4 of *Spaced-Out Soup*.
5. Do Steps 1–5 of *State of Cornfusion*.
6. Do Steps 2–8 of *Baffled Bass*.
7. Do Step 6 of *State of Cornfusion*.
8. Do Steps 5–6 of *Spaced-Out Soup*.
9. Do Steps 1–4 of *Salad Snafu*.
10. Do Steps 3–4 of *Bungled Berries*.

Weekend Six Sunday

SHOPPING LIST

FRESH PRODUCE

VEGETABLES
2 pounds small zucchini
2 stalks celery
1 medium head lettuce
1 small red onion
1 clove garlic

HERBS
1/4 cup parsley (when chopped)

FRUIT
1 large ripe pineapple

CANS, JARS & BOTTLES

SOUP
1 can (10-1/2 ounces) chicken broth
1 can (10-1/2 ounces) beef broth

CONDIMENTS
2 tablespoons sweet pickle relish

PACKAGED GOODS

BAKED GOODS
1 loaf sandwich bread, unsliced
1 Bundt cake

DRIED FRUITS & NUTS
1/4 cup pecan bits

DESSERT & BAKING NEEDS
12 ounces butterscotch chips

WINES & SPIRITS

3 tablespoons dry sherry

REFRIGERATED PRODUCTS

DAIRY
3 tablespoons half-and-half
1 tablespoon sour cream
8 eggs
1/2 pound sliced Swiss cheese

DELI
4 slices bacon
1 pound sliced turkey

FROZEN GOODS

DESSERTS
1 pint caramel yogurt

STAPLES

- ❏ Butter
- ❏ Granulated sugar
- ❏ Powdered sugar
- ❏ Vegetable oil
- ❏ Rice vinegar
- ❏ Dijon mustard
- ❏ Mayonnaise
- ❏ Poppy seeds
- ❏ Dried basil
- ❏ Curry powder
- ❏ Ground cardamom
- ❏ Ground cinnamon
- ❏ Ground cloves
- ❏ Pepper
- ❏ Salt
- ❏ Rum extract

Weekend Six Sunday

She Soups to Conquer

4 slices bacon
2 pounds small zucchini
1/4 cup fresh parsley (when chopped)
1 clove garlic
1 teaspoon dried basil
1 can (10-1/2 ounces) chicken broth
1 can (10-1/2 ounces) beef broth
3 tablespoons dry sherry
Seasoning to taste

School For Sandwiches

8 eggs
2 stalks celery
1 small red onion
1 medium head lettuce
2 tablespoons sweet pickle relish
1/3 cup mayonnaise
1 tablespoon Dijon mustard
1-1/2 teaspoons curry powder
1/4 teaspoon ground cinnamon
1/8 teaspoon ground cardamom
1/8 teaspoon ground cloves
Seasoning to taste
1 loaf sandwich bread, unsliced
1 pound sliced turkey
1/2 pound sliced Swiss cheese

Pride and Pineapple

1 large ripe pineapple
3 tablespoons vegetable oil
2 tablespoons rice vinegar
1 tablespoon sour cream
1/2 teaspoon granulated sugar
1 teaspoon poppy seeds

The Liquor of Cakefield

12 ounces butterscotch chips
4 tablespoons butter
3 tablespoons half-and-half
2 teaspoons rum extract
2/3 cup powdered sugar
1 Bundt cake
1 pint caramel frozen yogurt
1/4 cup pecan bits

EQUIPMENT

Blender
Medium covered saucepan
Medium saucepan
Small saucepan
Small skillet
2 small mixing bowls
Whisk
Vegetable brush
Vegetable grater
Ice cream scoop
Plastic wrap
Kitchen knives
Measuring cups and spoons
Cooking utensils

Weekend Six Sunday

She Soups to Conquer

1. Chop the bacon and sauté it in a small skillet until crisp, about 7 minutes.

2. Drain the bacon on paper towels.

3. Scrub, trim, and grate the zucchini. Rinse and chop the parsley. Peel and mince the garlic.

4. In a medium saucepan, combine the zucchini, the parsley, the garlic, and the basil.

5. Add the broth and the sherry.

6. Season to taste, bring to a boil, cover, reduce the heat, and simmer until the zucchini is tender, about 5 minutes.

7. Transfer the soup to a blender and process until smooth.

8. Pour into individual soup bowls, top with the bacon, cover them with plastic wrap, and refrigerate them until you are ready to serve.

School For Sandwiches

1. In a medium saucepan, cover the eggs with water, bring to a boil, and cook until hard-boiled, about 12 minutes.

2. Drain the eggs, rinse them in cold water, and refrigerate them until you are ready to use.

3. Rinse, trim, and chop the celery. Peel and thinly slice the onion. Wash and dry the lettuce and separate it into leaves.

4. In a small bowl, combine the celery, the pickle relish, the mayonnaise, the mustard, the curry powder, the cinnamon, the cardamom, and the cloves. Season to taste.

5. Peel and slice the eggs.

6. Cut the bread in half lengthwise.

7. Spread both halves with the mayonnaise mixture. Top with the lettuce leaves. Add the turkey slices, the cheese slices, the egg slices, and the onion slices. Assemble the loaf and secure it with toothpicks. Cut the loaf into thick slices and serve.

Pride and Pineapple

1. Quarter the pineapple and cut away the core. With a sharp knife, slice the fruit from the shell but do not remove it. Cut into 4 wedges.

2. Place the quarters on individual salad plates.

3. In a small bowl, whisk together the oil, the vinegar, the sour cream, the sugar, and the poppy seeds.

4. Drizzle the dressing over the pineapple quarters.

The Liquor of Cakefield

1. In a small saucepan, combine the butter-scotch chips, the butter, the half-and-half, and the rum extract, and cook over low heat, stirring, until melted and smooth. Fold in the powdered sugar. Set the pan aside to cool slightly.

2. Spread the cooled butterscotch over the Bundt cake, letting it drizzle down the sides. Refrigerate the cake until you are ready to serve.

3. Fill the center of the cake with the frozen yogurt. Sprinkle with the pecans.

COUNTDOWN

1. Assemble the ingredients and the equipment.
2. Do Steps 1–2 of *The Liquor of Cakefield*.
3. Do Steps 1–8 of *She Soups to Conquer*.
4. Do Step 1 of *School For Sandwiches*.
5. Do Steps 1–3 of *Pride and Pineapple*.
6. Do Steps 2–7 of *School For Sandwiches*.
7. Do Step 4 of *Pride and Pineapple*.
8. Do Step 3 of *The Liquor of Cakefield*.

Weekend Seven Saturday

SHOPPING LIST

MEAT & POULTRY

4 boneless, skinless chicken breast halves
(about 1-1/2 pounds)

FRESH PRODUCE

VEGETABLES
1/2 pound baby carrots
1 medium head Boston lettuce
2 medium tomatoes
1 medium shallot
2 scallions (green onions)

HERBS
2 tablespoons parsley (when chopped)

FRUIT
1 small ripe pineapple
2 medium ripe mangoes
1 medium lemon

CANS, JARS & BOTTLES

SOUP
1 can (14 ounces) vegetable broth

FRUIT
4 maraschino cherries

CONDIMENTS
1 can (14 ounces) artichoke hearts

PACKAGED GOODS

PASTA, RICE & GRAINS
1 cup long-grain white rice

DRIED FRUITS & NUTS
1/2 cup walnut pieces

WINES & SPIRITS

1/2 cup dry white wine

REFRIGERATED PRODUCTS

DAIRY
1/4 cup whipped cream

FROZEN GOODS

DESSERTS
1 pint coffee ice cream

STAPLES

- ❑ Butter
- ❑ Granulated sugar
- ❑ Dark brown sugar
- ❑ Olive oil
- ❑ Vegetable oil
- ❑ White wine vinegar
- ❑ Lemon juice
- ❑ Worcestershire sauce
- ❑ Beef bouillon cube
- ❑ Whole black peppercorns
- ❑ Pepper
- ❑ Salt

Weekend Seven Saturday

MENU

Chicanery

2 tablespoons whole black peppercorns
4 boneless, skinless chicken breast halves
   (about 1-1/2 pounds)
1 medium lemon
1/2 pound baby carrots
2 tablespoons fresh parsley (when
   chopped)
1 can (14 ounces) artichoke hearts
5 tablespoons butter
1/2 cup dry white wine
1/2 cup vegetable broth
Seasoning to taste

Tricky Rice

1 medium shallot
2 tablespoons vegetable oil
1-1/4 cups vegetable broth
3/4 cup water
1 beef bouillon cube
1 cup long-grain white rice
2 teaspoons Worcestershire sauce
Seasoning to taste

Artful Salad

1 medium head Boston lettuce
2 medium fresh tomatoes
2 scallions (green onions)
1/2 cup walnut pieces
3 tablespoons olive oil
2 tablespoons white wine vinegar
1/2 teaspoon granulated sugar
Seasoning to taste

Deceptive Dessert

1 small fresh ripe pineapple
2 medium ripe mangoes
1 tablespoon lemon juice
1 tablespoon granulated sugar
2 tablespoons butter
1/4 cup dark brown sugar
1 pint coffee ice cream
1/4 cup whipped cream
4 maraschino cherries

EQUIPMENT

Blender
Medium covered saucepan
Medium saucepan
Large covered skillet
Medium skillet
Large shallow bowl
Small mixing bowl
Whisk
Citrus grater
Citrus juicer
Mallet
Ice cream scoop
Plastic bag
Kitchen knives
Measuring cups and spoons
Cooking utensils

Weekend Seven Saturday

Chicanery

1. Bring water to a boil in a medium saucepan.

2. Put the peppercorns in a plastic bag, crush them with a mallet, and place them in a large shallow bowl.

3. Rinse and pat dry the chicken and dredge the breasts in the peppercorns.

4. Grate 2 teaspoons of lemon peel and juice the lemon.

5. Rinse and trim the carrots and cook them in the boiling water for 5 minutes.

6. Rinse and chop the parsley. Drain the artichokes and cut them in half.

7. Drain the carrots.

8. Melt 2 tablespoons of the butter in a large skillet and sauté the chicken until golden, about 5 minutes per side. Remove the chicken and keep it warm.

9. Melt the remaining 3 tablespoons butter in the skillet and sauté the carrots for 2 minutes. Return the chicken to the skillet, add the lemon peel, the lemon juice, the parsley, the wine, and the broth. Bring to a boil, cover, reduce the heat, and simmer for 5 minutes.

10. Fold in the artichokes, season to taste, cover, and simmer for 5 minutes more.

Tricky Rice

1. Peel and mince the shallot.

2. Heat the oil in a medium saucepan and sauté the shallot until golden, about 5 minutes.

3. Add the broth, the water, and the bouillon cube. Bring to a boil and cook, stirring, until the bouillon cube is dissolved. Add the rice and the Worcestershire sauce, season to taste, cover, reduce the heat, and simmer until the liquid is absorbed and the rice is tender, about 20 minutes.

4. Fluff with a fork before serving.

Artful Salad

1. Wash and dry the lettuce and arrange the leaves on individual salad plates. Rinse and slice the tomatoes and arrange the slices over the lettuce. Trim and chop the scallions and sprinkle them over the tomatoes. Sprinkle the walnuts over the salads.

2. In a small bowl, whisk together the oil, the vinegar, and the sugar.

3. Season to taste and drizzle the dressing over the salads.

Deceptive Dessert

1. Peel, core, and slice the pineapple into 4 thick rings. Peel, pit, and chunk the mangoes.

2. Combine the mangoes, the lemon juice, and the granulated sugar in a blender and process until smooth. Set aside until you are ready to use.

3. Melt the butter with the brown sugar in a medium skillet and sauté the pineapple rings until well glazed, about 3 minutes on each side. Set aside until you are ready to use.

4. Arrange the pineapple slices on individual dessert plates. Fill the centers with scoops of ice cream, and top with the mango sauce. Garnish with a dollop of whipped cream and a maraschino cherry.

COUNTDOWN

1. Assemble the ingredients and the equipment.
2. Do Steps 1–3 of *Deceptive Dessert*.
3. Do Steps 1–7 of *Chicanery*.
4. Do Steps 1–2 of *Artful Salad*.
5. Do Steps 1–3 of *Tricky Rice*.
6. Do Steps 8–10 of *Chicanery*.
7. Do Step 4 of *Tricky Rice*.
8. Do Step 3 of *Artful Salad*.
9. Do Step 4 of *Deceptive Dessert*.

Weekend Seven Sunday

MEAT & POULTRY

1-1/2 pounds lean boneless pork loin

FRESH PRODUCE

VEGETABLES

1 medium carrot
2 small Japanese eggplants
1/2 pound Chinese snow peas
1/2 pound mushrooms
4 ounces bean sprouts
4 radishes
1 medium onion
3 scallions (green onions)
2 cloves garlic

FRUIT

1 small orange

CANS, JARS & BOTTLES

SOUP

2 cans (14 ounces each) chicken broth
1 can (14 ounces) beef broth

VEGETABLES

1 can (6 ounces) whole baby corn

FRUIT

2 cans (11 ounces each) mandarin
   oranges

PACKAGED GOODS

INTERNATIONAL FOODS

8 ounces rice noodles

WINES & SPIRITS

2 tablespoons dry red wine

REFRIGERATED PRODUCTS

DAIRY

2 eggs

FROZEN GOODS

DESSERTS

1 pint orange sherbet

STAPLES

- ❏ Cornstarch
- ❏ Granulated sugar
- ❏ Dark brown sugar
- ❏ Vegetable oil
- ❏ Sesame oil
- ❏ Soy sauce
- ❏ Sesame seeds
- ❏ Chinese five-spice powder
- ❏ Ground cinnamon
- ❏ Ground ginger
- ❏ Pepper
- ❏ Salt
- ❏ Almond extract

Weekend Seven Sunday

MENU

Sing Song Soup

3 scallions (green onions)
1/2 pound Chinese snow peas
4 radishes
2 eggs
2 cans (14 ounces each) chicken broth
1 teaspoon soy sauce
1 tablespoon cornstarch
1/4 cup water
Seasoning to taste

Peek In Pork

1-1/2 pounds lean boneless pork loin
1 medium onion
2 cloves garlic
2 small Japanese eggplants
1 medium carrot
1/2 pound fresh mushrooms
4 ounces fresh bean sprouts
1 can (6 ounces) whole baby corn
3 tablespoons soy sauce
1/2 teaspoon ground ginger
2 tablespoons dry red wine
1 tablespoon granulated sugar
2 tablespoons vegetable oil
1 teaspoon sesame oil
2 teaspoons cornstarch
1 tablespoon water
Seasoning to taste
1 tablespoon sesame seeds

Ooh Long Noodles

1 can (14 ounces) beef broth
1/2 teaspoon Chinese five-spice powder
8 ounces rice noodles

Boo Da Zert

1 small orange
2 cans (11 ounces each) mandarin
   oranges
1/3 cup dark brown sugar
1 teaspoon almond extract
1 pint orange sherbet
1 teaspoon ground cinnamon

EQUIPMENT

Wok	Citrus grater
Large covered saucepan	Citrus juicer
Medium covered saucepan	Vegetable brush
	Vegetable peeler
Medium saucepan	Ice cream scoop
Large shallow bowl	Kitchen knives
Small mixing bowl	Measuring cups and spoons
Strainer	Cooking utensils

Sing Song Soup

1. Trim and chop the scallions. Rinse and string the snow peas. Trim and slice the radishes.

2. Beat the eggs in a small bowl.

3. Bring the broth and the soy sauce to a boil in a large saucepan.

4. Combine the cornstarch and the water and add it to the soup, stirring to blend for 1 minute.

5. Add the snow peas and the scallions. Return the soup to a boil.

6. Drizzle the egg into the soup, stirring continuously.

7. Season to taste, cover, and keep warm.

8. Distribute the radishes among individual soup bowls and ladle the soup over the radishes.

Peek In Pork

1. Rinse and pat dry the pork and cut it into thin strips. Peel and chop the onion. Peel and mince the garlic. Scrub, trim, and slice the eggplant. Peel the carrot and slice it into matchsticks. Rinse, pat dry, and slice the mushrooms. Rinse and blot the bean sprouts. Drain the corn.

2. In a large shallow bowl, combine the soy sauce, the ginger, the wine, and the sugar. Add the pork and marinate it for 20 minutes, turning occasionally to coat.

3. Heat the vegetable and sesame oils in a wok.

4. Add the onion, the garlic, the eggplants, and the carrot, and stir-fry for 2 minutes.

5. Drain the pork, reserving the marinade, and add it to the wok. Stir-fry until the meat is tender and cooked through, about 3 minutes.

6. Mix the cornstarch and the water with the reserved marinade, and add it to the wok. Add the mushrooms, the bean sprouts, and the corn, season to taste, and stir-fry until the sauce begins to thicken, about 2 minutes more.

7. Sprinkle with the sesame seeds.

Ooh Long Noodles

1. Bring the broth and the Chinese five-spice powder to a boil in a medium saucepan.

2. Add the noodles to the broth and cook until just tender, about 2 minutes.

3. Drain the noodles, return them to the saucepan, and cover to keep warm.

Boo Da Zert

1. Grate the orange peel and juice the orange.

2. Place the orange peel, the orange juice, the undrained mandarin oranges, and the brown sugar in a medium saucepan. Bring to a boil, reduce the heat, and simmer until the sauce begins to thicken, about 15 minutes.

3. Remove the pan from the heat and fold in the almond extract. Refrigerate until you are ready to serve.

4. Place scoops of sherbet in individual dessert bowls, top with the orange sauce, and sprinkle with the ground cinnamon.

COUNTDOWN

1. Assemble the ingredients and the equipment.
2. Do Steps 1–3 of *Boo Da Zert*.
3. Do Steps 1–2 of *Peek In Pork*.
4. Do Steps 1–7 of *Sing Song Soup*.
5. Do Steps 1–3 of *Ooh Long Noodles*.
6. Do Steps 3–7 of *Peek In Pork*.
7. Do Step 8 of *Sing Song Soup*.
8. Do Step 4 of *Boo Da Zert*.

Weekend Eight Saturday

SHOPPING LIST

MEAT & POULTRY
2 pounds sirloin steak

FRESH PRODUCE

VEGETABLES
2 stalks celery
1 medium head green cabbage
1 pint cherry tomatoes
1 large green bell pepper
1 large orange bell pepper
1 small jicama
1 small onion
1 large sweet onion
5 cloves garlic

HERBS
2 tablespoons chives (when chopped)
1 tablespoon dill (when chopped)
1 tablespoon parsley (when chopped)

FRUIT
2 pints strawberries

CANS, JARS & BOTTLES

SPREADS
1/3 cup red currant jelly

PACKAGED GOODS

BAKED GOODS
1 loaf French bread
4 individual tart shells

WINES & SPIRITS
2 tablespoons brandy

REFRIGERATED PRODUCTS

DAIRY
2 tablespoons sour cream
2/3 cup whipping cream

CHEESE
3/4 pound mascarpone cheese

STAPLES

- ☐ Butter
- ☐ Granulated sugar
- ☐ Powdered sugar
- ☐ Apple cider vinegar
- ☐ Rice vinegar
- ☐ Lemon juice
- ☐ Worcestershire sauce
- ☐ Mayonnaise
- ☐ Ground allspice
- ☐ Cayenne pepper
- ☐ Ground cumin
- ☐ Pepper
- ☐ Salt

Weekend Eight Saturday

MENU

Steak 'Em Up

2 pounds sirloin steak
1 small onion
1 clove garlic
1/4 teaspoon ground cumin
1 teaspoon lemon juice
1 teaspoon apple cider vinegar
1 teaspoon Worcestershire sauce
Seasoning to taste
1 pint cherry tomatoes
1 large green bell pepper
1 large orange bell pepper
1 large sweet onion

Against the Slaw

1 medium head green cabbage
1 small jicama
2 stalks celery
2 tablespoons fresh chives (when chopped)
1 tablespoon fresh dill (when chopped)
1 tablespoon fresh parsley (when chopped)
2 tablespoons mayonnaise
2 tablespoons sour cream
3 tablespoons rice vinegar
1/2 teaspoon granulated sugar
1/2 teaspoon cayenne pepper

Gimme the Dough

4 cloves garlic
4 tablespoons butter
1/2 teaspoon ground allspice
1 loaf French bread

Just Desserts

3/4 pound mascarpone cheese
2 pints fresh strawberries
1/3 cup red currant jelly
2 tablespoons brandy
2/3 cup whipping cream
3 tablespoons powdered sugar
4 individual tart shells

EQUIPMENT

Electric mixer
2 small saucepans
8 large skewers
Large shallow bowl
Large mixing bowl
Medium mixing bowl
Small mixing bowl
Whisk
Vegetable grater
Vegetable peeler
Plastic wrap
Aluminum foil
Kitchen knives
Measuring cups and spoons
Cooking utensils

Weekend Eight Saturday

Steak 'Em Up

1. Prepare the grill.

2. Trim any excess fat from the steak and cut it into 16 cubes.

3. Peel and grate the small onion. Peel and mince the garlic.

4. In a large shallow bowl, combine the onion, the garlic, the cumin, the lemon juice, the vinegar, and the Worcestershire sauce. Season to taste.

5. Roll the beef cubes in the mixture until well coated on all sides.

6. Set the beef aside for 30 minutes.

7. Rinse and stem the tomatoes. Rinse, stem, seed, and chunk the bell peppers. Peel the sweet onion and cut it into 8 wedges.

8. Thread 8 large skewers with the beef, the tomatoes, the peppers, and the onion.

9. Grill, turning occasionally, until done to taste, about 10 minutes for rare.

Against the Slaw

1. Trim and grate the cabbage. Peel, trim, and grate the jicama. Rinse, trim, and mince the celery. Rinse and chop the chives. Rinse and chop the dill. Rinse

and chop the parsley. Combine the vegetables in a large bowl.

2. In a small bowl, whisk together the mayonnaise, the sour cream, the vinegar, the sugar, and the cayenne pepper.

3. Toss the salad with the dressing, cover the bowl with plastic wrap, and refrigerate it until you are ready to serve.

Gimme the Dough

1. Peel and mince the garlic.

2. Melt the butter in a small saucepan and sauté the garlic for 2 minutes.

3. Blend in the allspice.

4. Cut the bread in half lengthwise. Spread both halves with the garlic mixture. Reassemble the loaf and wrap it in aluminum foil.

5. Place the wrapped bread at the back of the grill to heat through.

Just Desserts

1. Set the mascarpone out to soften.

2. Chill a medium bowl and the beaters of an electric mixer in the refrigerator for at least 10 minutes.

3. Wash and hull the strawberries. Reserve 4 whole berries for garnish and slice the remaining berries.

4. In a small saucepan, melt the red currant jelly with the brandy. Set the pan aside.

5. In the chilled bowl, whip the cream until stiff. Fold in the mascarpone. Fold in the powdered sugar.

6. Lightly cover the bottom of individual tart shells with the cheese mixture. Top with the sliced berries. Drizzle the jelly mixture over the berries. Top with the remaining cheese mixture. Garnish with a whole berry, stem side down. Refrigerate until you are ready to serve.

COUNTDOWN

1. Assemble the ingredients and the equipment.
2. Do Steps 1–6 of *Just Desserts*.
3. Do Steps 1–6 of *Steak 'Em Up*.
4. Do Steps 1–3 of *Against the Slaw*.
5. Do Steps 1–3 of *Gimme the Dough*.
6. Do Steps 7–9 of *Steak 'Em Up*.
7. Do Steps 4–5 of *Gimme the Dough*.

Weekend Eight Sunday

MEAT & POULTRY

1-1/2 pounds boneless, skinless
  chicken breast

FRESH PRODUCE

VEGETABLES

1 pound green beans
1 package (16 ounces) spinach
2 stalks celery
1 medium tomato
1 medium onion
1 small sweet onion

HERBS

1/4 cup chives (when chopped)

FRUIT

1 small ripe cantaloupe
1/4 small seedless watermelon
2 large ripe nectarines
1 medium orange
1 small lemon
1 pint blueberries

CANS, JARS & BOTTLES

SOUP

2 cans (14 ounces each) chicken broth
1 can (10-1/2 ounces) beef consommé

PACKAGED GOODS

BAKED GOODS

4 English muffins

DRIED FRUITS & NUTS

1/2 cup raisins

WINES & SPIRITS

2 tablespoons dry sherry

REFRIGERATED PRODUCTS

DAIRY

1/2 cup plain yogurt

CHEESE

1 container (4 ounces) herbed
  cream cheese spread

DELI

6 slices bacon

STAPLES

❑ Granulated sugar
❑ Vegetable oil
❑ Balsamic vinegar
❑ Raspberry vinegar
❑ White Worcestershire sauce
❑ Dijon mustard
❑ Poppy seeds
❑ Bay leaf
❑ Dried dill
❑ Dried thyme
❑ Ground nutmeg
❑ Paprika
❑ Pepper
❑ Salt
❑ Orange extract

Weekend Eight Sunday

Stunning Soup

1 small lemon
1 medium onion
2 stalks celery
1/4 cup fresh chives (when chopped)
2 cans (14 ounces each) chicken broth
1 can (10-1/2 ounces) beef consommé
1 tablespoon white Worcestershire sauce
2 tablespoons dry sherry
1 bay leaf
1-1/4 teaspoons dried thyme
1/2 teaspoon granulated sugar
Seasoning to taste

Salad Daze

1-1/2 pounds boneless, skinless chicken
   breast
1 pound fresh green beans
6 slices bacon
1 small sweet onion
1 package (16 ounces) fresh spinach
1/2 cup raisins
Seasoning to taste
1/3 cup balsamic vinegar
2 teaspoons Dijon mustard
1/2 teaspoon ground nutmeg

Muffin Mania

1 container (4 ounces) herbed cream
   cheese spread
4 English muffins
1 medium fresh tomato
1 tablespoon dried dill
1/2 teaspoon paprika

Infruitable

1 medium orange
1/4 cup granulated sugar
1/2 cup plain yogurt
1 tablespoon vegetable oil
2 tablespoons raspberry vinegar
1 teaspoon orange extract
1 tablespoon poppy seeds
1/4 small seedless watermelon
1 small ripe cantaloupe
2 large ripe nectarines
1 pint fresh blueberries

EQUIPMENT

2 large saucepans
Large skillet
Strainer
2 large mixing bowls
2 small mixing bowls
Citrus grater
Citrus juicer
Plastic wrap
Kitchen knives
Measuring cups and spoons
Cooking utensils

Stunning Soup

1. Grate the lemon peel and juice the lemon. Peel and quarter the onion. Rinse the celery and cut the stalks in half. Rinse and chop the chives.

2. In a large saucepan, combine the lemon peel, the lemon juice, the onion, the celery, the broth, the consommé, the Worcestershire sauce, the sherry, the bay leaf, the thyme, and the sugar.

3. Bring the mixture to a boil. Reduce the heat and simmer for 15 minutes.

4. Strain the soup, discarding the vegetables and the bay leaf.

5. Garnish with the chives.

Salad Daze

1. Rinse, pat dry, and cube the chicken. Rinse and trim the green beans and cut them into 1-inch pieces.

2. Bring water to a boil in a large saucepan.

3. Add the chicken and the green beans to the saucepan, and cook until the chicken is tender and opaque throughout and the beans are crisp-tender, about 7 minutes.

4. Dice the bacon. Peel and chop the onion. Rinse, pat dry, and stem the spinach.

5. Drain the chicken and beans, rinse well under cold water, and place them in a large bowl. Fold in the raisins.

6. Sauté the bacon in a large skillet until it is almost crisp, about 5 minutes. Add the spinach, season to taste, and sauté until the spinach wilts, about 2 minutes. Blend in the vinegar, the mustard, and the nutmeg.

7. Toss the spinach mixture with the chicken mixture.

Muffin Mania

1. Set the cream cheese spread out to soften.

2. Split and toast the muffins.

3. Rinse and chop the tomato.

4. In a small bowl, combine the tomato, the dill, and the paprika.

5. Spread the muffins lightly with the softened cheese, and top with the tomato mixture.

Infruitable

1. Grate 1 tablespoon of orange peel and juice the orange.

2. In a small bowl, combine the orange peel, the orange juice, the sugar, the yogurt, the oil, the vinegar, the orange extract, and the poppy seeds. Blend well. Cover the bowl with plastic wrap and refrigerate it until you are ready to use.

3. Chunk the melons. Rinse, pit, and slice the nectarines. Rinse and blot the blueberries. Combine the fruit in a large bowl, cover it with plastic wrap, and refrigerate it until you are ready to use.

4. Distribute the fruit among individual dessert dishes and top with the sauce.

COUNTDOWN

1. Assemble the ingredients and the equipment.
2. Do Steps 1–3 of *Infruitable*.
3. Do Steps 1–3 of *Stunning Soup*.
4. Do Step 1 of *Muffin Mania*.
5. Do Steps 1–7 of *Salad Daze*.
6. Do Steps 4–5 of *Stunning Soup*.
7. Do Steps 2–5 of *Muffin Mania*.
8. Do Step 4 of *Infruitable*.

Weekend Nine Saturday

FISH

1 whole salmon (about 6 pounds)

FRESH PRODUCE

VEGETABLES

2 ears corn on the cob
1 stalk celery
1/4 pound mushrooms
1 medium head Boston lettuce
3 medium tomatoes
3 large cucumbers
1 medium green bell pepper
1 small onion
1 large sweet onion
3 scallions (green onions)
1 clove garlic

HERBS

6 dill sprigs
1/2 cup dill (when chopped)
2 tablespoons parsley (when chopped)

FRUIT

2 large lemons
1 pint strawberries

CANS, JARS & BOTTLES

1 can (14 ounces) vegetable broth

PACKAGED GOODS

PASTA, RICE & GRAINS
1 cup long-grain white rice

BAKED GOODS
4 almond macaroons

DRIED FRUITS & NUTS
1/4 cup sliced almonds

WINES & SPIRITS

1/2 cup dry white wine
3 tablespoons Grand Marnier

REFRIGERATED PRODUCTS

DAIRY

2-1/4 cups sour cream
1/2 cup whipping cream

FROZEN PRODUCTS

DESSERTS

1 pint French vanilla ice cream

STAPLES

❑ Butter
❑ Granulated sugar
❑ Powdered sugar
❑ Vegetable oil
❑ Red wine vinegar
❑ Lemon juice
❑ Worcestershire sauce
❑ Dried oregano
❑ Ground cumin
❑ Paprika
❑ Pepper
❑ Salt

Weekend Nine Saturday

MENU

Salmon Snead

3 large cucumbers
1/2 cup fresh dill (when chopped)
2-1/4 cups sour cream
2 tablespoons lemon juice
3/4 teaspoon salt
3/8 teaspoon paprika
1 whole salmon (about 6 pounds)
1 large sweet onion
2 large lemons
6 fresh dill sprigs
1/2 cup dry white wine
1 teaspoon Worcestershire sauce
Seasoning to taste

Nick Rice

1 clove garlic
1 small onion
1 stalk celery
1/4 pound fresh mushrooms
2 tablespoons butter
1 cup long-grain white rice
1 can (14 ounces) vegetable broth
1/4 cup water
1/2 teaspoon ground cumin
Seasoning to taste

Putting Greens

1 tablespoon granulated sugar
2 ears fresh corn on the cob
1 medium head Boston lettuce
3 medium fresh tomatoes
1 medium green bell pepper
3 scallions (green onions)

2 tablespoons fresh parsley (when chopped)
3 tablespoons vegetable oil
2 tablespoons red wine vinegar
1/2 teaspoon dried oregano
Seasoning to taste

Berry Middlecoff

1 pint French vanilla ice cream
1 teaspoon butter
1/4 cup sliced almonds
4 almond macaroons
1/2 cup whipping cream
3 tablespoons Grand Marnier
1 pint fresh strawberries
3 tablespoons granulated sugar
1-1/2 teaspoons powdered sugar

EQUIPMENT

Electric mixer	Vegetable brush
Large saucepan	Vegetable peeler
2 medium covered saucepans	Mallet
Small skillet	Aluminum foil
1-quart soufflé dish	Plastic wrap
Large mixing bowl	Plastic bag
Medium mixing bowl	Kitchen knives
Small mixing bowl	Measuring cups and spoons
Whisk	Cooking utensils

Weekend Nine Saturday

Salmon Snead

1. Prepare the grill.

2. Peel and mince the cucumbers and drain them well. Rinse and chop the dill.

3. In a medium bowl, beat the sour cream with the lemon juice until stiff. Blend in the salt and paprika. Fold in the cucumbers and the dill. Cover the bowl with plastic wrap and refrigerate it until you are ready to use.

4. Rinse and pat dry the fish. Peel and thinly slice the onion. Scrub and thinly slice the lemons. Rinse and pat dry the dill sprigs.

5. Lay the fish on a long sheet of aluminum foil.

6. Combine the wine and the Worcestershire sauce, and drizzle it over the fish.

7. Spread the onion slices, the lemon slices, and the dill sprigs over the fish. Season to taste.

8. Seal the fish tightly in the foil and grill until the fish flakes easily with a fork, 40 to 50 minutes, depending on the size of the fish and the heat of the grill.

9. Remove the salmon from the grill, open the foil, and let the fish cool to room temperature. Serve with the sauce.

Nick Rice

1. Peel and mince the garlic. Peel and mince the onion. Rinse, trim, and chop the celery. Rinse, pat dry, and chop the mushrooms.

2. Melt the butter in a medium saucepan and sauté the garlic, the onion, and the celery for 1 minute. Add the mushrooms and sauté for 1 minute. Add the rice and sauté until lightly browned, about 3 minutes. Add the broth, the water, and the cumin. Season to taste and bring to a boil. Cover, reduce the heat, and simmer until the liquid is absorbed and the rice is tender, about 20 minutes.

3. Fluff the rice with a fork.

Putting Greens

1. Bring a small amount of water and 2 teaspoons of the sugar to a boil in a large saucepan.

2. Shuck, scrub, and trim the corn. Blanch it in the boiling water for 2 minutes. Drain and rinse to cool.

3. Wash and dry the lettuce and arrange the leaves on individual salad plates. Rinse and slice the tomatoes and arrange the slices over the lettuce. Rinse, stem, seed, and slice the bell pepper and arrange the slices over the tomatoes.

4. Trim and chop the scallions and sprinkle them over the salads. Cut the corn from the cob and sprinkle it over the salads. Rinse and chop the parsley.

5. In a small bowl, whisk together the oil, the vinegar, the remaining teaspoon of sugar, and the oregano. Season to taste.

6. Drizzle the dressing over the salads. Sprinkle with the parsley.

Berry Middlecoff

1. Chill a large bowl and the beaters of an electric mixer in the refrigerator for at least 10 minutes.

2. Set the ice cream out to soften.

3. Melt the butter in a small skillet and sauté the almonds until lightly golden, about 3 minutes. Remove the pan from the heat and set it aside.

4. Place the macaroons in a plastic bag and crush them lightly with a mallet.

5. In the chilled bowl, whip the cream until stiff. Fold in the softened ice cream. Fold in the macaroons. Fold in 1-1/2 table-spoons of the Grand Marnier. Turn the mixture into a 1-quart soufflé dish, cover with plastic wrap, and freeze for at least 1 hour.

6. Rinse, hull, and slice the strawberries. Combine the berries and the granulated sugar in a medium saucepan. Toss to coat and heat through.

7. Remove the berries from the heat and stir in the remaining 1-1/2 tablespoons Grand Marnier. Cover to keep warm.

8. Remove the soufflé from the freezer and let it stand for 10 minutes.

9. Sprinkle the soufflé with the toasted almonds and the powdered sugar. Serve with the warm strawberry sauce.

COUNTDOWN

1. Assemble the ingredients and the equipment.
2. Do Steps 1–5 of *Berry Middlecoff*.
3. Do Steps 1–8 of *Salmon Snead*.
4. Do Steps 1–2 of *Nick Rice*.
5. Do Steps 1–5 of *Putting Greens*.
6. Do Steps 6–7 of *Berry Middlecoff*.
7. Do Step 9 of *Salmon Snead*.
8. Do Step 3 of *Nick Rice*.
9. Do Step 6 of *Putting Greens*.
10. Do Steps 8–9 of *Berry Middlecoff*.

Weekend Nine Sunday

SHOPPING LIST

MEAT & POULTRY
1 pound sweet Italian sausage

FRESH PRODUCE

VEGETABLES
1 medium zucchini
3 medium carrots
1 stalk celery
1 medium head lettuce
1 medium red bell pepper
1 medium orange bell pepper
1 small bunch radishes
1 medium onion
3 scallions (green onions)
2 cloves garlic

HERBS
1/4 cup chives (when chopped)
3 tablespoons parsley (when chopped)

FRUIT
4 large ripe peaches

CANS, JARS & BOTTLES
2 cans (14 ounces each) beef broth
1 can (14 ounces) chicken broth

VEGETABLES
1 can (28 ounces) diced tomatoes

FRUIT
4 maraschino cherries

CONDIMENTS
1 tablespoon capers

PACKAGED GOODS

PASTA, RICE & GRAINS
1 cup orzo

BAKED GOODS
1 small loaf Italian bread
4 large sugar cookies

DRIED FRUITS & NUTS
2 tablespoons pecan pieces

WINES & SPIRITS
3 tablespoons dry sherry

REFRIGERATED PRODUCTS

DAIRY
1 pint peach yogurt

STAPLES

❏ Butter
❏ Dark brown sugar
❏ Olive oil
❏ White wine vinegar
❏ Lemon juice
❏ Grated Parmesan cheese
❏ Dried basil
❏ Dried tarragon
❏ Italian seasoning
❏ Pepper
❏ Salt
❏ Vanilla extract

Weekend Nine Sunday

Soupercalifragilistic-expealidocious

1 pound sweet Italian sausage
3 medium carrots
1 medium onion
1 stalk celery
3 tablespoons fresh parsley (when chopped)
1 clove garlic
2 tablespoons butter
2 cans (14 ounces each) beef broth
1 can (14 ounces) chicken broth
3 tablespoons dry sherry
1 can (28 ounces) diced tomatoes
1 cup orzo
1 teaspoon Italian seasoning
Grated Parmesan cheese

Juliennedrews

1 medium head lettuce
1 medium zucchini
1 medium red bell pepper
1 medium orange bell pepper
1 small bunch radishes
3 scallions (green onions)
1 tablespoon capers
3 tablespoons olive oil
2 tablespoons white wine vinegar
1/2 teaspoon dried tarragon
Seasoning to taste

Aca-dough-my Award

1 small loaf Italian bread
1 clove garlic
1/4 cup fresh chives (when chopped)
6 tablespoons olive oil
1 teaspoon dried basil

Chim Chim Cherry

4 large ripe peaches
2 tablespoons lemon juice
4 large sugar cookies
1 pint peach yogurt
1 teaspoon vanilla extract
2 tablespoons pecan pieces
1 tablespoon dark brown sugar
4 maraschino cherries

EQUIPMENT

Dutch oven	Mallet
Large mixing bowl	Plastic bag
3 small mixing bowls	Kitchen knives
Whisk	Measuring cups and spoons
Vegetable peeler	Cooking utensils
Pastry brush	

Weekend Nine Sunday

Soupercalifragilistic-expealidocious

1. Place the sausage in the freezer for 10 minutes.

2. Slice the sausage into 1/4-inch rounds. Peel and chop the carrots. Peel and chop the onion. Rinse, trim, and chop the celery. Rinse and chop the parsley. Peel and mince the garlic.

3. Place the sausage in a Dutch oven and sauté until browned, about 10 minutes.

4. Remove the sausage and set it aside.

5. Drain off any excess fat from the Dutch oven.

6. Add the butter, the carrots, the celery, and the onion to the Dutch oven, and sauté until the vegetables are softened, about 8 minutes.

7. Return the sausage to the Dutch oven. Add the broth, the sherry, the parsley, and the undrained tomatoes. Fold in the orzo and the Italian seasoning.

8. Bring the mixture to a boil, reduce the heat, and simmer for 20 minutes.

9. Sprinkle with the Parmesan cheese.

Julienndrews

1. Wash and dry the lettuce and tear it into bite-sized pieces. Rinse, trim, and julienne the zucchini. Rinse, stem, seed, and julienne the bell peppers. Trim and slice the radishes. Rinse, trim, and chop the scallions. Combine the vegetables in a large bowl.

2. In a small bowl, whisk together the capers, the oil, the vinegar, and the tarragon. Season to taste.

3. Toss the salad with the dressing.

Aca-dough-my Award

1. Cut the bread into thick slices and toast it on both sides.

2. Peel and mince the garlic. Rinse and chop the chives.

3. In a small bowl, combine the oil, the garlic, the basil, and the chives.

4. Brush the oil mixture over the warm bread.

Chim Chim Cherry

1. Rinse, pit, and halve the peaches. Scoop out a teaspoon of the flesh from each peach half to form a larger cavity. Place the flesh in a small bowl. Sprinkle the peach halves with the lemon juice and place them in individual dessert bowls.

2. Place the cookies in a plastic bag, crush them lightly with a mallet, and add them to the peach flesh. Fold in the yogurt and the vanilla. Spoon the mixture into the peach halves, mounding it over the whole half of the peach. Sprinkle with the pecan pieces and the brown sugar, and top with a maraschino cherry. Refrigerate until you are ready to serve.

COUNTDOWN

1. Assemble the ingredients and the equipment.
2. Do Step 1 of *Soupercalifragilistic-expealidocious*.
3. Do Steps 1–2 of *Chim Chim Cherry*.
4. Do Steps 2–8 of *Soupercalifragilistic-expealidocious*.
5. Do Steps 1–2 of *Juliennedrews*.
6. Do Steps 1–4 of *Aca-dough-my Award*.
7. Do Step 3 of *Juliennedrews*.
8. Do Step 9 of *Soupercalifragilisticex-pealidocious*.

Weekend Ten Saturday

SHOPPING LIST

MEAT & POULTRY

3 pounds chicken pieces

FRESH PRODUCE

VEGETABLES

1 pound green beans
1/2 pound mushrooms
1 small tomato
1 medium shallot
1 clove garlic

HERBS

1/4 cup chives (when chopped)
2 tablespoons parsley (when chopped)

FRUIT

2 large oranges
1 large lemon

CANS, JARS & BOTTLES

DESSERT & BAKING NEEDS

1/4 cup marshmallow crème

PACKAGED GOODS

PASTA, RICE & GRAINS

1 cup acini di pepe pasta

BAKED GOODS

1 package (9 ounces) chocolate wafers

DESSERT & BAKING NEEDS

1 square (1 ounce) semisweet chocolate

WINES & SPIRITS

2 tablespoons dry white wine
2 tablespoons brandy
2 tablespoons Kahlúa

REFRIGERATED PRODUCTS

DAIRY

1/4 cup whipping cream
3 eggs

CHEESE

1/4 pound Swiss cheese
3 packages (8 ounces each) cream
cheese

DELI

3 slices prosciutto

STAPLES

- ❐ Butter
- ❐ Cornstarch
- ❐ Granulated sugar
- ❐ Olive oil
- ❐ Vegetable oil
- ❐ Lemon juice
- ❐ Lime juice
- ❐ Coffee
- ❐ Chicken bouillon cube
- ❐ Dried tarragon
- ❐ Dried thyme
- ❐ Paprika
- ❐ Pepper
- ❐ Salt
- ❐ Vanilla extract

Weekend Ten Saturday

Admirable Bird

3 pounds chicken pieces
2 large oranges
1 large lemon
1/4 pound Swiss cheese
2 tablespoons fresh parsley (when chopped)
4 tablespoons butter
2 tablespoons vegetable oil
1/2 teaspoon dried tarragon
1/2 cup whipping cream
2 tablespoons brandy
2 tablespoons dry white wine
Seasoning to taste
1 tablespoon cornstarch
1/4 teaspoon paprika

Ricicles

1 clove garlic
1/4 cup fresh chives (when chopped)
1 small fresh tomato
1 chicken bouillon cube
1 cup acini di pepe pasta
2 tablespoons butter
Seasoning to taste

Polar Beans

1 medium shallot
1 pound fresh green beans
1/2 pound fresh mushrooms
3 slices prosciutto
3 tablespoons olive oil
1-1/2 tablespoons lime juice
1/2 teaspoon dried thyme
Seasoning to taste

Arctic Circle

1/4 cup strong coffee (when brewed)
3 packages (8 ounces each) cream cheese
1 package (9 ounces) chocolate wafers
3 tablespoons butter
3/4 cup + 1-1/2 tablespoons granulated sugar
1 square (1 ounce) semisweet chocolate
2 tablespoons Kahlúa
1/4 cup whipping cream
1 teaspoon vanilla extract
3 eggs
1/2 teaspoon lemon juice
1/4 cup marshmallow crème

EQUIPMENT

Electric mixer
Medium covered saucepan
Small saucepan
Large covered skillet
Large skillet
Small skillet
9 × 13-inch glass baking dish
Springform pan
Large mixing bowl
Medium mixing bowl

Strainer
Whisk
Cheese grater
Citrus grater
Citrus juicer
Plastic wrap
Plastic bag
Mallet
Kitchen knives
Measuring cups and spoons
Cooking utensils

Admirable Bird

1. Rinse and pat dry the chicken pieces.

2. Grate 1 teaspoon of peel from one of the oranges and juice the oranges to 3/4 cup. Grate 1 teaspoon of peel from the lemon and juice the lemon to 1/4 cup. Grate the cheese. Rinse and chop the parsley.

3. Melt the butter with the oil in a large skillet and sauté the chicken until golden and almost cooked through, about 20 minutes. Transfer the chicken to a 9 × 13-inch glass baking dish.

4. Preheat the oven to 350°F.

5. To the skillet, add the orange peel, 1/2 cup of the orange juice, the lemon peel, the lemon juice, and the tarragon. Cook, stirring, until well blended. Whisk in the cream. Whisk in the brandy and the wine. Season to taste.

6. Dissolve the cornstarch in the remaining 1/4 cup orange juice and whisk the mixture into the skillet. Cook, stirring, until the sauce begins to thicken.

7. Pour the sauce over the chicken, sprinkle with the cheese, the parsley, and the paprika, and bake for 30 minutes.

Ricicles

1. Peel and mince the garlic. Rinse and chop the chives. Rinse and chop the tomato.

2. In a medium saucepan, bring water for the pasta to a boil. Add the bouillon cube.

3. Cook the pasta in the boiling water until it is almost tender, about 5 minutes.

4. Drain the pasta and return it to the saucepan. Cover to keep warm.

5. Melt the butter in a small skillet and sauté the garlic and the tomato for 2 minutes. Fold in the chives, season to taste, and toss with the pasta.

Polar Beans

1. Peel and mince the shallot. Rinse and trim the beans. Rinse, pat dry, and slice the mushrooms. Chop the proscuitto.

2. Heat the oil in a large skillet and sauté the shallot for 2 minutes. Add the beans and the mushrooms, and sauté for 4 minutes. Add the prosciutto and sauté for 1 minute more. Stir in the lime juice and the thyme, and season to taste. Cover to keep warm.

Arctic Circle

1. Brew the coffee.

2. Set the cream cheese out to soften. Grease a springform pan.

3. Place the wafers in a plastic bag and crush them with a mallet. Melt the butter.

4. In a medium bowl, combine the wafer crumbs, the butter, and 1-1/2 tablespoons

of the sugar. Turn the mixture into the springform pan, pressing it firmly and evenly onto the bottom and up the sides. Refrigerate for 10 minutes.

5. Preheat the oven to 350°F.

6. Bake the cake crust for 8 minutes.

7. In a small saucepan, combine the brewed coffee and the chocolate, and stir until the chocolate is melted and the mixture is smooth. Stir in the Kahlúa.

8. In a large bowl, beat the cream cheese with an electric mixer until smooth and fluffy. Beat in the remaining 3/4 cup sugar, the cream, and the vanilla. Beat in the eggs, one at a time. Fold in the coffee mixture. Fold in the lemon juice.

9. Turn the mixture into the crust, and bake until the sides are firm when tapped with a spoon and the center is soft, about 35 minutes.

10. Remove from the oven, and allow to cool for 20 minutes. Cover the pan loosely with plastic wrap and refrigerate it for at least 2 hours.

11. Remove the sides of the springform pan, and garnish with dollops of marshmallow crème.

COUNTDOWN

1. Assemble the ingredients and the equipment.
2. Do Steps 1–10 of *Arctic Circle*.
3. Do Steps 1–7 of *Admirable Bird*.
4. Do Steps 1–2 of *Ricicles*.
5. Do Step 1 of *Polar Beans*.
6. Do Step 3 of *Ricicles*.
7. Do Step 2 of *Polar Beans*.
8. Do Steps 4–5 of *Ricicles*.
9. Do Step 11 of *Arctic Circle*.

Weekend Ten Sunday

SHOPPING LIST

FRESH PRODUCE

VEGETABLES
1 medium carrot
2 stalks celery
1 medium head lettuce
1 medium cucumber
1 medium onion
1 small red onion
1 clove garlic

HERBS
3 tablespoons chives (when chopped)

FRUIT
1/2 pound seedless green grapes
1/2 pound seedless red grapes

PACKAGED GOODS

PASTA, RICE & GRAINS
1 pound curly egg noodles

BAKED GOODS
4 individual tart shells

REFRIGERATED PRODUCTS

DAIRY
1-1/2 cups milk
1/2 cup sour cream
2 eggs

CHEESE
1/2 cup small-curd cottage cheese
1 cup shredded Colby/Monterey Jack
   cheese

FROZEN GOODS

VEGETABLES
1 package (10 ounces) green peas

DESSERTS
1 pint lemon yogurt

STAPLES

❑ Butter
❑ Flour
❑ Baking powder
❑ Granulated sugar
❑ Powdered sugar
❑ Olive oil
❑ Balsamic vinegar
❑ Rice vinegar
❑ Lemon juice
❑ White Worcestershire sauce
❑ Grated Parmesan cheese
❑ Plain breadcrumbs
❑ Dried oregano
❑ Ground cinnamon
❑ Pepper
❑ Salt

Noodle In a Haystack

1 package (10 ounces) frozen green peas
1 medium onion
1 egg
1 cup milk
1 pound curly egg noodles
2 tablespoons butter
2 tablespoons flour
1/2 cup small-curd cottage cheese
1 cup shredded Colby/Monterey Jack cheese
1 teaspoon white Worcestershire sauce
Seasoning to taste
1/4 cup plain breadcrumbs
2 tablespoons grated Parmesan cheese

Beleaf It or Not

1 medium head lettuce
1 medium cucumber
1 medium carrot
2 stalks celery
1 small red onion
1 clove garlic
3 tablespoons olive oil
1-1/2 tablespoons rice vinegar
2 teaspoons balsamic vinegar
1/4 teaspoon dried oregano
1/2 teaspoon granulated sugar
Seasoning to taste

Yokels

1/2 cup sour cream
1/2 cup milk

4 tablespoons butter
3 tablespoons fresh chives (when chopped)
2 cups flour
1 tablespoon baking powder
1/4 teaspoon salt
1 egg

Grapes of Wrath

1/2 pound seedless green grapes
1/2 pound seedless red grapes
2 tablespoons lemon juice
1/2 teaspoon ground cinnamon
1/4 cup powdered sugar
1 pint lemon frozen yogurt
4 individual tart shells

EQUIPMENT

Stockpot	Whisk
Medium skillet	Vegetable peeler
2-quart casserole	Vegetable grater
Muffin tin	Ice cream scoop
Colander	Kitchen knives
2 large mixing bowls	Measuring cups and spoons
2 medium mixing bowls	Cooking utensils
4 small mixing bowls	

Weekend Ten Sunday

RECIPES

Noodle In a Haystack

1. Set the peas in a small bowl of hot water to thaw.

2. Preheat the oven to 400°F. Butter a 2-quart casserole. Bring water for the noodles to a boil in a stockpot.

3. Peel and chop the onion.

4. In a small bowl, beat the egg with the milk.

5. Cook the noodles until they are almost tender, about 8 minutes.

6. Melt the butter in a medium skillet and sauté the onion for 2 minutes. Stir in the flour. Stir in the egg mixture. Bring to a boil, reduce the heat, fold in the cottage cheese and the Colby/Monterey Jack cheese, and simmer until the cheeses are melted and the sauce is well blended. Blend in the Worcestershire sauce and season to taste.

7. Drain the noodles, and return them to the stockpot. Fold in the peas. Add the cheese sauce to the noodles and peas and combine. Pour the noodle mixture into the casserole, and sprinkle with the breadcrumbs and the Parmesan cheese.

8. Bake until hot and bubbly, about 20 minutes.

Beleaf It or Not

1. Wash and dry the lettuce and tear it into bite-sized pieces. Scrub and slice the cucumber. Peel and grate the carrot. Rinse, trim, and slice the celery. Peel and thinly slice the onion. Combine the vegetables in a large bowl. Peel and mince the garlic.

2. In a small bowl, whisk together the garlic, the oil, the vinegars, the oregano, and the sugar. Season to taste and toss with the salad.

Yokels

1. Set the sour cream and milk out for 20 minutes.

2. Grease a muffin tin. Melt the butter. Rinse and chop the chives.

3. In a large bowl, combine the flour, the baking powder, and the salt.

4. In a medium bowl, combine the sour cream, the milk, the butter, and the chives. Add the egg and blend well.

5. Combine the egg mixture with the flour mixture. Divide the batter evenly among the muffin cups.

6. Bake at 400°F until a toothpick inserted in the center comes out clean, about 15 minutes.

Grapes of Wrath

1. Wash, dry, stem, and halve the grapes, and place them in a medium bowl.

2. In a small bowl, combine the lemon juice, the cinnamon, and the powdered sugar. Pour the mixture over the grapes and stir to combine. Refrigerate the mixture until you are ready to use.

3. Place scoops of frozen yogurt into 4 individual tart shells and spoon the grape mixture over the tops.

COUNTDOWN

1. Assemble the ingredients and the equipment.
2. Do Steps 1–2 of *Yokels*.
3. Do Steps 1–2 of *Grapes of Wrath*.
4. Do Steps 1–8 of *Noodle In a Haystack*.
5. Do Steps 3–6 of *Yokels*.
6. Do Steps 1–2 of *Beleaf It or Not*.
7. Do Step 3 of *Grapes of Wrath*.

Weekend Eleven Saturday

MEAT & POULTRY

1 crown roast of pork (about 9 ribs)

FRESH PRODUCE

VEGETABLES

1 pound Brussels sprouts
2 stalks celery
1 head Boston lettuce
3 medium tomatoes
1 large red bell pepper
3 scallions (green onions)
2 cloves garlic

HERBS

4 mint sprigs

CANS, JARS & BOTTLES

SOUP

1 can (14 ounces) chicken broth

PACKAGED GOODS

PASTA, RICE & GRAINS

1 cup long-grain white rice

DRIED FRUITS & NUTS

1/4 pound apricots
1/2 cup pecan bits

DESSERT & BAKING NEEDS

1/4 cup rock candy (when crushed)

WINES & SPIRITS

1/2 cup dry white wine
1/4 cup dry sherry
1 split champagne

FROZEN GOODS

DESSERTS

1 pint raspberry sherbet

STAPLES

- [ ] Butter
- [ ] Dark brown sugar
- [ ] Vegetable oil
- [ ] Rice vinegar
- [ ] Lime juice
- [ ] Dijon mustard
- [ ] Dried rosemary
- [ ] Dried sage
- [ ] Dried thyme
- [ ] Paprika
- [ ] Pepper
- [ ] Saffron threads
- [ ] Salt

Weekend Eleven Saturday

MENU

Jewel In the Crown

2 cloves garlic
1 teaspoon dried sage
1/2 teaspoon dried rosemary
1/2 teaspoon dried thyme
Seasoning to taste
1 crown roast of pork (about 9 ribs)
6 tablespoons butter
1/2 cup dry white wine
1/4 pound dried apricots
2 stalks celery
1 can (14 ounces) chicken broth
1/4 cup dry sherry
1 teaspoon saffron threads
1 cup long-grain white rice
1/2 cup pecan bits

Rubies and Emeralds

1 pound Brussels sprouts
1 large red bell pepper
1 tablespoon vegetable oil
2 tablespoons lime juice
2 teaspoons dark brown sugar
Seasoning to taste

Diamonds In the Roughage

1 head Boston lettuce
3 medium fresh tomatoes
3 scallions (green onions)
1/4 cup rock candy (when crushed)
3 tablespoons vegetable oil
2 tablespoons rice vinegar

1/2 teaspoon Dijon mustard
1/4 teaspoon paprika
Seasoning to taste

Champagne Sparklers

1 split champagne
4 fresh mint sprigs
1 pint raspberry sherbet

EQUIPMENT

Double boiler	Meat thermometer
Medium covered saucepan	Pastry brush
Small saucepan	Mallet
Medium skillet	Plastic bag
Small skillet	Aluminum foil
Large roasting pan	Ice cream scoop
Roasting rack	Kitchen knives
Steamer insert	Measuring cups and spoons
2 small mixing bowls	Cooking utensils
Whisk	

Jewel In the Crown

1. Preheat the oven to 350°F.

2. Peel and mince the garlic. In a small bowl, combine the garlic, the sage, the rosemary, and the thyme. Season to taste. Rub the mixture into the pork. Place the pork on a rack in a large roasting pan. Cover the rib bones with aluminum foil to keep them from browning. Stuff the center of the pork with crumpled aluminum foil to maintain the crown's shape.

3. Roast the pork until a meat thermometer stuck in the fleshy part of the meat registers 165°F, about 25 minutes per pound.

4. In a small saucepan, melt 4 tablespoons of the butter with the wine. Baste the pork frequently with the mixture.

5. Slice the apricots. Rinse, trim, and chop the celery.

6. Bring water to a boil in the bottom of a double boiler. In the top of the double boiler, combine the broth, the sherry, the saffron, and the rice. Cover, reduce the heat, and simmer for 15 minutes.

7. Fold the apricots into the rice and continue simmering until the liquid is absorbed and the rice is tender, about 20 minutes.

8. Melt the remaining 2 tablespoons butter in a small skillet, and sauté the celery and the pecans for 5 minutes. Fold the mixture into the rice.

9. Remove the roast from the oven and place it on a platter. Remove the foil. Fill the center of the roast with the rice. Place paper frills on the tips of the bones, if desired.

Rubies and Emeralds

1. Bring water to a boil in a medium saucepan.

2. Rinse and trim the sprouts and cut X's in the bottoms. Rinse, stem, seed, and chunk the bell pepper.

3. Arrange the sprouts in a steamer insert, place the insert in the saucepan, cover, and steam until the sprouts are crisp-tender, 8 to 10 minutes.

4. Heat the oil in a medium skillet and sauté the bell pepper for 3 minutes. Blend in the lime juice and the brown sugar. Season to taste.

5. Drain the sprouts and add them to the skillet. Toss to coat and combine.

Diamonds In the Roughage

1. Wash and dry the lettuce and arrange the leaves on individual salad plates. Rinse and slice the tomatoes and arrange the slices over the lettuce. Trim and chop the scallions and sprinkle them over the

tomatoes. Place the rock candy in a plastic bag and crush it with a mallet.

2. In a small bowl, whisk together the oil, the vinegar, the mustard, and the paprika. Season to taste.

3. Drizzle the dressing over the salad. Top with the crushed rock candy.

Champagne Sparklers

1. Refrigerate the champagne for at least 1 hour.

2. Place 4 dessert glasses in the freezer for 20 minutes.

3. Rinse and pat dry the mint sprigs.

4. Place scoops of the sherbet into the frosted dessert glasses. Top with the champagne. Garnish with the mint sprigs.

COUNTDOWN

1. Assemble the ingredients and the equipment.
2. Do Step 1 of *Champagne Sparklers*.
3. Do Steps 1–6 of *Jewel In the Crown*.
4. Do Steps 1–2 of *Diamonds In the Roughage*.
5. Do Step 7 of *Jewel In the Crown*.
6. Do Steps 1–3 of *Rubies and Emeralds*.
7. Do Step 8 of *Jewel In the Crown*.
8. Do Steps 4–5 of *Rubies and Emeralds*.
9. Do Step 9 of *Jewel In the Crown*.
10. Do Step 3 of *Diamonds In the Roughage*.
11. Do Steps 2–4 of *Champagne Sparklers*.

Weekend Eleven Sunday

FISH

4 red snapper fillets
(about 1-1/2 pounds)

FRESH PRODUCE

VEGETABLES
1 medium eggplant
1 medium zucchini
1 medium turnip
2 stalks celery
1/2 pound button mushrooms
1 small head red leaf lettuce
1 medium green bell pepper
1 small jicama
1 medium onion
1 clove garlic

FRUIT
3 small oranges

CANS, JARS & BOTTLES

VEGETABLES
1 can (14-1/2 ounces) diced tomatoes
1 can (11 ounces) whole kernel corn

JUICE
1/2 cup tomato juice

PACKAGED GOODS

BAKED GOODS
1 loaf French bread, sliced

WINES & SPIRITS

2 tablespoons dry white wine

REFRIGERATED PRODUCTS

DAIRY
2-1/2 cups milk
3 eggs

JUICE
1/2 cup orange juice

STAPLES

- ☐ Butter
- ☐ Cornstarch
- ☐ Granulated sugar
- ☐ Dark brown sugar
- ☐ Vegetable oil
- ☐ White wine vinegar
- ☐ Lemon juice
- ☐ Worcestershire sauce
- ☐ Dried basil
- ☐ Dried cilantro
- ☐ Dried oregano
- ☐ Pepper
- ☐ Salt
- ☐ Vanilla extract

Weekend Eleven Sunday

Fish Out of Water

1 medium eggplant
1 medium turnip
1 clove garlic
1 medium onion
2 stalks celery
1 can (11 ounces) whole kernel corn
1 can (14-1/2 ounces) diced tomatoes
1/2 cup tomato juice
2 tablespoons dry white wine
1 teaspoon Worcestershire sauce
1 teaspoon granulated sugar
1/2 teaspoon dried basil
1/4 teaspoon dried oregano
1 medium green bell pepper
1 medium zucchini
1/2 pound fresh button mushrooms
4 red snapper fillets (about
    1-1/2 pounds)
2 tablespoons vegetable oil
Seasoning to taste

Once-Over Salad

1 small jicama
1/2 cup orange juice
1 small head red leaf lettuce
3 small oranges
2 tablespoons vegetable oil
1 tablespoon white wine vinegar
1/2 teaspoon dried cilantro
Seasoning to taste

Pudding Up With It

1 loaf French bread, sliced
3 eggs
2-1/2 cups milk
3 tablespoons butter
1/4 cup dark brown sugar
2 teaspoons vanilla extract
1 cup boiling water
1/2 cup granulated sugar
1 tablespoon cornstarch
1-1/2 tablespoons lemon juice

EQUIPMENT

Large saucepan
2 small saucepans
9 × 13-inch glass
  baking dish
1-1/2-quart
  casserole
Medium mixing
  bowl
Small mixing bowl
Whisk

Vegetable brush
Vegetable peeler
Pastry brush
Plastic wrap
Kitchen knives
Measuring cups
  and spoons
Cooking utensils

Weekend Eleven Sunday

RECIPES

Fish Out of Water

1. Peel and cube the eggplant. Peel and dice the turnip. Peel and mince the garlic. Peel and chop the onion. Rinse, trim, and slice the celery. Drain the corn.

2. In a large saucepan, combine the eggplant, the turnip, the garlic, the onion, and the celery.

3. Add the corn, the canned tomatoes, the tomato juice, the wine, the Worcestershire sauce, the sugar, the basil, and the oregano.

4. Bring the mixture to a boil, reduce the heat, and simmer for 30 minutes.

5. Rinse, stem, seed, and chunk the bell pepper. Scrub, trim, and chunk the zucchini. Rinse and pat dry the mushrooms.

6. Add the bell pepper, the zucchini, and the mushrooms to the saucepan and continue simmering for 15 minutes more.

7. Preheat the oven to 350°F.

8. Rinse and pat dry the fish.

9. Brush both sides of the fillets with the oil, season to taste, and arrange them in a 9 × 13-inch glass baking dish.

10. Bake for 10 minutes.

11. Top the fish with the vegetables and bake for 5 minutes more.

Once-Over Salad

1. Peel and dice the jicama. Place it in a small bowl with the orange juice. Toss to combine. Cover the bowl with plastic wrap and refrigerate it for at least 1 hour.

2. Wash and dry the lettuce and arrange the leaves on individual salad plates. Peel and slice the oranges and arrange the slices over the lettuce.

3. Drain the jicama, reserving the juice, and spoon it over the orange slices.

4. To the reserved orange juice, add the oil, the vinegar, and the cilantro. Season to taste and whisk to blend.

5. Drizzle the dressing over the salads.

Pudding Up With It

1. Lay the bread slices out to dry for at least 2 hours.

2. Preheat the oven to 350°F. Grease a 1-1/2 quart casserole.

3. Tear the bread into small pieces and arrange them in the bottom of the casserole.

4. In a medium bowl, beat the eggs lightly with a fork.

5. Heat the milk in a small saucepan and slowly add it to the beaten eggs. Melt 1 tablespoon of the butter in the saucepan and add it to the egg mixture. Blend in the brown sugar and the vanilla, and pour the mixture over the bread pieces. Let them soak for 5 minutes, then bake until set, about 50 minutes.

6. Bring the water to a boil in the saucepan. Add the granulated sugar and the cornstarch, and cook, stirring constantly. Add the remaining 2 tablespoons butter and the lemon juice and blend. Pour the sauce over the hot bread pudding.

COUNTDOWN

1. Assemble the ingredients and the equipment.
2. Do Step 1 of *Pudding Up With It.*
3. Do Step 1 of *Once-Over Salad.*
4. Do Steps 1–4 of *Fish Out of Water.*
5. Do Steps 2–5 of *Pudding Up With It.*
6. Do Steps 5–10 of *Fish Out of Water.*
7. Do Steps 2–4 of *Once-Over Salad.*
8. Do Step 11 of *Fish Out of Water.*
9. Do Step 5 of *Once-Over Salad.*
10. Do Step 6 of *Pudding Up With It.*

Weekend Twelve Saturday

SHOPPING LIST

MEAT & POULTRY

4 beef tenderloins (about 2 pounds)

FRESH PRODUCE

VEGETABLES

1 pound asparagus
2 stalks celery
1 medium head cabbage
1 small daikon radish
1 small shallot
4 scallions (green onions)
1 clove garlic

CANS, JARS & BOTTLES

SOUP

1 can (14 ounces) chicken broth
1 can (14 ounces) beef broth

FRUIT

1 can (8 ounces) pineapple tidbits

SPREADS

1/2 cup strawberry preserves

INTERNATIONAL FOODS

1 can (8 ounces) sliced water chestnuts

PACKAGED GOODS

PASTA, RICE & GRAINS

1 cup wild rice

BAKED GOODS

1 package (3 ounces) ladyfingers

WINES & SPIRITS

1/2 cup dry sherry
2 tablespoons brandy

REFRIGERATED PRODUCTS

DAIRY

1 container (8 ounces) lemon yogurt
1/4 cup whipped cream

FROZEN GOODS

DESSERTS

1 pint lemon sherbet

STAPLES

❑ Cornstarch
❑ Granulated sugar
❑ Dark brown sugar
❑ Sesame oil
❑ Vegetable oil
❑ Rice vinegar
❑ Lemon juice
❑ Prepared horseradish
❑ Soy sauce
❑ Mayonnaise
❑ Sesame seeds
❑ Chinese five-spice powder
❑ Candied ginger
❑ Pepper
❑ Salt

Kowloon

1 clove garlic
1 small shallot
1 tablespoon candied ginger (when chopped)
4 beef tenderloins (about 2 pounds)
2 tablespoons dark brown sugar
1/2 cup dry sherry
3 tablespoons lemon juice
3 tablespoons soy sauce
Seasoning to taste
1 tablespoon cornstarch
2 tablespoons water

Rice Bowl

1 cup wild rice
1 can (8 ounces) sliced water chestnuts
1 can (14 ounces) chicken broth
1 can (14 ounces) beef broth
1/2 teaspoon Chinese five-spice powder
4 scallions (green onions)

Chopped Sticks

1 pound fresh asparagus
2 stalks celery
2 tablespoons vegetable oil
1 teaspoon granulated sugar
Seasoning to taste
1 tablespoon sesame seeds

Rickslaw

1 medium head cabbage
1 small daikon radish
1 can (8 ounces) pineapple tidbits
2 tablespoons mayonnaise
1 tablespoon vegetable oil
1/2 teaspoon sesame oil
2 tablespoons rice vinegar
1/4 teaspoon prepared horseradish
Seasoning to taste

Lemon Junk

1 pint lemon sherbet
1 package (3 ounces) ladyfingers
1 container (8 ounces) lemon yogurt
1/2 cup strawberry preserves
2 tablespoons brandy
1/4 cup whipped cream

EQUIPMENT

Double boiler	Whisk
2 small saucepans	Vegetable grater
Large covered skillet	Vegetable peeler
Strainer	Plastic wrap
Large shallow bowl	Kitchen knives
2 large mixing bowls	Measuring cups and spoons
Small mixing bowl	Cooking utensils

Weekend Twelve Saturday

RECIPES

Kowloon

1. Peel and mince the garlic. Peel and mince the shallot. Chop the ginger.

2. Rinse and pat dry the beef tenderloins and place them in a large shallow bowl. Cover the meat with the garlic, the shallot, and the ginger. Add the brown sugar, the sherry, the lemon juice, and the soy sauce. Season to taste, turn the beef to coat, cover the bowl with plastic wrap, and refrigerate it for at least 1 hour.

3. Preheat the broiler.

4. Remove the beef, reserving the marinade, and place the tenderloins on a broiler pan. Broil until the beef is done to taste, about 5 minutes per side for medium rare.

5. Bring the reserved marinade to boil in a small saucepan and cook for 1 minute. Strain the liquid and return it to the saucepan.

6. Dissolve the cornstarch in the water. Whisk the mixture into the reserved marinade and cook, stirring, until the sauce is thickened and clear, about 1 minute. Remove the pan from the heat and cover to keep warm.

7. Spoon the sauce over the beef.

Rice Bowl

1. Rinse and drain the rice well. Drain the water chestnuts.

2. Bring water to a boil in the bottom of a double boiler. Place the rice, the water chestnuts, the broth, and the Chinese five-spice powder in the top of the double boiler. Cover, reduce the heat, and simmer until the liquid is absorbed and the rice is tender, about 45 minutes.

3. Trim and chop the scallions. Fold the scallions into the rice and fluff with a fork.

Chopped Sticks

1. Rinse the asparagus, remove and discard the tough ends, and slice the spears into 1-1/2-inch diagonals. Rinse and trim the celery and slice it into 1-1/2-inch diagonals.

2. Heat the oil with the sugar in a large skillet and sauté the asparagus and the celery until crisp-tender, about 5 minutes. Season to taste, remove the pan from the heat, and cover to keep warm.

3. Sprinkle with the sesame seeds.

Rickslaw

1. Trim and grate the cabbage. Peel and grate the daikon. Drain the pineapple, reserving 1 tablespoon of the juice. Combine the prepared ingredients in a large bowl and toss with the mayonnaise.

2. In a small bowl, whisk together the reserved pineapple juice, the vegetable

and sesame oils, the vinegar, and the horseradish. Season to taste and toss with the salad.

Lemon Junk

1. Set the sherbet out to soften.

2. Cut each ladyfinger in half crosswise and separate the halves. Stand the ladyfinger halves, round side up, around the edges of individual dessert bowls. Lay any remaining halves in the bottoms of the dishes.

3. In a large bowl, combine the softened sherbet and the yogurt. Spoon the mixture into the dessert bowls. Freeze until you are ready to serve.

4. In a small saucepan, combine the preserves and the brandy, and heat through. Spoon the mixture over the sherbet mixture and garnish with a dollop of whipped cream.

COUNTDOWN

1. Assemble the ingredients and the equipment.
2. Do Step 1 of *Lemon Junk*.
3. Do Steps 1–2 of *Kowloon*.
4. Do Steps 2–3 of *Lemon Junk*.
5. Do Steps 1–2 of *Rice Bowl*.
6. Do Steps 1–2 of *Rickslaw*.
7. Do Step 1 of *Chopped Sticks*.
8. Do Steps 3–6 of *Kowloon*.
9. Do Step 2 of *Chopped Sticks*.
10. Do Step 3 of *Rice Bowl*.
11. Do Step 3 of *Chopped Sticks*.
12. Do Step 7 of *Kowloon*.
13. Do Step 4 of *Lemon Junk*.

Weekend Twelve Sunday

MEAT & POULTRY

1/2 pound Italian sausage

FRESH PRODUCE

VEGETABLES

1 package (10 ounces) spinach
1 medium cucumber
1 medium onion
1 small red onion
2 cloves garlic

HERBS

1/4 cup basil (when chopped)
2 tablespoons chives (when chopped)
1 tablespoon parsley (when chopped)

FRUIT

4 small bananas

PACKAGED GOODS

PASTA, RICE & GRAINS

1 pound fettuccine

DRIED FRUITS & NUTS

1/4 cup pecan bits

WINES & SPIRITS

1/4 cup dry white wine

REFRIGERATED PRODUCTS

DAIRY

3/4 cup buttermilk
1 cup half-and-half

CHEESE

1/2 cup shredded mozzarella cheese

DELI

8 slices bacon
1/4 pound pepperoni, sliced

FROZEN GOODS

DESSERTS

1 pint cinnamon-swirl ice cream

- ❏ Butter
- ❏ Vegetable shortening
- ❏ Flour
- ❏ Baking powder
- ❏ Baking soda
- ❏ Granulated sugar
- ❏ Dark brown sugar
- ❏ Olive oil
- ❏ Vegetable oil
- ❏ Lemon juice
- ❏ White Worcestershire sauce
- ❏ Ground cinnamon
- ❏ Dry mustard
- ❏ Ground nutmeg
- ❏ Pepper
- ❏ Salt
- ❏ Vanilla extract

Weekend Twelve Sunday

Primarily Pasta

2 cloves garlic
1 medium onion
8 slices bacon
1/4 pound pepperoni, sliced
1/2 pound Italian sausage
1/4 cup fresh basil (when chopped)
1 tablespoon fresh parsley (when chopped)
2 tablespoons olive oil
1 pound fettuccine
1 cup half-and-half
1/4 cup dry white wine
Seasoning to taste
1/2 cup shredded mozzarella cheese

Essentially Salad

1 package (10 ounces) fresh spinach
1 medium cucumber
1 small red onion
3 tablespoons vegetable oil
2 tablespoons lemon juice
1/2 teaspoon dry mustard
1/2 teaspoon white Worcestershire sauce
1/2 teaspoon granulated sugar
Seasoning to taste

Basically Biscuits

2 tablespoons fresh chives (when chopped)
2 cups flour
1 teaspoon granulated sugar
1 tablespoon baking powder
1/2 teaspoon salt
1/4 teaspoon baking soda
1/2 cup vegetable shortening
3/4 cup buttermilk

Fundamentally Fruit

3 tablespoons butter
3 tablespoons dark brown sugar
1/2 teaspoon ground cinnamon
1/2 teaspoon ground nutmeg
4 small bananas
1 teaspoon vanilla extract
1 pint cinnamon-swirl ice cream
1/4 cup pecan bits

EQUIPMENT

Stockpot	Whisk
Large skillet	Vegetable peeler
Medium covered skillet	Pastry blender
Baking sheet	Biscuit cutter
Breadboard	Ice cream scoop
Colander	Kitchen knives
2 large mixing bowls	Measuring cups and spoons
Small mixing bowl	Cooking utensils

Weekend Twelve Sunday

Primarily Pasta

1. Bring water for the pasta to a boil in a stockpot.

2. Peel and mince the garlic. Peel and chop the onion. Dice the bacon. Dice the pepperoni. Remove the casings from the sausage.

3. Rinse and chop the basil. Rinse and chop the parsley.

4. Heat the oil in a large skillet and sauté the garlic and the onion for 1 minute.

5. Add the bacon, the pepperoni, and the sausage, and sauté for 10 minutes.

6. Cook the pasta in the boiling water, 2 to 3 minutes if you are using fresh pasta, 6 to 7 minutes if you are using dry pasta.

7. Drain all but 2 tablespoons of the fat from the skillet.

8. Add the half-and-half and the wine to the skillet. Season to taste, reduce the heat, and simmer for 5 minutes.

9. Drain the pasta, return it to the stockpot, and toss it with the cheese.

10. Fold the basil and the parsley into the sauce, and combine it with the pasta.

Essentially Salad

1. Rinse, stem, and dry the spinach and tear into bite-sized pieces. Peel and chop the cucumber. Peel and thinly slice the onion. Combine the vegetables in a large bowl.

2. In a small bowl, whisk together the oil, the lemon juice, the mustard, the Worcestershire sauce, and the sugar. Season to taste.

3. Toss the salad with the dressing.

Basically Biscuits

1. Preheat the oven to 450°F. Lightly flour a breadboard. Flour a biscuit cutter.

2. Rinse and chop the chives.

3. In a large bowl, combine the flour, the sugar, the baking powder, the salt, and the baking soda. Cut in the shortening with a pastry blender until the mixture resembles fine crumbs. Fold in the buttermilk and the chives, and blend until the dough forms a ball.

4. Turn the dough out on the breadboard and knead lightly until smooth, 8–10 times. Pat the dough out to a 1/2-inch thickness and cut it with the biscuit cutter. Place the biscuits on a baking sheet.

5. Bake until the biscuits are golden, about 10 minutes.

Fundamentally Fruit

1. Melt the butter in a medium skillet. Add the brown sugar, the cinnamon, and the nutmeg. Bring to a boil and cook, stirring, until the sugar is dissolved and the sauce begins to thicken, about 3 minutes. Remove the pan from the heat.

2. Peel and chunk the bananas, and fold them into the sauce. Fold in the vanilla. Stir to combine and cover to keep warm.

3. Place scoops of ice cream in individual dessert bowls and top with the banana-caramel sauce. Garnish with the nuts.

COUNTDOWN

1. Assemble the ingredients and the equipment.
2. Do Steps 1–2 of *Essentially Salad*.
3. Do Steps 1–4 of *Basically Biscuits*.
4. Do Steps 1–2 of *Fundamentally Fruit*.
5. Do Steps 1–5 of *Primarily Pasta*.
6. Do Step 5 of *Basically Biscuits*.
7. Do Steps 6–10 of *Primarily Pasta*.
8. Do Step 3 of *Essentially Salad*.
9. Do Step 3 of *Fundamentally Fruit*.

Weekend Thirteen Saturday

FISH

1 pound cooked crabmeat

FRESH PRODUCE

VEGETABLES

1 pound green beans
1 small red bell pepper
1 small jicama
1 medium shallot
2 cloves garlic

FRUIT

2 medium ripe pears
2 ripe kiwifruits
1 large ripe papaya
1 small lemon

PACKAGED GOODS

BAKED GOODS

12 small almond cookies

WINES & SPIRITS

1/2 cup amaretto

REFRIGERATED PRODUCTS

DAIRY

3/4 cup milk
2 cups half-and-half
1/4 cup whipped cream
6 eggs

FROZEN GOODS

DESSERTS

1 pint honey almond gelato

❑ Butter
❑ Flour
❑ Baking powder
❑ Granulated sugar
❑ Powdered sugar
❑ Vegetable oil
❑ Lemon juice
❑ Worcestershire sauce
❑ Dijon mustard
❑ Honey
❑ Dried tarragon
❑ Ground allspice
❑ Pepper
❑ Salt

Weekend Thirteen Saturday

Classic Crab

6 tablespoons butter
4 tablespoons flour
2 cups half-and-half
Seasoning to taste
1 medium shallot
1 small red bell pepper
1 pound cooked crabmeat
5 eggs
1/4 teaspoon dried tarragon
1/2 teaspoon Dijon mustard

Better Beans

1 pound fresh green beans
2 cloves garlic
1 small jicama
2 tablespoons vegetable oil
1 teaspoon Worcestershire sauce
2 teaspoons lemon juice
1/2 teaspoon granulated sugar
Seasoning to taste

Matchless Muffins

1 small lemon
1 egg
3/4 cup milk
1/3 cup vegetable oil
2 tablespoons honey
2 cups flour
1 tablespoon baking powder
1/4 teaspoon salt
1/4 teaspoon ground allspice

Pearfect

1 pint honey almond gelato
12 small almond cookies
2 medium ripe pears
2 ripe kiwifruits
1 large ripe papaya
1/2 cup amaretto
1/4 cup powdered sugar
1/4 cup whipped cream

EQUIPMENT

Electric mixer
2 medium saucepans
Large skillet
2-quart casserole
Large shallow baking pan
Muffin tin
2 large mixing bowls
2 medium mixing bowls
Small mixing bowl
Whisk

Citrus grater
Citrus juicer
Vegetable peeler
Vegetable grater
Mallet
Ice cream scoop
Plastic wrap
Plastic bag
Kitchen knives
Measuring cups and spoons
Cooking utensils

Weekend Thirteen Saturday

Classic Crab

1. Melt 4 tablespoons of the butter in a medium saucepan. Whisk in the flour. Add the half-and-half, season to taste, and cook, stirring constantly, until the sauce is thick and smooth, about 5 minutes.

2. Peel and mince the shallot. Rinse, stem, seed, and mince the bell pepper. Clean and flake the crabmeat. Separate the eggs, placing the yolks in a medium bowl and the whites in a large bowl.

3. With an electric mixer, beat the egg whites until they are stiff, about 3 minutes. Beat the egg yolks until they are thick and lemon-colored, about 2 minutes.

4. Preheat the oven to 350°F.

5. Melt the remaining 2 tablespoons butter in a large skillet and sauté the shallot and the bell pepper for 5 minutes.

6. Fold the half-and-half mixture into the skillet. Fold the egg yolks into the skillet. Blend in the crab, the tarragon, and the mustard.

7. Fold the crab mixture into the egg whites and pour the entire mixture into a 2-quart casserole. Set the casserole in a large shallow baking pan of hot water, and bake until the soufflé rises and is golden, about 40 minutes.

Better Beans

1. Bring water to a boil in a medium saucepan.

2. Rinse and trim the green beans. Peel and mince the garlic. Peel and grate the jicama.

3. Blanch the green beans in the boiling water for 2 minutes. Drain and rinse the beans in cold water.

4. Heat the oil in the saucepan and sauté the garlic for 2 minutes. Add the jicama and sauté for 2 minutes. Add the green beans, the Worcestershire sauce, the lemon juice (from the Matchless Muffins), and the sugar. Season to taste and toss to combine and heat through.

Matchless Muffins

1. Grease a muffin tin.

2. Grate 2 teaspoons of the lemon peel. Juice the lemon and reserve the juice for the green beans.

3. In a small bowl, combine the egg, the milk, the oil, the honey, and the lemon peel.

4. In a medium bowl, combine the flour, the baking powder, the salt, and the allspice.

5. Make a well in the center of the dry ingredients, pour in the egg mixture, and fold to combine. Divide the batter evenly among the muffin cups.

6. Bake at 350°F until the muffins are golden, about 25 minutes.

Pearfect

1. Set the gelato out to soften.

2. Place 8 of the almond cookies in a plastic bag and crumble them with a mallet.

3. Peel and chunk the pears. Peel and chunk the kiwifruits. Peel, seed, and chunk the papaya. Place the fruit in a large bowl and toss with 1/4 cup of the amaretto and the powdered sugar. Cover the bowl with plastic wrap and refrigerate it until you are ready to use.

4. Blend the remaining 1/4 cup amaretto into the softened gelato and return it to the freezer.

5. Place half the cookie crumbs in the bottom of individual dessert glasses. Add half of fruit and half of the gelato mixture. Repeat. Garnish with dollops of whipped cream and a whole cookie on the edge of each glass.

COUNTDOWN

1. Assemble the ingredients and the equipment.
2. Do Steps 1–4 of *Pearfect.*
3. Do Steps 1–7 of *Classic Crab.*
4. Do Steps 1–6 of *Matchless Muffins.*
5. Do Steps 1–4 of *Better Beans.*
6. Do Step 5 of *Pearfect.*

Weekend Thirteen Sunday

MEAT & POULTRY

3 pounds chicken pieces

FRESH PRODUCE

VEGETABLES
4 medium yams
1/2 pound sugar-snap peas
1 large carrot
1 small onion
2 scallions (green onions)
2 cloves garlic

FRUIT
2 medium apples

CANS, JARS & BOTTLES

DESSERT & BAKING NEEDS
1 can (14 ounces) sweetened
   condensed milk

PACKAGED GOODS

DESSERT & BAKING NEEDS
1 small package instant devil's food
   pudding mix

REFRIGERATED PRODUCTS

DAIRY
2 cups buttermilk
1 cup whipping cream

FROZEN GOODS

VEGETABLES
1 package (10 ounces) green peas

FRUIT
1 package (10 ounces) raspberries

- ☐ Butter
- ☐ Vegetable shortening
- ☐ Flour
- ☐ Cornmeal
- ☐ Dark brown sugar
- ☐ Cocoa powder
- ☐ Lemon juice
- ☐ Tabasco sauce
- ☐ Dried sage
- ☐ Dried savory
- ☐ Ground cinnamon
- ☐ Ground nutmeg
- ☐ Paprika
- ☐ Pepper
- ☐ Salt
- ☐ Rum extract

Weekend Thirteen Sunday

MENU

For Frying Out Loud

2 cloves garlic
1 small onion
2 cups buttermilk
1 teaspoon Tabasco sauce
3 pounds chicken pieces
1 teaspoon dried sage
1 cup cornmeal
1 cup flour
1/2 teaspoon paprika
Seasoning to taste
2 cups vegetable shortening

I'll Be Yammed

4 medium yams
2 medium apples
1 tablespoon lemon juice
1/4 cup dark brown sugar
1/4 teaspoon ground cinnamon
2 tablespoons butter

Legumania

1 package (10 ounces) frozen green
   peas
1/2 pound fresh sugar-snap peas
1 large carrot
2 scallions (green onions)
2 tablespoons butter
1/2 teaspoon ground nutmeg
1/2 teaspoon dried savory

The Devil Made Me Do It

1 package (10 ounces) frozen
   raspberries
1 small package instant devil's food
   pudding mix
1 can (14 ounces) sweetened condensed
   milk
1 tablespoon cocoa powder
1 cup cold water
1 cup whipping cream
1 teaspoon rum extract

EQUIPMENT

Electric mixer

Large saucepan

2 large covered
   skillets

9 × 13-inch glass
   baking dish

Large shallow bowl

2 large mixing
   bowls

Medium mixing
   bowl

2 small mixing
   bowls

Vegetable peeler

Vegetable grater

Plastic wrap

Kitchen knives

Measuring cups
   and spoons

Cooking utensils

Weekend Thirteen Sunday

For Frying Out Loud

1. Peel and mince the garlic. Peel and mince the onion.

2. In a large bowl, combine the buttermilk, the Tabasco sauce, the garlic, and the onion. Put the chicken pieces into the mixture, cover the bowl with plastic wrap, and refrigerate it for at least 1 hour.

3. In a large shallow bowl, stir together the sage, the cornmeal, the flour, and the paprika. Season to taste.

4. Remove the chicken pieces from the buttermilk, allowing the excess to drip away. Coat the pieces evenly with the flour mixture.

5. Melt the shortening in a large skillet. Arrange the chicken pieces in the skillet, skin side down, with the dark meat in the middle. The pieces can touch slightly, but do not overcrowd the pan. Cook until the chicken is golden brown, about 12 minutes.

6. Turn the chicken, cover the pan, and cook for 10 minutes more.

7. Uncover the pan, turn the chicken again, and cook until it is crisp and cooked through, about 10 more minutes.

8. Drain the chicken well on paper towels before serving.

I'll Be Yammed

1. Butter a 9 × 13-inch glass baking dish.

2. Bring water to a boil in a large saucepan.

3. Peel and slice the yams, add them to the saucepan, and cook them until they are almost tender, about 6 minutes.

4. Peel and core the apples, cut them into thin wedges, and sprinkle them with the lemon juice.

5. Drain the potatoes and rinse them under cold water to cool.

6. In a small bowl, combine the brown sugar and the cinnamon.

7. Melt the butter.

8. Arrange half the potatoes in the bottom of the baking dish. Add half of the apples. Sprinkle with half of the brown sugar mixture. Drizzle with half of the butter. Repeat.

9. Preheat the oven to 350°F.

10. Bake until cooked through, about 30 minutes.

Legumania

1. Set the package of green peas in a small bowl of hot water to thaw.

2. Rinse and string the sugar-snap peas. Peel and grate the carrot. Trim and chop the scallions.

3. Melt the butter with the nutmeg and the savory in a large skillet, and sauté the snap peas and the carrot for 3 minutes. Add the green peas and the scallions, and sauté for 2 minutes more. Remove the pan from the heat and cover to keep warm.

The Devil Made Me Do It

1. Set the berries out to thaw slightly.

2. In a large bowl, combine the pudding mix, the condensed milk, the cocoa powder, and the cold water and beat well. Place the mixture in the freezer for 10 minutes.

3. In a medium bowl, whip the cream until stiff peaks form. Fold in the rum extract.

4. Fold the whipped cream into the pudding mixture. Spoon some of the raspberries into the bottoms of individual dessert glasses. Add the pudding mixture and top with the remaining raspberries. Refrigerate until you are ready to serve.

COUNTDOWN

1. Assemble the ingredients and the equipment.
2. Do Steps 1–2 of *For Frying Out Loud.*
3. Do Step 1 of *Legumania.*
4. Do Steps 1–4 of *The Devil Made Me Do It.*
5. Do Steps 1–9 of *I'll Be Yammed.*
6. Do Steps 3–4 of *For Frying Out Loud.*
7. Do Step 10 of *I'll Be Yammed.*
8. Do Steps 5–7 of *For Frying Out Loud.*
9. Do Steps 2–3 of *Legumania.*
10. Do Step 8 of *For Frying Out Loud.*

Autumn

Weekend One Saturday

MEAT & POULTRY

4 beef tenderloins (about 2 pounds)

FRESH PRODUCE

VEGETABLES
1-1/2 pounds baking potatoes
1 pound parsnips
2 stalks celery
4 medium mushrooms
2 medium onions
3 scallions (green onions)
2 cloves garlic

HERBS
2 tablespoons dill (when chopped)

CANS, JARS & BOTTLES

SOUP
1 can (10-1/2 ounces) beef broth

PACKAGED GOODS

BAKED GOODS
2 cups plain crackers (when crushed)

DRIED FRUITS & NUTS
1/2 cup golden raisins
1 cup pecan bits

DESSERT & BAKING NEEDS
1 envelope unflavored gelatin
8 ounces butterscotch chips

WINES & SPIRITS
1/4 cup rum
2 tablespoons Kahlúa

REFRIGERATED PRODUCTS

DAIRY
1 cup whipping cream
3 eggs

JUICE
1 cup orange juice

STAPLES

- ❏ Butter
- ❏ Granulated sugar
- ❏ Powdered sugar
- ❏ Vegetable oil
- ❏ Balsamic vinegar
- ❏ Dried oregano
- ❏ Chili powder
- ❏ Pepper
- ❏ Salt
- ❏ Vanilla extract

Weekend One Saturday

Beef Encounter

4 medium fresh mushrooms
2 medium onions
2 cloves garlic
3 tablespoons butter
1/2 cup beef broth
1/4 cup rum
2 teaspoons chili powder
1 teaspoon dried oregano
4 beef tenderloins (about 2 pounds)
Seasoning to taste

Illicit Potatoes

1-1/2 pounds baking potatoes
3 scallions (green onions)
2 stalks celery
2 tablespoons fresh dill (when chopped)
3 tablespoons vegetable oil
3/4 cup beef broth
2 tablespoons balsamic vinegar
Seasoning to taste

Private Parsnips

1/2 cup golden raisins
1/2 cup hot water
1 pound parsnips
2 tablespoons butter
1 cup orange juice
Seasoning to taste

Affair of the Tart

2 cups plain crackers (when crushed)
1 cup whipping cream
2 tablespoons powdered sugar
2 tablespoons Kahlúa
3 eggs
1-1/4 cups granulated sugar
1 envelope unflavored gelatin
1-1/2 teaspoons vanilla extract
8 ounces butterscotch chips
1 cup pecan bits

EQUIPMENT

Electric mixer

Medium covered saucepan

Large covered skillet

Medium covered skillet

Pie plate

Large mixing bowl

Medium mixing bowl

Small mixing bowl

Vegetable peeler

Plastic bag

Kitchen knives

Measuring cups and spoons

Cooking utensils

Beef Encounter

1. Rinse, pat dry, and thinly slice the mushrooms. Peel and chop the onions. Peel and mince the garlic.

2. Melt the butter in a medium skillet and sauté the mushrooms for 1 minute.

3. Remove the mushrooms and set them aside. Add the garlic and the onions to the skillet and sauté for 2 minutes.

4. Add the broth, the rum, the chili powder, and the oregano. Bring the mixture to a boil, cover, reduce the heat, and simmer for 5 minutes.

5. Remove the skillet from the heat and let it cool for 5 minutes.

6. Place the beef tenderloins in the skillet, turning to coat, and let them stand at room temperature for 30 minutes.

7. Preheat the broiler.

8. Remove the tenderloins, reserving the sauce.

9. Season the tenderloins to taste, place them on a broiler pan, and broil to taste, 4 minutes per side for rare.

10. Return the mushrooms to the skillet and bring the sauce to a boil.

11. Spoon the sauce over the tenderloins.

Illicit Potatoes

1. Peel and thinly slice the potatoes. Trim and chop the scallions. Rinse, trim, and slice the celery into 1/2-inch diagonals. Rinse and chop the dill.

2. Heat the oil in a large skillet and sauté the potatoes for 5 minutes. Add the celery and sauté until it begins to soften, about 3 minutes. Add the broth, the vinegar, and the dill. Season to taste, cover, reduce the heat, and simmer until the potatoes are tender, about 10 minutes.

3. Toss with the scallions.

Private Parsnips

1. In a small bowl, soak the raisins in the hot water for 10 minutes.

2. Peel and chunk the parsnips.

3. Melt the butter in a medium saucepan and sauté the parsnips for 2 minutes. Add the orange juice and bring to a boil. Reduce the heat, cover, and simmer for 10 minutes.

4. Drain the raisins and add them to the parsnips. Season to taste, toss to combine, and simmer for 2 minutes more.

Affair of the Tart

1. Chill a medium bowl and the beaters of an electric mixer in the refrigerator for at least 10 minutes.

2. Preheat the oven to 350°F. Grease a pie plate.

3. Place the crackers in a plastic bag and crush them.

4. In the chilled bowl, whip the cream until soft peaks form. Fold in the powdered sugar and beat until stiff. Fold in the Kahlúa. Refrigerate until you are ready to use.

5. In a large bowl, beat the eggs until they are light and fluffy, about 5 minutes. Blend in the granulated sugar and the gelatin. Add the cracker crumbs, the vanilla, the butterscotch chips, and the pecans, and blend well.

6. Pour the mixture into the pie plate and bake for 30 minutes.

7. Remove the tart from the oven and let it cool.

8. Spread the whipped cream over the tart.

COUNTDOWN

1. Assemble the ingredients and the equipment.
2. Do Steps 1–7 of *Affair of the Tart*.
3. Do Steps 1–6 of *Beef Encounter*.
4. Do Steps 1–2 of *Private Parsnips*.
5. Do Steps 1–2 of *Illicit Potatoes*.
6. Do Step 3 of *Private Parsnips*.
7. Do Steps 7–9 of *Beef Encounter*.
8. Do Step 4 of *Private Parsnips*.
9. Do Step 3 of *Illicit Potatoes*.
10. Do Steps 10–11 of *Beef Encounter*.
11. Do Step 8 of *Affair of the Tart*.

Weekend One Sunday

SHOPPING LIST

MEAT & POULTRY

4 lean loin pork chops
   (about 1-1/2 pounds)

FRESH PRODUCE

VEGETABLES

1 large bunch broccoli
2 stalks celery
1 medium head romaine lettuce
1 small green bell pepper
1 large onion
1 large shallot
1 clove garlic

FRUIT

1 medium red apple
1 medium yellow apple
1 medium banana
1/4 pound seedless green grapes

CANS, JARS & BOTTLES

VEGETABLES

1 can (14-1/2 ounces) diced tomatoes
1 can (11 ounces) whole kernel corn

PACKAGED GOODS

PASTA, RICE & GRAINS

1 cup brown rice

DRIED FRUITS & NUTS

1/4 cup walnut bits

DESSERT & BAKING NEEDS

1 small package instant chocolate
   pudding mix

WINES & SPIRITS

2 tablespoons Grand Marnier

REFRIGERATED PRODUCTS

DAIRY

2 cups milk
2 tablespoons sour cream

FROZEN GOODS

1 container (8 ounces) whipped topping

STAPLES

- ☐ Butter
- ☐ Granulated sugar
- ☐ Chocolate sprinkles
- ☐ Vegetable oil
- ☐ Apple cider vinegar
- ☐ Lemon juice
- ☐ Mayonnaise
- ☐ Dried sage
- ☐ Dried tarragon
- ☐ Ground allspice
- ☐ Pepper
- ☐ Salt
- ☐ Orange extract

Weekend One Sunday

Pork It Over

4 lean loin pork chops (about
    1-1/2 pounds)
Seasoning to taste
1 clove garlic
1 small green bell pepper
1 large shallot
1 can (11 ounces) whole kernel corn
3 tablespoons butter
1 cup brown rice
1 can (14-1/2 ounces) diced tomatoes
1-1/2 cups water
1 teaspoon ground allspice
1/2 teaspoon dried sage

Broccoli Bribery

1 large bunch broccoli
1 large onion
3 tablespoons vegetable oil
1 tablespoon lemon juice
1/2 teaspoon dried tarragon
Seasoning to taste

Apple-Licious Salad

1 medium head romaine lettuce
1 medium red apple
1 medium yellow apple
1 medium banana
2 stalks celery
1/4 pound seedless green grapes
1/4 cup walnuts bits
4 tablespoons mayonnaise
2 tablespoons apple cider vinegar

2 tablespoons sour cream
2 teaspoons granulated sugar
Seasoning to taste

Pudding On a Smile

2 cups milk
1 small package instant chocolate
    pudding mix
1/2 teaspoon orange extract
2 tablespoons Grand Marnier
1 container (8 ounces) frozen whipped
    topping
Chocolate sprinkles for garnish

EQUIPMENT

Electric mixer
2 large skillets
9 × 9-inch glass baking dish
Large mixing bowl
Medium mixing bowl
Small mixing bowl
Whisk
Aluminum foil
Kitchen knives
Measuring cups and spoons
Cooking utensils

Weekend One Sunday

Pork It Over

1. Rinse and pat dry the pork chops and season them to taste.

2. Peel and mince the garlic. Rinse, stem, seed, and chop the bell pepper. Peel and chop the shallot. Drain the corn.

3. Melt the butter in a large skillet and sauté the garlic for 1 minute.

4. Add the pork chops and sauté until they are browned, about 5 minutes per side.

5. Remove the chops and place them in a 9 × 9-inch glass baking dish.

6. Preheat the oven to 350°F.

7. Add the rice to the skillet and sauté it in the drippings until lightly browned, about 5 minutes.

8. Add the bell pepper, the shallot, the corn, and the tomatoes. Stir to combine. Add the water, the allspice, and the sage. Bring the mixture to a boil and cook for 1 minute.

9. Pour the mixture over the chops. Cover the dish with aluminum foil and bake until the liquid is absorbed and the rice is tender, 25 to 30 minutes.

Broccoli Bribery

1. Rinse and trim the broccoli and cut it into bite-sized florets. Peel the onion and cut it into 6 wedges.

2. Heat the oil in a large skillet and sauté the broccoli and the onion wedges until the broccoli is bright green and crisp-tender, about 6 minutes.

3. Blend in the lemon juice and the tarragon and season to taste.

Apple-Licious Salad

1. Wash and dry the romaine. Place half of the leaves on individual salad plates.

2. Tear the remainder of the romaine into bite-sized pieces. Rinse, core, and slice the apples. Peel and chunk the banana. Rinse, trim, and slice the celery. Rinse, stem, and halve the grapes. Combine the lettuce, the fruit, and the celery in a large bowl. Sprinkle with the walnuts.

3. In a small bowl, whisk together the mayonnaise, the vinegar, the sour cream, and the sugar. Season to taste and toss with the fruit salad. Spoon the salad over the lettuce leaves.

Pudding On a Smile

1. In a medium bowl, combine the milk and the pudding mix and beat with an electric mixer for 2 minutes.

2. Place the mixture in the refrigerator for 10 minutes.

3. Fold the orange extract and the Grand Marnier into the whipped topping.

4. Spoon half of the pudding into individual dessert glasses. Layer with half of the whipped topping. Repeat. Place in the refrigerator until you are ready to serve.

5. Garnish with the sprinkles.

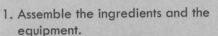

COUNTDOWN

1. Assemble the ingredients and the equipment.
2. Do Steps 1–4 of *Pudding On a Smile*.
3. Do Steps 1–9 of *Pork It Over*.
4. Do Steps 1–3 of *Apple-Licious Salad*.
5. Do Steps 1–3 of *Broccoli Bribery*.
6. Do Step 5 of *Pudding On a Smile*.

Weekend Two Saturday

SHOPPING LIST

MEAT & POULTRY

4 boneless, skinless chicken breast halves
(about 1-1/2 pounds)

FRESH PRODUCE

VEGETABLES

4 large tomatoes
1 medium red onion
2 scallions (green onions)
1 clove garlic

HERBS

3 tablespoons chives (when chopped)
3 tablespoons parsley (when chopped)

CANS, JARS & BOTTLES

SOUP

1 can (14 ounces) vegetable broth

PACKAGED GOODS

PASTA, RICE & GRAINS

1 cup long-grain white rice

BAKED GOODS

4 individual chocolate shells

DRIED FRUITS & NUTS

1/4 cup currants
1/4 cup slivered almonds

WINES & SPIRITS

1 tablespoon brandy

REFRIGERATED PRODUCTS

DAIRY

1 cup buttermilk
1/4 cup whipped cream

CHEESE

1 package (8 ounces) cream cheese

DELI

4 slices bacon

JUICE

1/2 cup orange juice

FROZEN GOODS

VEGETABLES

1 package (10 ounces) cut wax beans

FRUIT

1 package (10 ounces) raspberries

STAPLES

- ❏ Butter
- ❏ Granulated sugar
- ❏ Chocolate syrup
- ❏ Lemon juice
- ❏ Plain breadcrumbs
- ❏ Celery seed
- ❏ Dried oregano
- ❏ Dried thyme
- ❏ Curry powder
- ❏ Pepper
- ❏ Salt

Weekend Two Saturday

Swell Elegant Chicken

1 package (8 ounces) cream cheese
4 boneless, skinless chicken breast halves
    (about 1-1/2 pounds)
3 tablespoons fresh chives (when chopped)
3 tablespoons fresh parsley (when
    chopped)
4 slices bacon
2 tablespoons lemon juice
1/2 teaspoon dried thyme
1/2 teaspoon dried oregano
Seasoning to taste

Rhetorical Rice

1 medium red onion
2 tablespoons butter
1 cup long-grain white rice
1/2 teaspoon curry powder
1 can (14 ounces) vegetable broth
1/2 cup orange juice
1/4 cup dried currants
Seasoning to taste
1/4 cup slivered almonds

Articulate Tomatoes

1 package (10 ounces) frozen cut wax
    beans
1 clove garlic
2 scallions (green onions)
4 large fresh tomatoes
2 tablespoons butter
1/2 teaspoon celery seed
Seasoning to taste
1/4 cup plain breadcrumbs

Extravagant Raspberries

1 package (10 ounces) frozen
    raspberries
1 cup buttermilk
1/2 cup granulated sugar
1 tablespoon brandy
4 individual chocolate shells
1/2 cup chocolate syrup
1/4 cup whipped cream

EQUIPMENT

Blender
Medium covered saucepan
Medium skillet
9 × 9-inch glass baking dish
8 × 8-inch glass baking dish
Medium mixing bowl
3 small mixing bowls
Mallet
Ice cream scoop
Waxed paper
Kitchen knives
Measuring cups and spoons
Cooking utensils

Weekend Two Saturday

Swell Elegant Chicken

1. Set the cream cheese out to soften.

2. Preheat the oven to 350°F. Grease a 9 × 9-inch glass baking dish.

3. Place the chicken breasts between 2 sheets of waxed paper and pound to a 1/2-inch thickness. Rinse and chop the chives. Rinse and chop the parsley. Cut each bacon slice in half.

4. Combine the cream cheese, the lemon juice, the parsley, and the chives in a small bowl. Blend in the thyme and the oregano, and season to taste. Spoon a portion of the mixture on top of each chicken breast. Roll up the breasts and place them, seam side down, in the baking dish. Top each breast with the bacon.

5. Bake until the chicken is tender, about 20 minutes.

Rhetorical Rice

1. Peel and mince the onion.

2. Melt the butter in a medium saucepan and sauté the onion until it is soft, about 5 minutes. Add the rice and the curry powder, tossing to coat. Add the broth, the orange juice, and the currants. Season to taste, bring the mixture to a boil, reduce the heat, cover, and simmer until the liquid is absorbed and the rice is tender, about 20 minutes.

3. Fold in the almonds and fluff with a fork.

Articulate Tomatoes

1. Set the package of wax beans in a small bowl of hot water to thaw.

2. Peel and mince the garlic. Trim and chop the scallions. Rinse and dry the tomatoes, and cut off the tops. Carefully scoop out and reserve the pulp, leaving the shells. Turn the shells upside down on a paper towel to drain.

3. Melt the butter in a medium skillet and sauté the garlic for 1 minute. Add the beans, tossing to coat. Add the tomato pulp. Cook until the beans are crisp-tender, about 3 minutes.

4. Remove the pan from the heat and stir in the scallions and the celery seed. Season to taste.

5. Spoon the mixture into the tomato shells and top with the breadcrumbs.

6. Place the tomatoes in an 8 × 8-inch glass baking dish and bake at 350°F until heated through, about 10 minutes.

Extravagant
Raspberries

1. Set the package of raspberries in a small bowl of hot water to thaw.

2. Place the raspberries, the buttermilk, the sugar, and the brandy in a blender and process until smooth, about 30 seconds. Pour the mixture into a medium bowl and freeze until firm, at least 1 hour.

3. Place scoops of the frozen raspberry mixture into individual chocolate shells. Drizzle the shells with the chocolate sauce and top each with a dollop of whipped cream.

COUNTDOWN

1. Assemble the ingredients and the equipment.
2. Do Steps 1–2 of *Extravagant Raspberries*.
3. Do Steps 1–2 of *Articulate Tomatoes*.
4. Do Steps 1–5 of *Swell Elegant Chicken*.
5. Do Steps 1–2 of *Rhetorical Rice*.
6. Do Steps 3–6 of *Articulate Tomatoes*.
7. Do Step 3 of *Rhetorical Rice*.
8. Do Step 3 of *Extravagant Raspberries*.

Weekend Two Sunday

FRESH PRODUCE

VEGETABLES
1 small bunch broccoli
1 small head cauliflower
1/2 pound green beans
2 medium carrots
1 package (10 ounces) spinach
1 small head Belgian endive
8 large sweet onions
1 medium shallot

FRUIT
4 medium ripe pears
1 large lemon

CANS, JARS & BOTTLES

SOUP
2 cans (14 ounces each) chicken broth
2 cans (14 ounces each) beef broth

JUICE
8 ounces pineapple juice

DESSERT & BAKING NEEDS
1/4 cup marshmallow crème

PACKAGED GOODS

BAKED GOODS
4 slices French bread (about
   1/2-inch thick)
4 large sugar cookies

WINES & SPIRITS
1/4 cup dry sherry

REFRIGERATED PRODUCTS

CHEESE
4 ounces Gruyère cheese

FROZEN GOODS

PASTRY
1 sheet puff pastry

STAPLES

- ☐ Butter
- ☐ Flour
- ☐ Cornstarch
- ☐ Granulated sugar
- ☐ Multicolored sprinkles
- ☐ Olive oil
- ☐ Vegetable oil
- ☐ Dijon mustard
- ☐ Honey
- ☐ Dried basil
- ☐ Dried dill
- ☐ Ground nutmeg
- ☐ Pepper
- ☐ Salt

Weekend Two Sunday

MENU

Viva la Soup

1 sheet frozen puff pastry
8 large sweet onions
4 ounces Gruyère cheese
4 tablespoons butter
1 tablespoon olive oil
2 teaspoons granulated sugar
1 teaspoon salt
4 tablespoons flour
2 cans (14 ounces each) chicken broth
2 cans (14 ounces each) beef broth
1/4 cup dry sherry
Seasoning to taste
4 slices French bread (about 1/2-inch thick)

Joie de Veg

1 package (10 ounces) fresh spinach
1 small head Belgian endive
1 medium shallot
1/2 pound fresh green beans
2 medium carrots
1 small head cauliflower
1 small bunch broccoli
1 large lemon
1 teaspoon dried basil
1 teaspoon dried dill
3 tablespoons vegetable oil
1 teaspoon Dijon mustard
1/2 teaspoon honey
Seasoning to taste

C'est la Pear

4 medium ripe pears
8 ounces pineapple juice
1/2 teaspoon ground nutmeg
4 large sugar cookies
1 tablespoon cornstarch
2 tablespoons cold water
1/4 cup marshmallow crème
1 tablespoon multicolored sprinkles

EQUIPMENT

2 large covered saucepans
Medium covered saucepan
2-1/2-quart casserole
Steamer insert
Breadboard
Small mixing bowl
Whisk
Citrus juicer
Vegetable peeler
Rolling pin
Kitchen knives
Measuring cups and spoons
Cooking utensils

Viva la Soup

1. Set the puff pastry out to thaw.

2. Peel and thinly slice the onions. Cube the cheese.

3. Melt the butter with the oil in a large saucepan. Add the onions, cover, and simmer, stirring occasionally, until the onions are soft, about 20 minutes.

4. Add the sugar and the salt and continue cooking until the onions are golden, 40 to 50 minutes.

5. Blend in the flour. Add the chicken broth, the beef broth, and the sherry, and season to taste. Bring to a boil, reduce the heat, cover, and simmer for 10 minutes.

6. Lightly toast the French bread. Cut it into cubes.

7. Lightly flour a breadboard.

8. Lay the puff pastry out on the breadboard and roll it out to fit over the top of a 2-1/2-quart casserole. Prick the top of the pastry all over with a fork.

9. Spoon the soup into the casserole. Top with the French bread cubes and the cheese. Lay the pastry over the top and press around the edges to seal the pastry tightly.

10. Preheat the oven to 400°F.

11. Bake until the pastry is golden, about 8 minutes.

Joie de Veg

1. Rinse, trim, and dry the spinach and tear it into bite-sized pieces. Rinse and dry the endive and tear it into bite-sized pieces. Peel and mince the shallot. Arrange the greens on individual salad plates. Top with the shallot.

2. Rinse, trim, and cut the green beans into 2-inch pieces. Peel and julienne the carrots. Rinse the cauliflower and cut it into bite-sized florets. Rinse the broccoli and cut it into bite-sized florets.

3. Bring water to a boil in a large saucepan.

4. Arrange the green beans, the carrots, the cauliflower, and the broccoli in a steamer insert. Place the insert in the saucepan, cover, and steam the vegetables for 5 minutes.

5. Juice the lemon. In a small bowl, whisk together the lemon juice, the basil, the dill, the vegetable oil, the mustard, and the honey. Season to taste.

6. Drain the vegetables and spoon them over the greens. Drizzle the salads with the dressing.

C'est la Pear

1. Peel, core, and slice the pears.

2. Combine the pineapple juice and the nutmeg in a medium saucepan. Add the pears, bring to a boil, cover, reduce the heat, and simmer until the pears are just tender, about 5 minutes.

3. Remove the pan from the heat and set it aside.

4. Place the cookies on individual dessert plates. Arrange the pears over the cookies.

5. Dissolve the cornstarch in the water. Add the mixture to the pineapple liquid and cook, stirring, until thickened, about 2 minutes.

6. Pour the sauce over the pears and garnish each plate with a dollop of marshmallow crème and a splash of sprinkles.

COUNTDOWN

1. Assemble the ingredients and the equipment.
2. Do Steps 1–4 of *Viva la Soup*.
3. Do Steps 1–3 of *C'est la Pear*.
4. Do Steps 5–10 of *Viva la Soup*.
5. Do Steps 1–3 of *Joie de Veg*.
6. Do Step 11 of *Viva la Soup*.
7. Do Steps 4–6 of *Joie de Veg*.
8. Do Steps 4–6 of *C'est la Pear*.

Weekend Three Saturday

MEAT & POULTRY

1 lean boneless pork loin
(about 1-1/2 pounds)

FRESH PRODUCE

VEGETABLES
4 medium yams
1 pound asparagus
1 medium shallot
1 clove garlic

HERBS
1/4 cup parsley (when chopped)

FRUIT
1 large orange

CANS, JARS & BOTTLES

VEGETABLES
1 can (4 ounces) button mushrooms

PACKAGED GOODS

DESSERT & BAKING NEEDS
2 envelopes unflavored gelatin

WINES & SPIRITS

1/4 cup dry white wine
3 tablespoons brandy

REFRIGERATED PRODUCTS

DAIRY
1/4 cup half-and-half
1/2 cup sour cream
1-1/2 cups whipping cream
1/2 cup plain yogurt
2 eggs

FROZEN GOODS

FRUIT
1 package (10 ounces) sliced strawberries

STAPLES

- ❏ Butter
- ❏ Cornstarch
- ❏ Granulated sugar
- ❏ Dark brown sugar
- ❏ Lemon juice
- ❏ Plain breadcrumbs
- ❏ Beef bouillon cube
- ❏ Dried thyme
- ❏ Ground nutmeg
- ❏ Pepper
- ❏ Salt
- ❏ Orange extract
- ❏ Vanilla extract

Weekend Three Saturday

Swine With Wine

1 lean boneless pork loin (about
   1-1/2 pounds)
Seasoning to taste
1 medium shallot
1/4 cup fresh parsley (when chopped)
1 can (4 ounces) button mushrooms
2 tablespoons butter
1 teaspoon dried thyme
1/4 cup dry white wine
1 beef bouillon cube
1/4 cup half-and-half
1 tablespoon cornstarch
2 tablespoons water

Yamboree

4 medium yams
1 large orange
1/4 cup dark brown sugar
1/4 cup water
2 tablespoons butter
1 teaspoon orange extract
1 teaspoon ground nutmeg

Spear Pressure

2 eggs
1 pound fresh asparagus
1 clove garlic
4 tablespoons butter
3 tablespoons plain breadcrumbs
1-1/2 tablespoons lemon juice
Seasoning to taste

Dream Cream

1 package (10 ounces) frozen sliced
   strawberries
2 envelopes unflavored gelatin
1/2 cup + 2 tablespoons water
1-1/2 cups whipping cream
3/4 cup granulated sugar
1/2 cup plain yogurt
1/2 cup sour cream
2 teaspoons vanilla extract
3 tablespoons brandy

EQUIPMENT

Electric mixer	Large mixing bowl
Large covered saucepan	Small mixing bowl
Medium covered saucepan	Whisk
Medium saucepan	Citrus grater
2 small saucepans	Citrus juicer
Large covered skillet	Vegetable peeler
Small skillet	Plastic wrap
9 × 13-inch glass baking dish	Kitchen knives
Steamer insert	Measuring cups and spoons
	Cooking utensils

Swine With Wine

1. Cut the pork loin into 4 portions and season it to taste.

2. Peel and chop the shallot. Rinse and coarsely chop the parsley. Drain the mushrooms, reserving the liquid.

3. Melt the butter in a large skillet and sauté the shallot for 2 minutes. Add the pork and cook until it is lightly browned, 3 to 4 minutes per side. Cover the skillet, reduce the heat, and simmer until the pork is white throughout but still moist, about 15 minutes.

4. Remove the pork from the skillet and cover to keep it warm.

5. Add the thyme, the wine, the reserved mushroom liquid, and the bouillon cube to the skillet, and blend well. Blend in the half-and-half. Combine the cornstarch with the water and add it to the skillet, whisking until the sauce is thickened and smooth, about 5 minutes.

6. Add the mushrooms and the parsley, heat through, and spoon the sauce over the pork.

Yamboree

1. Trim and peel the yams and cut them in half lengthwise. Cover them with water in a large saucepan. Bring the water to a boil. Cover the pan, reduce the heat, and

simmer until the yams are tender, about 20 minutes.

2. Grate the peel from the orange and juice the orange.

3. Grease a 9 × 13-inch glass baking dish.

4. Drain the yams and set them aside.

5. In the same saucepan, combine the sugar, the water, the butter, and the orange juice. Bring the mixture to a boil and simmer until the sugar has dissolved and the syrup is clear, about 5 minutes. Stir in the orange extract.

6. Preheat the oven to 350°F.

7. Place the yams, cut side down, in the baking dish. Pour the syrup over the potatoes and sprinkle with the nutmeg.

8. Bake until the yams are heated through, about 15 minutes.

Spear Pressure

1. Cover the eggs with water in a small saucepan. Bring to a boil and hard-boil the eggs, 10 to 12 minutes.

2. Remove and discard the tough ends from the asparagus. Peel and mince the garlic.

3. Drain the eggs.

4. Bring a small amount of water to a boil in a medium saucepan.

5. Arrange the asparagus in a steamer insert, place the insert in the saucepan, cover,

and steam until the spears are crisp-tender, 3 to 8 minutes, depending on their thickness.

6. Melt the butter in a small skillet and sauté the garlic for 1 minute. Peel and finely chop the eggs and add them to the melted butter. Blend in the breadcrumbs and the lemon juice, and season to taste. Cover to keep warm.

7. Drain the asparagus and spoon the topping over the spears.

Dream Cream

1. Set the package of strawberries in a small bowl of warm water to thaw.

2. In a medium saucepan, combine the gelatin with 2 tablespoons of the water, and let stand for 5 minutes.

3. Add the whipping cream and 1/4 cup of the sugar, and heat, stirring, until the gelatin is dissolved, 6 to 8 minutes. Do not let the mixture boil.

4. Remove the pan from the heat, pour the gelatin mixture into a large bowl, and refrigerate it for 15 minutes.

5. With an electric mixer, beat the yogurt, the sour cream, and the vanilla into the gelatin mixture.

6. Cover the bowl tightly with plastic wrap and chill it for 2 hours.

7. Combine the strawberries, the remaining 1/2 cup sugar, and the remaining 1/2 cup water in a small saucepan. Bring to a boil and cook until the sugar is dissolved. Add the brandy, stir to combine, remove the pan from the heat, and let the mixture cool to room temperature.

8. Spoon the cream into individual dessert bowls and top with the strawberry sauce.

COUNTDOWN

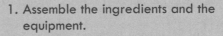

1. Assemble the ingredients and the equipment.
2. Do Steps 1–7 of *Dream Cream*.
3. Do Step 1 of *Yamboree*.
4. Do Steps 1–3 of *Spear Pressure*.
5. Do Steps 1–3 of *Swine With Wine*.
6. Do Steps 2–8 of *Yamboree*.
7. Do Steps 4–6 of *Spear Pressure*.
8. Do Steps 4–6 of *Swine With Wine*.
9. Do Step 7 of *Spear Pressure*.
10. Do Step 8 of *Dream Cream*.

Weekend Three Sunday

MEAT & POULTRY

1 pound sweet Italian bulk sausage

FRESH PRODUCE

VEGETABLES

1 medium head green cabbage
1 package (10 ounces) mixed salad
  greens
1 medium onion
2 cloves garlic

HERBS

1/4 cup chives (when chopped)
2 tablespoons coriander (when chopped)

FRUIT

2 medium yellow apples

CANS, JARS & BOTTLES

SOUP

1 can (10-1/2 ounces) beef broth

FRUIT

1 can (15 ounces) pineapple chunks

PACKAGED GOODS

PASTA, RICE & GRAINS

1 pound spaghetti

BAKED GOODS

1 loaf Italian bread

REFRIGERATED PRODUCTS

DAIRY

1/3 cup milk

CHEESE

1 package (3 ounces) cream cheese
1 cup shredded Cheddar cheese

FROZEN GOODS

DESSERTS

1 pint coffee ice cream

STAPLES

- ❏ Butter
- ❏ Granulated sugar
- ❏ Powdered sugar
- ❏ Multicolored sprinkles
- ❏ Olive oil
- ❏ Vegetable oil
- ❏ Apple cider vinegar
- ❏ Lemon juice
- ❏ Lime juice
- ❏ Dijon mustard
- ❏ Prepared horseradish
- ❏ Instant coffee
- ❏ Dried marjoram
- ❏ Pepper
- ❏ Salt
- ❏ Rum extract

Weekend Three Sunday

Impressive Pasta

1 medium head green cabbage
1 medium onion
2 cloves garlic
2 tablespoons fresh coriander (when chopped)
1 tablespoon olive oil
1 pound sweet Italian bulk sausage
1/2 teaspoon dried marjoram
1 can (10-1/2 ounces) beef broth
Seasoning to taste
1 pound spaghetti

Salad Encore

1 package (10 ounces) mixed salad greens
2 medium yellow apples
1 tablespoon lime juice
1 can (15 ounces) pineapple chunks
1/4 cup fresh chives (when chopped)
3 tablespoons vegetable oil
2 tablespoons apple cider vinegar
1 teaspoon Dijon mustard
1 teaspoon granulated sugar
Seasoning to taste

Larger Than Loaf

1 loaf Italian bread
1 package (3 ounces) cream cheese
2 tablespoons milk
1 cup shredded Cheddar cheese
1 tablespoon prepared horseradish
1 teaspoon lemon juice
Seasoning to taste

Jolt of Java

1/4 cup butter
1 1/2 cups powdered sugar
2 tablespoons instant coffee
4 tablespoons milk
1 teaspoon rum extract
1 pint coffee ice cream
Multicolored sprinkles

EQUIPMENT

Stockpot
Medium covered saucepan
Small covered saucepan
Large skillet
Baking sheet
Colander
Medium mixing bowl
2 small mixing bowls
Whisk
Ice cream scoop
Kitchen knives
Measuring cups and spoons
Cooking utensils

Weekend Three Sunday

Impressive Pasta

1. Bring water for the pasta to a boil in a stockpot.

2. Rinse, trim, and chop the cabbage. Place the cabbage in a medium saucepan, cover it with water, and bring to a boil.

3. Immediately remove the pan from the heat, drain the cabbage, and set it aside.

4. Peel and chop the onion. Peel and mince the garlic. Rinse and chop the coriander.

5. Heat the oil in a large skillet and sauté the onion, the garlic, and the coriander for 3 minutes.

6. Add the sausage and sauté until it is golden, about 10 minutes

7. Add the marjoram, the cabbage, and the broth. Season to taste, cover, reduce the heat, and simmer for 10 minutes.

8. Cook the pasta until it is almost tender, 2 to 3 minutes if you are using fresh pasta, 5 to 6 minutes if you are using dry pasta.

9. Drain the pasta and toss it with the sausage mixture.

Salad Encore

1. Wash and dry the salad greens and arrange them on individual salad plates.

2. Rinse, core, and chop the apples. Place them in a medium bowl and sprinkle them with the lime juice. Drain the pineapple and combine it with the apples. Arrange the fruit over the greens.

3. Rinse and chop the chives.

4. In a small bowl, whisk together the oil, the vinegar, the mustard, and the sugar. Season to taste.

5. Drizzle the dressing over the salads and sprinkle with the chives.

Larger Than Loaf

1. Preheat the oven to 350°F.

2. Split the bread in half lengthwise.

3. In a small bowl, combine the cream cheese and the milk. Fold in the Cheddar cheese, the horseradish, and the lemon juice. Season to taste. Spread the mixture on the cut sides of both halves of the bread. Place the bread, cut sides up, on a baking sheet and bake until heated through, about 10 minutes.

Jolt of Java

1. In a small saucepan, combine the butter, the sugar, the instant coffee, the milk, and the rum extract. Heat, stirring, until the butter is melted and the sauce is smooth, about 2 minutes. Cover the pan, remove it from the heat, and set it aside.

2. Place scoops of ice cream in individual dessert bowls. Pour the sauce over the ice cream and garnish with the sprinkles.

COUNTDOWN

1. Assemble the ingredients and the equipment.
2. Do Step 1 of *Jolt of Java*.
3. Do Steps 1–4 of *Salad Encore*.
4. Do Steps 1–7 of *Impressive Pasta*.
5. Do Steps 1–3 of *Larger Than Loaf*.
6. Do Steps 8–9 of *Impressive Pasta*.
7. Do Step 5 of *Salad Encore*.
8. Do Step 2 of *Jolt of Java*.

Weekend Four Saturday

SHOPPING LIST

FISH
1-1/2 pounds scallops

FRESH PRODUCE

VEGETABLES
1 small head romaine lettuce
1 bunch watercress
1 head Belgian endive
1 pint cherry tomatoes
1 medium orange bell pepper
1 medium sweet onion
3 scallions (green onions)
2 cloves garlic

HERBS
2 tablespoons basil (when chopped)

FRUIT
1 small lemon

CANS, JARS & BOTTLES

VEGETABLES
1 can (11 ounces) whole kernel corn
1 can (14 ounces) hearts of palm

PACKAGED GOODS

PASTA, RICE & GRAINS
12 ounces spinach noodles

DRIED FRUITS & NUTS
1 cup walnut bits

DESSERT & BAKING NEEDS
1-1/2 cups graham cracker crumbs

WINES & SPIRITS
1 cup dry white wine

REFRIGERATED PRODUCTS

DAIRY
1 cup plain yogurt
1/4 cup whipped cream
5 eggs

DELI
4 slices bacon

STAPLES

- [ ] Butter
- [ ] Flour
- [ ] Baking powder
- [ ] Baking soda
- [ ] Granulated sugar
- [ ] Vegetable oil
- [ ] Tarragon vinegar
- [ ] Worcestershire sauce
- [ ] Dried savory
- [ ] Pepper
- [ ] Salt
- [ ] Vanilla extract

MENU

Savory Scallops

4 slices bacon
1 medium sweet onion
1-1/2 pounds scallops
1 pint cherry tomatoes
1 can (11 ounces) whole kernel corn
1 small lemon
2 tablespoons butter
1 cup dry white wine
1 teaspoon dried savory
Seasoning to taste

Palatable Pasta

12 ounces spinach noodles
2 cloves garlic
2 tablespoons butter
Seasoning to taste

Sensible Salad

1 bunch watercress
1 head Belgian endive
1 small head romaine lettuce
3 scallions (green onions)
1 can (14 ounces) hearts of palm
1 medium orange bell pepper
3 tablespoons vegetable oil
2 tablespoons tarragon vinegar
1/2 teaspoon Worcestershire sauce
Seasoning to taste

Mellow Muffins

2 tablespoons fresh basil (when chopped)
1 cup plain yogurt

1/3 cup vegetable oil
1 egg
2 cups flour
1 tablespoon baking powder
1/2 teaspoon baking soda
1/4 teaspoon salt

Tempting Torte

4 large egg whites (reserving the yolks
    for use on Sunday)
1 cup granulated sugar
1-1/2 teaspoons baking powder
1-1/2 teaspoons vanilla extract
1-1/2 cups graham cracker crumbs
1 cup walnut bits
1/4 cup whipped cream

EQUIPMENT

Electric mixer	2 medium mixing bowls
Large covered saucepan	2 small mixing bowls
Large skillet	Whisk
Small skillet	Kitchen knives
Muffin tin	Measuring cups and spoons
Pie plate	Cooking utensils
Colander	

Weekend Four Saturday

Savory Scallops

1. Dice the bacon. Peel and chop the onion. Rinse and pat dry the scallops. Rinse and halve the tomatoes. Drain the corn.

2. Thinly slice the lemon.

3. In a large skillet, sauté the bacon with the onion for 5 minutes.

4. Add the butter, the tomatoes, the wine, and the savory. Season to taste and bring to a boil.

5. Add the scallops and the corn, reduce the heat, and simmer until the scallops are opaque, 3 to 4 minutes.

6. Garnish with the lemon slices.

Palatable Pasta

1. Bring water for the pasta to a boil in a large saucepan.

2. Cook the pasta until it is almost tender, 2 to 3 minutes if you are using fresh pasta, 6 to 7 minutes if you are using dry pasta.

3. Peel and mince the garlic. Melt the butter in a small skillet and sauté the garlic for 1 minute.

4. Drain the pasta, return it to the saucepan, and toss it with the garlic-butter mixture. Season to taste. Cover to keep warm.

Sensible Salad

1. Wash and dry the watercress, the endive, and the romaine. Tear them into bite-sized pieces and distribute among individual salad plates.

2. Trim and chop the scallions and sprinkle them over the greens. Drain and quarter the hearts of palm and arrange them over the scallions. Rinse, stem, seed, and chop the bell pepper and arrange it over the hearts of palm.

3. In a small bowl, whisk together the oil, the vinegar, and the Worcestershire sauce. Season to taste.

4. Drizzle the dressing over the salads.

Mellow Muffins

1. Increase the oven temperature to 400°F. Grease a muffin tin.

2. Rinse and chop the basil.

3. In a small bowl, whisk together the basil, the yogurt, the oil, and the egg.

4. In a medium bowl, combine the flour, the baking powder, the baking soda, and the salt. Fold the yogurt mixture into the flour mixture.

5. Divide the batter evenly among the muffin cups and bake until the muffins are golden, about 15 minutes.

Tempting Torte

1. Preheat the oven to 350°F. Grease a pie plate.

2. Separate the eggs, covering the yolks and reserving them in the refrigerator for use on Sunday.

3. In a medium bowl, beat the egg whites with an electric mixer until soft peaks form.

4. Gradually add the sugar, the baking powder, and the vanilla, and beat until very stiff and glossy.

5. Fold in the graham cracker crumbs. Fold in the walnuts.

6. Pour the mixture into the pie plate and bake until puffed and golden, 25 to 30 minutes.

7. Top with dollops of whipped cream.

COUNTDOWN

1. Assemble the ingredients and the equipment.
2. Do Steps 1–6 of *Tempting Torte*.
3. Do Steps 1–3 of *Sensible Salad*.
4. Do Steps 1–2 of *Savory Scallops*.
5. Do Step 1 of *Palatable Pasta*.
6. Do Steps 1–5 of *Mellow Muffins*.
7. Do Steps 2–4 of *Palatable Pasta*.
8. Do Steps 3–6 of *Savory Scallops*.
9. Do Step 4 of *Sensible Salad*.
10. Do Step 7 of *Tempting Torte*.

Weekend Four Sunday

MEAT & POULTRY

1 lean beef roast (about 4 pounds)

FRESH PRODUCE

VEGETABLES
1-1/2 pounds small new red potatoes
1 medium turnip
1 medium rutabaga
4 medium carrots
3 stalks celery
2 medium onions
1 head Bibb lettuce
1 box cherry tomatoes
1 medium cucumber
2 cloves garlic

HERBS
1/4 cup chives (when chopped)

FRUIT
1 medium lime

CANS, JARS & BOTTLES

FRUIT
1 can (16 ounces) whole cranberry sauce

JUICE
1 cup cranberry juice

DESSERT & BAKING NEEDS
1/4 cup marshmallow crème

PACKAGED GOODS

BAKED GOODS
1 shortbread pie shell

DESSERT & BAKING NEEDS
1 small package lime gelatin

WINES & SPIRITS

1 cup dry red wine

REFRIGERATED PRODUCTS

DAIRY
1 cup milk
4 egg yolks, reserved from Saturday

CHEESE
1/2 cup shredded Cheddar cheese

FROZEN GOODS

DESSERTS
1 pint vanilla ice cream

STAPLES

❑ Butter
❑ Flour
❑ Baking powder
❑ Granulated sugar
❑ Olive oil
❑ White wine vinegar
❑ Worcestershire sauce
❑ Dijon mustard
❑ Beef bouillon cubes
❑ Caraway seeds
❑ Bay leaf
❑ Dried rosemary
❑ Dried thyme
❑ Cayenne pepper
❑ Pepper
❑ Salt

Weekend Four Sunday

Sunday Kind of Beef

Seasoning to taste
1 lean beef roast (about 4 pounds)
2 cloves garlic
2 medium onions
4 medium carrots
1 medium turnip
1 medium rutabaga
3 stalks celery
1-1/2 pounds small new red potatoes
2 beef bouillon cubes
1 bay leaf
1 cup dry red wine
1 cup water
1 teaspoon dried rosemary
1 teaspoon dried thyme

Sally Salad

1 head Bibb lettuce
1 medium cucumber
1 box cherry tomatoes
1/4 cup fresh chives (when chopped)
3 tablespoons olive oil
2 tablespoons white wine vinegar
1 teaspoon white Worcestershire sauce
1/2 teaspoon granulated sugar
1/4 teaspoon cayenne pepper
Seasoning to taste

The Muffin Man

1/4 cup butter
2 cups flour
1 tablespoon baking powder
4 egg yolks (reserved from Saturday)

1 cup milk
1-1/2 tablespoons Dijon mustard
1/2 cup shredded Cheddar cheese
1 teaspoon caraway seeds

Parfait Pie

1 pint vanilla ice cream
1 medium lime
1 cup cranberry juice
1 small package lime gelatin
1/2 cup water
1 can (16 ounces) whole cranberry sauce
1 shortbread pie shell
1/4 cup marshmallow crème

EQUIPMENT

Medium saucepan	Whisk
Small saucepan	Citrus grater
Medium roasting pan	Citrus juicer
Muffin tin	Vegetable brush
Meat thermometer	Vegetable peeler
2 large mixing bowls	Kitchen knives
Medium mixing bowl	Measuring cups and spoons
2 small mixing bowls	Cooking utensils

Weekend Four Sunday

Sunday Kind of Beef

1. Preheat the oven to 400°F.

2. Season the roast to taste and place it, fat side up, in a medium roasting pan.

3. Peel and halve the garlic. Peel and quarter the onions. Peel and chunk the carrots. Peel and quarter the turnip. Peel and quarter the rutabaga. Rinse, trim, and chunk the celery. Scrub the potatoes and cut them in half.

4. Place the vegetables around the meat. Add the bouillon cubes, the bay leaf, the wine, the water, the rosemary, and the thyme.

5. Place the pan in the oven and roast until the beef begins to brown, about 15 minutes.

6. Reduce the oven temperature to 325°F, and roast until a meat thermometer inserted in the thickest part of the roast registers 160°F, about 2-1/2 hours for rare. Occasionally turn the vegetables for even browning.

7. Let the meat stand for 10 minutes before carving.

Sally Salad

1. Rinse and dry the lettuce and tear into bite-sized pieces. Peel and slice the cucumber. Rinse, dry, and halve the tomatoes. Combine the ingredients in a large bowl.

2. Rinse, pat dry, and chop the chives.

3. In a small bowl, whisk together the oil, the vinegar, the Worcestershire sauce, the sugar, and the cayenne pepper. Season to taste.

4. Toss the salad with the dressing. Sprinkle with the chives.

The Muffin Man

1. Increase the oven temperature to 425°F.

2. Melt the butter in a small saucepan.

3. In a large bowl, combine the flour and the baking powder.

4. In a small bowl, whisk together the egg yolks, the butter, the milk, and the mustard.

5. Make a well in the center of the dry ingredients. Pour in the egg mixture and stir to combine. Fold in the cheese and the caraway seeds.

6. Divide the batter evenly among the muffin cups, and bake until the muffins are golden, about 15 minutes.

Parfait Pie

1. Set the ice cream out to soften.

2. Grate 1 teaspoon of the lime peel and juice the lime.

3. In a medium saucepan, bring the cranberry juice to a boil. Add the lime gelatin and stir to dissolve.

4. Remove the pan from the heat and stir in the water. Add the ice cream and stir until melted. Pour the mixture into a medium bowl and refrigerate it for 30 minutes.

5. Stir the lime peel and the lime juice into the ice cream mixture. Fold in the cranberry sauce. Pour the mixture into the pie shell and refrigerate it for at least 1 hour.

6. Garnish with dollops of marshmallow crème.

COUNTDOWN

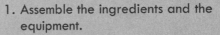

1. Assemble the ingredients and the equipment.
2. Do Steps 1–6 of *Sunday Kind of Beef.*
3. Do Steps 1–5 of *Parfait Pie.*
4. Do Steps 1–5 of *The Muffin Man.*
5. Do Step 7 of *Sunday Kind of Beef.*
6. Do Steps 1–3 of *Sally Salad.*
7. Do Step 6 of *The Muffin Man.*
8. Do Step 4 of *Sally Salad.*
9. Do Step 6 of *Parfait Pie.*

Weekend Five Saturday

MEAT & POULTRY

1 capon (about 5 pounds)

FRESH PRODUCE

VEGETABLES

1 pound green beans
1 stalk celery
1 medium onion
1 small onion
2 cloves garlic

HERBS

2 tablespoons basil (when chopped)
2 tablespoons parsley (when chopped)

CANS, JARS & BOTTLES

SPREADS

3/4 cup apricot preserves

CONDIMENTS

1 can (3-1/2 ounces) pitted black olives
1 jar (2 ounces) diced pimiento

PACKAGED GOODS

PASTA, RICE & GRAINS

6 ounces egg noodles

DRIED FRUITS & NUTS

1/4 cup sliced almonds

WINES & SPIRITS

1/4 cup dry white wine
1/2 cup Madeira

REFRIGERATED PRODUCTS

DAIRY

1/4 cup milk
2 tablespoons half-and-half
1/4 cup sour cream
1 cup whipping cream

FROZEN GOODS

PASTRY

4 puff pastry shells

STAPLES

- ☐ Butter
- ☐ Flour
- ☐ Granulated sugar
- ☐ Powdered sugar
- ☐ Olive oil
- ☐ Lemon juice
- ☐ Kitchen Bouquet
- ☐ Beef bouillon cube
- ☐ Dried thyme
- ☐ Pepper
- ☐ Salt
- ☐ Almond extract

Weekend Five Saturday

MENU

Al Capon

1 medium onion
2 cloves garlic
2 tablespoons parsley (when chopped)
6 ounces egg noodles
7 tablespoons butter
1/2 cup Madeira
1/4 teaspoon dried thyme
2 tablespoons half-and-half
Seasoning to taste
1 capon (about 5 pounds)
1/4 cup dry white wine
1 tablespoon Kitchen Bouquet

Gangster Gravy

1 small onion
1 stalk celery
Giblets and neck from the capon
2 cups water
1 beef bouillon cube
1/4 cup milk
3 tablespoons flour
1/4 cup sour cream
Seasoning to taste

Machine-Gun Beans

1 pound fresh green beans
2 tablespoons fresh basil (when chopped)
1 can (3-1/2 ounces) pitted black olives
1 jar (2 ounces) diced pimiento
1 tablespoon olive oil
2 tablespoons lemon juice
1/2 teaspoon granulated sugar
Seasoning to taste

Angels With Dirty Faces

4 frozen puff pastry shells
1 cup whipping cream
2 tablespoons powdered sugar
1 teaspoon almond extract
3/4 cup apricot preserves
1/4 cup sliced almonds

EQUIPMENT

Electric mixer	Strainer
Stockpot	Medium mixing bowl
2 medium covered saucepans	
	Whisk
Small saucepan	Baster
Medium skillet	Meat thermometer
Small skillet	Skewers
Medium roasting pan	Plastic wrap
	Kitchen knives
Roasting rack	Measuring cups and spoons
Baking sheet	
Colander	Cooking utensils

Weekend Five Saturday

RECIPES

Al Capon

1. Peel and chop the onion. Peel and mince the garlic. Rinse and chop the parsley.

2. Bring water for the pasta to a boil in a stockpot.

3. Cook the noodles for 5 minutes.

4. Drain the noodles well, return them to the stockpot, and toss with 1 tablespoon of the butter. Cover the stockpot and let it stand.

5. Melt 2 tablespoons of the butter in a small skillet and sauté the onion and the garlic for 3 minutes. Add the Madeira and cook for 2 minutes.

6. Add the thyme and the parsley. Stir in the half-and-half and season to taste. Pour the mixture over the noodles and combine thoroughly.

7. Rinse and pat dry the capon and season it to taste. Stuff the bird with the noodle dressing. Close the cavity with skewers.

8. Melt the remaining 4 tablespoons of butter in a small saucepan. Stir in the wine and the Kitchen Bouquet.

9. Place the capon on a rack in a medium roasting pan, breast side down. Baste the bird with half of the butter mixture and roast it at 400°F until golden, about 25 minutes.

10. Reduce the oven temperature to 350°F. Turn the bird over and baste it with the remaining butter mixture. Insert a meat thermometer in the fleshy part of the thigh, and continue to cook until the capon is tender and the thermometer registers 180°F, about 1-1/2 hours, basting occasionally with the pan juices.

11. Remove the capon from the roasting pan and let it sit for 10 minutes. Reserve the pan juices for the gravy.

12. Remove the stuffing, carve the capon, and serve with the gravy.

Gangster Gravy

1. Peel and quarter the onion. Rinse, trim, and chunk the celery. Rinse and pat dry the giblets and neck.

2. Place the onion, the celery, the giblets, and the neck in a medium saucepan. Cover the ingredients with the water. Add the bouillon cube and bring the mixture to a boil. Cover, reduce the heat, and simmer for 3 hours, checking occasionally to make sure the liquid does not boil out.

3. Strain the liquid, discarding the meat and the vegetables, and return it to the saucepan. Add the pan juices from the capon. Blend together the milk and the flour until smooth. Gradually add the mixture to the saucepan, blend in the sour cream, season to taste, and whisk until heated through and thickened.

Machine-Gun Beans

1. Rinse and trim the green beans and cut them into 3-inch pieces. Rinse and chop

the basil. Drain the olives. Drain the pimiento.

2. Bring water to a boil in a medium saucepan.

3. Cook the beans until crisp-tender, about 5 minutes.

4. Drain the beans, return them to the saucepan, and cover to keep warm.

5. Heat the oil in a medium skillet and sauté the basil for 3 minutes. Fold in the olives, the pimiento, the green beans, the lemon juice, and the sugar. Season to taste and heat through. Cover to keep warm.

Angels With Dirty Faces

1. Preheat the oven to 400°F.

2. Chill a medium bowl and the beaters of an electric mixer in the refrigerator for at least 10 minutes.

3. Place the pastry shells on an ungreased baking sheet and bake until the shells are golden brown and puffed, about 20 minutes.

4. In the chilled bowl, whip the cream until thick, about 3 minutes. Fold in the powdered sugar and the almond extract. Cover the bowl with plastic wrap and refrigerate it until you are ready to use.

5. Remove and discard the tops from the pastry shells. Return the shells to the oven and cook for 5 minutes more.

6. Remove the shells from the oven and let them cool.

7. Fill the pastry shells with the whipped cream. Spoon the apricot preserves over the tops and sprinkle with the almonds.

COUNTDOWN

1. Assemble the ingredients and the equipment.
2. Do Steps 1–6 of *Angels With Dirty Faces*.
3. Do Steps 1–2 of *Gangster Gravy*.
4. Do Steps 1–10 of *Al Capon*.
5. Do Steps 1–5 of *Machine-Gun Beans*.
6. Do Step 11 of *Al Capon*.
7. Do Step 3 of *Gangster Gravy*.
8. Do Step 12 of *Al Capon*.
9. Do Step 7 of *Angels With Dirty Faces*.

Weekend Five Sunday

MEAT & POULTRY

1-1/2 pounds chorizo sausage

FRESH PRODUCE

VEGETABLES

2 stalks celery
4 large mushrooms
1 small head lettuce
3 medium tomatoes
1 medium ripe avocado
1 large onion
3 cloves garlic

HERBS

2 tablespoons chives (when chopped)
3 tablespoons cilantro (when chopped)

CANS, JARS & BOTTLES

SOUP

2 cans (14 ounces each) chicken broth

VEGETABLES

2 cans (15 ounces each) black beans
1 can (15 ounces) cream style corn

PACKAGED GOODS

INTERNATIONAL FOODS

4 flour tortillas

REFRIGERATED PRODUCTS

DAIRY

1 cup milk
1/2 cup sour cream
2 eggs

FROZEN GOODS

DESSERTS

1 pint chocolate almond ice cream

STAPLES

- ☐ Flour
- ☐ Cornmeal
- ☐ Baking powder
- ☐ Baking soda
- ☐ Granulated sugar
- ☐ Powdered sugar
- ☐ Chocolate syrup
- ☐ Olive oil
- ☐ Vegetable oil
- ☐ Red wine vinegar
- ☐ Lemon juice
- ☐ Bay leaves
- ☐ Dried oregano
- ☐ Cayenne pepper
- ☐ Ground cinnamon
- ☐ Ground cumin
- ☐ Pepper
- ☐ Salt

Weekend Five Sunday

MENU

Guadalupe Soupe

3 cloves garlic
1 large onion
2 stalks celery
2 tablespoons fresh chives (when chopped)
3 tablespoons fresh cilantro (when chopped)
1-1/2 pounds chorizo sausage
2 cans (15 ounces each) black beans
1 tablespoon olive oil
2 cans (14 ounces each) chicken broth
1 teaspoon dried oregano
2 teaspoons ground cumin
2 bay leaves
Seasoning to taste
1/2 cup sour cream

Tomato Ensalada

1 small head lettuce
3 medium fresh tomatoes
4 large fresh mushrooms
1 medium ripe avocado
3 tablespoons vegetable oil
2 tablespoons red wine vinegar
1 tablespoon lemon juice
1/2 teaspoon granulated sugar
1/4 teaspoon cayenne pepper
Seasoning to taste

Mexicornbread

1 cup flour
1 cup cornmeal
4 teaspoons baking powder
1/2 teaspoon baking soda
1/4 teaspoon salt
2 tablespoons granulated sugar
1 cup milk
2 eggs
1/4 cup vegetable oil
1 can (15 ounces) cream style corn

Buñuelos

1 cup vegetable oil
1/2 cup powdered sugar
1 tablespoon ground cinnamon
4 flour tortillas
1 pint chocolate almond ice cream
Chocolate syrup

EQUIPMENT

Dutch oven

Large skillet

8 × 8-inch baking pan

Large mixing bowl

3 small mixing bowls

Whisk

Ice cream scoop

Kitchen knives

Measuring cups and spoons

Cooking utensils

Guadalupe Soupe

1. Peel and mince the garlic. Peel and mince the onion. Rinse, trim, and chop the celery. Rinse and chop the chives. Rinse and chop the cilantro.

2. Remove the casings from the sausage. Drain the beans.

3. Heat the oil in a Dutch oven and sauté the sausage until it is lightly browned, about 5 minutes.

4. Pour off all but 3 tablespoons of the fat.

5. Add the garlic, the onion, and the celery, and sauté until the onion is soft, about 5 minutes.

6. Add the beans, the broth, the oregano, the cumin, and the bay leaves. Season to taste.

7. Bring to a boil, reduce the heat, and simmer for 30 minutes.

8. Discard the bay leaves and serve the soup with the sour cream, the chives, and the cilantro.

Tomato Ensalada

1. Wash and dry the lettuce and distribute the leaves among individual salad plates.

2. Rinse and chop the tomatoes. Rinse, pat dry, and thinly slice the mushrooms. Peel, pit, and slice the avocado.

3. In a small bowl, whisk together the oil, the vinegar, the lemon juice, the sugar, and the cayenne pepper. Season to taste.

4. Top the lettuce leaves with the tomatoes, the mushrooms, and the avocado.

5. Drizzle with the dressing.

Mexicornbread

1. Grease an 8 × 8-inch baking pan.

2. In a large bowl, combine the flour, the cornmeal, the baking powder, the baking soda, the salt, and the sugar.

3. In a small bowl, beat together the milk, the eggs, and the oil.

4. Make a well in the center of the dry ingredients and fold in the egg mixture. Fold in the corn. Pour the mixture into the baking pan.

5. Preheat the oven to 425°F.

6. Bake until the cornbread is golden, 20 to 25 minutes.

Buñuelos

1. Heat the vegetable oil in a large skillet.

2. In a small bowl, combine the powdered sugar and the cinnamon.

3. Cook each tortilla in the hot oil until it is crisp, about 30 seconds per side.

4. Remove the tortillas to paper towels and blot them well. Sprinkle them with the sugar and cinnamon mixture.

5. Place each tortilla on an individual serving plate, top with scoops of ice cream, and drizzle with the chocolate syrup.

COUNTDOWN

1. Assemble the ingredients and the equipment.
2. Do Steps 1–5 of *Mexicornbread.*
3. Do Steps 1–7 of *Guadalupe Soupe.*
4. Do Step 6 of *Mexicornbread.*
5. Do Steps 1–5 of *Tomato Ensalada.*
6. Do Step 8 of *Guadalupe Soupe.*
7. Do Steps 1–5 of *Buñuelos.*

Weekend Six Saturday

MEAT & POULTRY

2 pounds lean boneless beef steak
1/2 pound lean cooked ham steak

FRESH PRODUCE

VEGETABLES
1-1/2 pounds small new potatoes
1/2 pound baby carrots
1 medium head green leaf lettuce
2 medium ripe avocados
2 medium sweet onions
12 small boiling onions
1 head garlic

FRUIT
2 medium ripe pears

CANS, JARS & BOTTLES

SOUP
2 cans (10-1/2 ounces each)
    beef consommé

VEGETABLES
1 can (4 ounces) button mushrooms

PACKAGED GOODS

DRIED FRUITS & NUTS
1/2 cup raisins
1/2 cup pecan pieces

DESSERT & BAKING NEEDS
1/2 cup flaked coconut

WINES & SPIRITS

1-1/2 cups Burgundy wine
1/4 cup brandy

REFRIGERATED PRODUCTS

DAIRY
1/4 cup whipped cream
2 eggs

FROZEN GOODS

PASTRY
1 pie shell

STAPLES

- ❏ Butter
- ❏ Flour
- ❏ Granulated sugar
- ❏ Dark brown sugar
- ❏ Olive oil
- ❏ Vegetable oil
- ❏ Apple cider vinegar
- ❏ Lime juice
- ❏ Honey
- ❏ Poppy seeds
- ❏ Dried marjoram
- ❏ Dried rosemary
- ❏ Dried thyme
- ❏ Dry mustard
- ❏ Pepper
- ❏ Salt
- ❏ Rum extract

MENU

Spirited Beef

2 pounds lean boneless beef steak
1/2 pound lean cooked ham steak
2 medium sweet onions
1/2 pound baby carrots
12 small boiling onions
1 can (4 ounces) button mushrooms
1/4 cup flour
Seasoning to taste
3 tablespoons butter
2 cans (10-1/2 ounces each) beef
    consommé
1 teaspoon dried thyme
1 teaspoon dried marjoram
1/4 cup brandy
1-1/2 cups Burgundy wine

Intrepid Potatoes

1-1/2 pounds small new potatoes
1 head garlic
1/3 cup olive oil
1 tablespoon dried rosemary
Seasoning to taste

Stalwart Salad

1 medium head green leaf lettuce
2 medium ripe avocados
2 medium ripe pears
1/4 cup lime juice
3 tablespoons vegetable oil
1 tablespoon honey
1/2 teaspoon dry mustard
1 tablespoon poppy seeds
Seasoning to taste

Impieous

1 frozen pie shell
1/2 cup butter
2 eggs
1/4 cup dark brown sugar
1/2 cup granulated sugar
2 teaspoons apple cider vinegar
2 teaspoons rum extract
1/2 cup pecan pieces
1/2 cup flaked coconut
1/2 cup raisins
1/4 cup whipped cream

EQUIPMENT

Electric mixer
Dutch oven
Small saucepan
9 × 13-inch baking pan
Large shallow bowl
Large mixing bowl
2 medium mixing bowls
Whisk
Kitchen knives
Measuring cups and spoons
Cooking utensils

Spirited Beef

1. Cut the beef steak into 1-1/2 inch cubes. Cube the ham steak. Peel and chop the sweet onions. Rinse and trim the baby carrots. Peel the boiling onions. Drain the mushrooms.

2. Place the flour in a large shallow bowl and season to taste. Dredge the beef cubes in the seasoned flour.

3. Melt the butter in a Dutch oven and sauté the beef cubes until they are seared on all sides, about 10 minutes.

4. Add the ham cubes and lightly brown them, about 5 minutes.

5. Add the consommé, the chopped onions, the carrots, the thyme, and the marjoram.

6. Cover and simmer for 1 hour.

7. Add the brandy, the Burgundy, the whole boiling onions, and the mushrooms to the mixture and simmer until the beef is very tender, about 45 minutes longer.

Intrepid Potatoes

1. Rinse the potatoes and cut them in half. Peel the garlic and cut the cloves in half.

2. Place the oil in a large bowl. Add the potatoes, the garlic, and the rosemary. Season to taste and toss to coat.

3. Increase the oven temperature to 400°F.

4. Place the potatoes and the garlic in a 9 × 13-inch baking pan. Drizzle the oil mixture over the potatoes and bake until the potatoes and garlic are tender, 35 to 40 minutes.

Stalwart Salad

1. Wash and dry the lettuce and arrange the leaves on individual salad plates.

2. Peel, pit, and thinly slice the avocados. Rinse, peel, core, and thinly slice the pears.

3. Combine the avocados and the pears in a medium bowl and toss with the lime juice.

4. Using a slotted spoon, alternately place the avocados and the pears on the lettuce.

5. Reserve the lime juice.

6. Whisk the oil, the honey, the mustard, and the poppy seeds into the lime juice. Season to taste and spoon the dressing over the salad.

Impieous

1. Set the pie shell out to thaw.

2. Preheat the oven to 325°F.

3. Melt the butter in a small saucepan.

4. In a medium bowl, beat the eggs with an electric mixer until thick and lemony.

5. Add the brown sugar, the granulated sugar, the butter, the vinegar, and the rum extract, and beat until well blended.

6. Fold in the pecans, the coconut, and the raisins. Pour the mixture into the pie shell and bake until a toothpick inserted into the center comes out clean, about 45 minutes.

7. Garnish with dollops of whipped cream.

COUNTDOWN

1. Do Steps 1–6 of *Spirited Beef*.
2. Do Steps 1–2 of *Intrepid Potatoes*.
3. Do Steps 1–6 of *Impieous*.
4. Do Step 7 of *Spirited Beef*.
5. Do Steps 3–4 of *Intrepid Potatoes*.
6. Do Steps 1–6 of *Stalwart Salad*.
7. Do Step 7 of *Impieous*.

Weekend Six Sunday

SHOPPING LIST

MEAT & POULTRY

1 whole chicken (about 4 pounds)

FRESH PRODUCE

VEGETABLES
1 pound green beans
2 stalks celery
1 small head Boston lettuce
2 medium orange bell peppers
1 large onion
1 medium shallot

HERBS
1/4 cup parsley (when chopped)

FRUIT
2 medium apples

CANS, JARS & BOTTLES

SOUP
1 can (10-1/2 ounces) chicken broth

PACKAGED GOODS

PASTA, RICE & GRAINS
1 cup orzo

REFRIGERATED PRODUCTS

DAIRY
1/2 cup half-and-half
1 cup whipping cream

STAPLES

❒ Butter
❒ Granulated sugar
❒ Powdered sugar
❒ Chocolate syrup
❒ Vegetable oil
❒ White wine vinegar
❒ Worcestershire sauce
❒ Dijon mustard
❒ Instant coffee
❒ Bay leaf
❒ Whole allspice
❒ Ground cloves
❒ Ground ginger
❒ Pepper
❒ Salt
❒ Vanilla extract

Weekend Six Sunday

Chicken From Castile

2 stalks celery
1 large onion
1 whole chicken (about 4 pounds)
Seasoning to taste
4 tablespoons butter
1 bay leaf
3 whole allspice
1 cup water
2 medium apples
1-1/2 teaspoons ground ginger
1 can (10-1/2 ounces) chicken broth
1/2 cup half-and-half

The Mark of Orzo

1 medium shallot
1/4 cup fresh parsley (when chopped)
1 cup orzo
2 tablespoons butter
1/2 teaspoon ground cloves
Seasoning to taste

Second Fiddle Salad

1 small head Boston lettuce
1 pound fresh green beans
2 medium orange bell peppers
2 teaspoons granulated sugar
3 tablespoons vegetable oil
2 tablespoons white wine vinegar
1 teaspoon Dijon mustard
1/2 teaspoon Worcestershire sauce
Seasoning to taste

The Black Rose

1 cup whipping cream
2 tablespoons powdered sugar
1 teaspoon vanilla extract
1 tablespoon instant coffee
2/3 cup chocolate syrup

EQUIPMENT

Electric mixer

Medium roasting pan

Large saucepan

2 medium saucepans

Medium covered skillet

Roasting rack

Strainer

Medium mixing bowl

Small mixing bowl

Whisk

Kitchen knives

Measuring cups and spoons

Cooking utensils

Weekend Six Sunday

RECIPES

Chicken From Castile

1. Preheat the oven to 400°F.

2. Rinse, trim, and chunk the celery. Peel and quarter the onion. Rinse and pat dry the chicken.

3. Place the celery pieces in a medium roasting pan. Rub the chicken with the onion. Season the chicken to taste, inside and out, and place it on a rack in the roasting pan. Place one onion quarter inside the chicken, and place the other quarters in the pan.

4. Melt the butter in a medium saucepan.

5. Spoon 1 tablespoon of the melted butter evenly over the bird, reserving the rest. Add the bay leaf, the allspice, and the 1 cup of water to the roasting pan, and roast the chicken until it is golden, about 20 minutes.

6. Turn the chicken over, reduce the oven temperature to 350°F, and continue roasting until a leg moves easily, about 50 minutes more.

7. Peel, core, and slice the apples.

8. Add the ginger to the reserved butter. Cook for 1 minute, stirring to mix well. Add the apple slices, tossing to coat. Add the broth and the half-and-half. Bring the mixture to a boil, stirring occasionally. Cook until the sauce thickens, about 10 minutes.

9. Carve the chicken and serve it with the sauce.

The Mark of Orzo

1. Peel and chop the shallot. Rinse and chop the parsley.

2. Bring water to a boil in a large saucepan.

3. Cook the orzo until it is almost tender, about 5 minutes.

4. Melt the butter in a medium skillet and mix in the cloves. Sauté the shallot in the butter until it is translucent, about 3 minutes.

5. Drain the orzo and combine it with the shallot. Season to taste and sprinkle with the parsley.

Second Fiddle Salad

1. Wash and dry the lettuce and distribute the leaves among individual salad plates. Rinse and trim the green beans. Rinse, stem, seed, and julienne the bell peppers.

2. Bring a small amount of water to a boil in a medium saucepan.

3. Add the beans and the sugar, and cook the beans for 5 minutes. Add the bell peppers and cook for 2 minutes more.

4. In a small bowl, whisk together the oil, the vinegar, the mustard, and the Worcester-shire sauce. Season to taste.

5. Drain the vegetables and toss them with the dressing. Spoon the warm vegetables over the lettuce.

The Black Rose

1. Chill a medium bowl and the beaters of an electric mixer in the refrigerator for at least 10 minutes.

2. In the chilled bowl, whip the cream until stiff peaks form, about 3 minutes.

3. Fold in the powdered sugar, the vanilla, and the coffee. Fold in the chocolate syrup.

4. Spoon the mixture into individual dessert glasses and refrigerate until you are ready to serve.

COUNTDOWN

1. Assemble the ingredients and the equipment.
2. Do Steps 1–5 of *Chicken From Castile*.
3. Do Steps 1–4 of *The Black Rose*.
4. Do Step 6 of *Chicken From Castile*.
5. Do Steps 1–2 of *The Mark of Orzo*.
6. Do Steps 1–2 of *Second Fiddle Salad*.
7. Do Steps 7–8 of *Chicken From Castile*.
8. Do Step 3 of *Second Fiddle Salad*.
9. Do Steps 3–4 of *The Mark of Orzo*.
10. Do Steps 4–5 of *Second Fiddle Salad*.
11. Do Step 5 of *The Mark of Orzo*.
12. Do Step 9 of *Chicken From Castile*.

Weekend Seven Saturday

FISH

4 swordfish steaks (about 1-1/2 pounds)

FRESH PRODUCE

VEGETABLES

1 pound asparagus
1 medium carrot
1 stalk celery
1 small green bell pepper
1 small yellow bell pepper
1 medium onion
3 scallions (green onions)
1 clove garlic

CANS, JARS & BOTTLES

FRUIT

1 can (11 ounces) mandarin oranges
1 can (16 ounces) pitted dark cherries

SPREADS

1/2 cup red currant jelly

PACKAGED GOODS

PASTA, RICE & GRAINS

1/2 cup long-grain white rice
1/2 cup wild rice

DRIED FRUITS & NUTS

1/4 cup cashew pieces

DESSERT & BAKING NEEDS

1 large package cherry gelatin

WINES & SPIRITS

1/4 cup dry white wine
1/2 cup port

REFRIGERATED PRODUCTS

DAIRY

1/2 cup whipping cream

JUICE

1-1/4 cups orange juice

STAPLES

- ☐ Butter
- ☐ Cornstarch
- ☐ Powdered sugar
- ☐ Lemon juice
- ☐ Tabasco sauce
- ☐ Chicken bouillon cube
- ☐ Dried savory
- ☐ Ground cinnamon
- ☐ Pepper
- ☐ Salt

Weekend Seven Saturday

MENU

A Sordid Affair

4 swordfish steaks (about 1-1/2 pounds)
1 clove garlic
4 tablespoons butter
1-1/4 cups orange juice
Seasoning to taste
2 tablespoons cornstarch
1/4 cup dry white wine
1/4 cup red currant jelly
1/4 cup lemon juice
1/4 teaspoon Tabasco sauce
1 can (11 ounces) mandarin oranges

Rendezvous With Rice

1 medium onion
1 medium carrot
1 stalk celery
1 small yellow bell pepper
1 small green bell pepper
3 scallions (green onions)
1/2 cup long-grain white rice
1/2 cup wild rice
1 chicken bouillon cube
2-1/4 cups water
2 tablespoons butter
1/2 teaspoon dried savory
Seasoning to taste

Amorous Asparagus

1/4 cup cashew pieces
1 pound fresh asparagus
3 tablespoons butter
1 tablespoon lemon juice
Seasoning to taste

A Couple of Cherries

1 can (16 ounces) pitted dark cherries
1/2 cup port
2 cups water
1 large package cherry gelatin
1/2 cup whipping cream
1 tablespoon powdered sugar
1/2 teaspoon ground cinnamon

EQUIPMENT

Electric mixer
Double boiler
Medium covered saucepan
Medium saucepan
2 small saucepans
2 large covered skillets
9 × 13-inch glass baking dish
Large mixing bowl
2 medium mixing bowls

Vegetable peeler
Pastry brush
Mallet
Plastic bag
Plastic wrap
Kitchen knives
Measuring cups and spoons
Cooking utensils

Weekend Seven Saturday

A Sordid Affair

1. Grease a 9 × 13-inch glass baking dish.

2. Rinse and pat dry the swordfish steaks. Peel and mince the garlic.

3. Melt 2 tablespoons of the butter in a small saucepan. Blend in 1/4 cup of the orange juice. Arrange the fish in the baking dish and brush it with some of the butter mixture. Season to taste.

4. Combine the cornstarch and the remaining 1 cup orange juice in a medium sauce-pan. Add the wine, the currant jelly, the lemon juice, the Tabasco sauce, and the garlic. Simmer, stirring, until the mixture thickens, about 3 minutes. Drain the mandarin oranges and fold them into the orange mixture. Remove the pan from the heat and cover to keep warm.

5. Preheat the broiler.

6. Broil the swordfish for 5 minutes. Turn the steaks, baste with the remaining butter mixture, and broil until the fish flakes easily with a fork, about 3 minutes.

7. Spoon the mandarin orange sauce over the fish.

Rendezvous With Rice

1. Peel and chop the onion. Peel and chop the carrot. Rinse, trim, and chop the celery. Rinse, stem, seed, and chop the bell peppers. Trim and chop the scallions.

2. Bring water to a boil in the bottom of a double boiler. Combine the rice, the bouillon cube, and the 2-1/4 cups water in the top of the double boiler. Cover, reduce the heat, and simmer until the liquid is absorbed and the rice is tender, 30 to 40 minutes.

3. Melt the butter in a large skillet and sauté the onion, the carrot, and the bell peppers until crisp-tender, about 8 minutes. Add the savory, and season to taste.

4. Fold the rice into the vegetables and toss with the scallions. Cover to keep warm.

Amorous Asparagus

1. Bring a small amount of water to a boil in a large skillet.

2. Place the cashews in a plastic bag and crush them with a mallet. Rinse the asparagus and remove and discard the tough ends.

3. Add the asparagus to the skillet, cover, reduce the heat, and simmer until the spears are crisp-tender, 3 to 8 minutes, depending on their thickness.

4. Melt the butter in a small saucepan. Blend in the lemon juice and the cashews, and season to taste.

5. Drain the asparagus and top with the butter sauce.

A Couple of Cherries

1. Drain the cherries, reserving the liquid in a large bowl. Place the cherries in a medium bowl, add the wine, cover, and set aside for 30 minutes.

2. Bring the water to a boil in a medium saucepan. Add the gelatin, stirring to dissolve.

3. Drain the wine from the cherries and add it to the reserved cherry liquid. Add enough cold water to make 1-1/2 cups. Add the gelatin to the wine mixture and refrigerate until partially set, about 30 minutes. Fold in the reserved cherries and pour the mixture into individual dessert glasses. Chill until firm, about 2 hours.

4. Chill a medium bowl and the beaters of an electric mixer in the refrigerator for at least 10 minutes.

5. In the chilled bowl, whip the cream until soft peaks form. Fold in the powdered sugar and the cinnamon, and beat until stiff. Cover the bowl with plastic wrap and refrigerate it until you are ready to serve.

6. Top each dessert with dollops of whipped cream.

COUNTDOWN

1. Assemble the ingredients and the equipment.
2. Do Steps 1–5 of *A Couple of Cherries*.
3. Do Steps 1–2 of *Rendezvous With Rice*.
4. Do Steps 1–5 of *A Sordid Affair*.
5. Do Steps 1–4 of *Amorous Asparagus*.
6. Do Step 6 of *A Sordid Affair*.
7. Do Steps 3–4 of *Rendezvous With Rice*.
8. Do Step 5 of *Amorous Asparagus*.
9. Do Step 7 of *A Sordid Affair*.
10. Do Step 6 of *A Couple of Cherries*.

Weekend Seven Sunday

SHOPPING LIST

FRESH PRODUCE

VEGETABLES
1 package (10 ounces) spinach
1 medium head romaine lettuce
1 large tomato
1 medium red bell pepper
1 small onion
3 cloves garlic

HERBS
1/4 cup parsley (when chopped)

CANS, JARS & BOTTLES

VEGETABLES
1 can (15 ounces) garbanzo beans

CONDIMENTS
1 can (3-1/2 ounces) pitted black olives

PACKAGED GOODS

PASTA, RICE & GRAINS
1 pound penne
2-1/2 cups bran cereal

BAKED GOODS
1 loaf peasant bread

REFRIGERATED PRODUCTS

DAIRY
2 tablespoons half-and-half
1 egg

CHEESE
1/4 cup shredded mozzarella cheese

DELI
4 ounces proscuitto

STAPLES

- ☐ Butter
- ☐ Vegetable shortening
- ☐ Flour
- ☐ Baking powder
- ☐ Baking soda
- ☐ Granulated sugar
- ☐ Dark brown sugar
- ☐ Molasses
- ☐ Olive oil
- ☐ Vegetable oil
- ☐ Red wine vinegar
- ☐ Grated Parmesan cheese
- ☐ Coffee
- ☐ Celery seed
- ☐ Ground cinnamon
- ☐ Ground cumin
- ☐ Ground ginger
- ☐ Italian seasoning
- ☐ Dry mustard
- ☐ Pepper
- ☐ Red pepper flakes
- ☐ Salt
- ☐ Vanilla extract

Weekend Seven Sunday

Penne From Heaven

1 medium red bell pepper
2 cloves garlic
1 package (10 ounces) fresh spinach
4 ounces prosciutto
1 pound penne
2 tablespoons butter
2 tablespoons olive oil
1 teaspoon Italian seasoning
1/4 teaspoon red pepper flakes
Seasoning to taste
1/4 cup shredded mozzarella cheese
1/2 cup grated Parmesan cheese

Down to Earth Salad

1 medium head romaine lettuce
1/4 cup fresh parsley (when chopped)
1 large fresh tomato
1 can (15 ounces) garbanzo beans
1 can (3-1/2 ounces) pitted black olives
1 clove garlic
1 teaspoon ground cumin
2 tablespoons red wine vinegar
1 teaspoon dry mustard
3 tablespoons vegetable oil
Seasoning to taste

Beyond the Bread

1 loaf peasant bread
1 small onion
2 tablespoons butter
1 teaspoon celery seed
Seasoning to taste

Jubilee Bars

2 tablespoons butter
1 cup strong coffee (when brewed)
4 tablespoons vegetable shortening
1/3 cup granulated sugar
1 egg
1/2 cup molasses
2-1/2 cups bran cereal
1-1/2 cups flour
1 tablespoon baking powder
1/4 teaspoon baking soda
1/4 teaspoon salt
1/2 teaspoon ground cinnamon
1/4 teaspoon ground ginger
1 teaspoon vanilla extract
2/3 cup dark brown sugar
2 tablespoons half-and-half

EQUIPMENT

Electric mixer	2 small mixing bowls
Stockpot	Whisk
Large skillet	Pastry brush
9 × 9-inch baking pan	Kitchen knives
Baking sheet	Measuring cups and spoons
Colander	Cooking utensils
2 large mixing bowls	

Penne From Heaven

1. Bring water for the pasta to a boil in a stockpot.

2. Rinse, stem, seed, and chop the bell pepper. Peel and mince the garlic. Rinse, pat dry, and stem the spinach. Chop the prosciutto.

3. Cook the pasta in the boiling water until it is almost tender, 7 to 9 minutes.

4. Melt the butter with the oil in a large skillet.

5. Add the garlic and the bell pepper, and sauté until the pepper begins to soften, 2 to 3 minutes.

6. Add the prosciutto, the Italian seasoning, and the red pepper flakes, toss to combine, and heat through.

7. Add the spinach to the skillet and sauté for 1 minute. Season to taste.

8. Drain the pasta, return it to the stockpot, and toss it with the mozzarella cheese.

9. Toss the spinach mixture with the pasta, and sprinkle with the Parmesan cheese.

Down to Earth Salad

1. Wash and dry the romaine and tear it into bite-sized pieces. Rinse and chop the parsley. Rinse and chop the tomato. Drain the beans. Drain the olives. Combine the ingredients in a large bowl.

2. Peel and mince the garlic.

3. In a small bowl, whisk together the garlic, the cumin, the vinegar, the mustard, and the oil. Season to taste.

4. Toss the salad with the dressing.

Beyond the Bread

1. Preheat the oven to 350°F.

2. Cut the bread in half lengthwise.

3. Peel and mince the onion.

4. Melt the butter.

5. Brush both halves of the bread with the melted butter. Sprinkle the onion over both halves. Top with celery seed, and season to taste.

6. Place the bread halves on a baking sheet, cut sides up, and bake until lightly brown, about 10 minutes.

Jubilee Bars

1. Set the butter out to soften. Brew the coffee.

2. Preheat the oven to 350°F. Grease and flour a 9 × 9-inch baking pan.

3. Combine the shortening and the granulated sugar in a large bowl and beat with an electric mixer until soft and fluffy. Beat in the egg, the molasses, and the coffee. Fold in the cereal, the flour, the baking powder, the baking soda, the salt, the cinnamon, the ginger, and the vanilla. Pour the mixture into the baking pan. Bake for 30 minutes.

4. In a small bowl, combine the softened butter, the brown sugar, and the half-and-half, spread the mixture over the warm cake, and cut it into bars to serve.

COUNTDOWN

1. Assemble the ingredients and the equipment.
2. Do Steps 1–4 of *Jubilee Bars*.
3. Do Steps 1–3 of *Down to Earth Salad*.
4. Do Steps 1–6 of *Beyond the Bread*.
5. Do Steps 1–9 of *Penne From Heaven*.
6. Do Step 4 of *Down to Earth Salad*.

Weekend Eight Saturday

FISH

3/4 pound medium shrimp, shelled and deveined
3/4 pound scallops
12 hard-shell clams
12 mussels

FRESH PRODUCE

VEGETABLES

1/2 pound red potatoes
2 stalks celery
1/4 pound mushrooms
1 medium head red leaf lettuce
1 small bunch watercress
1 pint cherry tomatoes
1 medium ripe avocado
2 small white radishes
1 medium onion
1 clove garlic

HERBS

1/2 cup chives (when chopped)

FRUIT

2 large ripe red pears
1 large orange
1 small lemon

CANS, JARS & BOTTLES

SOUP

1 can (10-3/4 ounces) tomato soup

JUICE

8 ounces clam juice

WINES & SPIRITS

1/2 cup dry sherry
3 tablespoons Grand Marnier

REFRIGERATED PRODUCTS

DAIRY

3 cups milk
2 cups half-and-half
2 eggs

STAPLES

- ❏ Butter
- ❏ Flour
- ❏ Granulated sugar
- ❏ Olive oil
- ❏ Lemon juice
- ❏ Dijon mustard
- ❏ Dried basil
- ❏ Dried thyme
- ❏ Lemon-pepper seasoning
- ❏ Pepper
- ❏ Salt

Weekend Eight Saturday

Crowded Chowder

3/4 pound medium shrimp, shelled and deveined
3/4 pound scallops
2 cups half-and-half
1/2 pound red potatoes
1 medium onion
2 stalks celery
1/2 cup fresh chives (when chopped)
12 mussels
12 hard-shell clams
2 tablespoons butter
2 cups milk
1 can (10-3/4 ounces) tomato soup
8 ounces clam juice
1 teaspoon lemon-pepper seasoning
1/4 teaspoon dried thyme
Seasoning to taste
1/2 cup dry sherry
4 tablespoons flour

Sizeable Salad

1 small lemon
1 medium head red leaf lettuce
1 small bunch watercress
1 pint cherry tomatoes
2 small white radishes
1/4 pound fresh mushrooms
1 medium ripe avocado
1 clove garlic
3 tablespoons olive oil
2 teaspoons Dijon mustard
1/2 teaspoon dried basil
Seasoning to taste

Prodigious Popovers

1 cup flour
1/2 teaspoon salt
2 tablespoons butter
1 cup milk
2 eggs

Pearasols

2 large ripe red pears
2 tablespoons lemon juice
1 large orange
1/2 cup granulated sugar
1/4 cup butter
3 tablespoons Grand Marnier

EQUIPMENT

Electric mixer	Citrus grater
Dutch oven	Citrus juicer
Medium covered saucepan	Vegetable brush
Small saucepan	Vegetable peeler
Popover pan	Pastry brush
2 large mixing bowls	Plastic wrap
2 small mixing bowls	Kitchen knives
Whisk	Measuring cups and spoons
	Cooking utensils

Weekend Eight Saturday

Crowded Chowder

1. Rinse and pat dry the shrimp and the scallops. Combine the shellfish in a large bowl. Pour the half-and-half over the shellfish and let stand for 30 minutes.

2. Scrub and cube the potatoes. Peel and chop the onion. Rinse, trim, and chop the celery. Rinse and chop the chives.

3. Scrub and debeard the mussels. Scrub the clams.

4. In a Dutch oven, cover the potatoes with water and cook until tender, about 10 minutes.

5. Drain the potatoes and return them to the Dutch oven.

6. Melt the butter in a medium saucepan. Add the onion and the celery, and sauté until just softened, about 3 minutes. Add the vegetables to the Dutch oven.

7. In the same saucepan, cover the mussels with water, bring to a boil, cover, and cook until the mussels open, discarding any that do not. With a slotted spoon, remove the mussels from the saucepan and set them aside. Add the clams to the saucepan, cover, and steam until they open, discarding any that do not.

8. Add the milk to the potato mixture. Add the shrimp, the scallops, the half-and-half, the tomato soup, the clam juice, the lemon-pepper seasoning, and the thyme. Season to taste. Blend together the sherry and the flour, and whisk the mixture into the soup. Add the mussels and the clams, and heat through.

9. Garnish with the chives.

Sizeable Salad

1. Grate 1 tablespoon of the lemon peel and juice the lemon.

2. Wash and dry the lettuce and arrange the leaves on individual salad plates.

3. Wash, dry, and chop the watercress and sprinkle it over the lettuce. Rinse and halve the tomatoes. Rinse, trim, and slice the radishes. Rinse, pat dry, and slice the mushrooms. Arrange the vegetables over the watercress.

4. Peel, pit, and slice the avocado. Sprinkle the slices with 1 tablespoon of the lemon juice and add them to the salad.

5. Peel and mince the garlic.

6. In a small bowl, combine the garlic, the oil, the remaining lemon juice, the mustard, and the basil. Season to taste.

7. Drizzle the dressing over the salads. Sprinkle with the lemon peel.

Prodigious Popovers

1. Preheat the oven to 425°F. Grease a popover pan. Place the greased pan in the oven to preheat.

2. Combine the flour and salt in a large mixing bowl.

3. Melt the butter.

4. In a small bowl, combine the milk, the eggs, and the butter.

5. Pour the egg mixture into the flour and beat with an electric mixer until smooth, 2 to 3 minutes.

6. Fill the popover cups half full and bake for 15 minutes.

7. Reduce the oven temperature to 325°F and bake until the popovers puff and turn golden, about 25 minutes.

Pearasols

1. Rinse and core the pears and cut them in half lengthwise. Brush both sides of the pears with the lemon juice to prevent browning.

2. Place a pear half on individual dessert plates, cut side down. Without cutting all the way through, cut each half lengthwise into 1/8-inch slices. Cover the plates with plastic wrap and set them aside.

3. Grate the orange peel and juice the orange.

4. Combine the orange juice, the sugar, the butter, and the Grand Marnier in a small saucepan and cook until the sugar is

dissolved and the butter has melted. Cover and set aside.

5. Gently press down on each pear half with the heel of your hand to fan out the pears. Sprinkle the orange peel around the pears and pour the warm syrup over the top.

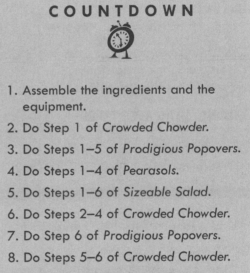

COUNTDOWN

1. Assemble the ingredients and the equipment.
2. Do Step 1 of *Crowded Chowder*.
3. Do Steps 1–5 of *Prodigious Popovers*.
4. Do Steps 1–4 of *Pearasols*.
5. Do Steps 1–6 of *Sizeable Salad*.
6. Do Steps 2–4 of *Crowded Chowder*.
7. Do Step 6 of *Prodigious Popovers*.
8. Do Steps 5–6 of *Crowded Chowder*.
9. Do Step 7 of *Prodigious Popovers*.
10. Do Steps 7–9 of *Crowded Chowder*.
11. Do Step 7 of *Sizeable Salad*.
12. Do Step 5 of *Pearasols*.

Weekend Eight Sunday

MEAT & POULTRY

1-1/2 pounds boneless, skinless
chicken breast

FRESH PRODUCE

VEGETABLES
1/2 pound medium carrots
3 stalks celery
1 medium head lettuce
1 medium cucumber
1 medium red onion

HERBS
1/4 cup parsley (when chopped)

FRUIT
1 medium pink grapefruit
1 medium white grapefruit

CANS, JARS & BOTTLES

SOUP
3 cans (10-1/2 ounces each) chicken
broth

VEGETABLES
1 can (11 ounces) whole kernel corn

CONDIMENTS
1 jar (4 ounces) sliced pimiento

PACKAGED GOODS

PASTA, RICE & GRAINS
1 cup long-grain white rice

DRIED FRUITS & NUTS
1 cup walnut pieces

DESSERT & BAKING GOODS

2 squares (1 ounce each)
unsweetened chocolate
6 ounces chocolate chips

WINES & SPIRITS

2 tablespoons Madeira

REFRIGERATED PRODUCTS

DAIRY
2 tablespoons milk
1/2 cup whipping cream
2 eggs

FROZEN GOODS

VEGETABLES
1 package (10 ounces) pearl onions
1 package (10 ounces) green peas

PASTRY
1 package puff pastry sheets

DESSERTS
1 pint vanilla ice cream

STAPLES

- ❏ Butter
- ❏ Flour
- ❏ Granulated sugar
- ❏ Vegetable oil
- ❏ White wine vinegar
- ❏ Dried thyme
- ❏ Ground allspice
- ❏ Pepper
- ❏ Salt
- ❏ Vanilla extract

Weekend Eight Sunday

Tummy-Tempting Chicken

1 package (10 ounces) frozen pearl onions
1 package (10 ounces) frozen green peas
1 package frozen puff pastry sheets
1-1/2 pounds boneless, skinless chicken breast
1/2 pound medium carrots
3 stalks celery
1 can (11 ounces) whole kernel corn
1 jar (4 ounces) sliced pimiento
1 stick butter
2/3 cup flour
3 cans (10-1/2 ounces each) chicken broth
1/2 cup whipping cream
Seasoning to taste
2 tablespoons milk

Down the Hatch Rice

1/4 cup fresh parsley (when chopped)
1 cup long-grain white rice
2 cups water
2 tablespoons Madeira
1/4 teaspoon ground allspice

Slurpy Salad

1 medium head lettuce
1 medium pink grapefruit
1 medium white grapefruit
1 medium red onion
1 medium cucumber
3 tablespoons vegetable oil
2 tablespoons white wine vinegar
1/2 teaspoon granulated sugar
1/4 teaspoon dried thyme
Seasoning to taste

Better Than Brownies

1/2 cup butter
2 squares (1 ounce each) unsweetened chocolate
2 eggs
1 cup granulated sugar
2 teaspoons vanilla extract
1 cup flour
1 cup walnut pieces
6 ounces chocolate chips
1 pint vanilla ice cream

EQUIPMENT

Electric mixer	2 medium mixing bowls
Dutch oven	Small mixing bowl
Double boiler	Whisk
Small saucepan	Vegetable peeler
10 × 15-inch glass baking dish	Rolling pin
9 × 9-inch baking pan	Pastry brush
Baking sheet	Ice cream scoop
Breadboard	Kitchen knives
Colander	Measuring cups and spoons
Large mixing bowl	Cooking utensils

Tummy-Tempting Chicken

1. Set the onions and the package of peas in a medium bowl of hot water to thaw. Set the pastry sheets out to thaw.

2. Bring water to a boil in a Dutch oven.

3. Rinse, pat dry, and cut the chicken into bite-sized pieces.

4. Peel and slice the carrots. Rinse, trim, and slice the celery. Drain the corn. Drain the pimiento.

5. Cook the carrots and the celery in the boiling water for 10 minutes.

6. Lightly flour a breadboard.

7. Roll out the pastry sheets on the breadboard. Invert a 10 × 15-inch glass baking dish over the pastry and cut around the edges of the dish, leaving an inch to spare.

8. Add the chicken to the Dutch oven and cook 5 minutes more.

9. Add the onions, the peas, the corn, and the pimiento to the Dutch oven, and cook a scant 2 minutes more. Drain the mixture and set it aside.

10. Melt the butter in the Dutch oven. Whisk in the flour until well blended and crumbly. Add the broth and bring to a boil. Remove the Dutch oven from the heat and add the cream, whisking to blend. Return the chicken and the vegetables to the Dutch oven, season to taste, blend well, and heat thoroughly.

11. Turn the mixture into the baking dish. Top with the pastry, fluting the edges with a fork or a finger to seal. With a knife, make slits in the top of the pastry to vent. Roll out any remaining pastry, cut it into decorative shapes, and arrange them on top of the pie. Brush the pastry with the milk.

12. Increase the oven temperature to 425°F.

13. Place the baking dish on a large baking sheet and bake until the crust is lightly browned, about 30 minutes.

14. Serve over the rice.

Down the Hatch Rice

1. Bring water to a boil in the bottom of a double boiler.

2. Rinse and chop the parsley.

3. Place the rice, the 2 cups water, the Madeira, and the allspice in the top of the double boiler. Cover, reduce the heat, and simmer until the liquid is absorbed and the rice is tender, 30 to 40 minutes.

4. Fluff the rice and fold in the parsley.

Slurpy Salad

1. Wash and dry the lettuce and arrange the leaves on individual salad plates.

2. Peel and section the grapefruits and place the sections in a medium bowl.

3. Peel and thinly slice the onion and the cucumber, and add them to the grapefruits.

4. In a small bowl, whisk together the oil, the vinegar, the sugar, and the thyme. Season to taste, add to the grapefruit mixture, and toss to blend.

5. Spoon the fruit mixture over the lettuce.

Better Than Brownies

1. Preheat oven to 350°F. Grease and flour a 9 × 9-inch baking pan.

2. Combine the butter and the unsweetened chocolate in a small saucepan and simmer, whisking, until melted and smooth.

3. In a large bowl, beat the eggs, the sugar, and the vanilla with an electric mixer until smooth. Blend in the chocolate mixture. Fold in the flour until well blended.

4. Fold in the walnut pieces and the chocolate chips. Pour the batter into the baking dish, spreading evenly.

5. Bake until a toothpick inserted in the center comes out clean, 20 to 25 minutes.

6. Cut into squares and top each square with a scoop of vanilla ice cream.

COUNTDOWN

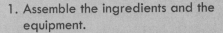

1. Assemble the ingredients and the equipment.
2. Do Steps 1–5 of *Better Than Brownies*.
3. Do Steps 1–12 of *Tummy-Tempting Chicken*.
4. Do Steps 1–3 of *Down the Hatch Rice*.
5. Do Step 13 of *Tummy-Tempting Chicken*.
6. Do Steps 1–5 of *Slurpy Salad*.
7. Do Step 4 of *Down the Hatch Rice*.
8. Do Step 14 of *Tummy-Tempting Chicken*.
9. Do Step 6 of *Better Than Brownies*.

Weekend Nine Saturday

SHOPPING LIST

MEAT & POULTRY
2 pounds lean boneless sirloin steak

FRESH PRODUCE

VEGETABLES
1-1/2 pounds baking potatoes
1 pound green beans
1 medium onion
2 scallions (green onions)
1 clove garlic

HERBS
2 tablespoons dill (when chopped)

CANS, JARS & BOTTLES

SOUP
1 can (14 ounces) beef broth

CONDIMENTS
1 jar (2 ounces) diced pimiento

PACKAGED GOODS

PASTA, RICE & GRAINS
1 cup corn flakes cereal (when crushed)

REFRIGERATED PRODUCTS

DAIRY
2/3 cup milk
1/2 cup half-and-half
1/2 cup sour cream
2-1/3 cups whipping cream
6 eggs

CHEESE
1 cup shredded Cheddar cheese

STAPLES

❐ Butter
❐ Granulated sugar
❐ Dark brown sugar
❐ Vegetable oil
❐ Lemon juice
❐ Worcestershire sauce
❐ Dried savory
❐ Ground cinnamon
❐ Pepper
❐ Salt
❐ Vanilla extract

Weekend Nine Saturday

MENU

London Broil

1 clove garlic
2 pounds lean boneless sirloin steak
1 tablespoon butter
1 tablespoon vegetable oil
1 teaspoon lemon juice
1 tablespoon Worcestershire sauce
Seasoning to taste

Piccadilly Potatoes

1-1/2 pounds baking potatoes
2 scallions (green onions)
2 tablespoons fresh dill (when chopped)
1 cup corn flakes cereal (when crushed)
1/2 cup sour cream
1 cup shredded Cheddar cheese
1 can (14 ounces) beef broth
1/2 cup half-and-half
3 egg whites
Seasoning to taste
2 tablespoons butter

Brighton Beans

1 medium onion
1 pound fresh green beans
1 jar (2 ounces) diced pimiento
1 tablespoon vegetable oil
1/4 teaspoon dried savory
Seasoning to taste

Canterbury Cream

3 egg yolks
3 eggs

2-1/3 cups whipping cream
1/2 cup granulated sugar
2/3 cup milk
1 teaspoon vanilla extract
3/4 cup dark brown sugar
1 teaspoon ground cinnamon

EQUIPMENT

Medium saucepan
Small saucepan
Medium skillet
Small skillet
9 × 13-inch glass baking dish
Large baking pan
4 individual custard cups
2 medium mixing bowls
Small mixing bowl
Whisk
Vegetable peeler
Pastry brush
Aluminum foil
Plastic bag
Plastic wrap
Kitchen knives
Measuring cups and spoons
Cooking utensils

Weekend Nine Saturday

London Broil

1. Peel and mince the garlic. Trim any excess fat from the meat.

2. In a small skillet, melt the butter with the oil and sauté the garlic for 1 minute. Blend in the lemon juice and the Worcestershire sauce, and season to taste.

3. Brush the steak with half of the garlic mixture.

4. Preheat the broiler.

5. Place the steak on a broiler rack and broil for 5 minutes. Turn the meat, brush with the remaining garlic mixture, and broil until the steak is done to taste, about 5 minutes for rare.

6. To serve, slice the steak diagonally across the grain.

Piccadilly Potatoes

1. Peel and slice the potatoes. Trim and chop the scallions. Rinse and chop the dill. Place the corn flakes in a plastic bag and lightly crush them.

2. Grease a 9 × 13-inch glass baking dish. Arrange the potato slices in the dish and top them with the scallions and the dill.

3. In a medium bowl, combine the sour cream, the cheese, the broth, the half-and-half, and the egg whites. Season to taste and pour the mixture over the potatoes.

4. Increase the oven temperature to 350°F.

5. Melt the butter in a small saucepan. Fold in the crushed corn flakes. Spread the mixture over the potatoes.

6. Cover the dish with aluminum foil and bake until the potatoes are tender, about 1-1/2 hours.

7. Remove the potatoes from the oven and keep them covered.

8. Remove the aluminum foil and place the potatoes under the broiler until the top is lightly browned, about 2 minutes.

Brighton Beans

1. Peel and finely chop the onion. Rinse and trim the green beans and cut them into 2-inch pieces. Drain the pimiento.

2. Heat the oil in a medium skillet and sauté the onion for 3 minutes. Add the beans and sauté until they are crisp-tender, about 4 minutes.

3. Add the pimiento and the savory, and season to taste.

Canterbury Cream

1. Separate 3 of the eggs, reserving the whites for the potatoes.

2. In a medium bowl, whisk the eggs and the egg yolks until well blended.

3. In a medium saucepan, combine the cream, the granulated sugar, and the milk, and heat until small bubbles form around the edge. Remove the pan from the heat and let it cool.

4. Preheat the oven to 300°F.

5. Gradually add the egg mixture to the cream mixture. Return the pan to the heat and simmer, stirring constantly, until the mixture coats the back of a spoon, 3 to 4 minutes. Fold in the vanilla.

6. Pour the mixture into individual custard cups. Set the dishes in a large baking pan and fill the pan with hot water to the level of the custard.

7. Bake until the center of the custard is set, 40 to 45 minutes.

8. Cool the custards for 10 minutes.

9. Cover the cooled custards with plastic wrap and refrigerate then until you are ready to serve.

10. Preheat the broiler.

11. In a small bowl, combine the brown sugar and the cinnamon. Sprinkle the mixture over the custards.

12. Place the custards under the broiler, watching closely, until browned, but not burned, about 1-1/2 minutes.

COUNTDOWN

1. Assemble the ingredients and the equipment.
2. Do Steps 1–9 of *Canterbury Cream.*
3. Do Steps 1–6 of *Piccadilly Potatoes.*
4. Do Step 1 of *Brighton Beans.*
5. Do Steps 1–3 of *London Broil.*
6. Do Step 7 of *Piccadilly Potatoes.*
7. Do Steps 4–5 of *London Broil.*
8. Do Steps 2–3 of *Brighton Beans.*
9. Do Step 6 of *London Broil.*
10. Do Step 8 of *Piccadilly Potatoes.*
11. Do Steps 10–12 of *Canterbury Cream.*

Weekend Nine Sunday

FRESH PRODUCE

VEGETABLES
1 stalk celery
1 medium head lettuce
1 small head Belgian endive
1 small onion
2 scallions (green onions)

HERBS
3 tablespoons chives (when chopped)

FRUIT
2 small oranges
1 large lemon

CANS, JARS & BOTTLES

SOUP
2 cans (14 ounces each) chicken broth

FISH
1 can (6 ounces) solid white tuna

PACKAGED GOODS

PASTA, RICE & GRAINS
1 cup brown rice

DRIED FRUITS & NUTS
1 cup golden raisins

WINES & SPIRITS
3 tablespoons dry sherry

REFRIGERATED PRODUCTS

DAIRY
1/2 cup milk
3 tablespoons sour cream
1/4 cup whipped cream
4 eggs

CHEESE
1 package (3 ounces) cream cheese

STAPLES

- ☐ Butter
- ☐ Flour
- ☐ Baking powder
- ☐ Granulated sugar
- ☐ Dark brown sugar
- ☐ Vegetable oil
- ☐ Red wine vinegar
- ☐ Lemon juice
- ☐ Honey
- ☐ Soy sauce
- ☐ Grated Parmesan cheese
- ☐ Dried basil
- ☐ Paprika
- ☐ Pepper
- ☐ Salt
- ☐ Rum extract

Weekend Nine Sunday

MENU

Lively Lemon Soup

3 tablespoons fresh chives (when chopped)
1 large lemon
2 eggs
2 cans (14 ounces each) chicken broth
3 tablespoons dry sherry
Seasoning to taste

Merry Muffins

1 cup brown rice
2-1/2 cups water
2 scallions (green onions)
1 stalk celery
1 tablespoon lemon juice
1 can (6 ounces) solid white tuna
2 eggs
1 tablespoon baking powder
3 tablespoons sour cream
2 tablespoons cream cheese
1 teaspoon dried basil
1 tablespoon soy sauce
4 tablespoons grated Parmesan cheese
Seasoning to taste

Spry Salad

1 medium head lettuce
1 small head Belgian endive
2 small oranges
1 small onion
3 tablespoons vegetable oil
2 tablespoons red wine vinegar
1 teaspoon honey

1/2 teaspoon paprika
Seasoning to taste

Happy Cake

1 cup flour
1/8 teaspoon salt
1 tablespoon baking powder
2/3 cup granulated sugar
4 tablespoons cream cheese
1 cup golden raisins
1/2 cup milk
2 cups water
1 cup dark brown sugar
3 tablespoons butter
1 teaspoon rum extract
1/4 cup whipped cream

EQUIPMENT

Large saucepan

Medium covered saucepan

Medium saucepan

9 × 9-inch glass baking dish

Muffin tin

2 large mixing bowls

3 small mixing bowls

Whisk

Citrus grater

Citrus juicer

Kitchen knives

Measuring cups and spoons

Cooking utensils

Weekend Nine Sunday

Lively Lemon Soup

1. Rinse and chop the chives. Grate the lemon peel and squeeze 1/4 cup lemon juice.

2. In a small bowl, whisk the lemon juice and the eggs until frothy.

3. In a large saucepan, bring the broth to a boil.

4. Slowly whisk 1/2 cup of the hot broth into the into the egg mixture until thick. Pour the mixture into the saucepan. Blend in the sherry, season to taste, and simmer until you are ready to serve.

5. Pour the soup into individual bowls and garnish with the lemon peel and the chives.

Merry Muffins

1. Combine the rice and the water in a medium saucepan and bring to a boil. Cover the saucepan, reduce the heat, and simmer until the liquid is absorbed and the rice is tender, about 40 minutes.

2. Remove the rice from the heat and set it aside.

3. Trim and thinly slice the scallions. Rinse, trim, and mince the celery.

4. In a large bowl, combine 2 cups of the cooked rice, the scallions, the celery, and the lemon juice.

5. Drain and flake the tuna and add it to the mixture. Fold in the eggs, the baking powder, the sour cream, the cream cheese, the basil, and the soy sauce. Mix well. Fold in the Parmesan cheese and season to taste.

6. Increase the oven temperature to 375°F. Grease a muffin tin.

7. Spoon the mixture into the muffin tin, filling the cups and mounding the tops, and bake until the muffins are golden, about 40 minutes.

Spry Salad

1. Wash and dry the lettuce and tear the leaves into bite-sized pieces. Wash and dry the endive and tear it into bite-sized pieces. Distribute the greens among individual salad plates.

2. Peel and thinly slice the oranges. Peel and thinly slice the onion, and separate it into rings. Arrange the orange slices over the greens. Arrange the onion slices over the oranges.

3. In a small bowl, combine the oil, the vinegar, the honey, and the paprika. Season to taste and drizzle the dressing over the salads.

Happy Cake

1. Preheat the oven to 350°F. Butter a 9 × 9-inch glass baking dish.

2. In a large bowl, combine the flour, the salt, and the baking powder.

3. In a small bowl, blend together the granulated sugar and the cream cheese. Fold in the raisins and the milk.

4. Add the cheese mixture to the flour mixture, and blend well. Pour the batter into the baking dish.

5. In a medium saucepan, combine the water with the brown sugar and the butter. Bring to a boil, stirring to blend, until the sugar is dissolved. Fold in the rum extract. Pour over the flour mixture.

6. Bake until a toothpick inserted in the center comes out clean, 30 to 35 minutes.

7. Top with dollops of whipped cream.

COUNTDOWN

1. Assemble the ingredients and the equipment.
2. Do Step 1 of *Merry Muffins*.
3. Do Steps 1–6 of *Happy Cake*.
4. Do Steps 1–4 of *Lively Lemon Soup*.
5. Do Steps 2–7 of *Merry Muffins*.
6. Do Steps 1–3 of *Spry Salad*.
7. Do Step 5 of *Lively Lemon Soup*.
8. Do Step 7 of *Happy Cake*.

Weekend Ten Saturday

SHOPPING LIST

MEAT & POULTRY

1 lean boneless pork loin
(about 4 pounds)

FRESH PRODUCE

VEGETABLES

1 pound asparagus
1 medium red bell pepper
1 medium onion
1 small shallot
2 cloves garlic

FRUIT

4 medium very ripe bananas
2 medium bananas

CANS, JARS & BOTTLES

SOUP

1 can (10-1/2 ounces) beef broth
1 can (10-1/2 ounces) chicken broth

FRUIT

1 can (8 ounces) pineapple tidbits

PACKAGED GOODS

PASTA, RICE & GRAINS

1 cup long-grain white rice

WINES & SPIRITS

2 tablespoons dry sherry

REFRIGERATED PRODUCTS

DAIRY

2 cups whipping cream
2 eggs

STAPLES

- ❏ Butter
- ❏ Vegetable shortening
- ❏ Flour
- ❏ Baking powder
- ❏ Baking soda
- ❏ Granulated sugar
- ❏ Powdered sugar
- ❏ Vegetable oil
- ❏ Rice vinegar
- ❏ Lemon juice
- ❏ White Worcestershire sauce
- ❏ Dried sage
- ❏ Dried tarragon
- ❏ Ground cinnamon
- ❏ Curry powder
- ❏ Pepper
- ❏ Salt
- ❏ Banana extract

Weekend Ten Saturday

MENU

Palette of Pork

1 lean boneless pork loin (about 4 pounds)
1 medium onion
2 tablespoons ground cinnamon
2 teaspoons granulated sugar
1/2 teaspoon dried sage
1 teaspoon white Worcestershire sauce
2 tablespoons dry sherry
Seasoning to taste

Study In Rice

1 small shallot
1 clove garlic
1 can (8 ounces) pineapple tidbits
1 tablespoon butter
1 can (10-1/2 ounces) beef broth
1 can (10-1/2 ounces) chicken broth
1 cup long-grain white rice
1/2 teaspoon curry powder
Seasoning to taste

Asparagus Artistry

1 pound fresh asparagus
1 clove garlic
1 medium red bell pepper
2 tablespoons vegetable oil
1 tablespoon rice vinegar
1 teaspoon dried tarragon
Seasoning to taste

Still Life

4 medium very ripe bananas
1/2 cup vegetable shortening

2 eggs
1-1/2 teaspoons banana extract
1-2/3 cups flour
1-1/4 cups granulated sugar
2-1/2 teaspoons baking powder
1/2 teaspoon baking soda
1/2 teaspoon + 1/8 teaspoon salt
2 cups whipping cream
1/4 cup powdered sugar
2 tablespoons lemon juice
2 medium bananas

EQUIPMENT

Electric mixer

Medium covered saucepan

Large skillet

Medium roasting pan

2 round cake pans

Roasting rack

2 large mixing bowls

Medium mixing bowl

2 small mixing bowls

Cake rack

Meat thermometer

Kitchen knives

Measuring cups and spoons

Cooking utensils

Palette of Pork

1. With a sharp knife, score the pork loin by making several cuts in the fat across the top, about 1/8-inch deep.

2. Peel and mince the onion.

3. In a small bowl, combine the onion, the cinnamon, the sugar, the sage, the Worcestershire sauce, and the sherry. Season to taste. Rub the mixture over the pork and into the scoring. Place the pork on a rack in a medium roasting pan and refrigerate it for at least 1 hour.

4. Reduce the oven temperature to 350°F.

5. Insert a meat thermometer into the thickest part of the pork loin. Roast until the thermometer reads 170°F, about 1-1/2 hours.

6. Let the pork stand for 5 minutes before slicing it.

Study In Rice

1. Peel and chop the shallot. Peel and mince the garlic. Drain the pineapple, reserving the juice.

2. Melt the butter in a medium saucepan and sauté the shallot and the garlic for 3 minutes.

3. Add the reserved pineapple juice, the broth, the rice, and the curry powder. Season to taste, cover, reduce the heat, and simmer until the liquid is absorbed and the rice is tender, about 25 minutes.

4. Add the pineapple to the rice and fluff with a fork.

Asparagus Artistry

1. Trim and discard the tough ends from the asparagus and cut the spears into 2-inch pieces. Peel and mince the garlic. Rinse, stem, seed, and julienne the bell pepper.

2. Heat the oil in a large skillet and sauté the garlic for 1 minute. Add the asparagus and the bell pepper, and sauté until crisp-tender, about 5 minutes.

3. Add the vinegar and the tarragon, and season to taste.

Still Life

1. Preheat the oven to 375°F. Grease and flour 2 round cake pans.

2. Peel and mash the 4 very ripe bananas in a medium bowl. Blend in the shortening, the eggs, and 1 teaspoon of the banana extract.

3. In a large bowl, combine the flour, the granulated sugar, the baking powder, the baking soda, and 1/2 teaspoon of the salt.

4. Fold the banana mixture into the flour mixture and beat with an electric mixer until smooth, about 5 minutes.

5. Turn the mixture into the 2 cake pans and bake until a toothpick inserted in the center comes out clean, about 25 minutes.

6. Rinse the beaters of the electric mixer and chill them and a large bowl in the refrigerator for at least 10 minutes.

7. In the chilled bowl, beat the cream until soft peaks form, about 5 minutes. Fold in the powdered sugar and the remaining 1/8 teaspoon salt, and continue beating until stiff, about 2 minutes. Fold in the remaining 1/2 teaspoon banana extract and refrigerate until you are ready to use.

8. Remove the cake pans from the oven and let them cool for 10 minutes.

9. Remove the cakes from the pans and set them on a rack to cool completely.

10. Place one layer of the cake on a serving plate. Spread the top with 1/4 of the whipped cream frosting. Place the second cake layer on top. Completely frost the sides and the top. Refrigerate until you are ready to serve.

11. Place the lemon juice in a small bowl. Peel and slice the remaining bananas. Dip the slices in the lemon juice and arrange them around the top edge of the cake.

COUNTDOWN

1. Assemble the ingredients and the equipment.
2. Do Steps 1–3 of *Palette of Pork*.
3. Do Steps 1–9 of *Still Life*.
4. Do Steps 4–5 of *Palette of Pork*.
5. Do Steps 1–3 of *Study In Rice*.
6. Do Step 10 of *Still Life*.
7. Do Steps 1–3 of *Asparagus Artistry*.
8. Do Step 6 of *Palette of Pork*.
9. Do Step 4 of *Study In Rice*.
10. Do Step 11 of *Still Life*.

Weekend Ten Sunday

SHOPPING LIST

MEAT & POULTRY

2 pounds lean boneless beef steak

FRESH PRODUCE

VEGETABLES

1-1/2 pounds new red potatoes
4 medium carrots
2 stalks celery
1 large parsnip
2 medium tomatoes
1 large onion
1 clove garlic

HERBS

3 tablespoons parsley (when chopped)

CANS, JARS & BOTTLES

SOUP

1 can (10-1/2 ounces) beef consommé

DESSERT & BAKING NEEDS

1 can (20 ounces) raspberry pie filling

PACKAGED GOODS

BAKED GOODS

1 chocolate pie shell

DESSERT & BAKING NEEDS

3-1/2 cups mini marshmallows

WINES & SPIRITS

1/2 cup dry red wine

REFRIGERATED PRODUCTS

DAIRY

3/4 cup + 2 tablespoons milk
1 cup buttermilk
1/2 cup whipping cream
1 egg

STAPLES

- ☐ Butter
- ☐ Flour
- ☐ Baking powder
- ☐ Baking soda
- ☐ Granulated sugar
- ☐ Beef bouillon cube
- ☐ Poppy seeds
- ☐ Bay leaf
- ☐ Pepper
- ☐ Salt
- ☐ Vanilla extract

Weekend Ten Sunday

MENU

Beef Friendly

2 pounds lean boneless beef steak
1 large onion
1 clove garlic
4 medium carrots
2 stalks celery
1 large parsnip
1-1/2 pounds new red potatoes
2 medium fresh tomatoes
3 tablespoons fresh parsley (when chopped)
3 tablespoons flour
Seasoning to taste
3 tablespoons butter
1 can (10-1/2 ounces) beef consommé
1 cup water
1/2 cup dry red wine
1 beef bouillon cube
1 bay leaf

Soft-Spoken Muffins

1-3/4 cups flour
1 tablespoon granulated sugar
3 teaspoons baking powder
1/2 teaspoon baking soda
1/4 teaspoon salt
4 tablespoons butter
1 cup buttermilk
1 egg
2 tablespoons milk
1/4 teaspoon poppy seeds

Pleasant Pie

3-1/2 cups mini marshmallows
1 can (20 ounces) raspberry pie filling
3/4 cup milk
1/2 cup whipping cream
1/2 teaspoon vanilla extract
1 chocolate pie shell

EQUIPMENT

Electric mixer
Dutch oven
Large covered saucepan
Muffin tin
Large shallow bowl
Large mixing bowl
Medium mixing bowl
Small mixing bowl
Vegetable peeler
Kitchen knives
Measuring cups and spoons
Cooking utensils

Weekend Ten Sunday

Beef Friendly

1. Cube the beef. Peel and chop the onion. Peel and mince the garlic. Peel and chunk the carrots. Rinse, trim, and chunk the celery. Peel and chunk the parsnip. Rinse and quarter the potatoes. Rinse and quarter the tomatoes. Rinse and chop the parsley.

2. Place the flour in a large shallow bowl and season to taste. Dredge the beef cubes in the seasoned flour.

3. Melt the butter with the garlic in a Dutch oven.

4. Add the beef and brown the cubes on all sides, about 10 minutes.

5. Add the onion and sauté for 3 minutes.

6. Add the consommé, the water, the wine, the bouillon cube, and the bay leaf.

7. Cover the Dutch oven and simmer for 30 minutes.

8. Add the carrots, the celery, the parsnip, the potatoes, and the tomatoes, and continue to cook until the meat is tender and the vegetables are cooked through, about 30 minutes.

9. Remove the bay leaf and garnish the stew with the parsley.

Soft-Spoken Muffins

1. Preheat the oven to 400°F. Grease a muffin tin.

2. In a large bowl, combine the flour, the sugar, the baking powder, the baking soda, and the salt.

3. Melt the butter.

4. In a small bowl, combine the buttermilk, the egg, and the milk. Fold in the butter.

5. Make a well in the dry ingredients. Pour the egg mixture into the well and fold it in.

6. Divide the batter evenly among the muffin cups, sprinkle with the poppy seeds, and bake until a toothpick inserted in the center of a muffin comes out clean, about 15 minutes.

Pleasant Pie

1. Reserve 1/2 cup of the marshmallows and 1/2 cup of the pie filling for garnish.

2. Combine the remaining marshmallows with the milk in a large saucepan and simmer, stirring, until the marshmallows are melted.

3. Cover the saucepan and refrigerate it for 30 minutes.

4. Chill a medium bowl and the beaters of electric mixer in the refrigerator for at least 10 minutes.

5. In the chilled bowl, whip the cream until soft peaks form. Fold in the vanilla and beat until stiff. Fold the whipped cream into the marshmallow mixture.

6. Spoon half of the mixture into the pie shell. Layer with the remaining pie filling.

7. Fold the reserved marshmallows into the remaining whipped cream and spread it over the pie filling. Garnish with the reserved pie filling. Refrigerate the pie until it is set, about 2 hours.

COUNTDOWN

1. Assemble the ingredients and the equipment.
2. Do Steps 1–7 of *Pleasant Pie*.
3. Do Steps 1–8 of *Beef Friendly*.
4. Do Steps 1–6 of *Mild-Mannered Muffins*.
5. Do Step 9 of *Beef Friendly*.

Weekend Eleven Saturday

SHOPPING LIST

MEAT & POULTRY

2 Rock Cornish game hens

FRESH PRODUCE

VEGETABLES

2 large baking potatoes
1 medium onion
1 medium shallot
2 cloves garlic

HERBS

Parsley sprigs for garnish

CANS, JARS & BOTTLES

VEGETABLES

2 cans (15 ounces each) sliced beets

DESSERT & BAKING NEEDS

1 can (16 ounces) pumpkin

PACKAGED GOODS

BAKED GOODS

1 package (9 ounces) gingersnap
   cookies

WINES & SPIRITS

1/2 cup dry white wine

REFRIGERATED PRODUCTS

DAIRY

1/4 cup whipped cream

FROZEN GOODS

DESSERTS

1 quart vanilla ice cream

STAPLES

- ❏ Butter
- ❏ Dark brown sugar
- ❏ Apple cider vinegar
- ❏ White Worcestershire sauce
- ❏ Dijon mustard
- ❏ Honey
- ❏ Dried rosemary
- ❏ Dried thyme
- ❏ Ground allspice
- ❏ Ground cinnamon
- ❏ Ground ginger
- ❏ Ground nutmeg
- ❏ Paprika
- ❏ Pepper
- ❏ Salt

Weekend Eleven Saturday

The Name of the Game

2 Rock Cornish game hens
Seasoning to taste
2 cloves garlic
Parsley sprigs for garnish
2 tablespoons butter
1-1/2 tablespoons Dijon mustard
1 tablespoon dark brown sugar
1/2 teaspoon dried rosemary
1/2 cup dry white wine

One Potato, Two Potato

2 large baking potatoes
1 medium shallot
4 tablespoons butter
1/4 teaspoon paprika
1/2 teaspoon dried thyme
1/4 teaspoon white Worcestershire sauce
Seasoning to taste

Between You and Me

1 medium onion
2 cans (15 ounces each) sliced beets
2 tablespoons butter
1/4 cup honey
2 tablespoons apple cider vinegar

That's How the Cookie Crumbles

1 package (9 ounces) gingersnap cookies
3 tablespoons butter
1 can (16 ounces) pumpkin
1 quart vanilla ice cream
1/4 cup dark brown sugar
1/4 teaspoon ground allspice
1/4 teaspoon ground ginger
1/4 teaspoon ground cinnamon
1/2 teaspoon ground nutmeg
1/4 cup whipped cream

EQUIPMENT

Blender
Medium saucepan
2 small saucepans
Small skillet
9 × 13-inch baking pan
9 × 9-inch glass baking dish
Pie plate
Vegetable brush
Pastry brush
Mallet
Plastic wrap
Plastic bag
Kitchen knives
Measuring cups and spoons
Cooking utensils

Weekend Eleven Saturday

RECIPES

The Name of the Game

1. Preheat the oven to 450°F. Grease a 9 × 13-inch baking pan.

2. Rinse and pat dry the game hens, season them to taste, and cut them in half lengthwise.

3. Peel and mince the garlic. Rinse and pat dry the parsley.

4. Melt the butter in a small skillet and sauté the garlic for 1 minute.

5. Blend in the mustard, the brown sugar, and the rosemary.

6. Coat the hens with the mustard mixture and lay them, skin side up, in the baking pan.

7. Add the wine and bake until the hens begin to brown, about 20 minutes.

8. Turn the hens over and continue to cook until they are tender, about 20 minutes.

9. Garnish with the parsley sprigs.

One Potato, Two Potato

1. Grease a 9 × 9-inch glass baking dish.

2. Rinse and scrub the potatoes and cut them in half lengthwise. Cut each half lengthwise into 4 wedges.

3. Peel and mince the shallot.

4. Melt the butter in a small saucepan.

5. Add the shallot, the paprika, the thyme, and the Worcestershire sauce. Season to taste and sauté until the shallot is soft, about 3 minutes.

6. Brush the shallot mixture on the cut sides of the potatoes and place the potatoes, skin side down, in the baking dish.

7. Bake with the game hens until the potatoes are tender, about 40 minutes.

Between You and Me

1. Peel and slice the onion and separate it into rings.

2. Drain the beets, reserving 2 tablespoons of the liquid.

3. Melt the butter in a medium saucepan and sauté the onion rings for 2 minutes.

4. Blend in the reserved beet liquid, the honey, and the vinegar.

5. Add the beets and simmer until heated through, about 5 minutes.

That's How the Cookie Crumbles

1. Place the gingersnaps in a plastic bag and crush them with a mallet.

2. Melt the butter in a small saucepan.

3. Blend the cookie crumbs into the butter and press the mixture evenly into a pie plate.

4. Bake for 10 minutes.

5. Remove the pie shell from the oven and let it cool for 10 minutes.

6. In a blender, combine the pumpkin, the ice cream, the brown sugar, the allspice, the ginger, the cinnamon, and the nutmeg, and process until well blended, about 2 minutes. Pour the mixture into the pie shell. Cover the pie with plastic wrap and freeze it until it is firm, about 2 hours.

7. Remove the pie from the freezer, and let it sit out for 5 minutes before cutting. Top each serving with a dollop of whipped cream.

COUNTDOWN

1. Assemble the ingredients and the equipment.
2. Do Steps 1–6 of *That's How the Cookie Crumbles.*
3. Do Steps 1–6 of *One Potato, Two Potato.*
4. Do Steps 1–7 of *The Name of the Game.*
5. Do Step 7 of *One Potato, Two Potato.*
6. Do Step 8 of *The Name of the Game.*
7. Do Steps 1–5 of *Between You and Me.*
8. Do Step 9 of *The Name of the Game.*
9. Do Step 7 of *That's How the Cookie Crumbles.*

Weekend Eleven Sunday

FRESH PRODUCE

VEGETABLES
2 medium red bell peppers
2 large ripe avocados
1 medium sweet onion
3 medium red onions
1 clove garlic

FRUIT
1 small red apple

CANS, JARS & BOTTLES

SOUP
2 cans (14 ounces each) chicken broth

VEGETABLES
1 jar (22 ounces) sauerkraut

JUICE
1 cup apple cider

PACKAGED GOODS

BAKED GOODS
1 loaf rye bread, unsliced

DESSERT & BAKING GOODS
1 cup chocolate chips

WINES & SPIRITS

3 tablespoons dry sherry

REFRIGERATED PRODUCTS

DAIRY
1 cup whipping cream
2 eggs

DELI
8 thick slices cooked corned beef
8 slices Swiss cheese

STAPLES

- [ ] Butter
- [ ] Flour
- [ ] Granulated sugar
- [ ] Powdered sugar
- [ ] Vegetable oil
- [ ] Dijon mustard
- [ ] Lemon juice
- [ ] Mayonnaise
- [ ] Caraway seeds
- [ ] Bay leaf
- [ ] Dried dill
- [ ] Whole allspice
- [ ] Ground cinnamon
- [ ] Dry mustard
- [ ] Pepper
- [ ] Salt
- [ ] Almond extract

Weekend Eleven Sunday

MENU

Gracie Soup

3 medium red onions
1 clove garlic
3 tablespoons butter
2 tablespoons flour
2 cans (14 ounces each) chicken broth
3 tablespoons dry sherry
1 bay leaf
2 whole allspice
1 teaspoon granulated sugar
1 cup apple cider
Seasoning to taste
1 small red apple

Ruben Reubens

1 medium sweet onion
1 jar (22 ounces) sauerkraut
1 tablespoon caraway seeds
1 loaf rye bread, unsliced
4 tablespoons mayonnaise
3 tablespoons Dijon mustard
8 thick slices deli cooked corned beef
8 slices Swiss cheese

Belle du Jour

2 medium red bell peppers
2 large ripe avocados
3 tablespoons vegetable oil
2 tablespoons lemon juice
1 teaspoon dry mustard
1/2 teaspoon dried dill
Seasoning to taste

Ian His Cups

1 cup chocolate chips
2 tablespoons butter
2 eggs
1/4 cup warm water
1 cup whipping cream
2 tablespoons powdered sugar
1 teaspoon almond extract
2 tablespoons granulated sugar
1 teaspoon ground cinnamon

EQUIPMENT

Electric mixer

Large covered saucepan

Small saucepan

4 individual custard cups

2 baking sheets

3 medium mixing bowls

3 small mixing bowls

Whisk

Kitchen knives

Measuring cups and spoons

Cooking utensils

Gracie Soup

1. Peel and thinly slice the onions. Peel and mince the garlic.

2. Melt the butter in a large saucepan, and sauté the onions until they begin to turn golden, about 10 minutes.

3. Add the flour and the garlic, and sauté for 1 minute.

4. Add the broth, the sherry, the bay leaf, the allspice, the sugar, and the cider. Season to taste and blend well.

5. Bring to a boil, cover, reduce the heat, and simmer for 30 minutes.

6. Remove the bay leaf and the allspice.

7. Rinse, core, and slice the apple. Place a slice in each bowl before adding the soup.

Ruben Reubens

1. Peel and thinly slice the onion. Drain the sauerkraut. In a medium bowl, blend the caraway seeds into the sauerkraut.

2. Cut the bread into 8 thick slices and toast them lightly.

3. In a small bowl, combine the mayonnaise and the mustard. Spread the mixture on each slice of bread. Top with a slice of corned beef. Top the corned beef with the sauerkraut. Lay a slice of the Swiss cheese on top of the sauerkraut.

4. Preheat the broiler.

5. Arrange the open-faced sandwiches on a baking sheet and broil until they are hot and the cheese is melted and bubbly, about 2 minutes.

Belle du Jour

1. Rinse, stem, seed, and slice the bell peppers into rings. Peel, pit, and slice the avocados.

2. Arrange the avocado and the bell pepper slices on individual salad plates.

3. In a small bowl, whisk together the oil, the lemon juice, the mustard, and the dill and season to taste.

4. Drizzle the dressing over the salad.

Ian His Cups

1. Chill a medium bowl and the beaters of an electric mixer in the refrigerator for at least 10 minutes.

2. Place the chocolate chips and the butter in a small saucepan and simmer, stirring, until melted.

3. Separate the eggs, placing the yolks in a small bowl and the whites in a medium bowl.

4. Beat the yolks with the warm water and blend them into the melted chocolate.

5. Remove the pan from the heat and chill it in the refrigerator for 10 minutes.

6. In the chilled bowl, whip the cream until thick. Fold in the powdered sugar and the almond extract.

7. Fold the whipped cream into the chocolate mixture, and spoon it into individual custard cups.

8. Whisk the egg whites until soft peaks form, about 1 minute.

9. Gradually add the granulated sugar, and beat until very stiff and glossy, about 2 minutes.

10. Cover each custard cup with the meringue and sprinkle with the cinnamon.

11. Refrigerate until you are ready to use.

12. Preheat the broiler.

13. Arrange the custard cups on a baking sheet and broil until the tops are lightly browned, about 3 minutes.

COUNTDOWN

1. Assemble the ingredients and the equipment.
2. Do Steps 1–11 of *Ian His Cups*.
3. Do Steps 1–5 of *Gracie Soup*.
4. Do Steps 1–3 of *Belle du Jour*.
5. Do Steps 1–5 of *Ruben Reubens*.
6. Do Steps 6–7 of *Gracie Soup*.
7. Do Step 4 of *Belle du Jour*.
8. Do Steps 12–13 of *Ian His Cups*.

Weekend Twelve Saturday

MEAT & POULTRY

4 beef tenderloins (about 2 pounds)

FRESH PRODUCE

VEGETABLES

1 pound green beans
1/2 pound mushrooms
1 medium red bell pepper
1 medium orange bell pepper
1 small onion
1 large red onion
4 small shallots

HERBS

3 tablespoons parsley (when chopped)

FRUIT

2 medium ripe pears
2 large oranges

PACKAGED GOODS

BAKED GOODS

1 chocolate pie shell

DRIED FRUITS & NUTS

3/4 cup sliced almonds

DESSERT & BAKING NEEDS

1 small package instant devil's food
   pudding mix

WINES & SPIRITS

1/2 cup dry red wine
1/4 cup Kahlúa

REFRIGERATED PRODUCTS

DAIRY

1 cup milk
1 cup whipping cream
1 egg

FROZEN GOODS

PASTRY

8 puff pastry shells

STAPLES

- ❏ Butter
- ❏ Flour
- ❏ Cornstarch
- ❏ Granulated sugar
- ❏ Dark brown sugar
- ❏ Olive oil
- ❏ Lemon juice
- ❏ Plain breadcrumbs
- ❏ Beef bouillon cube
- ❏ Ground cinnamon
- ❏ Ground nutmeg
- ❏ Paprika
- ❏ Pepper
- ❏ Salt
- ❏ Almond extract

Weekend Twelve Saturday

Beef Swellington

8 frozen puff pastry shells
4 beef tenderloins (about 2 pounds)
Seasoning to taste
1/2 pound fresh mushrooms
4 small shallots
1/4 teaspoon ground nutmeg
1 small onion
3 tablespoons fresh parsley (when chopped)
4 tablespoons butter
1/4 cup plain breadcrumbs
1/4 cup + 1 tablespoon water
1 egg
1/2 cup dry red wine
1 beef bouillon cube
2 tablespoons flour
1 tablespoon lemon juice
1/4 teaspoon pepper

Gay Blades

1 pound fresh green beans
1 medium red bell pepper
1 medium orange bell pepper
1 large red onion
2 tablespoons olive oil
2 tablespoons butter
1 teaspoon dark brown sugar
Seasoning to taste
1/2 teaspoon paprika

Poised Pears

2 medium ripe pears
2 large oranges

2 tablespoons lemon juice
1-1/2 cups + 2 tablespoons water
1/4 cup granulated sugar
1 tablespoon cornstarch
1/2 teaspoon ground cinnamon

Distinguished Dessert

3/4 cup sliced almonds
1 cup whipping cream
1 teaspoon almond extract
1 cup milk
1 small package instant devil's food pudding mix
1/4 cup Kahlúa
1 chocolate pie shell

EQUIPMENT

Electric mixer	Medium mixing bowl
Medium covered saucepan	Small mixing bowl
Medium saucepan	Whisk
Large skillet	Rolling pin
Medium skillet	Pastry brush
Small skillet	Kitchen knives
Baking sheet	Measuring cups and spoons
Breadboard	Cooking utensils
Large mixing bowl	

Weekend Twelve Saturday

Beef Swellington

1. Set the pastry out to thaw. Lightly flour a breadboard.

2. Season the beef to taste.

3. Rinse, pat dry, and mince the mushrooms. Peel and mince the shallots. Combine the mushrooms and the shallots in a small bowl and sprinkle with the nutmeg. Peel and mince the onion. Rinse and mince the parsley.

4. Melt the butter in a large skillet. Sear the beef, about 2 minutes per side. Remove the beef and set it aside.

5. Add the onion to the skillet and sauté for 2 minutes. Add the shallots and the mushrooms, and sauté for 2 minutes. Remove the skillet from the heat and fold in half the parsley.

6. Preheat the oven to 450°F.

7. Roll out the pastry shells on the breadboard. Sprinkle the breadcrumbs in the middle of 4 of the shells. Place a tenderloin on top of the breadcrumbs. Top each tenderloin with 1/4 of the mushroom mixture. Place a second pastry shell over each tenderloin and seal the edges.

8. Whisk together 1 tablespoon of the water with the egg.

9. Brush the pastry with the egg mixture.

10. Bake until the pastry is golden and the meat is done, about 20 minutes for medium rare.

11. In a small skillet, combine the wine, the remaining 1/4 cup water, and the bouillon cube, and bring to a boil. Blend in the flour, 1 tablespoon at a time, until smooth. Add the lemon juice, the remaining parsley, and the pepper. Serve with the beef.

Gay Blades

1. Rinse and trim the green beans. Rinse, stem, seed, and julienne the bell peppers. Peel and thinly slice the onion, and separate it into rings.

2. Bring water to a boil in a medium saucepan.

3. Cook the beans until they are crisp-tender, about 5 minutes.

4. Heat the oil in a medium skillet, and sauté the onion rings for 3 minutes. Add the bell peppers and sauté until soft, about 3 minutes. Blend in the butter and the sugar.

5. Drain the beans, add them to the onion mixture, and toss to combine. Season to taste and sprinkle with the paprika.

Poised Pears

1. Peel, core, and slice the pears, and sprinkle them with the lemon juice to prevent browning. Peel and section the oranges.

2. Place the pears in a medium saucepan. Add 1-1/2 cups of the water and the sugar. Cook until the pears begin to soften, about 10 minutes.

3. Combine the cornstarch and the remaining 2 tablespoons water, and add it to the pears. Add the orange sections and cook until the sauce is thick and clear, about 3 minutes. Fold in the cinnamon. Cover to keep warm.

Distinguished Dessert

1. Chill a medium bowl and the beaters of an electric mixer in the refrigerator for at least 10 minutes.

2. Preheat the oven to 250°F.

3. Arrange the almonds on a baking sheet and toast them in the oven for 5 minutes. Remove the pan from the oven and set it aside.

4. In the chilled bowl, whip the cream until soft peaks form. Fold in the almond extract and beat until stiff.

5. In a large bowl, combine the milk, the pudding mix, and the Kahlúa, and beat until well blended. Fold the whipped cream into the chocolate mixture, and turn it into the pie shell, smoothing it out to the edges. Sprinkle with the almonds and refrigerate the pie until you are ready to serve.

C O U N T D O W N

1. Assemble the ingredients and the equipment.
2. Do Steps 1–5 of *Distinguished Dessert*.
3. Do Steps 1–10 of *Beef Swellington*.
4. Do Steps 1–2 of *Poised Pears*.
5. Do Steps 1–2 of *Gay Blades*.
6. Do Step 11 of *Beef Swellington*.
7. Do Step 3 of *Poised Pears*.
8. Do Steps 3–5 of *Gay Blades*.

Weekend Twelve Sunday

SHOPPING LIST

MEAT & POULTRY

1/2 pound boneless, skinless chicken breast

FISH

1/2 pound medium shrimp, shelled and deveined

FRESH PRODUCE

VEGETABLES

2 stalks celery
1 small head lettuce
2 medium tomatoes
1 medium onion

FRUIT

1 large ripe banana
1 medium ripe papaya
2 ripe kiwifruits
1/4 pound seedless red grapes

CANS, JARS & BOTTLES

SOUP

2 cans (14 ounces each) chicken broth

VEGETABLES

1 can (11 ounces) whole kernel corn

JUICE

8 ounces clam juice

PACKAGED GOODS

PASTA, RICE & GRAINS

1 cup long-grain white rice

BAKED GOODS

4 individual shortbread tart shells

DRIED FRUITS & NUTS

1/2 cup pecan bits

WINES & SPIRITS

1/4 cup dry sherry

REFRIGERATED PRODUCTS

DAIRY

1/4 cup whipped cream

DELI

1/2 pound sliced cooked ham

FROZEN GOODS

VEGETABLES

1 package (10 ounces) whole okra

DESSERTS

1 pint French vanilla ice cream

STAPLES

- ☐ Butter
- ☐ Flour
- ☐ Granulated sugar
- ☐ Maple syrup
- ☐ Vegetable oil
- ☐ Raspberry vinegar
- ☐ Honey
- ☐ Bay leaf
- ☐ Dried coriander
- ☐ Dried thyme
- ☐ Cayenne pepper
- ☐ Ground cumin
- ☐ Pepper
- ☐ Salt

Weekend Twelve Sunday

Jumbo Gumbo

1 package (10 ounces) frozen whole okra
1 medium onion
2 medium fresh tomatoes
2 stalks celery
1/2 pound sliced cooked deli ham
1/2 pound boneless, skinless chicken breast
1/2 pound medium shrimp, shelled and deveined
1 can (11 ounces) whole kernel corn
3 tablespoons vegetable oil
2 tablespoons flour
1 bay leaf
1/2 teaspoon dried thyme
1/2 teaspoon cayenne pepper
1 teaspoon granulated sugar
1/4 cup dry sherry
2 cans (14 ounces each) chicken broth
8 ounces clam juice

Ridiculous Rice

1 cup long-grain white rice
2-1/4 cups water
1/2 teaspoon ground cumin
1/2 teaspoon dried coriander

Foolish Fruit

1 small head lettuce
1 large banana
1 medium ripe papaya
2 ripe kiwifruits
1/4 pound seedless red grapes
3 tablespoons vegetable oil

2 tablespoons raspberry vinegar
1/2 teaspoon honey
Seasoning to taste

Maple Madness

2 tablespoons butter
1 cup maple syrup
1/2 cup pecan bits
1 pint French vanilla ice cream
4 individual shortbread tart shells
1/4 cup whipped cream

EQUIPMENT

Dutch oven

Double boiler

Small covered saucepan

Large covered skillet

Medium mixing bowl

2 small mixing bowls

Whisk

Ice cream scoop

Kitchen knives

Measuring cups and spoons

Cooking utensils

Jumbo Gumbo

1. Set the okra in a small bowl of hot water to thaw.

2. Peel and dice the onion. Rinse and chop the tomatoes. Rinse, trim, and chop the celery. Chop the ham. Cube the chicken. Rinse and pat dry the shrimp. Drain the corn. Cut the okra into 1/2-inch pieces.

3. Heat the oil in a large skillet and sauté the okra for 5 minutes.

4. Stir in the flour, cover the skillet, reduce the heat, and simmer for 5 minutes.

5. Remove the skillet from the heat and set it aside.

6. Combine the bay leaf, the thyme, the cayenne pepper, the sugar, the sherry, the broth, and the clam juice in a Dutch oven. Add the celery, the onion, and the tomatoes, and simmer until the vegetables are crisp-tender, about 10 minutes.

7. Add the chicken and the corn, and simmer for 5 minutes more.

8. Add the shrimp and the okra, and simmer, stirring, until the shrimp turn bright pink, about 3 minutes.

9. Remove the bay leaf before serving.

Ridiculous Rice

1. Bring water to a boil in the bottom of a double boiler. Place the rice, the 2-1/4 cups water, the cumin, and the coriander in the top of the double boiler. Cover, reduce the heat, and simmer until all the liquid is absorbed and the rice is tender, 30 to 40 minutes.

2. Fluff the rice with a fork and serve with the gumbo.

Foolish Fruit

1. Wash and dry the lettuce and distribute the leaves among individual salad plates.

2. Peel and slice the banana. Peel, seed, and slice the papaya. Peel and slice the kiwifruits. Rinse, stem, and halve the grapes. Combine the fruit in a medium bowl.

3. In a small bowl, whisk together the oil, the vinegar, and the honey. Season to taste and toss with the fruit.

4. Spoon the mixture over the lettuce.

Maple Madness

1. In a small saucepan, combine the butter, the maple syrup, and the pecans. Bring to a boil, reduce the heat, and simmer until the sauce begins to thicken, about 3 minutes.

2. Cover the saucepan and remove it from the heat.

3. Place a scoop of ice cream in each individual tart shell. Spoon the maple sauce over the top.

4. Garnish with the whipped cream.

COUNTDOWN

1. Assemble the ingredients and the equipment.
2. Do Steps 1–2 of *Maple Madness*.
3. Do Step 1 of *Ridiculous Rice*.
4. Do Steps 1–6 of *Jumbo Gumbo*.
5. Do Steps 1–2 of *Foolish Fruit*.
6. Do Step 7 of *Jumbo Gumbo*.
7. Do Step 3 of *Foolish Fruit*.
8. Do Steps 8–9 of *Jumbo Gumbo*.
9. Do Step 2 of *Ridiculous Rice*.
10. Do Step 4 of *Foolish Fruit*.
11. Do Steps 3–4 of *Maple Madness*.

Weekend Thirteen Saturday

MEAT & POULTRY

3 pounds chicken pieces

FRESH PRODUCE

VEGETABLES

2 pounds baking potatoes
1 pound Brussels sprouts
1/2 pound baby carrots
3 stalks celery
1/4 pound small mushrooms
1 head escarole
12 small boiling onions
4 scallions (green onions)
1 clove garlic

HERBS

1/4 cup parsley (when chopped)
2 tablespoons rosemary (when chopped)

FRUIT

1 medium green apple
1 medium red apple
3 cups cranberries

PACKAGED GOODS

DRIED FRUITS & NUTS

1/3 cup walnut bits
8 walnut halves

WINES & SPIRITS

1-1/2 cups dry white wine

REFRIGERATED PRODUCTS

DAIRY

1/4 cup whipped cream
1 egg

JUICE

1/4 cup orange juice

STAPLES

- ❑ Butter
- ❑ Flour
- ❑ Cornstarch
- ❑ Granulated sugar
- ❑ Olive oil
- ❑ Vegetable oil
- ❑ Balsamic vinegar
- ❑ Lemon juice
- ❑ Plain breadcrumbs
- ❑ Bay leaf
- ❑ Dried savory
- ❑ Ground allspice
- ❑ Pepper
- ❑ Salt
- ❑ Vanilla extract

Weekend Thirteen Saturday

MENU

Luscious Chicken

3 pounds chicken pieces
12 small boiling onions
1/2 pound baby carrots
4 scallions (green onions)
1/4 cup fresh parsley (when chopped)
1/4 pound small fresh mushrooms
1 cup plain breadcrumbs
1/2 cup flour
Seasoning to taste
3 tablespoons vegetable oil
1-1/2 cups dry white wine
1 bay leaf

Pie-Eyed Potatoes

2 pounds baking potatoes
2 tablespoons fresh rosemary (when chopped)
1 clove garlic
4 tablespoons butter
Seasoning to taste

Spontaneous Sprouts

1 pound Brussels sprouts
1 tablespoon butter
1 teaspoon lemon juice
1/2 teaspoon dried savory
Seasoning to taste

On an Escarole

1 head escarole
3 stalks celery
1 medium green apple
1 medium red apple
3 tablespoons olive oil
2 tablespoons balsamic vinegar
1 teaspoon granulated sugar
1/4 teaspoon ground allspice
Seasoning to taste

Tipsy Tart

1/3 cup walnut bits
1 cup flour
1-3/4 cups granulated sugar
4 tablespoons butter
1 egg
3 cups fresh cranberries
1/4 cup orange juice
3 tablespoons cornstarch
1/3 cup water
1 teaspoon vanilla extract
1/4 cup whipped cream
8 walnut halves

EQUIPMENT

Dutch oven	Small mixing bowl
Large saucepan	Whisk
Medium saucepan	Vegetable peeler
Springform pan	Mallet
Pie plate	Pastry blender
Large shallow bowl	Plastic bag
2 large mixing bowls	Kitchen knives
Medium mixing bowl	Measuring cups and spoons
	Cooking utensils

Weekend Thirteen Saturday

Luscious Chicken

1. Rinse and pat dry the chicken. Trim and peel the onions. Rinse the carrots. Rinse and trim the scallions, and cut them into thirds. Rinse and chop the parsley. Rinse and pat dry the mushrooms.

2. Combine the breadcrumbs and the flour in a large shallow bowl, and season to taste. Dredge the chicken pieces in the mixture, shaking off the excess.

3. Heat the oil in a Dutch oven and brown the chicken pieces well on all sides, about 10 minutes. Remove the chicken and set it aside. Pour off all but 2 tablespoons of the fat from the Dutch oven. Add the onions, the carrots, and the scallions, and sauté until the onions begin to turn golden, about 6 minutes.

4. Return the chicken to the Dutch oven. Pour the wine over the chicken, and add the bay leaf. Cover, reduce the heat, and simmer, for 35 minutes.

5. Add the mushrooms and continue to simmer until the chicken is tender, about 20 minutes longer.

6. Remove the bay leaf and garnish with the parsley.

Pie-Eyed Potatoes

1. Grease a springform pan.

2. Peel and slice the potatoes. Place them in a large bowl of ice water and set it aside.

Rinse and chop the rosemary. Peel and mince the garlic. Melt the butter.

3. Drain and pat dry the potatoes. Arrange 1/4 of the slices in the pan, overlapping to fill the bottom. Sprinkle with 1 teaspoon of the rosemary, and season to taste. Add 1 tablespoon of the melted butter. Repeat 3 times. Sprinkle with the garlic.

4. Increase the oven temperature to 450°F.

5. Bake for 55 minutes.

6. Remove the sides of the springform pan and turn the potatoes onto a warm platter. Cut into wedges.

Spontaneous Sprouts

1. Bring water to a boil in a medium saucepan

2. Rinse and trim the sprouts and cut small X's in the bottoms of the stems. Add the sprouts to the boiling water, and cook until they are crisp-tender, about 10 minutes.

3. Drain the sprouts, return them to the saucepan, and toss them with the butter, the lemon juice, and the savory. Season to taste and toss again.

On an Escarole

1. Wash and dry the escarole and cut it into bite-sized pieces. Rinse, trim, and slice the celery into thin diagonals. Rinse, core, quarter, and thinly slice the apples. Combine the ingredients in a large bowl.

2. In a small bowl, whisk together the oil, the vinegar, the sugar, and the allspice. Season to taste.

3. Toss the salad with the dressing.

Tipsy Tart

1. Preheat the oven to 400°F. Lightly grease a pie plate.

2. Place the walnut bits in a plastic bag and pound them with a mallet until finely chopped. Combine the walnuts, the flour, 1/4 cup of the sugar, and the butter in a medium bowl. Blend with a pastry blender until the mixture resembles small peas. Blend in the egg. Form the dough into a ball and set it aside.

3. Rinse the cranberries and discard any that are soft or discolored.

4. Press the dough into the pie plate, smoothing it evenly over the bottom and up the sides. Prick the dough all over with the tines of a fork. Bake until the pie shell is golden, about 10 minutes.

5. Remove the pie shell from the oven and let it cool. Reduce the oven temperature to 375°F.

6. Combine the cranberries, the orange juice, and the remaining 1-1/2 cups sugar in a large saucepan. Mix the cornstarch with the water and stir it into the cranberry mixture. Bring the mixture to a boil and cook until the cranberries begin to pop

and the mixture begins to thicken and is clear, about 10 minutes.

7. Stir in the vanilla, pour the mixture into the pie shell, and bake until the filling is set, about 25 minutes.

8. Garnish with dollops of whipped cream and the walnut halves.

COUNTDOWN

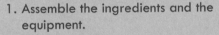

1. Assemble the ingredients and the equipment.
2. Do Steps 1–7 of *Tipsy Tart*.
3. Do Steps 1–4 of *Pie-Eyed Potatoes*.
4. Do Steps 1–4 of *Luscious Chicken*.
5. Do Step 5 of *Pie-Eyed Potatoes*.
6. Do Step 5 of *Luscious Chicken*.
7. Do Steps 1–2 of *On an Escarole*.
8. Do Steps 1–3 of *Spontaneous Sprouts*.
9. Do Step 6 of *Pie-Eyed Potatoes*.
10. Do Step 6 of *Luscious Chicken*.
11. Do Step 3 of *On an Escarole*.
12. Do Step 8 of *Tipsy Tart*.

Weekend Thirteen Sunday

FRESH PRODUCE

VEGETABLES

2 stalks celery
1 medium head red leaf lettuce
1 medium ripe avocado
1 medium green bell pepper
1 medium yellow bell pepper
1 large red onion
2 cloves garlic

HERBS

1/4 cup chives (when chopped)

FRUIT

1 small pink grapefruit
2 seedless tangerines

CANS, JARS & BOTTLES

SOUP

1 can (14 ounces) chicken broth

VEGETABLES

1 can (14-1/2 ounces) tomatoes with
    chilies
1 can (15 ounces) kidney beans
1 can (15 ounces) great Northern beans
1 can (11 ounces) whole kernel corn

DESSERT & BAKING NEEDS

1/4 cup marshmallow crème

PACKAGED GOODS

PASTA, RICE & GRAINS

1 cup long-grain white rice

BAKED GOODS

1 shortbread pie shell

DRIED FRUITS & NUTS

1/2 cup sliced almonds

DESSERT & BAKING NEEDS

1 small package instant coconut cream
    pudding mix
1 cup flaked coconut

WINES & SPIRITS

1/4 cup dry sherry

REFRIGERATED PRODUCTS

DAIRY

1-1/3 cups milk
1/2 cup sour cream
1 container (6 ounces) lemon yogurt
1 egg

STAPLES

- ☐ Flour
- ☐ Baking powder
- ☐ Baking soda
- ☐ Granulated sugar
- ☐ Olive oil
- ☐ Vegetable oil
- ☐ Tarragon vinegar
- ☐ Lemon juice
- ☐ Poppy seeds
- ☐ Chili powder
- ☐ Ground cumin
- ☐ Pepper
- ☐ Salt
- ☐ Almond extract

Weekend Thirteen Sunday

Chase the Chili

1 large red onion
2 cloves garlic
1 medium green bell pepper
1 medium yellow bell pepper
1 can (15 ounces) kidney beans
1 can (15 ounces) great Northern beans
1 can (11 ounces) whole kernel corn
2 tablespoons olive oil
1 can (14-1/2 ounces) tomatoes
    with chilies
1 can (14 ounces) chicken broth
1 cup long-grain white rice
1/4 cup water
1/4 cup dry sherry
1 teaspoon chili powder
1 teaspoon ground cumin
Seasoning to taste

Stalk the Salad

1 medium head red leaf lettuce
2 stalks celery
1 small pink grapefruit
2 seedless tangerines
1 medium ripe avocado
1/4 cup fresh chives (when chopped)
3 tablespoons olive oil
2 tablespoons tarragon vinegar
2 teaspoons granulated sugar
1/2 teaspoon almond extract
Seasoning to taste
1/2 cup sliced almonds

Mangle the Muffins

1/3 cup milk
1/4 cup vegetable oil
1 container (6 ounces) lemon yogurt
1 teaspoon lemon juice
1 egg
1-3/4 cups flour
1/4 cup granulated sugar
2 tablespoons poppy seeds
1 tablespoon baking powder
1/2 teaspoon baking soda
1/4 teaspoon salt

Follow that Pie

1 cup flaked coconut
1 small package instant coconut cream
    pudding mix
1 cup milk
1/2 cup sour cream
1 shortbread pie shell
1/4 cup marshmallow crème

EQUIPMENT

Dutch oven	Small mixing bowl
Muffin tin	Whisk
Baking sheet	Kitchen knives
2 large mixing bowls	Measuring cups and spoons
2 medium mixing bowls	Cooking utensils

Weekend Thirteen Sunday

RECIPES

Chase the Chili

1. Peel and chop the onion. Peel and mince the garlic. Rinse, stem, seed, and chop the bell peppers.

2. Drain the beans. Drain the corn.

3. Heat the oil in a Dutch oven.

4. Add the onion, the garlic, and the bell peppers, and sauté until tender, about 4 minutes.

5. Add the tomatoes with chilies, the beans, the corn, the broth, the rice, the water, the sherry, the chili powder, and the cumin. Season to taste and stir to combine.

6. Bring the mixture to a boil, reduce the heat, cover, and simmer until the liquid is absorbed, and the rice is tender, about 30 minutes.

Stalk the Salad

1. Wash and dry the lettuce. Place 4 whole leaves on individual salad plates, and tear the remainder into bite-sized pieces.

2. Rinse, trim, and slice the celery. Peel and section the grapefruit. Peel and section the tangerines. Peel, pit, and slice the avocado. Rinse and chop the chives. Combine the fruit and vegetables in a large bowl.

3. In a small bowl, whisk together the oil, the vinegar, the sugar, and the almond extract. Season to taste

4. Toss the fruit and vegetables with the dressing and distribute the mixture over the lettuce leaves.

5. Sprinkle the salads with the sliced almonds.

Mangle the Muffins

1. Preheat the oven to 400°F. Grease a muffin tin.

2. In a large bowl, combine the milk, the oil, the yogurt, the lemon juice, and the egg.

3. In a medium bowl, combine the flour, the sugar, the poppy seeds, the baking powder, the baking soda, and the salt.

4. Fold the flour mixture into the yogurt mixture.

5. Divide the batter evenly among the muffin cups and bake until the muffins are golden, about 15 minutes.

Follow that Pie

1. Preheat the broiler.

2. Spread the coconut on a baking sheet and toast until it is golden, about 4 minutes.

3. In a medium bowl, combine the pudding mix, the milk, and the sour cream, and beat until well blended.

4. Pour the mixture into the pie shell and refrigerate it until you are ready to serve.

5. Top the pie with the toasted coconut, and garnish with dollops of marshmallow crème.

COUNTDOWN

1. Assemble the ingredients and the equipment.
2. Do Steps 1–4 of *Follow that Pie.*
3. Do Steps 1–6 of *Chase the Chili.*
4. Do Steps 1–5 of *Mangle the Muffins.*
5. Do Steps 1–5 of *Stalk the Salad.*
6. Do Step 5 of *Follow that Pie.*

Holidays

New Year's Day Brunch

SHOPPING LIST

FISH

1/2 pound smoked salmon, sliced

FRESH PRODUCE

VEGETABLES

1 pound asparagus
1 large sweet onion
1 small red onion
1 small red bell pepper

HERBS

3 tablespoons basil (when chopped)
3 tablespoons dill (when chopped)
3 tablespoons parsley (when chopped)

FRUIT

1 large ripe pineapple
1 medium ripe honeydew melon
1 medium ripe cantaloupe
2 medium ripe papayas
1 small lemon
1/2 pound seedless red grapes
1/2 pound seedless green grapes

CANS, JARS & BOTTLES

CONDIMENTS

2 tablespoons capers

PACKAGED GOODS

BAKED GOODS

1 small loaf black bread, sliced

REFRIGERATED PRODUCTS

DAIRY

3/4 cup milk
1 cup sour cream
1/4 cup whipping cream
11 eggs

CHEESE

1 package (8 ounces) cream cheese

DELI

1/2 pound bacon
1/2 pound breakfast link sausage

STAPLES

- [ ] Butter
- [ ] Flour
- [ ] Baking powder
- [ ] Granulated sugar
- [ ] Dark brown sugar
- [ ] Vegetable oil
- [ ] Red wine vinegar
- [ ] Dijon mustard
- [ ] Honey
- [ ] Poppy seeds
- [ ] Dried sage
- [ ] Ground allspice
- [ ] Ground cinnamon
- [ ] Pepper
- [ ] Salt

New Year's Day Brunch

MENU

Startup Salmon

1 package (8 ounces) cream cheese
1 large sweet onion
1/2 pound smoked salmon, sliced
1 small loaf black bread, sliced
2 tablespoons capers

Equinox Eggs

3 tablespoons fresh basil (when chopped)
3 tablespoons fresh parsley (when chopped)
3 tablespoons fresh dill (when chopped)
10 eggs
1/4 cup whipping cream
Seasoning to taste
4 tablespoons butter

Party Pork

1 small red onion
1 small red bell pepper
1/2 pound breakfast link sausage
1/2 pound bacon
1/2 teaspoon dried sage

That's the Spear-It

1 pound fresh asparagus
2 tablespoons butter
2 teaspoons red wine vinegar
1 teaspoon Dijon mustard
1/2 teaspoon granulated sugar
Seasoning to taste

Go Ahead, Bake My Day

2 cups flour
1 tablespoon baking powder

1/4 teaspoon salt
1/4 cup poppy seeds
1/2 teaspoon ground cinnamon
1/4 teaspoon ground allspice
3/4 cup milk
1/3 cup vegetable oil
1/4 cup honey
1 egg

Fruit Bowl

1 large fresh ripe pineapple
1 medium ripe honeydew melon
1 medium ripe cantaloupe
1/2 pound seedless red grapes
1/2 pound seedless green grapes
2 medium ripe papayas
1 small lemon
1/4 cup dark brown sugar
1 cup sour cream

EQUIPMENT

2 large covered skillets	Whisk
9 × 13-inch glass baking dish	Citrus grater
Muffin tin	Citrus juicer
Large shallow bowl	Plastic wrap
2 large mixing bowls	Aluminum foil
Medium mixing bowl	Kitchen knives
Small mixing bowl	Measuring cups and spoons
	Cooking utensils

New Year's Day Brunch

Startup Salmon

1. Set the cream cheese out to soften.

2. Peel and thinly slice the sweet onion. Roll up the salmon slices. Cut the bread into triangles. Drain the capers.

3. Set the cream cheese in the middle of a platter. Arrange the bread triangles around half of the platter. Arrange the salmon rolls around the other half of the platter. Sprinkle the onion slices and the capers over the salmon.

Equinox Eggs

1. Preheat the oven to 350°F.

2. Rinse and chop the basil. Rinse and chop the parsley. Rinse and chop the dill.

3. In large bowl, beat the eggs with the cream until frothy. Fold in the herbs and season to taste.

4. Melt the butter in a 9 × 13-inch glass baking dish. Pour the egg mixture into the dish and bake until a knife inserted in the center comes out clean, about 25 minutes.

Party Pork

1. Peel and mince the onion. Rinse, stem, seed, and dice the bell pepper.

2. Separate the sausage links and cook them in a large skillet, turning to brown them on all sides, about 15 minutes.

3. Drain the sausage on paper towels and cover it with aluminum foil to keep warm.

4. Wipe out the skillet, add the bacon, and cook until crisp, about 10 minutes.

5. Drain the bacon on paper towels.

6. Sauté the onion and the bell pepper with the sage in the bacon drippings until soft, about 5 minutes. Return the sausage and the bacon to the skillet and toss gently to combine. Cover to keep warm.

That's the Spear-It

1. Bring a small amount of water to a boil in a large skillet.

2. Remove and discard the tough ends from the asparagus.

3. Arrange the spears in the skillet, cover, and steam until crisp-tender, 3 to 8 minutes, depending on their thickness.

4. Drain the asparagus and return it to the skillet. Blend in the butter, the vinegar, the mustard, and the sugar. Season to taste, toss to coat, and heat through. Cover to keep warm.

Go Ahead, Bake My Day

1. Grease a muffin tin.

2. In a large bowl, combine the flour, the baking powder, the salt, the poppy seeds, the cinnamon, and the allspice.

3. In a medium bowl, combine the milk, the oil, the honey, the reserved lemon peel from the fruit bowl, and the egg, and whisk until well blended.

4. Fold the egg mixture into the flour mixture until just moistened. Divide the batter evenly among the muffin cups.

5. Bake at 350°F until the muffins are golden, about 25 minutes.

Fruit Bowl

1. Cut the pineapple into quarters and remove the core. With a sharp knife, separate the fruit from the rind but do not remove it. Cut each wedge into slices.

2. Cut the melons into quarters and remove the seeds. With a sharp knife, separate the fruit from the rind and cut each wedge into slices.

3. Rinse the grapes and separate into small bunches.

4. Cut the papayas in half, remove the peel and the seeds, and cut the fruit into slices.

5. Grate the peel from the lemon and reserve it. Juice the lemon.

6. In a small bowl, combine the lemon juice, the brown sugar, and the sour cream. Place the bowl in the middle of a large shallow bowl and arrange the fruit up around the edges. Cover with plastic wrap and refrigerate until you are ready to serve.

COUNTDOWN

1. Assemble the ingredients and the equipment.
2. Do Step 1 of *Startup Salmon*.
3. Do Steps 1–6 of *Fruit Bowl*.
4. Do Steps 2–3 of *Startup Salmon*.
5. Do Steps 1–4 of *Go Ahead, Bake My Day*.
6. Do Steps 1–4 of *That's the Spear-It*.
7. Do Steps 1–4 of *Equinox Eggs*.
8. Do Step 5 of *Go Ahead, Bake My Day*.
9. Do Steps 1–6 of *Party Pork*.

Martin Luther King, Jr.'s Birthday

SHOPPING LIST

MEAT & POULTRY

1-1/2 pounds boneless, skinless
    chicken breast

FRESH PRODUCE

VEGETABLES
1 package (16 ounces) spinach
2 stalks celery
1/2 pound mushrooms
2 medium orange bell peppers
2 medium shallots
3 cloves garlic

CANS, JARS & BOTTLES

SOUP
1 can (14 ounces) chicken broth
2 cans (10-1/2 ounces each) beef broth

FRUIT
1 can (29 ounces) peach halves

CONDIMENTS
1 jar (2 ounces) diced pimiento

DESSERT & BAKING NEEDS
1 can (14 ounces) sweetened
    condensed milk

PACKAGED GOODS

DRIED FRUITS & NUTS
2 tablespoons sliced almonds

DESSERT & BAKING NEEDS
1 cup chocolate chips

WINES & SPIRITS

1/4 cup dry sherry
2 teaspoons rum

REFRIGERATED PRODUCTS

DAIRY
1 cup buttermilk
2/3 cup sour cream
1 cup half-and-half
1 egg

FROZEN GOODS

DESSERTS
1 container (8 ounces) whipped topping

STAPLES

- [ ] Butter
- [ ] Flour
- [ ] Baking powder
- [ ] Baking soda
- [ ] Cornmeal
- [ ] Cornstarch
- [ ] Granulated sugar
- [ ] Dark brown sugar
- [ ] Vegetable oil
- [ ] Worcestershire sauce
- [ ] Ground cinnamon
- [ ] Ground cumin
- [ ] Pepper
- [ ] Red pepper flakes
- [ ] Salt
- [ ] Almond extract

Martin Luther King, Jr.'s Birthday

Chicken a la King

1-1/2 pounds boneless, skinless chicken breast
2 cans (10-1/2 ounces each) beef broth
2 stalks celery
2 medium orange bell peppers
1/2 pound fresh mushrooms
1 jar (2 ounces) diced pimiento
2 tablespoons butter
1-1/2 cups chicken broth
1/3 cup flour
1 cup half-and-half
1/4 cup dry sherry
Seasoning to taste

Ebenezer Bread

1 tablespoon butter
1/2 teaspoon red pepper flakes
1 egg
1 cup buttermilk
1 cup flour
1 cup cornmeal
3 tablespoons granulated sugar
1 tablespoon baking powder
1/2 teaspoon salt
1/2 teaspoon ground cumin
1/2 teaspoon baking soda

Spiritual Spinach

2 medium shallots
3 cloves garlic
1 package (16 ounces) fresh spinach
2 tablespoons vegetable oil
2 teaspoons cornstarch

1/4 cup chicken broth
1 teaspoon Worcestershire sauce

Nobel Peach Prize

1 can (29 ounces) peach halves
2 teaspoons rum
2/3 cup sour cream
1 tablespoon dark brown sugar
1/2 teaspoon ground cinnamon

I Have a Cream

1 cup chocolate chips
1 can (14 ounces) sweetened condensed milk
1 teaspoon almond extract
1 container (8 ounces) frozen whipped topping
2 tablespoons sliced almonds

EQUIPMENT

Large covered saucepan	Large mixing bowl
Medium saucepan	2 small mixing bowls
Small saucepan	Whisk
Large covered skillet	Kitchen knives
Medium skillet	Measuring cups and spoons
9 × 13-inch glass baking dish	Cooking utensils
9 × 9-inch glass baking dish	

Martin Luther King, Jr.'s Birthday

RECIPES

Chicken a la King

1. Rinse and pat dry the chicken.

2. Combine the chicken and the beef broth in a large saucepan. Bring to a boil, cover, reduce the heat, and simmer until the chicken is tender and cooked throughout, about 15 minutes.

3. Drain the chicken. Rinse the breasts under cold water and cut them into bite-sized pieces.

4. Rinse, trim, and slice the celery. Rinse, stem, seed, and chop the bell peppers. Rinse, pat dry, and slice the mushrooms. Drain the pimiento.

5. Melt the butter in a medium skillet and sauté the celery for 2 minutes. Add the bell peppers and the mushrooms, and sauté for 5 minutes. Set the skillet aside.

6. Heat the chicken broth in the saucepan.

7. In a small bowl, blend the flour with the half-and-half. Add the mixture to the saucepan and simmer until the sauce begins to thicken. Return the chicken to the saucepan. Add the vegetables, the pimiento, and the sherry. Season to taste and heat through, but do not let the mixture boil. Remove the pan from the heat and cover to keep warm.

Ebenezer Bread

1. Grease a 9 × 9-inch glass baking dish.

2. In a small saucepan, melt the butter with the red pepper flakes. Remove the pan from the heat and blend in the egg and the buttermilk.

3. In a large bowl, combine the flour, the cornmeal, the sugar, the baking powder, the salt, the cumin, and the baking soda.

4. Fold the buttermilk mixture into the dry ingredients and stir until just blended. Turn the mixture into the baking dish.

5. Preheat the oven to 425°F.

6. Bake until a toothpick inserted in the center comes out clean, about 25 minutes.

Spiritual Spinach

1. Peel and mince the shallots. Peel and mince the garlic. Rinse and stem the spinach.

2. Heat 1 tablespoon of the oil in a large skillet and sauté half of the shallots until brown, about 10 minutes. Drain the shallots on paper towels.

3. In a small bowl, combine the cornstarch with the broth and the Worcestershire sauce.

4. Heat the remaining 1 tablespoon oil in the skillet and sauté the remaining half of the shallots with the garlic until just brown, about 7 minutes.

5. Add the spinach and the cornstarch mixture, and sauté until the spinach is just wilted and the sauce comes to a boil, about 1 minute. Remove the pan from the heat and cover to keep warm.

6. Sprinkle with the toasted shallot.

Nobel Peach Prize

1. Drain the peaches and arrange the halves, cut sides up, in a 9 × 13-inch baking dish.

2. Sprinkle the peaches with the rum. Spoon the sour cream over the peaches and sprinkle with the brown sugar and the cinnamon.

3. Preheat the broiler.

4. Broil the peaches until they are hot and the sugar begins to caramelize, about 3 minutes.

I Have a Cream

1. In a medium saucepan, slowly heat the chocolate chips with the condensed milk and blend until the chocolate is melted and the mixture is smooth.

2. Remove the pan from the heat and stir in the almond extract. Place the saucepan in the freezer for 30 minutes.

3. Fold the whipped topping into the chilled chocolate mixture, spoon into individual dessert dishes, and freeze until you are ready to serve.

4. Garnish with the sliced almonds.

COUNTDOWN

1. Assemble the ingredients and the equipment.
2. Do Steps 1–3 of *I Have a Cream*.
3. Do Steps 1–2 of *Chicken a la King*.
4. Do Steps 1–4 of *Ebenezer Bread*.
5. Do Step 1 of *Nobel Peach Prize*.
6. Do Steps 1–2 of *Spiritual Spinach*.
7. Do Step 3 of *Chicken a la King*.
8. Do Steps 5–6 of *Ebenezer Bread*.
9. Do Steps 3–5 of *Spiritual Spinach*.
10. Do Steps 4–7 of *Chicken a la King*.
11. Do Steps 2–3 of *Nobel Peach Prize*.
12. Do Step 6 of *Spiritual Spinach*.
13. Do Step 4 of *I Have a Cream*.
14. Do Step 4 of *Nobel Peach Prize*.

Super Bowl Sunday

MEAT & POULTRY

2 pounds lean beef stew meat

FRESH PRODUCE

VEGETABLES

1/2 pound green beans
4 medium carrots
4 stalks celery
1/4 pound mushrooms
1 medium head green leaf lettuce
2 medium tomatoes
1 large ripe avocado
1 small orange bell pepper
3 scallions (green onions)
1 clove garlic

HERBS

2 tablespoons chives (when chopped)

FRUIT

1 large banana

CANS, JARS & BOTTLES

SOUP

1 can (10-3/4 ounces) tomato soup
1 can (10-1/2 ounces) onion soup

SAUCES

1 jar (12 ounces) beef gravy

CONDIMENTS

1 jar (6-1/2 ounces) marinated
   artichoke hearts

DESSERT & BAKING NEEDS

1 jar (12 ounces) chocolate fudge
   topping

PACKAGED GOODS

PASTA, RICE & GRAINS

12 ounces curly egg noodles

BAKED GOODS

20 Oreo cookies

DRIED FRUITS & NUTS

1/2 cup pecan bits

WINES & SPIRITS

3/4 cup dry red wine

REFRIGERATED PRODUCTS

DAIRY

1/2 cup milk
1 cup sour cream
1 egg

FROZEN GOODS

DESSERTS

1 quart Cookies and Cream ice cream

STAPLES

- ❑ Butter
- ❑ Flour
- ❑ Baking powder
- ❑ Baking soda
- ❑ Granulated sugar
- ❑ Balsamic vinegar
- ❑ Worcestershire sauce
- ❑ Bay leaf
- ❑ Dried oregano
- ❑ Dried thyme
- ❑ Ground allspice
- ❑ Pepper
- ❑ Salt
- ❑ Brandy extract

Super Bowl Sunday

Quarterback Stew

2 pounds lean beef stew meat
1 can (10-3/4 ounces) tomato soup
1 can (10-1/2 ounces) onion soup
1 jar (12 ounces) beef gravy
3/4 cup dry red wine
1 teaspoon dried thyme
1 bay leaf
1/2 teaspoon ground allspice
4 medium carrots
4 stalks celery
1/2 pound fresh green beans
1/4 pound fresh mushrooms
Seasoning to taste
12 ounces curly egg noodles

First Down Salad

1 medium head green leaf lettuce
2 medium fresh tomatoes
1 small orange bell pepper
3 scallions (green onions)
1 jar (6-1/2 ounces) marinated artichoke
   hearts
2 tablespoons balsamic vinegar
1/2 teaspoon Worcestershire sauce
1/2 teaspoon granulated sugar
1/2 teaspoon dried oregano
Seasoning to taste
1 large ripe avocado

Halftime Muffins

2 tablespoons fresh chives (when
   chopped)
1 clove garlic

4 tablespoons butter
1 cup sour cream
1/2 cup milk
1 egg
2 cups flour
1 tablespoon baking powder
1/2 teaspoon baking soda
1/4 teaspoon salt

Refereeze

1 quart Cookies and Cream ice cream
3 tablespoons butter
20 Oreo cookies
2 teaspoons brandy extract
1 large banana
1 jar (12 ounces) chocolate fudge
   topping
1/2 cup pecan bits

EQUIPMENT

Stockpot	Small mixing bowl
6-quart ovenproof casserole	Whisk
Small saucepan	Vegetable peeler
Muffin tin	Mallet
Pie plate	Plastic wrap
Colander	Plastic bag
2 large mixing bowls	Kitchen knives
3 medium mixing bowls	Measuring cups and spoons
	Cooking utensils

Super Bowl Sunday

Quarterback Stew

1. Preheat the oven to 325°F.

2. Rinse, trim, and cube the beef, and place the cubes in the bottom of a 6-quart ovenproof casserole.

3. Cover the beef with the tomato soup, the onion soup, the beef gravy, the wine, the thyme, the bay leaf, and the allspice. Stir to combine.

4. Cover and bake for 3 hours.

5. Peel and slice the carrots. Rinse, trim, and slice the celery. Rinse and trim the green beans and cut them into 1-inch pieces. Rinse, pat dry, and slice the mushrooms.

6. Add the vegetables to the beef, season to taste, cover, and continue cooking for 1 more hour.

7. Bring water for the pasta to a boil in a stockpot.

8. Remove the stew from the oven and let sit, covered, for 20 minutes. Remove the bay leaf.

9. Cook the noodles until they are almost tender, about 7 minutes.

10. Drain the noodles and serve them with the stew.

First Down Salad

1. Wash and dry the lettuce and tear it into bite-sized pieces. Rinse and chop the tomatoes. Rinse, stem, seed, and chop the bell pepper. Trim and chop the scallions. Drain the artichokes, reserving the marinade. Combine the vegetables in a large bowl.

2. In a small bowl, whisk together the reserved marinade with the vinegar, the Worcestershire sauce, the sugar, and the oregano. Season to taste.

3. Toss the salad with the dressing. Peel, pit, and slice the avocado and arrange the slices over the salad.

Halftime Muffins

1. Rinse and chop the chives. Peel and mince the garlic.

2. Melt the butter.

3. In a large bowl, blend together the chives, the garlic, the melted butter, the sour cream, the milk, and the egg.

4. In a medium bowl, combine the flour, the baking powder, the baking soda, and the salt. Fold the dry ingredients into the egg mixture until just moistened.

5. Grease a muffin tin and divide the batter evenly among the cups.

6. Increase the oven temperature to 400°F.

7. Bake until the muffins are golden, about 18 minutes.

Refereeze

1. Set the ice cream out to soften.

2. Melt the butter.

3. Place the cookies in a plastic bag and crush them with a mallet.

4. In a medium bowl, combine the melted butter and the cookie crumbs. Press the mixture evenly into the bottom and sides of a pie plate and freeze it for 10 minutes.

5. In a medium bowl, blend the brandy extract into the softened ice cream. Spread half of the ice cream mixture into the pie pan.

6. Peel and slice the banana and arrange the slices over the ice cream.

7. Spread the remaining ice cream mixture over the banana, cover the pie with plastic wrap, and freeze until firm, at least 2 hours.

8. In a small saucepan, heat the fudge topping with the nuts. Spread the mixture over the pie.

COUNTDOWN

1. Assemble the ingredients and the equipment.
2. Do Steps 1–4 of *Quarterback Stew*.
3. Do Steps 1–7 of *Refereeze*.
4. Do Steps 5–6 of *Quarterback Stew*.
5. Do Steps 1–5 of *Halftime Muffins*.
6. Do Steps 1–2 of *First Down Salad*.
7. Do Steps 7–8 of *Quarterback Stew*.
8. Do Steps 6–7 of *Halftime Muffins*.
9. Do Step 9 of *Quarterback Stew*.
10. Do Step 3 of *First Down Salad*.
11. Do Step 10 of *Quarterback Stew*.
12. Do Step 8 of *Refereeze*.

Chinese New Year's

FISH

1/2 pound baby cooked shrimp

FRESH PRODUCE

VEGETABLES

2 medium carrots
2 stalks celery
1/4 pound mushrooms
1/4 pound bean sprouts
1/2 pound baby bok choy
1 small head green cabbage
6 scallions (green onions)
2 cloves garlic

HERBS

2 tablespoons chives (when chopped)

CANS, JARS & BOTTLES

SOUP

2 cans (14 ounces each) chicken broth
1 can (14 ounces) beef broth

FRUIT

1 can (11 ounces) mandarin oranges

INTERNATIONAL FOODS

1 can (8 ounces) sliced water chestnuts
1 jar (7 ounces) plum sauce

PACKAGED GOODS

PASTA, RICE & GRAINS

1 cup long-grain white rice

BAKED GOODS

1 package (9 ounces) almond cookies

DESSERT & BAKING NEEDS

1 small package instant lemon pudding
   mix

WINES & SPIRITS

1 tablespoon dry white wine
2 tablespoons dry sherry

REFRIGERATED PRODUCTS

DAIRY

2 cups milk
1 cup half-and-half
2 eggs

FROZEN GOODS

VEGETABLES

1 package (10 ounces) green peas

STAPLES

- ☐ Flour
- ☐ Baking powder
- ☐ Dark brown sugar
- ☐ Vegetable oil
- ☐ Sesame oil
- ☐ Rice vinegar
- ☐ Soy sauce
- ☐ Ketchup
- ☐ Sesame seeds
- ☐ Chinese five-spice powder
- ☐ Ground ginger
- ☐ Pepper
- ☐ Red pepper flakes
- ☐ Salt
- ☐ Almond extract

Chinese New Year's

Dragon Dance Soup

1/2 pound baby bok choy
2 tablespoons fresh chives (when chopped)
1 can (8 ounces) sliced water chestnuts
2 cans (14 ounces each) chicken broth
2 tablespoons dry sherry
2 teaspoons soy sauce
1/4 teaspoon red pepper flakes
Seasoning to taste
2 teaspoons sesame oil

Chinese Pillows

1 small head green cabbage
2 medium carrots
3 scallions (green onions)
2 stalks celery
1/4 pound fresh bean sprouts
1 cup flour
1 tablespoon dark brown sugar
1 teaspoon baking powder
1 teaspoon ground ginger
1 cup half-and-half
1 egg
1 tablespoon soy sauce
1/4 teaspoon Chinese five-spice powder
Seasoning to taste
1/4 cup vegetable oil
1 jar (7 ounces) plum sauce
1-1/2 tablespoons rice vinegar
1 tablespoon sesame seeds

Year of the Rice

1 package (10 ounces) frozen green peas
1 cup long-grain white rice
1 can (14 ounces) beef broth

1/4 cup water
3 scallions (green onions)
1/4 pound fresh mushrooms
2 cloves garlic
1/2 pound baby cooked shrimp
1 tablespoons ketchup
2 tablespoons soy sauce
1 tablespoon dry white wine
1 egg
1/2 teaspoon rice vinegar
3 tablespoons vegetable oil

Good Fortune Pudding

1 small package instant lemon pudding mix
2 cups milk
1 teaspoon almond extract
1 package (9 ounces) almond cookies
1 can (11 ounces) mandarin oranges

EQUIPMENT

Electric mixer	Whisk
Wok	Vegetable peeler
Double boiler	Vegetable grater
Medium saucepan	Mallet
Small covered saucepan	Plastic bag
Large skillet	Kitchen knives
Large mixing bowl	Measuring cups and spoons
2 medium mixing bowls	Cooking utensils
3 small mixing bowls	

Chinese New Year's

Dragon Dance Soup

1. Thoroughly rinse, stem, and slice the bok choy. Rinse and chop the chives. Drain the water chestnuts.

2. In a medium saucepan, combine the broth, the sherry, the soy sauce, and the red pepper flakes. Bring to a boil. Add the water chestnuts and cook for 2 minutes.

3. Fold in the bok choy, season to taste, and cook for 2 minutes more.

4. Blend in the chives and the oil.

Chinese Pillows

1. Trim and grate the cabbage. Peel and grate the carrots. Trim and chop the scallions. Rinse, trim, and chop the celery. Rinse and pat dry the bean sprouts. Combine the vegetables in a large bowl.

2. In a medium bowl, combine the flour, the brown sugar, the baking powder, and the ginger. Gradually blend in the half-and-half. Whisk in the egg and the soy sauce. Blend in the Chinese five-spice powder. Season to taste.

3. Blend the egg mixture into the vegetable mixture.

4. Preheat the oven to 275°F.

5. Heat half of the oil in a large skillet. Drop half of the vegetable mixture by spoonfuls into the skillet, and flatten them into rounds. Cook until golden and puffy, about 3 minutes per side. Place them on an ovenproof plate in the oven to keep them warm. Repeat.

6. In a small saucepan, bring the plum sauce and the vinegar to a boil. Remove from the heat and fold in the sesame seeds. Cover to keep warm.

7. Spoon the sauce over the pillows.

Year of the Rice

1. Set the package of peas in a small bowl of hot water to thaw.

2. Bring water to a boil in the bottom of a double boiler. In the top of the double boiler, combine the rice, the broth, and the water. Cover, reduce the heat, and simmer until the liquid is absorbed and the rice is tender, about 40 minutes.

3. Trim and chop the scallions. Rinse, pat dry, and slice the mushrooms. Peel and mince the garlic. Rinse and pat dry the shrimp.

4. In a small bowl, combine the ketchup, the soy sauce, and the wine.

5. In another small bowl, beat the egg with the vinegar.

6. Heat the oil in a wok and stir-fry the garlic and the scallions for 1 minute. Fold in the rice and stir-fry until it is lightly browned, about 3 minutes.

7. Add the mushrooms, the peas, and the shrimp, and stir-fry for 2 minutes.

8. Blend in the ketchup mixture. Blend in the egg and stir-fry for 2 minutes more. Cover to keep warm.

Good Fortune Pudding

1. In a medium bowl, combine the pudding mix and the milk, and beat until well blended, about 2 minutes. Blend in the almond extract. Refrigerate for 20 minutes.

2. Place the cookies in a plastic bag and crush them with a mallet.

3. Drain the mandarin oranges.

4. Place half the cookie crumbs in the bottom of individual dessert glasses. Add half of the pudding. Top with half of the oranges. Repeat. Refrigerate until you are ready to serve.

COUNTDOWN

1. Assemble the ingredients and the equipment.
2. Do Steps 1–4 of *Good Fortune Pudding*.
3. Do Steps 1–5 of *Year of the Rice*.
4. Do Step 1 of *Chinese Pillows*.
5. Do Step 1 of *Dragon Dance Soup*.
6. Do Steps 6–8 of *Year of the Rice*.
7. Do Steps 2–6 of *Chinese Pillows*.
8. Do Step 2–4 of *Dragon Dance Soup*.
9. Do Step 7 of *Chinese Pillows*.

Valentine's Day

FISH
4 sole fillets (about 1-1/2 pounds)
1/2 pound crabmeat

FRESH PRODUCE

VEGETABLES
1 pound sugar-snap peas
1 stalk celery
1 medium head red leaf lettuce
1 medium cucumber
1 small red onion
2 scallions (green onions)

FRUIT
1 large pink grapefruit

CANS, JARS & BOTTLES

FRUIT
1 jar (6 ounces) maraschino cherries

PACKAGED GOODS

DRIED FRUITS & NUTS
1/4 cup pecan bits

DESSERT & BAKING NEEDS
2 squares (1 ounce each)
   unsweetened chocolate

REFRIGERATED PRODUCTS

DAIRY
1 cup + 2 tablespoons milk
1 cup half-and-half
3 eggs

- ❏ Butter
- ❏ Vegetable shortening
- ❏ Flour
- ❏ Baking soda
- ❏ Granulated sugar
- ❏ Dark brown sugar
- ❏ Powdered sugar
- ❏ Olive oil
- ❏ Red wine vinegar
- ❏ Lemon juice
- ❏ White Worcestershire sauce
- ❏ Honey
- ❏ Poppy seeds
- ❏ Dried tarragon
- ❏ Dry mustard
- ❏ Ground nutmeg
- ❏ Paprika
- ❏ Pepper
- ❏ Salt
- ❏ Vanilla extract

Valentine's Day

Sole Mates

2 eggs
4 sole fillets (about 1-1/2 pounds)
2 scallions (green onions)
1 stalk celery
1/2 pound fresh crabmeat
2 tablespoons butter
3 tablespoons flour
1 cup half-and-half
1/2 teaspoon dry mustard
1 teaspoon white Worcestershire sauce
Seasoning to taste
1/2 teaspoon paprika

Passionate Peas

1 pound fresh sugar-snap peas
3 tablespoons butter
3 tablespoons lemon juice
1-1/2 tablespoons dark brown sugar
1/4 teaspoon ground nutmeg
Seasoning to taste
1/4 cup pecan bits

Heart and Salad

1 medium head red leaf lettuce
1 large pink grapefruit
1 medium cucumber
1 small red onion
3 tablespoons olive oil
2 tablespoons red wine vinegar
1 tablespoon lemon juice
1 teaspoon honey
1/2 teaspoon dried tarragon

1 tablespoon poppy seeds
Seasoning to taste

Be My Valentine

1/3 cup butter
2 squares (1 ounce each) unsweetened
   chocolate
1 cup milk
1 jar (6 ounces) maraschino cherries
1/2 cup vegetable shortening
1 cup granulated sugar
1 egg
1-1/2 cups flour
1 teaspoon baking soda
1/2 teaspoon salt
3 cups powdered sugar
1-1/2 teaspoons vanilla extract

EQUIPMENT

Electric mixer

Medium saucepan

Small saucepan

Medium skillet

9 × 13-inch glass
   baking dish

Heart-shaped
   baking pan

2 large mixing
   bowls

Medium mixing
   bowl

2 small mixing
   bowls

Whisk

Kitchen knives

Measuring cups
   and spoons

Cooking utensils

Valentine's Day

Sole Mates

1. Grease a 9 × 13-inch glass baking dish.

2. In a small saucepan, cover the eggs with water, bring to a boil, and hard-boil the eggs, 10 to 12 minutes.

3. Rinse and pat dry the fish.

4. Trim and chop the scallions. Rinse, trim, and mince the celery. Flake and pick over the crabmeat.

5. Drain the eggs and rinse them in cold water to cool.

6. Melt the butter in a medium saucepan. Add the flour and blend well. Slowly blend in the half-and-half. Blend in the mustard and the Worcestershire sauce, and season to taste. Simmer, stirring, until the mixture begins to thicken, about 5 minutes.

7. Peel and chop the eggs. Add the eggs to the half-and-half mixture. Fold in the scallions, the celery, and the crabmeat.

8. Preheat the oven to 400°F.

9. Spoon a tablespoon of the crabmeat mixture onto each fish fillet. Roll the fillets up and place them, seam side down, in the baking dish. Spoon the remaining crab mixture over the fillets. Sprinkle with the paprika.

10. Bake until the fish flakes easily with a fork, about 20 minutes.

Passionate Peas

1. Rinse and trim the snap peas.

2. Melt the butter in a medium skillet and sauté the snap peas for 2 minutes.

3. Add the lemon juice, the brown sugar, and the nutmeg. Season to taste and sauté until the peas are crisp-tender, about 2 minutes more.

4. Garnish with the pecans.

Heart and Salad

1. Wash and dry the lettuce and tear it into bite-sized pieces. Peel and section the grapefruit. Peel and slice the cucumber. Peel and slice the red onion. Combine the ingredients in a large bowl.

2. In a small bowl, whisk together the oil, the vinegar, the lemon juice, the honey, the tarragon, and the poppy seeds. Season to taste.

3. Toss the salad with the dressing.

Be My Valentine

1. Preheat the oven to 325°F. Grease a heart-shaped baking pan.

2. Set the butter out to soften.

3. Melt the chocolate with 2 tablespoons of the milk.

4. Drain and chop the maraschino cherries, reserving the syrup.

5. In a large bowl, cream the shortening and the granulated sugar with an electric mixer until light and fluffy. Add the egg and beat well. Fold in the melted chocolate.

6. In a small bowl, combine the flour, the baking soda, and the salt. Alternating with small amounts of the milk, add small amounts of the flour mixture to the chocolate mixture, beating well after each addition. Fold in 1/4 cup of the chopped cherries and 2 tablespoons of the cherry syrup.

7. Pour the batter into the baking pan and bake until a toothpick inserted in the center comes out clean, about 40 minutes.

8 . In a medium bowl, beat the softened butter with the powdered sugar until smooth. Blend in the vanilla, the remaining cherries, and the remaining cherry syrup.

9. Remove the pan from the oven and let it cool.

10. Remove the cooled cake from the pan and place it on a platter. Frost the top and the sides.

COUNTDOWN

1. Assemble the ingredients and the equipment.
2. Do Steps 1–10 of *Be My Valentine*.
3. Do Steps 1–2 of *Heart and Salad*.
4. Do Steps 1–10 of *Sole Mates*.
5. Do Steps 1–4 of *Passionate Peas*.
6. Do Step 3 of *Heart and Salad*.

President's Day

MEAT & POULTRY

1 turkey breast with bone and skin
(about 2-1/2 pounds)

FRESH PRODUCE

VEGETABLES
3 small yellow squash
2 stalks celery
1 small head Boston lettuce
2 medium tomatoes
1 large onion
1 medium onion

HERBS
2 tablespoons parsley (when chopped)

FRUIT
1 small ripe pineapple
2 medium ripe pears
1 medium lime

CANS, JARS & BOTTLES

SOUP
2 cans (14 ounces each) chicken broth
1 can (10-1/2 ounces) beef consommé

VEGETABLES
1 can (11 ounces) whole kernel corn

PACKAGED GOODS

DRIED FRUITS & NUTS
6 walnut halves

BAKED GOODS
4 thick slices sourdough bread

WINES & SPIRITS
2 tablespoons dry sherry

REFRIGERATED PRODUCTS

DAIRY
1/4 cup milk
1/2 cup half-and-half
3 tablespoons sour cream
2 cups whipped cream
5 eggs

CHEESE
4 slices (about 1/4 pound) Swiss cheese

DELI
4 slices bacon

STAPLES

- ❏ Butter
- ❏ Flour
- ❏ Granulated sugar
- ❏ Powdered sugar
- ❏ Cocoa powder
- ❏ Dijon mustard
- ❏ Mayonnaise
- ❏ Kitchen Bouquet
- ❏ Bay leaf
- ❏ Dried sage
- ❏ Chili powder
- ❏ Pepper
- ❏ Salt
- ❏ Vanilla extract

President's Day

Squashington Soup

4 slices bacon
1 medium onion
3 small yellow squash
1 can (11 ounces) whole kernel corn
2 cans (14 ounces each) chicken broth
1/2 teaspoon granulated sugar
1/2 teaspoon chili powder
1/2 cup half-and-half
Seasoning to taste

Gobbledygook

3 tablespoons butter
1 turkey breast with bone and skin (about 2-1/2 pounds)
1 tablespoon Kitchen Bouquet
1 can (10-1/2 ounces) beef consommé
1/2 teaspoon dried sage
1 bay leaf
1 large onion
2 medium fresh tomatoes
4 tablespoons mayonnaise
2 teaspoons Dijon mustard
1/2 teaspoon granulated sugar
1/4 cup flour
1/4 cup milk
2 tablespoons dry sherry
Seasoning to taste
4 thick slices sourdough bread
4 slices (about 1/4 pound) Swiss cheese

Hail to the Leaf

1 medium lime
1 small head Boston lettuce
1 small ripe pineapple
2 medium ripe pears
2 stalks celery
2 tablespoons fresh parsley (when chopped)
3 tablespoons sour cream
1/2 teaspoon granulated sugar

Lincoln Log

5 eggs
1 cup granulated sugar
1/4 cup flour
3 tablespoons cocoa powder
1/4 teaspoon salt
1 teaspoon vanilla extract
1/2 cup powdered sugar
2 cups whipped cream
6 walnut halves

EQUIPMENT

Electric mixer	Whisk
Blender	Citrus grater
Large covered saucepan	Citrus juicer
Medium saucepan	Vegetable brush
Small roasting pan	Pastry brush
Jelly-roll pan	Baster
Meat thermometer	Waxed paper
2 large mixing bowls	Kitchen knives
Medium mixing bowl	Measuring cups and spoons
4 small mixing bowls	Cooking utensils

President's Day

Squashington Soup

1. Dice the bacon. Peel and chop the onion. Scrub, trim, and chop the squash. Drain the corn.

2. Cook the bacon in a large saucepan until it is crisp, about 7 minutes. Drain the bacon on paper towels, reserving the drippings in the saucepan.

3. Sauté the onion in the bacon drippings until it just begins to turn brown, about 7 minutes.

4. Add the squash and the corn to the saucepan, and stir to combine and coat. Add the broth, the sugar, and the chili powder, and bring the mixture to a boil. Cover, reduce the heat, and simmer until the vegetables are cooked through, about 35 minutes.

5. Remove the saucepan from the heat and let it cool for 10 minutes.

6. Puree the soup in a blender and return it to the saucepan. Stir in the half-and-half and season to taste. Return the soup to the heat and simmer, stirring frequently, until heated through, about 5 minutes.

7. Remove the pan from the heat and cover to keep warm.

8. Garnish with the bacon.

Gobbledygook

1. Melt the butter.

2. Rinse and pat dry the turkey breast and brush the skin side with the melted butter and the Kitchen Bouquet.

3. Place the turkey in a small roasting pan. Pour the consommé around the turkey. Add the sage and the bay leaf. Roast at 325°F until a thermometer inserted in the thickest part of the meat registers 170°F, about 1-1/2 hours. Baste occasionally.

4. Peel and slice the onion. Rinse and slice the tomatoes. In a small bowl, combine the mayonnaise, the mustard, and the sugar.

5. In another small bowl, whisk together the flour, the milk, and the sherry.

6. Remove the turkey from the roasting pan, reserving the pan juices, and let it stand for 10 minutes.

7. Transfer the pan juices to a medium saucepan. Remove and discard the bay leaf. Bring the pan juices to a boil. Whisk in the flour mixture and cook, whisking constantly, until the gravy thickens. Season to taste.

8. Slice the turkey. Spread the bread with the mayonnaise mixture. Layer with the turkey, the tomato slices, the onion slices, and the cheese slices. Top with the gravy.

Hail to the Leaf

1. Grate the peel from the lime and juice the lime.

2. Wash and dry the lettuce and arrange the leaves on individual salad plates. Peel, core, and chunk the pineapple. Peel, core, and chunk the pears. Rinse, trim, and chop the celery. Arrange the ingredients over the lettuce. Rinse and chop the parsley.

3. In a small bowl, combine the lime juice, the sour cream, and the sugar. Fold in the lime peel.

4. Spoon the sour cream mixture over the salads and garnish with the parsley.

Lincoln Log

1. Preheat the oven to 325°F. Line a jelly-roll pan with waxed paper. Lightly grease the waxed paper.

2. Separate the eggs, placing the whites in a large bowl and the yolks in a medium bowl. Beat the egg whites with an electric mixer until stiff. Gradually beat in half of the granulated sugar. Beat the egg yolks until thick and lemon-colored.

3. In a small bowl, combine the remaining 1/2 cup granulated sugar, the flour, the cocoa powder, and the salt.

4. Fold the flour mixture into the egg yolk mixture. Blend in the vanilla. Fold the egg yolk mixture into the egg white mixture.

5. Pour the batter evenly into the baking pan and bake until set, about 25 minutes.

6. Cool the cake roll for 5 minutes.

7. Spread out a dishtowel and sprinkle it with the powdered sugar. Invert the cake pan onto the towel. Peel the waxed paper off the cake roll and let stand for 5 minutes.

8. Trim the crust off the edges of the cake roll and roll the cake up in the towel. Place it in the refrigerator for 20 minutes.

9. Carefully unroll the cake, removing the towel. Spread the top side evenly with half of the whipped cream, roll it back up, place it seam side down on a platter, and refrigerate it until you are ready to serve.

10. Garnish the cake with dollops of the remaining whipped cream and the walnuts.

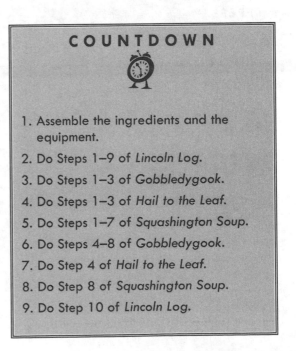

COUNTDOWN

1. Assemble the ingredients and the equipment.
2. Do Steps 1–9 of *Lincoln Log*.
3. Do Steps 1–3 of *Gobbledygook*.
4. Do Steps 1–3 of *Hail to the Leaf*.
5. Do Steps 1–7 of *Squashington Soup*.
6. Do Steps 4–8 of *Gobbledygook*.
7. Do Step 4 of *Hail to the Leaf*.
8. Do Step 8 of *Squashington Soup*.
9. Do Step 10 of *Lincoln Log*.

St. Patrick's Day

MEAT & POULTRY
1 corned beef brisket (about 4 pounds)

FRESH PRODUCE

VEGETABLES
4 medium baking potatoes
2 large carrots
1 large head cabbage
1 medium onion
1 clove garlic

HERBS
1/4 cup chives (when chopped)
2 tablespoons dill (when chopped)

FRUIT
1 large lime

CANS, JARS & BOTTLES

SPREADS
1/2 cup apricot preserves

WINES & SPIRITS
1 bottle ale
2 teaspoons crème de menthe

REFRIGERATED PRODUCTS

DAIRY
2 tablespoons sour cream
1/2 cup whipped cream
4 eggs

- ☐ Butter
- ☐ Granulated sugar
- ☐ Apple cider vinegar
- ☐ Lemon juice
- ☐ Worcestershire sauce
- ☐ Dijon mustard
- ☐ Ketchup
- ☐ Caraway seeds
- ☐ Bay leaves
- ☐ Whole allspice
- ☐ Whole cloves
- ☐ Ground nutmeg
- ☐ Pepper
- ☐ Salt

St. Patrick's Day

Saints Preserve Us

1 medium onion
1 corned beef brisket (about 4 pounds)
1 bottle ale
2 bay leaves
4 whole allspice
2 whole cloves
1/2 cup apricot preserves
2 tablespoons ketchup
1 teaspoon Worcestershire sauce
1 tablespoon Dijon mustard
2 tablespoons apple cider vinegar
Seasoning to taste

Dublin the Pleasure

1 large head cabbage
2 large carrots
3 tablespoons butter
1/4 cup lemon juice
1 teaspoon granulated sugar
Seasoning to taste
1/2 teaspoon caraway seeds

Leprechaun Potatoes

4 medium baking potatoes
1/4 cup fresh chives (when chopped)
1 clove garlic
2 tablespoons fresh dill (when chopped)
1 teaspoon granulated sugar
2 tablespoons sour cream
2 tablespoons butter
1/4 teaspoon ground nutmeg
Seasoning to taste

Limerick Pudding

1 large lime
4 eggs
6 tablespoons granulated sugar
2 tablespoons crème de menthe
1/2 cup whipped cream

EQUIPMENT

Electric mixer
Dutch oven
Small covered saucepan
Large covered skillet
1-quart casserole
2 large mixing bowls
Medium mixing bowl
Whisk
Citrus grater
Citrus juicer
Vegetable brush
Vegetable peeler
Vegetable grater
Aluminum foil
Kitchen knives
Measuring cups and spoons
Cooking utensils

St. Patrick's Day

RECITES

RECIPES

Saints Preserve Us

1. Peel and quarter the onion.

2. Place the onion, the corned beef, the ale, the bay leaves, the allspice, and the cloves in a Dutch oven.

3. Cover the ingredients with water and bring to a boil.

4. Reduce the heat and simmer until the corned beef is tender, 2-1/2 to 3 hours.

5. In a small saucepan, combine the apricot preserves, the ketchup, the Worcestershire sauce, the mustard, and the vinegar. Season to taste and cook, stirring, until the preserves are melted and the sauce is well blended, about 5 minutes. Remove the pan from the heat and cover to keep warm.

6. Remove the corned beef, discarding the cooking liquid. Slice the beef across the grain and serve it with the sauce.

Dublin the Pleasure

1. Trim and thinly slice the cabbage. Peel and grate the carrots.

2. Melt the butter in a large skillet. Add the cabbage, the carrots, the lemon juice, and the sugar, tossing to coat.

3. Cover the skillet and simmer until the vegetables are crisp-tender, about 5 minutes.

4. Season to taste and sprinkle with the caraway seeds.

Leprechaun Potatoes

1. Preheat the oven to 425°F.

2. Scrub the potatoes and prick them several times with a fork. Wrap each potato in a sheet of aluminum foil and bake until they are tender, about 1 hour.

3. Rinse and chop the chives. Peel and mince the garlic. Rinse and chop the dill.

4. Remove the foil wrapping, slice the potatoes in half lengthwise, and carefully scoop out the pulp, reserving the skins.

5. In a large bowl, combine the potato pulp, the chives, the garlic, the dill, the sugar, the sour cream, the butter, and the nutmeg. Season to taste and beat to combine.

6. Fill the potato skins with the mixture. Return the potatoes to the oven and heat through, about 10 minutes.

Limerick Pudding

1. Reduce the oven temperature to 350°F. Grease a 1-quart casserole.

2. Grate 2 tablespoons of peel from the lime and juice the lime.

3. Separate the eggs, placing the yolks in a large bowl and the whites in a medium bowl.

4. Beat the yolks with an electric mixer for 1 minute.

5. Blend in half of the sugar, the lime juice, and half of the lime peel.

6. Beat the egg whites until soft peaks form. Gradually add the remaining 3 tablespoons sugar and continue beating until stiff and glossy.

7. Fold the egg whites into the egg yolks and pour the mixture into the casserole.

8. Bake until the pudding is set and golden, about 25 minutes.

9. Fold the crème de menthe into the whipped cream, top each serving with a dollop of the whipped cream, and sprinkle with the remaining lime peel.

COUNTDOWN

1. Assemble the ingredients and the equipment.
2. Do Steps 1–4 of *Saints Preserve Us*.
3. Do Steps 1–2 of *Leprechaun Potatoes*.
4. Do Steps 1–8 of *Limerick Pudding*.
5. Do Steps 3–6 of *Leprechaun Potatoes*.
6. Do Step 5 of *Saints Preserve Us*.
7. Do Steps 1–3 of *Dublin the Pleasure*.
8. Do Step 6 of *Saints Preserve Us*.
9. Do Step 4 of *Dublin the Pleasure*.
10. Do Step 9 of *Limerick Pudding*.

Passover

SHOPPING LIST

MEAT & POULTRY

1 whole chicken (about 3-1/2 pounds)

FRESH PRODUCE

VEGETABLES

1-1/2 pounds baby red potatoes
4 medium carrots
4 stalks celery
2 medium parsnips
4 medium onions
3 cloves garlic

HERBS

2 tablespoons parsley (when chopped)

FRUIT

4 medium cooking apples

CANS, JARS & BOTTLES

SOUP

11 cups chicken broth

PACKAGED GOODS

PASTA, RICE & GRAINS

1-1/2 cups matzo meal

DRIED FRUITS & NUTS

1/2 cup raisins
1/2 cup walnut bits

WINES & SPIRITS

1/4 cup dry sherry

REFRIGERATED PRODUCTS

DAIRY

2 cups sour cream
7 eggs

CHEESE

3 packages (8 ounces each)
   cream cheese

STAPLES

- ❏ Butter
- ❏ Granulated sugar
- ❏ Dark brown sugar
- ❏ Lemon juice
- ❏ Bay leaf
- ❏ Whole allspice
- ❏ Whole cloves
- ❏ Ground cinnamon
- ❏ Pepper
- ❏ White pepper
- ❏ Salt
- ❏ Vanilla extract

Passover

Traditional Soup

1/4 cup butter or rendered chicken fat
4 eggs
10 cups chicken broth
1/2 teaspoon salt
1/4 teaspoon white pepper
1 cup matzo meal
1 medium onion
1 clove garlic
2 tablespoons fresh parsley (when chopped)
1 gallon water
3 whole allspice
1/4 cup dry sherry

Old-World Chicken

1 whole chicken (about 3-1/2 pounds)
Seasoning to taste
3 medium onions
2 cloves garlic
4 medium carrots
4 stalks celery
2 medium parsnips
1-1/2 pounds baby red potatoes
1 cup chicken broth
1 bay leaf
4 whole cloves
1 stick butter
1 cup hot water

Ceremonial Sauce

4 medium cooking apples
1 cup water
1/2 cup raisins

1/2 cup dark brown sugar
2 teaspoons ground cinnamon
1 teaspoon vanilla extract
1/2 cup walnut bits

Pale Cake

3 packages (8 ounces each) cream cheese
1/2 cup matzo meal
2/3 cup granulated sugar
3 eggs
1-1/4 teaspoons lemon juice
1 teaspoon vanilla extract
2 cups sour cream
3 tablespoons dark brown sugar

EQUIPMENT

Electric mixer
Dutch oven
Large saucepan
Medium covered saucepan
Large roasting pan
Springform pan
Roasting rack
2 large mixing bowls
Medium mixing bowl
Small mixing bowl

Whisk
Vegetable peeler
Vegetable brush
Baster
Ice cream scoop
Waxed paper
Plastic wrap
Kitchen knives
Measuring cups and spoons
Cooking utensils

Passover

Traditional Soup

1. Melt the butter or chicken fat.

2. Separate the eggs, placing the yolks in a large bowl and the whites in a medium bowl.

3. Beat the egg whites with an electric mixer until stiff.

4. Beat the egg yolks until lemon-colored. Whisk 1/2 cup of the broth, the salt, and the pepper into the melted fat. Fold in the matzo meal. Fold in the egg whites and blend well. Cover the bowl with plastic wrap and refrigerate it for at least 1 hour.

5. Peel and quarter the onion. Peel and halve the garlic. Rinse and chop the parsley.

6. Bring the water to a boil in a Dutch oven. Add the onion, the garlic, and the allspice.

7. With an ice cream scoop, make balls of the matzo mixture and drop them into the boiling water. Return to a boil, and carefully lift any balls off the bottom that have not risen to the surface. Partially cover the Dutch oven, reduce the heat, and simmer for 30 minutes.

8. Bring the remaining 9-1/2 cups of broth and the sherry to a boil in a large saucepan.

9. With a slotted spoon, transfer the matzo balls to the saucepan and cook for 5 minutes.

10. Ladle the matzo balls and the broth into individual soup bowl and garnish with the parsley.

Old-World Chicken

1. Preheat the oven to 425°F.

2. Rinse and pat dry the chicken, inside and out, and season to taste.

3. Place the chicken, breast side down, on a rack in the center of a large roasting pan.

4. Peel and quarter the onions. Peel and mince the garlic. Peel and chunk the carrots. Rinse, trim, and chunk the celery. Peel and chunk the parsnips. Scrub the potatoes.

5. Arrange the vegetables around the chicken. Add the broth. Add the bay leaf and the cloves.

6. Melt the butter in the hot water.

7. Baste the chicken with the butter mixture. Roast the chicken for 20 minutes.

8. Reduce the oven temperature to 350°F.

9. Turn the chicken breast side up and continue roasting, basting the bird and the vegetables every fifteen minutes, until the chicken is golden and cooked through and the juices run clear, about 1-1/4 hours longer.

10. Let the chicken sit for 10 minutes before carving. Remove the bay leaf and the cloves. Serve with the vegetables.

Ceremonial Sauce

1. Peel, core, and chunk the apples.

2. In a medium saucepan, combine the apples and the water. Bring to a boil, add the raisins, reduce the heat, and simmer until the apples are soft, about 20 minutes.

3. Remove the saucepan from the heat and stir in the brown sugar, the cinnamon, the vanilla, and the nuts. Remove the pan from the heat and cover to keep warm.

Pale Cake

1. Set the cream cheese out to soften.

2. Preheat the oven to 325°F. Grease a springform pan and press the matzo meal evenly into the bottom and sides.

3. Place the cream cheese in a large bowl and beat to fluff. Add the granulated sugar and beat well. Beat in the eggs, one at a time. Beat in 1 teaspoon of the lemon juice and the vanilla.

4. Pour the mixture into the springform pan and bake until the sides are set and beginning to brown, about 35 minutes.

5. Remove the cake from the oven and let it stand for 10 minutes.

6. In a small bowl, combine the sour cream, the brown sugar, and the remaining 1/4 teaspoon lemon juice. Spread the mixture carefully over the cake, return it to the oven, and bake for 10 minutes more.

7. Let the cake cool for 10 minutes.

8. Cover it with a sheet of waxed paper and refrigerate for at least 1 hour.

9. To serve, remove the waxed paper and the sides of the springform pan.

C O U N T D O W N

1. Assemble the ingredients and the equipment.
2. Do Steps 1–8 of *Pale Cake*.
3. Do Steps 1–4 of *Traditional Soup*.
4. Do Steps 1–9 of *Old-World Chicken*.
5. Do Steps 1–2 of *Ceremonial Sauce*.
6. Do Steps 5–7 of *Traditional Soup*.
7. Do Step 3 of *Ceremonial Sauce*.
8. Do Steps 8–9 of *Traditional Soup*.
9. Do Step 10 of *Old-World Chicken*.
10. Do Step 10 of *Traditional Soup*.
11. Do Step 9 of *Pale Cake*.

Easter Sunday

MEAT & POULTRY

1 boneless ham, fully cooked
(about 4 pounds)

FRESH PRODUCE

VEGETABLES

2 large tomatoes
1 medium red bell pepper
1 medium onion
1 small onion
1 clove garlic

CANS, JARS & BOTTLES

VEGETABLES

1 can (11 ounces) whole kernel corn

SPREADS

1 jar (16 ounces) apple jelly

PACKAGED GOODS

DRIED FRUITS & NUTS

2/3 cup golden raisins

DESSERT & BAKING NEEDS

12 Easter egg candies
1 red licorice whip
1 cup flaked coconut
3 drops green food coloring (optional)
3 squares (1 ounce each)
   semisweet chocolate

WINES & SPIRITS

1/4 cup dry white wine
2 tablespoons dry sherry

REFRIGERATED PRODUCTS

DAIRY

1 cup + 2 tablespoons milk
1/4 cup half-and-half
1 cup sour cream
5 eggs

DELI

2 slices bacon

FROZEN GOODS

VEGETABLES

1 package (10 ounces)
   baby lima beans

STAPLES

- ❏ Butter
- ❏ Flour
- ❏ Granulated sugar
- ❏ Powdered sugar
- ❏ Apple cider vinegar
- ❏ Dijon mustard
- ❏ Mayonnaise
- ❏ Grated Parmesan cheese
- ❏ Dried basil
- ❏ Dried oregano
- ❏ Ground cinnamon
- ❏ Whole cloves
- ❏ Pepper
- ❏ Salt
- ❏ Vanilla extract

Easter Sunday

MENU

Holiday Ham

1 medium onion
1 boneless ham, fully cooked (about
  4 pounds)
12 whole cloves
1 jar (16 ounces) apple jelly
3 tablespoons Dijon mustard
1/4 cup dry white wine
1 teaspoon ground cinnamon
2/3 cup golden raisins

Sunday Succotash

1 package (10 ounces) frozen baby lima
  beans
2 slices bacon
1 small onion
1 medium red bell pepper
1 can (11 ounces) whole kernel corn
1/4 cup half-and-half
1 tablespoon apple cider vinegar
1/2 teaspoon granulated sugar

Trinity Tomatoes

2 large fresh tomatoes
2 tablespoons dry sherry
1/2 teaspoon dried oregano
Seasoning to taste
4 tablespoons mayonnaise
2 tablespoons grated Parmesan cheese

Penitent Popovers

1 clove garlic
1 teaspoon dried basil
2 eggs
1 cup flour
1 cup milk
1/2 teaspoon salt

The Easter Basket

5 tablespoons butter
3 squares (1 ounce each) semisweet
  chocolate
3 eggs
1 cup granulated sugar
1 cup flour
1 cup sour cream
2 teaspoons vanilla extract
1 cup flaked coconut
3 drops green food coloring (optional)
1-1/2 cups powdered sugar
2 tablespoons milk
1 red licorice whip
12 Easter egg candies

EQUIPMENT

Electric mixer	3 small mixing bowls
2 small saucepans	Baster
Large skillet	Pastry brush
Medium roasting pan	Aluminum foil
8 × 8-inch glass baking dish	Kitchen knives
Popover pan	Measuring cups and spoons
9-inch round cake pan	Cooking utensils
3 medium mixing bowls	

Easter Sunday

Holiday Ham

1. Peel and slice the onion and lay the slices in the bottom of a medium roasting pan.

2. Score the top of the ham in a diamond pattern and stick a clove in the center of each diamond. Place the ham over the onion slices.

3. In a small saucepan, combine the apple jelly, the mustard, the wine, the cinnamon, and the raisins, and simmer until the jelly has melted and the mixture is well blended. Brush some of the mixture over the ham, reserving the remainder.

4. Bake the ham at 325°F, basting every 15 minutes, until heated through, about 1 hour.

5. Remove the ham from the oven and discard the cloves. Cover with aluminum foil.

6. Return the ham to the oven and reheat at 350°F for 10 minutes.

7. Reheat the jelly sauce and serve it with the ham.

Sunday Succotash

1. Set the package of lima beans in a small bowl of hot water to thaw.

2. Dice the bacon. Peel and mince the onion. Rinse, stem, seed, and chop the bell pepper. Drain the corn.

3. Sauté the bacon in a large skillet for 3 minutes. Add the onion and the bell pepper and sauté for 2 minutes. Add the corn and the lima beans and sauté for 3 minutes.

4. Blend in the half-and-half, the vinegar, and the sugar, and stir until heated through.

Trinity Tomatoes

1. Rinse the tomatoes, cut them in half, and arrange them, cut sides up, in an 8 × 8-inch glass baking dish. Sprinkle them with the sherry and the oregano, and season to taste. Let stand for 10 minutes.

2. Bake at 350°F for 5 minutes.

3. Remove the tomatoes from the oven and top with the mayonnaise and the cheese.

4. Return the tomatoes to the oven and bake for 10 minutes more.

Penitent Popovers

1. Grease a popover pan.

2. Peel and mince the garlic.

3. In a medium bowl, combine the garlic, the basil, and the eggs. Add the flour, the milk, and the salt, and beat until smooth.

4. Pour the batter evenly into the popover pan.

5. Increase the oven temperature to 450°F and bake for 20 minutes.

6. Reduce the oven temperature to 350°F and bake for 20 minutes more.

The Easter Basket

1. Preheat the oven to 325°F. Grease and flour a 9-inch round cake pan.

2. In a small saucepan, combine 3 tablespoons of the butter with the semisweet chocolate and slowly heat until melted.

3. Separate the eggs, placing the yolks in a small bowl and the whites in a medium bowl.

4. Beat the egg whites with an electric mixer until fluffy. Fold in 1/2 cup of the granulated sugar and beat until stiff and glossy.

5. Beat the egg yolks until lemon-colored. Fold in the remaining 1/2 cup granulated sugar, the flour, the sour cream, and 1 teaspoon of the vanilla, and blend well. Fold in the melted chocolate. Pour the mixture into the egg whites and blend well.

6. Pour the batter into the cake pan and bake until a toothpick inserted in the center comes out clean, about 30 minutes.

7. In a small bowl, combine the coconut and the food coloring, if desired, until the coconut turns green.

8. Remove the cake from the oven and let it cool.

9. Cream the remaining 2 tablespoons butter in a medium bowl. Blend in the powdered sugar and the milk. Blend in the remaining 1 teaspoon vanilla.

10. Remove the cake from the pan and frost the top and sides. Bend the licorice whip over the frosting, inserting it into the edge of the cake to form a handle. Sprinkle the coconut in the center of the cake, and nest the Easter candies on the coconut.

COUNTDOWN

1. Assemble the ingredients and the equipment.
2. Do Steps 1–10 of *The Easter Basket*.
3. Do Step 1 of *Sunday Succotash*.
4. Do Steps 1–4 of *Holiday Ham*.
5. Do Steps 1–4 of *Penitent Popovers*.
6. Do Step 5 of *Holiday Ham*.
7. Do Step 5 of *Penitent Popovers*.
8. Do Step 1 of *Trinity Tomatoes*.
9. Do Step 6 of *Penitent Popovers*.
10. Do Steps 2–4 of *Trinity Tomatoes*.
11. Do Step 6 of *Holiday Ham*.
12. Do Steps 2–4 of *Sunday Succotash*.
13. Do Step 7 of *Holiday Ham*.

April 15th

FRESH PRODUCE

VEGETABLES
1 medium zucchini
2 medium carrots
2 stalks celery
2 small turnips
1 medium head lettuce
1 medium cucumber
2 medium onions
3 scallions (green onions)
2 cloves garlic

HERBS
1/2 cup parsley (when chopped)

FRUIT
2 large limes

CANS, JARS & BOTTLES

SOUP
2 cans (14 ounces each) beef broth
1 can (14 ounces) chicken broth

VEGETABLES
1 can (14-1/2 ounces) stewed tomatoes
1 can (15 ounces) kidney beans
1 can (15 ounces) garbanzo beans

DESSERT & BAKING NEEDS
1 jar (7 ounces) marshmallow crème

PACKAGED GOODS

PASTA, RICE & GRAINS
6 ounces elbow macaroni

BAKED GOODS
4 small pita breads

DESSERT & BAKING NEEDS
1 envelope unflavored gelatin

WINES & SPIRITS
1 cup cheap dry red wine

REFRIGERATED PRODUCTS

DAIRY
3 eggs

STAPLES

- ❏ Butter
- ❏ Granulated sugar
- ❏ Vegetable oil
- ❏ Olive oil
- ❏ Balsamic vinegar
- ❏ Grated Parmesan cheese
- ❏ Sesame seeds
- ❏ Bay leaf
- ❏ Dried basil
- ❏ Dried oregano
- ❏ Pepper
- ❏ Salt

April 15th

Poor Man's Stew

2 medium onions
2 cloves garlic
2 medium carrots
2 small turnips
2 stalks celery
1 medium zucchini
1/2 cup fresh parsley (when chopped)
1 can (15 ounces) kidney beans
1 can (15 ounces) garbanzo beans
3 tablespoons olive oil
1 can (14-1/2 ounces) stewed tomatoes
2 cans (14 ounces each) beef broth
1 can (14 ounces) chicken broth
1 cup cheap dry red wine
1 bay leaf
1 teaspoon dried oregano
6 ounces elbow macaroni
Seasoning to taste
1 cup grated Parmesan cheese

Skimpy Salad

1 medium head lettuce
1 medium cucumber
3 scallions (green onions)
3 tablespoons vegetable oil
2 tablespoons balsamic vinegar
1/2 teaspoon dried basil
Seasoning to taste

Empty Pockets

1-1/2 tablespoons sesame seeds
3 tablespoons butter
4 small pita breads

Brother, Can You Spare a Lime?

1 envelope unflavored gelatin
1/2 cup water
2 large limes
3 eggs
3/4 cup granulated sugar
1/4 teaspoon salt
1 jar (7 ounces) marshmallow crème

EQUIPMENT

Electric mixer	Citrus grater
Double boiler	Citrus juicer
Dutch oven	Vegetable brush
Loaf pan	Vegetable peeler
2 large mixing bowls	Pastry brush
Medium mixing bowl	Aluminum foil
2 small mixing bowls	Kitchen knives
Whisk	Measuring cups and spoons
	Cooking utensils

Poor Man's Stew

1. Peel and chop the onions. Peel and mince the garlic. Peel and slice the carrots. Peel and chop the turnips. Rinse, trim, and chop the celery. Scrub, trim, and slice the zucchini. Rinse and chop the parsley. Rinse and drain the beans.

2. Heat the oil in a Dutch oven and sauté the onions and the garlic for 3 minutes. Add the tomatoes, the carrots, the turnips, and the celery, and sauté for 3 minutes.

3. Add the broth, the wine, the bay leaf, and the oregano. Bring the mixture to a boil, cover, reduce the heat, and cook for 15 minutes.

4. Add the zucchini, the beans, and the macaroni to the Dutch oven, season to taste, cover, and cook until the pasta is tender, about 10 minutes.

5. Fold in the parsley and the cheese.

Skimpy Salad

1. Wash and dry the lettuce and tear it into bite-sized pieces. Peel and slice the cucumber. Trim and chop the scallions. Combine the vegetables in a large bowl.

2. In a small bowl, whisk together the oil, the vinegar, and the basil. Season to taste and toss with the salad.

Empty Pockets

1. Preheat the broiler.

2. Spread the sesame seeds on a sheet of aluminum foil and broil until they begin to pop, about 2 minutes.

3. Melt the butter.

4. Preheat the oven to 275°F.

5. Cut the pita breads in half. Brush the insides with the melted butter and sprinkle with the toasted sesame seeds. Arrange the pita breads upright in a loaf pan and bake until heated through, about 10 minutes.

Brother, Can You Spare a Lime?

1. In a small bowl, combine the gelatin and the water and set it aside.

2. Grate the lime peel and juice the limes.

3. Bring water to a boil in the bottom of a double boiler.

4. Separate the eggs, placing the yolks in the top of the double boiler, and placing the whites in a medium bowl.

5. Blend 1/2 cup of the sugar, the salt, the lime peel, and the lime juice into the egg yolks and whisk until the mixture is thick, about 10 minutes.

6. Remove the pan from the heat, add the gelatin, and stir until dissolved. Fold 1 cup

of the marshmallow crème into the gelatin, pour the mixture into a large bowl, and refrigerate it for 10 minutes.

7. Beat the egg whites with an electric mixer until soft peaks form. Add the remaining 1/4 cup sugar and beat until stiff and glossy.

8. Fold the egg white mixture into the gelatin mixture. Spoon into individual dessert dishes, and chill until you are ready to serve.

9. Garnish with dollops of the remaining marshmallow crème.

COUNTDOWN

1. Assemble the ingredients and the equipment.
2. Do Steps 1–8 of *Brother, Can You Spare a Lime?*
3. Do Steps 1–3 of *Poor Man's Stew.*
4. Do Steps 1–4 of *Empty Pockets.*
5. Do Step 4 of *Poor Man's Stew.*
6. Do Step 5 of *Empty Pockets.*
7. Do Steps 1–2 of *Skimpy Salad.*
8. Do Step 5 of *Poor Man's Stew.*
9. Do Step 9 of *Brother, Can You Spare a Lime?*

Cinco de Mayo

SHOPPING LIST

MEAT & POULTRY

2 pounds lean boneless pork loin
1/2 pound chorizo sausage

FRESH PRODUCE

VEGETABLES

1/4 pound mushrooms
1 medium head lettuce
1/2 pound tomatoes
1 medium ripe avocado
1 medium cucumber
1 medium onion
4 cloves garlic

HERBS

2 tablespoons chives (when chopped)
2 tablespoons cilantro (when chopped)
2 tablespoons parsley (when chopped)

CANS, JARS & BOTTLES

SOUP

1 can (14 ounces) beef broth
1 can (14 ounces) chicken broth

INTERNATIONAL FOODS

1 can (4 ounces) diced green chilies
1 can (12 ounces) tomatillos

PACKAGED GOODS

PASTA, RICE & GRAINS

1 cup long-grain white rice

BAKED GOODS

1 chocolate pie shell

DESSERT & BAKING NEEDS

1 envelope unflavored gelatin

WINES & SPIRITS

1 cup dry red wine
1/4 cup Kahlúa

REFRIGERATED PRODUCTS

DAIRY

1-1/4 cups milk
1/4 cup sour cream
1/2 cup whipping cream
2 eggs

STAPLES

- ❏ Flour
- ❏ Granulated sugar
- ❏ Chocolate sprinkles
- ❏ Vegetable oil
- ❏ Lime juice
- ❏ Tabasco sauce
- ❏ Instant coffee
- ❏ Dried oregano
- ❏ Ground cumin
- ❏ Pepper
- ❏ Saffron threads
- ❏ Salt
- ❏ Vanilla extract

Cinco de Mayo

Porko Vallarta Stew

2 pounds lean boneless pork loin
1/2 pound chorizo sausage
1 medium onion
1 clove garlic
1/2 pound fresh tomatoes
1 can (12 ounces) tomatillos
1 can (4 ounces) diced green chilies
1/2 cup flour
Seasoning to taste
2 tablespoons vegetable oil
1 can (14 ounces) beef broth
1 cup dry red wine
1/2 teaspoon dried oregano
1/8 teaspoon granulated sugar
2 teaspoons ground cumin
1 medium ripe avocado

Rio Grande Rice

3 cloves garlic
1 tablespoon vegetable oil
1 cup long-grain white rice
1 can (14 ounces) chicken broth
1/4 cup water
2 teaspoons saffron threads
2 tablespoons fresh parsley (when chopped)

Ensalada

1 medium head lettuce
1 medium cucumber
1/4 pound fresh mushrooms
2 tablespoons fresh chives (when chopped)

2 tablespoons fresh cilantro (when chopped)
1/4 cup sour cream
2 tablespoons lime juice
1/4 teaspoon Tabasco sauce
1/2 teaspoon granulated sugar

Vera Crust

1 envelope unflavored gelatin
1/4 cup cold water
2 eggs
3 tablespoons instant coffee
1/2 cup granulated sugar
1-1/4 cups milk
1/4 cup Kahlúa
1 teaspoon vanilla extract
1/4 teaspoon salt
1/2 cup whipping cream
1 chocolate pie shell
Chocolate sprinkles for garnish

EQUIPMENT

Electric mixer	4 small mixing bowls
Dutch oven	Whisk
Double boiler	
Medium covered saucepan	Vegetable peeler
Large shallow bowl	Kitchen knives
2 large mixing bowls	Measuring cups and spoons
Medium mixing bowl	Cooking utensils

Cinco de Mayo

Porko Vallarta Stew

1. Trim and cube the pork. Slice the sausage.

2. Peel and chop the onion. Peel and mince the garlic. Rinse and chop the tomatoes. Drain and chop the tomatillos. Drain the chilies.

3. Place the flour in a large shallow bowl and season it to taste.

4. Roll the pork cubes in the flour to coat.

5. Heat the oil in a Dutch oven and sauté the sausage, the onion, and the garlic until the sausage is browned and cooked through, about 10 minutes. Drain the sausage mixture on paper towels, reserving the pan drippings in the Dutch oven.

6. Sauté the pork cubes in the Dutch oven until lightly browned on all sides.

7. Add the broth, the wine, and enough water to cover, if necessary. Cook until tender, about 1 hour.

8. Add the tomatoes, the tomatillos, the chilies, the oregano, the sugar, and the cumin. Cook for 5 minutes.

9. Return the sausage, the onion, and the garlic to the Dutch oven and cook until thickened, about 15 minutes.

10. Peel, pit, and slice the avocado. Arrange the slices over the stew and serve over the rice.

Rio Grande Rice

1. Peel and slice the garlic. Heat the oil in a medium saucepan and sauté the garlic for 5 minutes.

2. Add the rice, the broth, the water, and the saffron. Cover, reduce the heat, and simmer until the liquid is absorbed and the rice is tender, about 20 minutes.

3. Rinse and chop the parsley.

4. Fold the parsley into the rice and fluff with a fork.

Ensalada

1. Wash and dry the lettuce and tear it into bite-sized pieces. Peel and chop the cucumber. Rinse, pat dry, and slice the mushrooms. Rinse and chop the chives. Combine the ingredients in a large bowl. Rinse and chop the cilantro.

2. In a small bowl, whisk together the sour cream, the lime juice, the Tabasco sauce, and the sugar.

3. Toss the salad with the dressing and garnish with the cilantro.

Vera Crust

1. In a small bowl, combine the gelatin and the water and let stand until the gelatin has softened.

2. Bring water to a boil in the bottom of a double boiler.

3. Separate the eggs, placing the whites in a medium bowl and the yolks in the top of the double boiler.

4. Add the instant coffee and 1/4 cup of the sugar to the egg yolks. Gradually stir in the milk and cook, stirring, until the mixture thickens slightly, about 10 minutes.

5. Remove from the heat, add the gelatin mixture, and stir until dissolved. Fold in the Kahlúa and the vanilla, pour the mixture into a large bowl, and refrigerate until partially set, about 20 minutes.

6. With an electric mixer, beat the egg whites with the salt until soft peaks form. Gradually add the remaining 1/4 cup sugar and beat until stiff and glossy.

7. In a small bowl, whip the cream until stiff.

8. Beat the partially set gelatin mixture until fluffy. Fold in the egg whites. Fold in the whipped cream. Turn the mixture into the pie shell and refrigerate for at least 1 hour.

9. Garnish with the chocolate sprinkles.

COUNTDOWN

1. Assemble the ingredients and the equipment.
2. Do Steps 1–8 of *Vera Crust*.
3. Do Steps 1–7 of *Porko Vallarta Stew*.
4. Do Steps 1–2 of *Ensalada*.
5. Do Steps 1–3 of *Rio Grande Rice*.
6. Do Steps 8–9 of *Porko Vallarta Stew*.
7. Do Step 10 of *Porko Vallarta Stew*.
8. Do Step 4 of *Rio Grande Rice*.
9. Do Step 3 of *Ensalada*.
10. Do Step 9 of *Vera Crust*.

Mother's Day Brunch

FRESH PRODUCE

VEGETABLES
4 stalks celery
1 large onion

HERBS
1 tablespoon dill (when chopped)

FRUIT
1 medium ripe cantaloupe
1/2 pound cherries
1 small lemon
1 large lime

CANS, JARS & BOTTLES

JUICE
4 cups tomato juice

SPREADS
2 tablespoons orange marmalade

PACKAGED GOODS

BAKED GOODS
4 large croissants
1 cup corn flakes (when crushed)

DRIED FRUITS & NUTS
1 cup chopped walnuts

WINES & SPIRITS

1 tablespoon Grand Marnier

REFRIGERATED PRODUCTS

DAIRY
1/2 cup milk
1/2 cup sour cream
1/2 cup whipping cream
5 eggs

CHEESE
1 package (3 ounces) cream cheese

JUICE
1 cup orange juice

DELI
1 pound breakfast sausage links

STAPLES

- ☐ Butter
- ☐ Bisquick
- ☐ Cornstarch
- ☐ Granulated sugar
- ☐ Dark brown sugar
- ☐ Powdered sugar
- ☐ Vegetable oil
- ☐ Lemon juice
- ☐ Worcestershire sauce
- ☐ Tabasco sauce
- ☐ Ground cardamom
- ☐ Ground cinnamon
- ☐ Ground nutmeg
- ☐ Pepper
- ☐ Salt
- ☐ Lemon extract
- ☐ Vanilla extract

Mother's Day Brunch

Mild Marys

1/2 cup salt
1 large lime
4 stalks celery
4 cups tomato juice
1 teaspoon Worcestershire sauce
1/2 teaspoon Tabasco sauce
Seasoning to taste

Mumsy's Toast

1 package (3 ounces) cream cheese
4 large croissants
4 eggs
1/2 cup whipping cream
1/2 teaspoon vanilla extract
2 teaspoons cornstarch
1 tablespoon Grand Marnier
1 cup orange juice
2 tablespoons orange marmalade
5 tablespoons butter
2 tablespoons powdered sugar

Loving Links

1 large onion
1 tablespoon fresh dill (when chopped)
1 pound breakfast sausage links
1 tablespoon vegetable oil

Faithful Fruit

1/2 cup sour cream
1 tablespoon lemon juice
1 teaspoon dark brown sugar
1/4 teaspoon ground cinnamon

1/2 pound fresh cherries
1 medium ripe cantaloupe

Generation Cake

1 small lemon
5 tablespoons butter
2 cups Bisquick
1 cup chopped walnuts
1 egg
1/2 cup milk
1/2 cup dark brown sugar
1 teaspoon lemon extract
1 cup corn flakes (when crushed)
1/4 cup granulated sugar
1/2 teaspoon ground nutmeg
1/2 teaspoon ground cardamom

EQUIPMENT

Blender
Small covered saucepan
Large skillet
Medium covered skillet
8 × 8-inch baking pan
Large shallow bowl
Small shallow bowl
Medium mixing bowl

3 small mixing bowls
Whisk
Citrus juicer
Citrus grater
Kitchen knives
Measuring cups and spoons
Cooking utensils

Mother's Day Brunch

Mild Marys

1. Place the salt in a small shallow bowl.

2. Wet the rims of 4 tall glasses and dip the rims into the salt to coat well. Chill the glasses until you are ready to use.

3. Cut the lime in half. Cut one half into 4 wedges and juice the remaining half. Rinse and trim the celery.

4. In a blender, combine the tomato juice, the lime juice, the Worcestershire sauce, and the Tabasco sauce. Season to taste and refrigerate until you are ready to use.

5. Half-fill the chilled glasses with ice. Pour the tomato mixture over the ice. Stick a celery stalk into each glass, and affix a lime wedge to each rim.

Mumsy's Toast

1. Set the cream cheese out to soften.

2. Cut the croissants in half lengthwise.

3. In a large shallow bowl, whisk the eggs with the cream and the vanilla.

4. In a small saucepan, combine the cornstarch and the Grand Marnier. Add the orange juice, the marmalade, and 1 tablespoon of the butter. Simmer until the syrup runs clear and begins to thicken, about 5 minutes. Cover to keep warm.

5. Melt the remaining 4 tablespoons butter in a large skillet.

6. Dip the croissant halves in the egg mixture, coating both sides well, and cook in the skillet until crisp and golden on both sides, about 6 minutes.

7. Spread the cream cheese on the bottom halves of the croissants. Cover with the top halves of the croissants, sprinkle with the powdered sugar, and serve with the syrup.

Loving Links

1. Peel and slice the onion. Rinse and chop the dill. Separate the sausage links.

2. Heat the oil in a medium skillet and sauté the onion and the sausage with the dill until the onion is golden and the sausage is cooked through, about 10 minutes. Cover to keep warm.

Faithful Fruit

1. In a small bowl, combine the sour cream, the lemon juice, the brown sugar, and the cinnamon.

2. Rinse, pit, and halve the cherries. Quarter the melon and remove the seeds.

3. Spoon the cherries into the melon cavities and serve with the sauce.

Generation Cake

1. Preheat the oven to 400°F. Grease an 8 × 8-inch baking pan.

2. Grate the lemon peel and juice the lemon.

3. Melt the butter.

4. In a medium bowl, combine the Bisquick and 1/2 cup of the walnuts.

5. In a small bowl, combine the egg, the milk, the brown sugar, and 3 tablespoons of the melted butter. Fold into the Bisquick mixture and stir until moistened. Blend in the lemon peel, the lemon juice, and the lemon extract.

6. Pour the batter into the baking pan.

7. In a small bowl, combine the remaining 1/2 cup walnuts, the corn flakes, the granulated sugar, the nutmeg, and the cardamom. Blend in the remaining 2 tablespoons of butter, and spread the mixture over the cake batter.

8. Bake until golden, about 30 minutes.

COUNTDOWN

1. Assemble the ingredients and the equipment.
2. Do Steps 1–8 of *Generation Cake*.
3. Do Step 1 of *Mumsy's Toast*.
4. Do Steps 1–4 of *Mild Marys*.
5. Do Steps 1–2 of *Faithful Fruit*.
6. Do Steps 2–4 of *Mumsy's Toast*.
7. Do Steps 1–2 of *Loving Links*.
8. Do Steps 5–7 of *Mumsy's Toast*.
9. Do Step 5 of *Mild Marys*.
10. Do Step 3 of *Faithful Fruit*.

Memorial Day

MEAT & POULTRY

4 New York strip steaks (about 2 pounds)

FRESH PRODUCE

VEGETABLES

1 small bunch broccoli
1/2 pound green beans
2 medium carrots
2 stalks celery
2 medium tomatoes
2 large sweet onions
1 clove garlic

HERBS

1/4 cup dill (when chopped)

FRUIT

1 large ripe pineapple
2 medium bananas
1 pint strawberries
1 large lemon

PACKAGED GOODS

PASTA, RICE & GRAINS

12 ounces corkscrew
    pasta

WINES & SPIRITS

2 tablespoons brandy

REFRIGERATED PRODUCTS

DAIRY

1-1/2 cups half-and-half
1 container (8 ounces) vanilla yogurt
1/4 cup whipped cream
4 eggs

STAPLES

- ❑ Butter
- ❑ Flour
- ❑ Baking powder
- ❑ Baking soda
- ❑ Granulated sugar
- ❑ Vegetable oil
- ❑ Olive oil
- ❑ White wine vinegar
- ❑ Lemon juice
- ❑ Honey
- ❑ Dried rosemary
- ❑ Ground nutmeg
- ❑ Pepper
- ❑ Salt

Memorial Day

Bull Run

2 large sweet onions
4 New York strip steaks (about 2 pounds)
2 tablespoons butter
1 teaspoon dried rosemary
1/4 teaspoon ground nutmeg

They Shall Not Pasta

12 ounces corkscrew pasta
1 small bunch fresh broccoli
1/2 pound fresh green beans
2 medium carrots
2 stalks celery
2 medium fresh tomatoes
1/4 cup fresh dill (when chopped)
1 clove garlic
1/2 cup olive oil
1/4 cup white wine vinegar
Seasoning to taste

Brandywine

1/4 cup lemon juice
1/8 teaspoon salt
2 tablespoons honey
2 tablespoons brandy
1 large ripe pineapple
1 pint fresh strawberries
2 medium bananas

Maginot Muffins

1 container (8 ounces) vanilla yogurt
1 egg
1/3 cup vegetable oil
2 cups flour

1 tablespoon baking powder
1/2 teaspoon baking soda
1/2 teaspoon salt

Lemon Seoul-flé

2 tablespoons butter
1-1/2 cups half-and-half
1 large lemon
3 eggs
1 cup granulated sugar
1/4 cup flour
1/8 teaspoon salt
1/4 cup whipped cream

EQUIPMENT

Electric mixer
Stockpot
Small saucepan
Large covered skillet
Large skillet
2-quart casserole or soufflé dish
Baking pan
Muffin tin
Colander
4 large skewers
Pastry brush
3 large mixing bowls

Medium mixing bowl
3 small mixing bowls
Whisk
Citrus grater
Citrus juicer
Vegetable peeler
Plastic wrap
Aluminum foil
Kitchen knives
Measuring cups and spoons
Cooking utensils

Memorial Day

Bull Run

1. Prepare the grill.

2. Peel and thinly slice the onions.

3. Trim any excess fat from the steaks and grill them to taste, about 5 minutes per side for rare.

4. Melt the butter in a large skillet and sauté the onions for 10 minutes. Add the rosemary and the nutmeg, and sauté for 2 minutes more.

5. Top the steaks with the onion and mushroom mixture.

They Shall Not Pasta

1. Bring water for the pasta to a boil in a stockpot.

2. Cook the pasta until it is almost tender, about 8 minutes.

3. Rinse the broccoli and cut it into bite-sized florets. Rinse and trim the green beans and cut them into 2-inch lengths. Peel and slice the carrots. Rinse, trim, and slice the celery. Rinse and chop the tomatoes. Rinse and chop the dill.

4. Drain the pasta, rinse it well in cold water, and place it in a large bowl.

5. Bring a small amount of water to a boil in a large skillet. Place the broccoli, the green beans, the carrots, and the celery in the skillet, cover, and steam until the vegetables are crisp-tender, about 3 minutes.

6. Drain the vegetables, rinse them in cold water, and add them to the pasta. Add the tomatoes.

7. Peel and mince the garlic. In a small bowl, whisk together the garlic, the oil, and the vinegar. Season to taste and toss with the salad. Add the dill and toss to combine. Cover the bowl with plastic wrap and refrigerate it until you are ready to serve.

Brandywine

1. In a small bowl, combine the lemon juice, the salt, the honey, and the brandy.

2. Peel and core the pineapple and cut it into large chunks. Rinse and hull the strawberries. Peel and chunk the bananas.

3. Alternate the fruit onto skewers and lay the skewers on sheets of aluminum foil.

4. Brush the fruit with the sauce and grill, turning and basting frequently, until hot and bubbly.

Maginot Muffins

1. Preheat the oven to 400°F. Grease a muffin tin.

2. In a large bowl, whisk together the yogurt, the egg, and the oil. Fold in the flour, the baking powder, the baking soda, and the salt until just moistened.

3. Distribute the batter evenly among the muffin cups.

4. Bake until the muffins are golden, about 18 minutes.

Lemon Seoul-flé

1. Preheat the oven to 325°F. Butter a 2-quart casserole or souffle dish.

2. Melt the butter.

3. In a small saucepan, scald the half-and-half.

4. Grate the lemon peel and juice the lemon.

5. Separate the eggs, placing the whites in a large bowl and the yolks in a small bowl.

6. Beat the egg whites with an electric mixer until firm.

7. In a medium bowl, combine the sugar, the flour, the salt, and the melted butter. Stir in the lemon juice and the lemon peel.

8. Whisk the egg yolks until lemon-colored and whisk them into the half-and-half. Whisk the egg yolk mixture into the lemon mixture. Fold the lemon mixture into the egg whites.

9. Pour the mixture into the casserole. Set the casserole in a baking pan half-filled with warm water and bake until a toothpick inserted in the center comes out clean, about 45 minutes.

10. Cool the soufflé to room temperature, about 30 minutes.

11. Refrigerate it until you are ready to serve.

12. Garnish with whipped cream.

COUNTDOWN

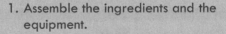

1. Assemble the ingredients and the equipment.
2. Do Steps 1–11 of *Lemon Seoul-flé*.
3. Do Steps 1–7 of *They Shall Not Pasta*.
4. Do Step 1 of *Bull Run*.
5. Do Steps 1–3 of *Maginot Muffins*.
6. Do Steps 1–3 of *Brandywine*.
7. Do Step 4 of *Maginot Muffins*.
8. Do Step 4 of *Brandywine*.
9. Do Steps 2–5 of *Bull Run*.
10. Do Step 12 of *Lemon Seoul-flé*.

Father's Day

MEAT & POULTRY

3 pounds boneless country-style
pork spareribs

FRESH PRODUCE

VEGETABLES
4 medium baking potatoes
1/4 pound mushrooms
1 medium onion
1 clove garlic

FRUIT
3 medium apples

CANS, JARS & BOTTLES

VEGETABLES
1 can (28 ounces) sauerkraut

PACKAGED GOODS

BAKED GOODS
4 individual tart shells

DRIED FRUITS & NUTS
3/4 cup sliced almonds
3/4 cup flaked coconut

WINES & SPIRITS

1 tablespoon amaretto

REFRIGERATED PRODUCTS

DAIRY
1 cup milk
1/2 cup sour cream
1/4 cup whipped cream
2 eggs

DELI
3 slices bacon

STAPLES

❒ Butter
❒ Flour
❒ Baking powder
❒ Dark brown sugar
❒ Vegetable oil
❒ Rice vinegar
❒ Worcestershire sauce
❒ Dijon mustard
❒ Steak sauce
❒ Honey
❒ Ketchup
❒ Ground allspice
❒ Pepper
❒ White pepper
❒ Salt

Father's Day

Spare the Rib, Spoil the Child

1 medium onion
1 clove garlic
1/4 cup vegetable oil
1/2 cup ketchup
2 tablespoons rice vinegar
1/2 cup water
1 teaspoon Worcestershire sauce
1 tablespoon Dijon mustard
2 tablespoons steak sauce
1/4 cup honey
3 pounds boneless country-style pork spareribs

Paternal Potatoes

4 medium baking potatoes
2 tablespoons vegetable oil
3 slices bacon
1/4 pound fresh mushrooms
2 tablespoons butter
3 tablespoons flour
1 cup milk
1/2 cup sour cream
1/8 teaspoon white pepper
Seasoning to taste

Apples & Sire-Kraut

3 medium apples
1 can (28 ounces) sauerkraut
3 tablespoons butter
1 teaspoon ground allspice
3 tablespoons dark brown sugar

My Tart Belongs to Daddy

3/4 cup sliced almonds
1/2 cup dark brown sugar
2 eggs
1 tablespoon amaretto
3/4 cup flaked coconut
2 teaspoons flour
1/2 teaspoon baking powder
4 individual tart shells
1/4 cup whipped cream

EQUIPMENT

Electric mixer
Medium saucepan
Large skillet
Small skillet
Baking sheet
Medium mixing bowl
Vegetable brush
Pastry brush
Aluminum foil
Kitchen knives
Measuring cups and spoons
Cooking utensils

Father's Day

Spare the Rib, Spoil the Child

1. Peel and mince the onion. Peel and mince the garlic.

2. In a medium saucepan, combine the onion, the garlic, the oil, the ketchup, the vinegar, the water, the Worcestershire sauce, the mustard, the steak sauce, and the honey, and simmer until well blended and thick, about 1 hour.

3. Prepare the grill.

4. Rinse and pat dry the ribs.

5. Lay the ribs on the grill and brush with some of the sauce. Cook, basting frequently, until well browned and cooked through, about 20 minutes per side.

Paternal Potatoes

1. Scrub the potatoes and brush them with the oil. Place each potato on a sheet of aluminum foil and seal the packets.

2. Grill the potatoes until tender, about one hour.

3. Dice the bacon and sauté it in a small skillet until crisp, about 5 minutes.

4. Drain the bacon on paper towels.

5. Rinse, pat dry, trim, and chop the mushrooms.

6. Melt the butter in the skillet and sauté the mushrooms until they are soft, about 3 minutes.

7. Blend in the flour. Add the milk, the sour cream, and the white pepper. Season to taste.

8. Remove the potatoes from the foil, split them down the middle, and top with the mushroom sauce. Sprinkle with the bacon.

Apples & Sire-Kraut

1. Peel, core, and chop the apples. Drain the sauerkraut.

2. Melt the butter in a large skillet and sauté the apples with the allspice and the brown sugar until crisp-tender, about 5 minutes.

3. Add the sauerkraut, toss to combine, and heat through, about 2 minutes.

My Tart Belongs to Daddy

1. Preheat the oven to 250°F.

2. Spread the almonds on a baking sheet and bake for 5 minutes.

3. In a medium bowl, beat the sugar, the eggs, and the amaretto with an electric mixer until well blended. Fold in the toasted almonds, the coconut, the flour, and the baking powder.

4. Spoon the mixture into the tart shells and bake until the tarts are golden, about 18 minutes.

5. Let the tarts cool at room temperature.

6. Garnish with dollops of whipped cream.

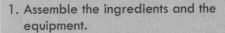

COUNTDOWN

1. Assemble the ingredients and the equipment.

2. Do Steps 1–5 of *My Tart Belongs to Daddy*.

3. Do Steps 1–4 of *Spare the Rib, Spoil the Child*.

4. Do Steps 1–2 of *Paternal Potatoes*.

5. Do Step 5 of *Spare the Rib, Spoil the Child*.

6. Do Steps 3–7 of *Paternal Potatoes*.

7. Do Steps 1–3 of *Apples & Sire-Kraut*.

8. Do Step 8 of *Paternal Potatoes*.

9. Do Step 6 of *My Tart Belongs to Daddy*.

Fourth of July

SHOPPING LIST

FISH
1 salmon fillet (about 3 pounds)

FRESH PRODUCE

VEGETABLES
1 pound asparagus
2 stalks celery
1 medium green bell pepper
1 small onion
3 scallions (green onions)
3 cloves garlic

HERBS
4 sprigs dill

FRUIT
1 medium orange
1 pint raspberries
1 pint blueberries

CANS, JARS & BOTTLES

SOUP
2 cans (10-1/2 ounces each) chicken broth
1 can (10-1/2 ounces) beef consommé

JUICE
3 cups tomato juice

CONDIMENTS
1 jar (6-1/2 ounces) marinated artichoke hearts
1 jar (2 ounces) diced pimiento
2 tablespoons capers

PACKAGED GOODS

PASTA, RICE & GRAINS
1 cup long-grain white rice

BAKED GOODS
1 graham cracker pie shell

DESSERT & BAKING NEEDS
1 large package cook-and-serve vanilla pudding mix

WINES & SPIRITS
1/4 cup dry white wine

REFRIGERATED PRODUCTS

DAIRY
3 cups milk
1/4 cup sour cream
1 cup whipping cream

CHEESE
1 package (8 ounces) cream cheese

STAPLES

☐ Butter
☐ Granulated sugar
☐ Powdered sugar
☐ Tarragon vinegar
☐ Lemon juice
☐ Worcestershire sauce
☐ Mayonnaise
☐ Whole cloves
☐ Pepper
☐ Salt
☐ Vanilla extract

Fourth of July

Salute the Soup

1 medium green bell pepper
1 clove garlic
1 can (10-1/2 ounces) beef consommé
3 cups tomato juice
2 tablespoons lemon juice
1 teaspoon Worcestershire sauce
1 teaspoon granulated sugar
3 whole cloves
1/4 cup sour cream

Uncle Salmon

1 small onion
4 sprigs fresh dill
4 tablespoons butter
1 salmon fillet (about 3 pounds)
Seasoning to taste
1/4 cup dry white wine
2 tablespoons lemon juice
2 tablespoons tarragon vinegar
2 tablespoons capers

Patriotic Asparagus

1 pound fresh asparagus
2 cloves garlic
1 medium orange
2 tablespoons butter

Grand Old Salad

1 cup long-grain white rice
2 cans (10-1/2 ounces each) chicken
  broth
3 scallions (green onions)
2 stalks celery

1 jar (6-1/2 ounces) marinated artichoke
  hearts
1 jar (2 ounces) diced pimiento
1/2 cup mayonnaise
Seasoning to taste

Fourth of July Pie

1 package (8 ounces) cream cheese
1 large package cook-and-serve vanilla
  pudding mix
3 cups milk
1 teaspoon vanilla extract
1 graham cracker pie shell
1 pint fresh raspberries
1 pint fresh blueberries
1 cup whipping cream
2 tablespoons powdered sugar

EQUIPMENT

Electric mixer

Double boiler

Large covered
  saucepan

Medium saucepan

Large covered
  skillet

Strainer

2 large mixing
  bowls

Medium mixing
  bowl

2 small mixing
  bowls

Whisk

Citrus grater

Citrus juicer

Pastry brush

Aluminum foil

Plastic wrap

Kitchen knives

Measuring cups
  and spoons

Cooking utensils

Fourth of July

Salute the Soup

1. Rinse, stem, seed, and chop the bell pepper. Peel and halve the garlic.

2. In a large saucepan, combine the bell pepper, the garlic, the consommé, the tomato juice, the lemon juice, the Worcestershire sauce, the sugar, and the cloves. Cover, bring to a boil, reduce the heat, and simmer until the bell pepper is tender, about 10 minutes.

3. Strain the soup into a large bowl, removing the bell pepper, the garlic, and the cloves. Chill until you are ready to serve.

4. Garnish the soup with dollops of sour cream.

Uncle Salmon

1. Prepare the grill.

2. Peel and mince the onion. Rinse and pat dry the dill.

3. Melt the butter.

4. Rinse and pat dry the salmon and season it to taste.

5. Brush half of the melted butter on a sheet of aluminum foil. Lay the fillet over the buttered foil and brush the remaining butter over the top of the fillet.

6. In a small bowl, combine the onion, the wine, the lemon juice, the vinegar, and the capers. Spread the mixture over the salmon. Top with the dill sprigs. Seal the aluminum foil around the fillet and grill the packet until the fish flakes easily with a fork, about 30 minutes.

Patriotic Asparagus

1. Rinse the asparagus and remove and discard the tough ends. Peel and mince the garlic. Grate the peel from the orange and juice the orange.

2. Bring a small amount of water to a boil in a large skillet. Place the asparagus spears in the skillet, cover, and steam until crisp-tender, 3 to 8 minutes, depending on their thickness.

3. Rinse the asparagus in cold water and set aside.

4. Melt the butter in the skillet and sauté the garlic for 1 minute. Add the orange juice and the orange peel, and cook for 1 minute. Return the asparagus to the skillet, toss to coat, and heat through.

Grand Old Salad

1. Bring water to a boil in the bottom of a double boiler. In the top of the double boiler, combine the rice and the broth. Cover, reduce the heat, and simmer until the liquid is absorbed and the rice is tender, about 40 minutes.

2. Trim and chop the scallions. Rinse, trim, and chop the celery. Drain and chop the ar-

tichokes, reserving the marinade. Drain the pimiento. Combine the ingredients in a large bowl.

3. In a small bowl, whisk together the reserved artichoke marinade with the mayonnaise. Season to taste.

4. Fold the rice into the vegetables, toss with the mayonnaise mixture, cover with plastic wrap, and refrigerate until you are ready to serve.

Fourth of July Pie

1. Set the cream cheese out to soften.

2. Chill a medium bowl and the beaters of an electric mixer in the refrigerator for at least 10 minutes.

3. In a medium saucepan, combine the pudding mix, the milk, and the vanilla, and cook, stirring constantly, until thickened, about 10 minutes.

4. Remove the saucepan from the heat and blend in the cream cheese. Pour the mixture into the pie shell and set it aside to cool.

5. Rinse and blot the berries.

6. In the chilled bowl, whip the cream until soft peaks form. Fold in the powdered sugar and beat until stiff. Spread the mixture over the cooled pie.

7. Arrange the berries over the whipped cream in the design of the flag and refrigerate until you are ready to serve.

COUNTDOWN

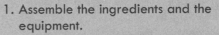

1. Assemble the ingredients and the equipment.
2. Do Step 1 of *Grand Old Salad.*
3. Do Steps 1–7 of *Fourth of July Pie.*
4. Do Steps 1–3 of *Salute the Soup.*
5. Do Steps 2–4 of *Grand Old Salad.*
6. Do Steps 1–6 of *Uncle Salmon.*
7. Do Steps 1–4 of *Patriotic Asparagus.*
8. Do Step 4 of *Salute the Soup.*

Labor Day

MEAT & POULTRY

2 lean cooked ham steaks (about
  2 pounds)

FRESH PRODUCE

VEGETABLES

4 ears corn on the cob
1 small head cabbage
1 medium green bell pepper
1 medium onion
2 scallions (green onions)
1 clove garlic

FRUIT

2 Granny Smith apples

CANS, JARS & BOTTLES

FRUIT

1 can (8 ounces) pineapple tidbits

SPREADS

1/3 cup red currant jelly

REFRIGERATED PRODUCTS

DAIRY

1-3/4 cups half-and-half
3 eggs

- ❏ Butter
- ❏ Flour
- ❏ Baking powder
- ❏ Granulated sugar
- ❏ Dark brown sugar
- ❏ Balsamic vinegar
- ❏ Lemon juice
- ❏ Prepared horseradish
- ❏ Mayonnaise
- ❏ Celery seed
- ❏ Sesame seeds
- ❏ Ground cinnamon
- ❏ Ground cloves
- ❏ Ground nutmeg
- ❏ Paprika
- ❏ Pepper
- ❏ Salt
- ❏ Almond extract

Labor Day

Ham and Haw

1/3 cup red currant jelly
2 tablespoons lemon juice
2 teaspoons prepared horseradish
1/2 teaspoon ground cloves
2 lean cooked ham steaks (about
2 pounds)

Aw Shucks

4 ears fresh corn on the cob
3 tablespoons butter
1 teaspoon balsamic vinegar
1/2 teaspoon ground nutmeg
1/2 teaspoon granulated sugar

Slaw Motion

1 small head cabbage
1 medium green bell pepper
1 medium onion
1 can (8 ounces) pineapple tidbits
1/2 cup mayonnaise
1/2 teaspoon paprika
1/2 teaspoon celery seed

Banal Biscuits

2 scallions (green onions)
1 clove garlic
2 cups flour
1 tablespoon baking powder
1/2 teaspoon salt
1 cup half-and-half
1 egg
2 tablespoons sesame seeds

Piece of Cake

2 Granny Smith apples
1/4 cup butter
1 cup granulated sugar
2 eggs
1 teaspoon almond extract
2 cups flour
1 tablespoon baking powder
1/4 teaspoon salt
3/4 cup half-and-half
3 tablespoons dark brown sugar
1 teaspoon ground cinnamon

EQUIPMENT

Electric mixer
2 small saucepans
9 × 9-inch glass
baking dish
Baking sheet
Breadboard
3 large mixing
bowls
Medium mixing
bowl
2 small mixing
bowls

Whisk
Vegetable grater
Pastry brush
Biscuit cutter
Aluminum foil
Plastic wrap
Kitchen knives
Measuring cups
and spoons
Cooking utensils

Labor Day

Ham and Haw

1. Prepare the grill.

2. In a small saucepan, combine the currant jelly, the lemon juice, the horseradish, and the cloves. Cook, stirring, until melted and well blended.

3. Brush one side of the ham steaks with the sauce and grill for 5 minutes.

4. Turn, brush with the remaining sauce, and grill for 5 minutes more.

5. Cut the ham steaks in half to serve.

Aw Shucks

1. Shuck the corn and lay each ear on a sheet of aluminum foil.

2. Melt the butter in a small saucepan. Blend in the vinegar, the nutmeg, and the sugar.

3. Brush the corn with the mixture, seal the foil around the ears, and grill for 10 minutes.

Slaw Motion

1. Trim and grate the cabbage. Rinse, stem, seed, and dice the bell pepper. Peel and dice the onion. Drain the pineapple, reserving the juice. Combine the ingredients in a large bowl.

2. In a small bowl, whisk together the reserved pineapple juice with the mayonnaise, the paprika, and the celery seed. Toss with the salad, cover the bowl with plastic wrap, and refrigerate it until you are ready to serve.

Banal Biscuits

1. Increase the oven temperature to 375°F. Flour a breadboard. Flour a biscuit cutter.

2. Rinse, trim, and chop the scallions. Peel and mince the garlic.

3. In a large bowl, combine the flour, the baking powder, the salt, the scallions, and the garlic.

4. Blend in the half-and-half until the dough forms a ball. Place the dough on the breadboard and knead it until smooth, 8–10 times. Pat out the dough to a half-inch thickness, and cut with the biscuit cutter. Arrange the biscuits on a baking sheet.

5. In a small bowl, whisk the egg until frothy. Brush the egg over the biscuits, and sprinkle with the sesame seeds.

6. Bake until golden, about 30 minutes.

Piece of Cake

1. Peel, core, and slice the apples.

2. Preheat the oven to 350°F. Grease a 9 × 9-inch glass baking dish.

3. In a large bowl, cream the butter with the granulated sugar with an electric mixer until fluffy. Beat in the eggs, one at a time, until well blended. Blend in the almond extract.

4. In a medium bowl, combine the flour, the baking powder, and the salt.

5. Beat the flour mixture into the egg mixture. Beat in the half-and-half until smooth. Pour the batter into the baking dish. Spread the apple slices over the batter. Sprinkle the brown sugar and the cinnamon over the apples.

6. Bake until the cake is golden, about 40 minutes.

COUNTDOWN

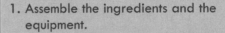

1. Assemble the ingredients and the equipment.
2. Do Steps 1–6 of *Piece of Cake*.
3. Do Steps 1–6 of *Banal Biscuits*.
4. Do Step 1 of *Ham and Haw*.
5. Do Steps 1–2 of *Slaw Motion*.
6. Do Step 2 of *Ham and Haw*.
7. Do Steps 1–3 of *Aw Shucks*.
8. Do Steps 3–5 of *Ham and Haw*.

Columbus Day Dinner

MEAT & POULTRY

2 pounds lean beef stew meat

FRESH PRODUCE

VEGETABLES
4 medium carrots
4 stalks celery
2 small parsnips
1 medium head lettuce
1 medium cucumber
1 small green bell pepper
1 large onion
3 scallions (green onions)

HERBS
2 tablespoons parsley (when chopped)

FRUIT
1 large orange

CANS, JARS & BOTTLES

SOUP
2 cans (14 ounces each) beef broth

VEGETABLES
1 can (28 ounces) diced tomatoes

CONDIMENTS
1 jar (6-1/2 ounces) marinated
    artichoke hearts

PACKAGED GOODS

PASTA, RICE & GRAINS
1 cup quick-cooking barley

BAKED GOODS
1 loaf Italian bread

DRIED FRUITS & NUTS
1/4 cup chopped walnuts

DESSERT & BAKING NEEDS
20 large marshmallows
4 chocolate cups

WINES & SPIRITS
1 cup dry red wine

REFRIGERATED PRODUCTS

DAIRY
1/2 cup milk
1 cup whipping cream

CHEESE
6 ounces provolone, sliced
6 ounces shredded mozzarella

FROZEN GOODS

VEGETABLES
1 package (10 ounces) cut green beans

STAPLES

- ☐ Butter
- ☐ Granulated sugar
- ☐ Cocoa powder
- ☐ Olive oil
- ☐ Red wine vinegar
- ☐ Dijon mustard
- ☐ Instant coffee
- ☐ Dried basil
- ☐ Dried oregano
- ☐ Dried thyme
- ☐ Paprika
- ☐ Pepper
- ☐ Salt
- ☐ Vanilla extract

Columbus Day Dinner

MENU

Fourteen Ninety-Stew

1 package (10 ounces) frozen cut green beans
4 stalks celery
4 medium carrots
2 small parsnips
1 large onion
1 can (28 ounces) diced tomatoes
2 pounds lean beef stew meat
2 cans (14 ounces each) beef broth
1 cup dry red wine
1 cup quick-cooking barley
1 teaspoon dried thyme
Seasoning to taste

Circumnavigate the Salad

1 medium head lettuce
1 medium cucumber
1 small green bell pepper
3 scallions (green onions)
1 jar (6-1/2 ounces) marinated artichoke hearts
1 large orange
2 tablespoons fresh parsley (when chopped)
3 tablespoons olive oil
2 tablespoons red wine vinegar
1 teaspoon Dijon mustard
1/2 teaspoon dried basil
1/2 teaspoon granulated sugar
Seasoning to taste

New World Bread

1 loaf Italian bread
2 tablespoons butter
6 ounces provolone cheese, sliced
6 ounces shredded mozzarella cheese
1/2 teaspoon dried oregano
1/2 teaspoon paprika

Discover the Dessert

1/2 cup milk
2 tablespoons cocoa powder
1 tablespoon instant coffee
20 large marshmallows
1 cup whipping cream
1 teaspoon vanilla extract
4 chocolate cups
1/4 cup chopped walnuts

EQUIPMENT

Electric mixer	2 small mixing bowls
Dutch oven	Whisk
Large saucepan	Vegetable peeler
Baking sheet	Kitchen knives
2 large mixing bowls	Measuring cups and spoons
Medium mixing bowl	Cooking utensils

Columbus Day Dinner

Fourteen Ninety-Stew

1. Set the package of green beans in a small bowl of hot water to thaw.

2. Rinse, trim, and chunk the celery. Peel and chunk the carrots. Peel and chunk the parsnips. Peel and chop the onion. Drain the tomatoes, reserving the liquid.

3. In a Dutch oven, combine the beef, the broth, the wine, and the reserved tomato liquid. Bring the mixture to a boil.

4. Add the celery, the carrots, the parsnips, the onion, the barley, and the thyme. Season to taste, cover, reduce the heat, and simmer until the beef is tender, about 2-1/2 hours.

5. Add the green beans and the tomatoes, and simmer, uncovered, for 30 minutes more.

Circumnavigate the Salad

1. Wash and dry the lettuce and tear it into bite-sized pieces. Peel and slice the cucumber. Rinse, stem, seed, and chop the bell pepper. Trim and slice the scallions. Drain and chop the artichokes. Combine the vegetables in a large bowl.

2. Peel and slice the orange. Rinse and chop the parsley.

3. In a small bowl, whisk together the oil, the vinegar, the mustard, the basil, and the sugar. Season to taste.

4. Toss the salad with the dressing. Arrange the orange slices on top and sprinkle with the parsley.

New World Bread

1. Preheat the broiler.

2. Cut the bread in half lengthwise and butter the cut sides. Place the bread, cut sides up, on a baking sheet.

3. Lay the provolone slices over the bread. Sprinkle the mozzarella over the provolone. Sprinkle the oregano and the paprika over the mozzarella.

4. Broil until bubbly, about 2 minutes.

Discover the Dessert

1. Chill a medium bowl and the beaters of an electric mixer in the refrigerator for at least 10 minutes.

2. In a large saucepan, heat the milk just to boiling. Reduce the heat and blend in the cocoa powder and the instant coffee. Add the marshmallows and cook over low heat, stirring, until the marshmallows are melted and the mixture is thick, about 10 minutes.

3. Turn the mixture into a large bowl and refrigerate for 20 minutes.

4. In the chilled bowl, whip the cream until it is stiff, about 5 minutes. Fold in the vanilla.

5. Fold the whipped cream into the marshmallow mixture and refrigerate until you are ready to use.

6. Spoon the marshmallow mixture into the chocolate cups and garnish with the chopped nuts.

COUNTDOWN

1. Assemble the ingredients and the equipment.

2. Do Steps 1–4 of *Fourteen Ninety-Stew*.

3. Do Steps 1–3 of *Discover the Dessert*.

4. Do Steps 1–3 of *Circumnavigate the Salad*.

5. Do Step 5 of *Fourteen Ninety-Stew*.

6. Do Steps 4–5 of *Discover the Dessert*.

7. Do Steps 1–4 of *New World Bread*.

8. Do Step 4 of *Circumnavigate the Salad*.

9. Do Step 6 of *Discover the Dessert*.

World Series

MEAT & POULTRY

4 boneless, skinless chicken breast halves
   (about 1-1/2 pounds)

FRESH PRODUCE

VEGETABLES

1 stalk celery
1 package (10 ounces) baby spinach
1/4 pound mushrooms
4 large red onions
4 scallions (green onions)
2 cloves garlic

CANS, JARS & BOTTLES

SOUP

1 can (14 ounces) chicken broth
1 can (10-1/2 ounces) beef broth

SPREADS

1/2 cup apricot preserves

PACKAGED GOODS

PASTA, RICE & GRAINS

1 cup wild rice

DRIED FRUITS & NUTS

3 tablespoons slivered almonds

DESSERT & BAKING NEEDS

2 squares (1 ounce each)
   unsweetened chocolate
8 ounces chocolate chips

REFRIGERATED PRODUCTS

DAIRY

1 cup plain yogurt
3 eggs

DELI

4 slices bacon

STAPLES

❏ Butter
❏ Flour
❏ Baking powder
❏ Granulated sugar
❏ Dijon mustard
❏ Ground nutmeg
❏ Pepper
❏ Salt
❏ Vanilla extract

World Series

Fowl Ball

1/2 cup flour
Seasoning to taste
2 tablespoons butter
4 boneless, skinless chicken breast halves
    (about 1-1/2 pounds)
1/2 cup apricot preserves
1 tablespoon Dijon mustard
1 cup plain yogurt
3 tablespoons slivered almonds

Wild Pitch Rice

1 cup wild rice
4 slices bacon
4 scallions (green onions)
1 stalk celery
1 clove garlic
1 can (14 ounces) chicken broth
1 cup beef broth
1/4 cup water
Seasoning to taste

Major League Onions

4 large red onions
1/4 pound fresh mushrooms
1 clove garlic
1 package (10 ounces) baby
    spinach
4 tablespoons butter
1/3 cup beef broth
Seasoning to taste
1/2 teaspoon ground nutmeg

Designated Dessert

1 stick butter
2 squares (1 ounce each) unsweetened
    chocolate
1 cup granulated sugar
3 eggs
1 teaspoon vanilla extract
3/4 cup flour
1 teaspoon baking powder
8 ounces chocolate chips

EQUIPMENT

Double boiler
Medium covered saucepan
Medium skillet
9 × 13-inch glass baking dish
9 × 9-inch glass baking dish
8 × 8-inch baking pan
Strainer
Large shallow bowl
Small mixing bowl
Kitchen knives
Measuring cups and spoons
Cooking utensils

World Series

Fowl Ball

1. Place the flour in a large shallow bowl and season it to taste. Melt the butter in a 9 × 13-inch glass baking dish.

2. Rinse and pat dry the chicken, and dredge it in the seasoned flour to coat evenly on all sides. Shake off any excess flour and lay the breasts in the baking dish.

3. In a small bowl, combine the preserves, the mustard, and the yogurt. Spread the mixture over the chicken.

4. Bake at 350°F for 15 minutes.

5. Sprinkle the almonds over the chicken and continue baking until the breasts are tender, about 15 minutes more.

Wild Pitch Rice

1. Rinse well and drain the rice.

2. Dice the bacon. Trim and chop the scallions. Rinse, trim, and chop the celery. Peel and mince the garlic.

3. Sauté the bacon in a medium saucepan until crisp. Drain the bacon on paper towels, reserving the drippings.

4. Add the celery and the garlic to the bacon drippings and sauté for 2 minutes.

5. Add the rice, the broth, and the 1/4 cup water to the saucepan, season to taste, and bring to a boil.

6. Cover, reduce the heat, and simmer until the liquid is absorbed and the rice is tender, about 40 minutes.

7. Fluff the rice and fold in the bacon and the scallions.

Major League Onions

1. Increase the oven temperature to 350°F. Grease a 9 × 9-inch glass baking dish.

2. Rinse and dry the onions. Do not peel. Cut a thin slice off the tops and bottoms. With a serrated knife, hollow out the centers of the onions, being careful not to pierce the sides or the bottoms. Chop and reserve the pulp.

3. Place the onion shells in the baking dish and bake for 15 minutes.

4. Rinse, pat dry, and chop the mushrooms. Peel and mince the garlic. Rinse, dry, and chop the spinach.

5. Melt half of the butter in a medium skillet and sauté the onion pulp, the mushrooms, and the garlic for 5 minutes. Fold in the spinach and the broth. Season to taste and cook just until the spinach is wilted and the liquid is evaporated, about 2 minutes.

6. Melt the remaining 2 tablespoons butter with the nutmeg.

7. Spoon the spinach mixture into the onion shells. Drizzle with the butter mixture.

8. Bake for 15 minutes longer.

9. Remove the onions skins before serving.

Designated Dessert

1. Preheat the oven to 325°F. Grease an
   8 × 8-inch baking pan.

2. Bring water to a boil in the bottom of a
   double boiler. Melt the butter with the
   chocolate in the top of the double boiler.
   Remove the double boiler from the heat,
   add the sugar, and blend well. Whisk in the
   eggs, one at a time. Blend in the vanilla.
   Stir in the flour, a little at a time, and blend
   well. Stir in the baking powder and blend
   well. Fold in the chocolate chips.

3. Spread the mixture evenly into the baking
   pan and bake until set, about 40 minutes.
   The top should be soft and springy, and a
   knife inserted in the middle should come
   out clean. Be careful not to overbake.

4. Let the brownies cool before cutting into
   2-inch squares.

COUNTDOWN

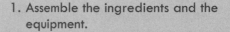

1. Assemble the ingredients and the
   equipment.
2. Do Steps 1–4 of *Designated Dessert*.
3. Do Steps 1–6 of *Wild Pitch Rice*.
4. Do Steps 1–2 of *Major League Onions*.
5. Do Steps 1–3 of *Fowl Ball*.
6. Do Step 3 of *Major League Onions*.
7. Do Step 4 of *Fowl Ball*.
8. Do Steps 4–8 of *Major League Onions*.
9. Do Step 5 of *Fowl Ball*.
10. Do Step 9 of *Major League Onions*.
11. Do Step 7 of *Wild Pitch Rice*.

Halloween

MEAT & POULTRY
1-1/2 pounds lean boneless pork loin

FRESH PRODUCE

VEGETABLES
1 pound medium carrots
1 medium head Boston lettuce
1 medium cucumber
2 medium green bell peppers
1 medium shallot

HERBS
2 tablespoons chives (when chopped)

FRUIT
1/2 pound seedless black grapes

CANS, JARS & BOTTLES

CONDIMENTS
2 tablespoons capers

DESSERT & BAKING NEEDS
1 can (16 ounces) pumpkin

PACKAGED GOODS

PASTA, RICE & GRAINS
12 ounces curly egg noodles

DRIED FRUITS & NUTS
1/2 cup chopped pecans

WINES & SPIRITS
1/2 cup dry white wine

REFRIGERATED PRODUCTS

DAIRY
1-1/2 cups sour cream
2 cups whipped cream

FROZEN GOODS

DESSERTS
1 pint orange yogurt

STAPLES

- ❏ Butter
- ❏ Flour
- ❏ Granulated sugar
- ❏ Dark brown sugar
- ❏ Maple syrup
- ❏ Olive oil
- ❏ Tarragon vinegar
- ❏ Lemon juice
- ❏ White Worcestershire sauce
- ❏ Ground allspice
- ❏ Ground cinnamon
- ❏ Ground nutmeg
- ❏ Pepper
- ❏ Salt

Halloween

Mostly Ghostly Pork

1 medium shallot
1/4 cup flour
Seasoning to taste
1-1/2 pounds lean boneless pork loin
2 tablespoons butter
12 ounces curly egg noodles
1/2 cup dry white wine
1-1/2 cups sour cream
1 teaspoon white Worcestershire sauce

Bedknobs and Broomsticks

1 pound medium carrots
1/2 pound seedless black grapes
2 tablespoons butter
2 tablespoons lemon juice
1/2 teaspoon ground allspice
1 teaspoon dark brown sugar

Green Slime Salad

1 medium head Boston lettuce
2 medium green bell peppers
1 medium cucumber
2 tablespoons fresh chives (when chopped)
3 tablespoons olive oil
2 tablespoons tarragon vinegar
1 teaspoon granulated sugar
2 tablespoons capers
Seasoning to taste

Jack O'Lanterns

1 can (16 ounces) pumpkin
1/4 cup maple syrup
1 teaspoon ground cinnamon
1/2 teaspoon ground nutmeg
2 cups whipped cream
1 pint orange frozen yogurt
1/2 cup chopped pecans

EQUIPMENT

Stockpot
Large skillet
Medium covered skillet
Colander
Large shallow bowl
Large mixing bowl
Small mixing bowl
Whisk
Vegetable peeler
Ice cream scoop
Kitchen knives
Measuring cups and spoons
Cooking utensils

Mostly Ghostly Pork

1. Peel and mince the shallot.

2. Place the flour in a large shallow bowl and season it to taste.

3. Pat dry the pork and cut it into 4 portions. Dredge the portions in the seasoned flour.

4. Melt the butter in a large skillet and sauté the shallot for 1 minute.

5. Add the pork and cook until white throughout, about 10 minutes per side.

6. Bring water for the pasta to a boil in a stockpot.

7. Cook the noodles in the stockpot until almost tender, about 8 minutes.

8. Remove the pork and cover to keep warm.

9. Add the wine to the skillet and cook until it evaporates.

10. Reduce the heat and stir in the sour cream and the Worcestershire sauce. Blend well and heat through.

11. Drain the noodles and serve with the pork and the sauce.

Bedknobs and Broomsticks

1. Rinse and peel carrots and cut them into sticks. Rinse and stem the grapes.

2. Melt the butter in a medium skillet and sauté the carrots until they are crisp-tender, about 5 minutes.

3. Blend in the lemon juice, the allspice, and the brown sugar. Fold in the grapes and heat through, about 2 minutes. Cover to keep warm.

Green Slime Salad

1. Wash and dry the lettuce and distribute the leaves among individual salad plates.

2. Rinse, stem, seed, and thinly slice the bell peppers. Scrub the cucumber, scrape down the length of it with the tines of a fork, and slice it.

3. Distribute the vegetables over the lettuce.

4. Rinse and chop the chives.

5. In a small bowl, whisk together the oil, the vinegar, the sugar, and the capers. Season to taste.

6. Drizzle the dressing over the salads and sprinkle with the chives.

Jack O'Lanterns

1. In a large bowl, combine the pumpkin, the maple syrup, the cinnamon, and the nutmeg.

2. Fold in the whipped cream.

3. Place a scoop of the frozen yogurt in the bottom of each individual dessert glass. Spoon on half of the pumpkin mixture. Repeat.

4. Freeze until you are ready to serve.

5. Garnish the parfaits with the nuts.

COUNTDOWN

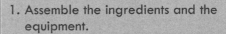

1. Assemble the ingredients and the equipment.

2. Do Steps 1–4 of *Jack O'Lanterns.*

3. Do Steps 1–5 of *Green Slime Salad.*

4. Do Step 1 of *Bedknobs and Broomsticks.*

5. Do Steps 1–6 of *Mostly Ghostly Pork.*

6. Do Steps 2–3 of *Bedknobs and Broomsticks.*

7. Do Steps 7–11 of *Mostly Ghostly Pork.*

8. Do Step 6 of *Green Slime Salad.*

9. Do Step 5 of *Jack O'Lanterns.*

Veteran's Day

SHOPPING LIST

FISH
1 whole red snapper (about
   1-1/2 pounds), cleaned and scaled

FRESH PRODUCE

VEGETABLES
4 medium baking potatoes
1 pound green beans
2 stalks celery
1 medium tomato
1 small red bell pepper
1 small onion
1 small shallot
2 scallions (green onions)
1 clove garlic

HERBS
2 tablespoons parsley (when chopped)
2 tablespoons rosemary (when chopped)

FRUIT
1 small lemon

CANS, JARS & BOTTLES

VEGETABLES
1 can (11 ounces) whole kernel corn

WINES & SPIRITS
1/2 cup dry white wine

REFRIGERATED PRODUCTS

DAIRY
1-1/2 cups buttermilk
4 eggs

STAPLES

- ☐ Butter
- ☐ Flour
- ☐ Baking powder
- ☐ Baking soda
- ☐ Granulated sugar
- ☐ Dark brown sugar
- ☐ Powdered sugar
- ☐ Vegetable oil
- ☐ Red wine vinegar
- ☐ Poppy seeds
- ☐ Dried dill
- ☐ Ground cinnamon
- ☐ Pepper
- ☐ Salt
- ☐ Orange extract

Veteran's Day

Snappy Sailor

2 tablespoons fresh rosemary (when chopped)
2 tablespoons fresh parsley (when chopped)
1 small lemon
1 whole red snapper (about 1-1/2 pounds), cleaned and scaled
Seasoning to taste
4 tablespoons butter
1/2 cup dry white wine

Marine Kernels

4 medium baking potatoes
2 stalks celery
2 scallions (green onions)
1 small red bell pepper
1 can (11 ounces) whole kernel corn
2 tablespoons butter
1/2 cup buttermilk
Seasoning to taste

Veteran Vegetables

1 pound fresh green beans
1 small onion
1 small shallot
1 clove garlic
1 medium fresh tomato
3 tablespoons vegetable oil
1 tablespoon red wine vinegar
1 teaspoon dried dill
1/2 teaspoon granulated sugar
Seasoning to taste

Doughboy

1/2 cup poppy seeds
1 cup buttermilk
2 sticks butter
1 cup granulated sugar
4 eggs
2-1/2 cups flour
1 tablespoon baking powder
1 teaspoon baking soda
1/2 teaspoon salt
1 teaspoon orange extract
2 tablespoons dark brown sugar
1 teaspoon ground cinnamon
2 tablespoons powdered sugar

EQUIPMENT

Electric mixer	2 large mixing bowls
Medium covered saucepan	2 medium mixing bowls
Large covered skillet	Small mixing bowl
Medium skillet	Vegetable brush
Shallow roasting pan	Aluminum foil
Bundt pan	Kitchen knives
Baking sheet	Measuring cups and spoons
Steamer insert	Cooking utensils

Veteran's Day

Snappy Sailor

1. Grease a shallow roasting pan.

2. Rinse and chop the rosemary. Rinse and chop the parsley. Scrub and slice the lemon.

3. Rinse and pat dry the fish.

4. Season the fish to taste inside and out and sprinkle with the rosemary. Place the fish in the roasting pan. Dot the fish with the butter. Drizzle the wine over the fish.

5. Bake the fish at 350°F for 20 minutes.

6. Arrange the lemon slices along the top of the snapper and bake until the fish flakes easily with a fork, about 5 minutes more.

7. Sprinkle with the parsley.

Marine Kernels

1. Scrub the potatoes and prick each of them several times with a fork. Wrap each potato in aluminum foil and bake at 350°F until slightly soft to the touch, about 1 hour.

2. Remove the potatoes and let them cool slightly.

3. Rinse, trim, and chop the celery. Trim and chop the scallions. Rinse, stem, seed, and chop the bell pepper. Drain the corn and place it in a medium bowl.

4. Melt the butter in a medium skillet and sauté the celery, the scallions, and the bell pepper for 3 minutes. Mix the vegetables with the corn.

5. Cut a thin slice from the top of each potato and carefully scoop out the flesh to 1/4 inch around the skins. Place the potato flesh in a large bowl. Blend the buttermilk with the potato flesh and season to taste.

6. Spoon the flesh back into the potato skins and top them with the vegetable mixture. Place the potatoes on a baking sheet, return them to the oven, and bake until they are heated through, about 10 minutes.

Veteran Vegetables

1. Rinse and trim the green beans. Peel and chop the onion. Peel and chop the shallot. Peel and mince the garlic. Rinse and chop the tomato.

2. Bring water to a boil in a medium saucepan. Arrange the beans in a steamer insert, place the insert in the saucepan, cover, and steam until crisp-tender, about 5 minutes.

3. Heat the oil in a large skillet and sauté the onion, the shallot, and the garlic for 3 minutes. Add the tomato and sauté for 2 minutes more.

4. Drain the beans and add them to the skillet. Add the vinegar, the dill, and the sugar, season to taste, and toss to combine. Cover to keep warm.

Doughboy

1. Preheat the oven to 350°F. Grease and flour a Bundt pan.

2. In a small bowl, combine the poppy seeds and the buttermilk, and let stand.

3. In a large bowl, cream the butter with the granulated sugar with an electric mixer until fluffy. Beat in the eggs, one at a time.

4. In a medium bowl, combine the flour, the baking powder, the baking soda, and the salt. Beat the flour mixture into the egg mixture. Blend in the poppy seed mixture and the orange extract.

5. Pour half of the batter into the Bundt pan, and sprinkle with the brown sugar and the cinnamon. Add the remaining batter.

6. Add to the oven and bake until a toothpick inserted in the center comes out clean, about 50 minutes.

7. Remove the cake from the oven and let cool for 10 minutes.

8. Invert the cake onto a platter and dust with the powdered sugar.

COUNTDOWN

1. Assemble the ingredients and the equipment.
2. Do Steps 1–6 of *Doughboy*.
3. Do Step 1 of *Marine Kernels*.
4. Do Step 1 of *Veteran Vegetables*.
5. Do Steps 1–5 of *Snappy Sailor*.
6. Do Step 7 of *Doughboy*.
7. Do Steps 2–6 of *Marine Kernels*.
8. Do Step 6 of *Snappy Sailor*.
9. Do Steps 2–4 of *Veteran Vegetables*.
10. Do Step 8 of *Doughboy*.
11. Do Step 7 of *Snappy Sailor*.

Thanksgiving

MEAT & POULTRY

1 pound bulk pork sausage
1 whole turkey (about 10 pounds)

FRESH PRODUCE

VEGETABLES

4 medium sweet potatoes
1-1/2 pounds Brussels sprouts
3 stalks celery
1 large onion
1 medium onion
4 scallions (green onions)
2 cloves garlic

FRUIT

2 Granny Smith apples

CANS, JARS & BOTTLES

SOUP

1 can (10-1/2 ounces) beef consommé

INTERNATIONAL FOODS

1 can (8 ounces) whole water chestnuts

FRUIT

1 can (20 ounces) crushed pineapple
1 can (16 ounces) whole cranberry sauce

DESSERT & BAKING NEEDS

1 can (16 ounces) pumpkin

PACKAGED GOODS

BAKED GOODS

10 slices whole wheat bread

DRIED FRUITS & NUTS

1/4 cup pecan bits

DESSERT & BAKING NEEDS

1 unbaked pie shell
1 cup mini marshmallows

WINES & SPIRITS

1/4 cup dry sherry
1/4 cup bourbon

REFRIGERATED PRODUCTS

DAIRY

1-1/2 cups half-and-half
1 cup sour cream
1/4 cup whipped cream
2 eggs

JUICE

1/2 cup orange juice

DELI

3 slices bacon

STAPLES

❒ Butter
❒ Flour
❒ Granulated sugar
❒ Dark brown sugar
❒ Kitchen Bouquet
❒ Plain breadcrumbs
❒ Bay leaf
❒ Whole allspice
❒ Ground cinnamon
❒ Ground ginger
❒ Ground nutmeg
❒ Poultry seasoning
❒ Pepper
❒ Salt

Thanksgiving

Well-Bread Bird

1 whole turkey (about 10 pounds)
10 slices whole wheat bread
1 medium onion
3 stalks celery
2 Granny Smith apples
1 can (8 ounces) whole water chestnuts
1 pound bulk pork sausage
1-1/2 sticks butter
2 tablespoons poultry seasoning
Seasoning to taste
2 cloves garlic
1 large onion
2 bay leaves
3 whole allspice
1 can (10-1/2 ounces) beef consommé
1/4 cup dry sherry
1/2 cup half-and-half
1/4 cup flour
2 tablespoons Kitchen Bouquet

Poised Potatoes

4 medium sweet potatoes
1/2 cup orange juice
1/4 cup granulated sugar
3 tablespoons butter
1 teaspoon ground cinnamon
1 cup mini marshmallows

Venerable Vegetables

1-1/2 pounds Brussels sprouts
3 slices bacon
4 scallions (green onions)
3 tablespoons butter
1-1/2 cups plain breadcrumbs
1/2 teaspoon dried oregano
Seasoning to taste

Celebrated Sauce

1 can (20 ounces) crushed pineapple
1 can (16 ounces) whole cranberry sauce
1 cup sour cream
1/4 cup pecan bits

Praiseworthy Pie

2 eggs
1 can (16 ounces) pumpkin
3/4 cup dark brown sugar
1/2 teaspoon ground ginger
1/4 teaspoon ground nutmeg
1 cup half-and-half
1/4 cup bourbon
1 unbaked pie shell
1/4 cup whipped cream

EQUIPMENT

Electric mixer	Strainer
Large saucepan	3 large mixing bowls
2 medium covered saucepans	
	Small mixing bowl
Small saucepan	Whisk
Large skillet	Baster
Medium skillet	Meat thermometer
Large roasting pan	Vegetable brush
Roasting rack	Plastic wrap
9 × 9-inch glass baking dish	Kitchen knives
Loaf pan	Measuring cups and spoons
Pie plate	Cooking utensils
Steamer insert	

Thanksgiving

Well-Bread Bird

1. Remove the giblet package from the turkey cavity or neck. Rinse the turkey inside and out and turn it upside down to drain.

2. Cover the giblets and the neck with water in a medium saucepan. Bring to a boil, cover, reduce the heat, and simmer until you are ready to use, checking to make sure the water does not boil away.

3. Toast the bread, cut it into small cubes, and place the cubes in a large bowl.

4. Peel and chop the medium onion. Rinse, trim, and mince the celery. Peel, core, and chop the apples. Drain and chop the water chestnuts. Add the ingredients to the bread cubes.

5. Brown the sausage in a large skillet. Drain the sausage on paper towels and add it to the bread mixture.

6. Melt 1/2 stick of the butter and drizzle it over the stuffing mixture. Blend in the poultry seasoning.

7. Peel and halve the garlic, adding 1 clove to the simmering giblets. Peel and quarter the large onion.

8. Preheat the oven to 325°F.

9. Rub the turkey with the remaining garlic clove.

10. Fill the turkey cavities with the stuffing and sew or skewer to close. Place the bird, breast side down, on a rack in a large roasting pan. Add the onion, the bay leaf, and the allspice to the pan. Pour the consommé over the turkey.

11. Melt the remaining 1 stick butter in a small saucepan. Blend in the sherry. Baste the turkey with the mixture and roast until golden and a meat thermometer reaches 175°F, about 4-1/2 hours. Baste every 15 minutes.

12. Strain the giblets and the garlic, reserving the cooking juice in the saucepan.

13. Remove the turkey from the roasting pan and let stand for 10 minutes before carving.

14. Strain the pan juices, add them to the saucepan, and bring to a rolling boil.

15. In a small bowl, combine the half-and-half and the flour, and whisk until smooth. Slowly add the mixture to the pan juices, whisking until the gravy is well blended and thick. Blend in the Kitchen Bouquet.

Poised Potatoes

1. Scrub the potatoes and cover them with water in a large saucepan. Bring to a boil and cook for 20 minutes.

2. Grease a 9 × 9-inch glass baking dish.

3. Drain the potatoes and rinse them under cold water to cool.

4. Pour the orange juice into the baking dish. Peel and slice the potatoes and arrange the slices over the orange juice. Sprinkle the potatoes with the sugar. Dot with the butter. Sprinkle with the cinnamon. Top with the marshmallows.

5. Bake at 325°F until the marshmallows are golden, about 35 minutes.

Venerable Vegetables

1. Rinse and trim the Brussels sprouts, cutting x's in the bottom of each stem. Dice the bacon. Trim and chop the scallions.

2. Bring water to a boil in a medium saucepan. Arrange the sprouts in a steamer insert. Place the insert in the saucepan, cover, and steam until the sprouts are crisp-tender, about 7 minutes.

3. Sauté the bacon in a medium skillet until crisp. Drain the bacon on paper towels, reserving the drippings in the pan.

4. Drain the sprouts.

5. Melt the butter in the bacon drippings and sauté the scallions for 1 minute. Add the bacon, the sprouts, the breadcrumbs, and the oregano. Season to taste and toss until the breadcrumbs are lightly browned and the mixture is heated through. Cover to keep warm.

Celebrated Sauce

1. Grease a loaf pan.

2. Drain the pineapple. Place the pineapple in a large bowl and blend in the cranberry sauce. Fold in the sour cream and the pecans. Pour the mixture into the loaf pan, cover with plastic wrap, and freeze until you are ready to use.

3. Invert the mold onto the platter and slice to serve.

Praiseworthy Pie

1. Preheat the oven to 425°F.

2. In a large bowl, beat the eggs with an electric mixer until lemon-colored. Beat in the pumpkin, the granulated sugar, the brown sugar, the cinnamon, the ginger, the nutmeg, the half-and-half, the bourbon, and the salt.

3. Place the pie shell in a pie plate, pour the mixture into the shell, and bake for 15 minutes.

4. Reduce the oven temperature to 350°F and continue baking until a knife inserted in the center comes out clean, about 40 minutes.

5. Garnish with dollops of whipped cream.

COUNTDOWN

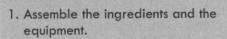

1. Assemble the ingredients and the equipment.
2. Do Steps 1–4 of *Praiseworthy Pie*.
3. Do Steps 1–11 of *Well-Bread Bird*.
4. Do Steps 1–2 of *Celebrated Sauce*.
5. Do Steps 1–5 of *Poised Potatoes*.
6. Do Steps 12–15 of *Well-Bread Bird*.
7. Do Steps 1–5 of *Venerable Vegetables*.
8. Do Step 3 of *Celebrated Sauce*.
9. Do Step 5 of *Praiseworthy Pie*.

Christmas

SHOPPING LIST

MEAT & POULTRY

1 standing rib roast (about 4 pounds)

FRESH PRODUCE

VEGETABLES

1 medium bunch broccoli
1 package (10 ounces) baby spinach
2 small ripe avocados
1 medium red onion
3 scallions (green onions)
3 cloves garlic

HERBS

2 tablespoons dill (when chopped)

FRUIT

1 large ripe pomegranate

PACKAGED GOODS

DESSERT & BAKING NEEDS

1/2 cup flaked coconut
1 cup chopped walnuts

WINES & SPIRITS

1 cup dry white wine

REFRIGERATED PRODUCTS

DAIRY

1 cup milk
2 tablespoons half-and-half
4 eggs

STAPLES

❒ Butter
❒ Flour
❒ Baking powder
❒ Granulated sugar
❒ Dark brown sugar
❒ Powdered sugar
❒ Vegetable oil
❒ Raspberry vinegar
❒ Worcestershire sauce
❒ Dijon mustard
❒ Honey
❒ Dried tarragon
❒ Ground nutmeg
❒ Pepper
❒ White pepper
❒ Salt
❒ Rum extract
❒ Vanilla extract

Christmas

Beef On Earth

1 standing rib roast (about 4 pounds)
2 cloves garlic
1/4 cup honey
3 tablespoons Dijon mustard
1 tablespoon Worcestershire sauce
1 cup dry white wine

Good Dill Toward Men

1 clove garlic
1 medium bunch broccoli
1 medium red onion
2 tablespoons fresh dill (when chopped)
3 tablespoons vegetable oil
Seasoning to taste

Jolly Holly Pudding

2 tablespoons butter
1 cup flour
1 teaspoon salt
1/8 teaspoon white pepper
1/2 teaspoon ground nutmeg
2 eggs
1 cup milk

Santa Salad

1 package (10 ounces) baby spinach
3 scallions (green onions)
3 tablespoons vegetable oil
2 tablespoons raspberry vinegar
1/2 teaspoon granulated sugar
1/4 teaspoon dried tarragon
Seasoning to taste
1 large ripe pomegranate
2 small ripe avocados

Nutcracker Sweet

1 cup + 3 tablespoons flour
1/2 teaspoon salt
3/4 teaspoon granulated sugar
2 sticks butter
1/2 cup flaked coconut
1 teaspoon baking powder
1-1/4 cups dark brown sugar
1 cup chopped walnuts
1 teaspoon rum extract
2 eggs
1-1/4 cups powdered sugar
2 tablespoons half-and-half
1/2 teaspoon vanilla extract

EQUIPMENT

Electric mixer	Whisk
Medium skillet	Meat thermometer
Medium roasting pan	Pastry brush
9 × 9-inch glass baking dish	Pastry blender
Springform pan	Aluminum foil
Large mixing bowl	Kitchen knives
Medium mixing bowl	Measuring cups and spoons
2 small mixing bowls	Cooking utensils

Christmas

Beef On Earth

1. Pat dry the roast and place it in a medium roasting pan.

2. Peel and mince the garlic.

3. In a small bowl, combine the garlic, the honey, the mustard, and the Worcestershire sauce. Brush the mixture over the entire roast and let stand for 1 hour.

4. Preheat the oven to 375°F.

5. Add the wine to the roasting pan and roast, basting occasionally, until a meat thermometer inserted in the thickest part of the roast reaches 150°F for medium rare, about 2 hours.

6. Remove the roast from the oven and cover with aluminum foil to keep warm.

Good Dill Toward Men

1. Peel and mince the garlic. Rinse and trim the broccoli and cut it into bite-sized florets. Peel the onion and cut it into 8 wedges. Rinse and chop the dill.

2. Heat the oil in a medium skillet and sauté the garlic for 1 minute. Add the broccoli and the onion. Season to taste and sauté until the broccoli is crisp-tender, about 5 minutes. Sprinkle with the dill.

Jolly Holly Pudding

1. Increase the oven temperature to 425°F.

2. Put the butter in a 9 × 9-inch glass baking dish and melt it in the oven.

3. In a large bowl, combine the flour, the salt, the pepper, and the nutmeg. Make a well in the center, add the eggs and the milk, and beat well until very smooth, about 2 minutes.

4. Remove the hot baking dish from the oven, spread the melted butter evenly over the bottom, pour the batter into the dish, and bake until the pudding is golden and puffy, about 20 minutes.

Santa Salad

1. Rinse, pat dry, and stem the spinach and arrange the leaves on individual salad plates. Trim and chop the scallions and sprinkle them over the spinach.

2. In a small bowl, whisk together the oil, the vinegar, the sugar, and the tarragon. Season to taste.

3. Cut the pomegranate in half, carefully remove and reserve the seeds, and discard the shell. Peel, pit, and slice the avocados. Arrange the avocado slices over the salad. Sprinkle the pomegranate seeds over the avocado, and drizzle with the dressing.

Nutcracker Sweet

1. Preheat the oven to 375°F. Grease a springform pan.

2. In a medium bowl, combine 1 cup of the flour, 1/4 teaspoon of the salt, and the granulated sugar.

3. With a pastry blender, cut in 1 stick of the butter until the mixture is the consistency of fine crumbs. Press the mixture into the bottom of the springform pan.

4. In the same bowl, combine the coconut, the remaining 3 tablespoons flour, the baking powder, the remaining 1/4 teaspoon salt, the brown sugar, the walnuts, the rum extract, and the eggs, and beat until well blended. Pour the mixture into the springform pan.

5. Bake for 35 minutes.

6. Remove the torte from the oven and let it cool for 30 minutes.

7. In the same bowl, cream together the remaining stick of butter, the powdered sugar, the half-and-half, and the vanilla. Spread the frosting over the cooled torte.

COUNTDOWN

1. Assemble the ingredients and the equipment.
2. Do Steps 1–7 of *Nutcracker Sweet*.
3. Do Steps 1–5 of *Beef On Earth*.
4. Do Steps 1–2 of *Santa Salad*.
5. Do Step 6 of *Beef On Earth*.
6. Do Steps 1–4 of *Jolly Holly Pudding*.
7. Do Step 3 of *Santa Salad*.
8. Do Steps 1–2 of *Good Dill Toward Men*.

New Year's Eve

SHOPPING LIST

MEAT & POULTRY

1 boneless ham, fully cooked
    (about 4 pounds)

FRESH PRODUCE

VEGETABLES

1 pound green beans

CANS, JARS & BOTTLES

SOUP

1 can (10-1/2 ounces) beef broth

FRUIT

4 maraschino cherries

PACKAGED GOODS

PASTA, RICE & GRAINS

6 ounces wide egg noodles

DESSERT & BAKING NEEDS

1 envelope unflavored gelatin
1 cup chocolate chips

WINES & SPIRITS

1/3 cup bourbon

REFRIGERATED PRODUCTS

DAIRY

2-1/4 cups milk
1 cup + 6 tablespoons whipping cream
1/4 cup whipped cream
5 eggs

CHEESE

1/2 cup small-curd cottage cheese
1 package (3 ounces) cream cheese

STAPLES

- ☐ Butter
- ☐ Granulated sugar
- ☐ Dark brown sugar
- ☐ Vegetable oil
- ☐ Lemon juice
- ☐ Dijon mustard
- ☐ Grated Parmesan cheese
- ☐ Dried sage
- ☐ Dried thyme
- ☐ Ground allspice
- ☐ Ground cinnamon
- ☐ Ground nutmeg
- ☐ Pepper
- ☐ Salt
- ☐ Vanilla extract

New Year's Eve

Father Thyme

1 boneless ham, fully cooked (about 4 pounds)
1/3 cup Dijon mustard
2 tablespoons dark brown sugar
2 tablespoons vegetable oil
1/3 cup bourbon
1/4 teaspoon dried thyme
1/2 teaspoon dried sage
1 can (10-1/2 ounces) beef broth

Happy Noodle Year

1 package (3 ounces) cream cheese
3 tablespoons butter
6 ounces wide egg noodles
2 eggs
1 egg white
1/2 cup small-curd cottage cheese
1/2 cup milk
1/4 teaspoon vanilla extract
1 tablespoon granulated sugar
1/4 teaspoon ground cinnamon
1/8 teaspoon ground nutmeg

It's Bean Great

2 tablespoons butter
6 tablespoons whipping cream
2 egg whites
1 tablespoon grated Parmesan cheese
1/8 teaspoon ground allspice
Seasoning to taste
2 tablespoons lemon juice
1 pound fresh green beans

Diet Tomorrow

3 egg yolks
1/4 cup granulated sugar
1 envelope unflavored gelatin
1/4 teaspoon salt
1-3/4 cups milk
1 cup chocolate chips
1 cup whipping cream
1 teaspoon vanilla extract
1/4 cup whipped cream
4 maraschino cherries

EQUIPMENT

Electric mixer	2 large mixing bowls
Large saucepan	2 medium mixing bowls
Medium covered saucepan	
Medium saucepan	2 small mixing bowls
Small covered saucepan	Whisk
Medium roasting pan	Pastry brush
	Baster
8 × 8-inch glass baking dish	Kitchen knives
Steamer insert	Measuring cups and spoons
Colander	Cooking utensils

New Year's Eve

Father Thyme

1. Preheat the oven to 325°F.

2. Cut deep scores into the top fat on the ham and place the ham in a medium roasting pan.

3. In a small bowl, combine the mustard, the brown sugar, the oil, the bourbon, the thyme, and the sage, and brush the mixture over the ham and into the scores.

4. Pour the broth into the bottom of the roasting pan and bake until heated through, about 1-1/2 hours, basting occasionally.

5. Slice the ham and serve with the sauce.

Happy Noodle Year

1. Set the cream cheese out to soften.

2. Bring water to a boil in a large saucepan.

3. Preheat the oven to 325°F. Melt the butter in an 8 × 8-inch glass baking dish in the warming oven.

4. Cook the noodles in the saucepan until almost tender, about 7 minutes.

5. In a large bowl, whip the eggs and the egg white until light and frothy. Fold in the cottage cheese, the softened cream cheese, the milk, the vanilla, the sugar, the cinnamon, and the nutmeg.

6. Drain the noodles, add them to the egg mixture, and blend well. Fold the noodle mixture into the melted butter and bake

until a knife inserted in the center comes out clean, about 35 minutes.

7. Cut into squares to serve.

It's Bean Great

1. Melt the butter in a small saucepan. Fold in 2 tablespoons of the cream and simmer for 5 minutes.

2. In a small bowl, whisk together the egg whites, the remaining 4 tablespoons cream, the cheese, and the allspice. Season to taste and whisk slowly into the butter mixture. Blend in the lemon juice and simmer until the sauce begins to thicken, about 2 minutes. Remove from the heat and cover to keep warm.

3. Bring water to a boil in a medium saucepan.

4. Rinse and trim the green beans. Arrange the beans in a steamer insert, place the insert in the saucepan, cover, and steam until the beans are crisp-tender, about 5 minutes.

5. Drain the beans and top with the sauce.

Diet Tomorrow

1. Place the egg yolks in a medium bowl, reserving the whites.

2. In a medium saucepan, combine the sugar, the gelatin, the salt, the milk, and the chocolate chips, and cook, stirring, until

the chocolate is melted and the gelatin is dissolved.

3. Stir 1/4 cup of the chocolate mixture into the egg yolks. Then stir the egg yolk mixture into the saucepan. Simmer, stirring, for 2 minutes. Do not let the mixture boil.

4. Pour the mixture into a large bowl, cover it with plastic wrap, and chill until partially set, about 1-1/2 hours.

5. Chill a medium bowl and the beaters of an electric mixer in the refrigerator for at least 10 minutes.

6. In the chilled bowl, whip the cream until stiff peaks form. Blend in the vanilla.

7. Fold the whipped cream mixture into the thickened chocolate mixture, spoon into individual dessert glasses, and refrigerate for 2 hours.

8. Garnish each glass with dollops of whipped cream and a maraschino cherry.

COUNTDOWN

1. Assemble the ingredients and the equipment.
2. Do Steps 1–7 of *Diet Tomorrow*.
3. Do Steps 1–4 of *Father Thyme*.
4. Do Steps 1–6 of *Happy Noodle Year*.
5. Do Steps 1–4 of *It's Bean Great*.
6. Do Step 5 of *Father Thyme*.
7. Do Step 7 of *Happy Noodle Year*.
8. Do Step 5 of *It's Bean Great*.
9. Do Step 8 of *Diet Tomorrow*.

Metric Conversion Table

LIQUID MEASUREMENTS

1/4 teaspoon = 1.25 milliliters
1/2 teaspoon = 2.5 milliliters
1 teaspoon = 5 milliliters
1 tablespoon = 15 milliliters
2 tablespoons = 30 milliliters
1/4 cup = 60 milliliters
1/3 cup = 80 milliliters
1/2 cup = 120 milliliters
2/3 cup = 160 milliliters
3/4 cup = 180 milliliters
1 cup = 240 milliliters
1 pint (2 cups) = 480 milliliters
1 quart (4 cups) = 960 milliliters (.96 liters)

EQUIVALENTS FOR DRY MEASUREMENTS

AMOUNT	FINE POWDER (FLOUR)	GRAIN/RICE
1 cup	140 grams	150 grams
3/4 cup	105 grams	113 grams
2/3 cup	93 grams	100 grams
1/2 cup	70 grams	75 grams
1/3 cup	47 grams	50 grams
1/4 cup	35 grams	38 grams
1/8 cup	18 grams	19 grams

AMOUNT	GRANULAR (SUGAR)	SOLIDS/BUTTER
1 cup	190 grams	200 grams
3/4 cup	143 grams	150 grams
2/3 cup	125 grams	133 grams
1/2 cup	95 grams	100 grams
1/3 cup	63 grams	67 grams
1/4 cup	48 grams	50 grams
1/8 cup	24 grams	15 grams

OVEN TEMPERATURES

	FAHRENHEIT	CELSIUS	GAS MARK
Freeze water	32°F	0°C	
Room temperature	68°F	20°C	
Boil water	212°F	100°C	
Bake	325°F	160°C	3
	350°F	180°C	4
	375°F	190°C	5
	400°F	200°C	6
	425°F	220°C	7
	450°F	230°C	8

EQUIVALENTS FOR WEIGHT

1 ounce = 30 grams
4 ounces = 120 grams
8 ounces = 240 grams
12 ounces = 3/4 pound = 360 grams
16 ounces = 1 pound = 480 grams

EQUIVALENTS FOR LENGTH

1 inch = 2.5 centimeters
6 inches = 1/2 foot = 15 centimeters
12 inches = 1 foot = 30 centimeters
36 inches = 3 feet = 1 yard = 90 centimeters
40 inches = 100 centimeters = 1 meter

INDEX